PLUNDER

In memory of Edward Said

PLUNDER
WHEN THE RULE OF LAW IS ILLEGAL

Ugo Mattei and Laura Nader

BLACKWELL PUBLISHING
350 Main Street, Malden, MA 02148-5020, USA
9600 Garsington Road, Oxford OX4 2DQ, UK
550 Swanston Street, Carlton, Victoria 3053, Australia

First published 2008 by Blackwell Publishing Ltd

1 2008

Library of Congress Cataloging-in-Publication Data

Mattei, Ugo.
Plunder: When the rule of law is illegal / Ugo Mattei & Laura Nader.
p. cm.
Includes bibliographical references and index.
ISBN 978-1-4051-7895-2 (hardcover : alk. paper) – ISBN 978-1-4051-7894-5 (pbk. : alk. paper)
1. Rule of law. 2. Law and ethics. 3. Law and anthropology. I. Nader, Laura. II. Title.

KZ1275.M38 2008
340′.11—dc22

2007026293

A catalogue record for this title is available from the British Library.

Set in 10.5/13pt Minion
by Graphicraft Limited, Hong Kong

For further information on
Blackwell Publishing, visit our website at
www.blackwellpublishing.com

Contents

Preface viii

Introduction 1

1: Plunder and the Rule of Law **10**

An Anatomy of Plunder 10
Plunder, Hegemony, and Positional Superiority 17
Law, Plunder, and European Expansionism 20
Institutionalizing Plunder: the Colonial Relationship and the Imperial Project 26
A Story of Continuity: Constructing the Empire of Law (lessness) 28

2: Neo-liberalism: Economic Engine of Plunder **35**

The Argentinean Bonanza 35
Neo-Liberalism: an Economic Theory of Simplification and a Spectacular Project 42
Structural Adjustment Programs and the Comprehensive Development Framework 53
Development Frameworks, Plunder, and the Rule of Law 58

3: Before Neo-liberalism: a Story of Western Plunder 64

The European Roots of Colonial Plunder 64
The Fundamental Structure of US Law as a Post-colonial Reception 65
A Theory of Lack, Yesterday and Today 67
Before Neo-liberalism: Colonial Practices and Harmonious Strategies – Yesterday and Now 76

4: Plunder of Ideas and the Providers of Legitimacy 81

Hegemony and Legal Consciousness 81
Intellectual Property as Plunder of Ideas 83
Providing Legitimacy: Law and Economics 88
Providing Legitimacy: Lawyers and Anthropologists 100

5: Constructing the Conditions for Plunder 111

The Plunder of Oil: Iraq and Elsewhere 111
The New World Order of Plunder 120
Not Only Iraq: Plunder, War, and Legal Ideologies of Intervention 123
Institutional Lacks as Conditions for Plunder: Real or Created? 128
"Double Standards Policy" and Plunder 130
Poverty: Justification for Intervention and Consequence of Plunder 133

6: International Imperial Law 137

Reactive Institutions of Imperial Plunder 137
US Rule of Law: Forms of Global Domination 142
Globalization of the American Way 144
An Ideological Institution of Global Governance: International Law 150

Holocaust Litigation: Back to the Future 155
The Swallowing of International Law by US Law 158
Economic Power and the US Courts as Imperial Agencies 164

7: Hegemony and Plunder: Dismantling Legality in the United States 168

Strategies to Subordinate the Rule of Law to Plunder 168
Plunder in High Places: Enron and its Aftermath 172
Plunder in Even Higher Places: Electoral Politics and Plunder 176
Plunder of Liberty: the War on Terror 179
Plunder Undisrupted: the Discourse of Patriotism 191

8: Beyond an Illegal Rule of Law? 196

Summing Up: Plunder and the Global Transformation of Law 196
Imperial Rule of Law or the People's Rule of Law? 202
The Future of Plunder 211

Notes to Text 217
Selected Further Reading 240
Documentary Film Resources 266
Index 273

Preface

This book resulted from an almost casual scholarly encounter. Independently from each other we produced, from our different academic perspectives, papers dealing broadly with the issue of legal and institutional transformations produced by the globalization of the economy. Having been good friends and UC colleagues for quite some time, we exchanged drafts. At the end of the reading, we concluded that we shared a vision about the past and present role of the law in violent political and economic transformations such as the ones we are living through today. Thus, we decided to deepen our exchange in order to make this common vision take better shape and possibly materialize in some joint effort.

It quickly appeared from our conversations that the issues we were discussing had broad political meaning and were potentially of general interest. They had to do with the role of law and politics in corporate capitalist expansion. Ideas such as the promotion of the "rule of law," a key tenet in American discourse on foreign policy, part of the "modern trinity" (democracy, the rule of law, and Christianity) whose promotion Woodrow Wilson considered an obligation of the US government, had rarely been the object of public discussion: this positive connotation has mostly been taken for granted, right up to recent dramatic global events.

Today, in the name of democracy and the rule of law, an intense wave of US-led war has crashed upon Islamic populations in the Middle East. It thus appears that while Christianization is no longer by itself a sufficient ideological justification for wars of aggression, the rule of law seems to have taken on its role in persuading public opinion in the West (particularly the United States) of the moral acceptability of military aggression and occupation of foreign countries. We believed it was important, for more educated political discussion of these fundamental civic questions, to explore the dark side of law, discussing its oppressive uses in a variety of social and historical contexts.

The book is thus fundamentally a comparison of the role of the rule of law in Euro-American practices of violent extraction (what we call plunder) by stronger international political actors victimizing weaker ones. Because of the breadth of our theme, we have selected our materials so that our examples, with different degrees of detail, cover quite a large part of the world. Because our main worry is to understand the present with the help of the past, we devote particular focus to the current dominating political power, the United States. Thus, the rule of law is discussed both domestically and in its international dimension. Our ultimate task was to remove the rule of law from its pedestal of sanctity by showing it as an institutional construct that can be used for good or – very often – for ill.

Among the many colleagues who helped us to shape the arguments of this book we need to mention Tarek Milleron, Ellen Hertz, Roberto González, Rik Pinxton, Charles Hirschkind, George Bisharat, Richard Boswell, Teemu Ruskola, James Gordley, Duncan Kennedy, Richard Delgado, Meir Dan Cohen, Elisabetta Grande, Mariella Pandolfi, Luca Pes, Jed Kroncke, George Akerlof, Monica Eppinger, Mark Goodale, Liza Grandia, David Price, Rob Borofsky, James Holston, and Elizabeth Colson.

We also contracted debts in the process of selecting a publisher that, perhaps because of the many friends that the rule of law has within the US intellectual industry, this time proved particularly long and difficult. We wish to thank Rosalie Robertson and anonymous referees at Blackwell Publishing, Brat Clark and anonymous referees and members of the editorial committee at Monthly Review Press, and Marion Berghahn at Berghahn Books.

We benefited from the generous support of a variety of editors and research assistants in the long process of production. Among those, particularly precious have been Bettina Lewis, Hoda Bandeh-Ahmadi, and librarian Suzanne Calpestri at UC Berkeley Anthropology, and Claire Harvey, Saki Bailey, Zia Gewaalla, and in particular Linda Weir and the library staff at Hastings.

Ugo Mattei benefited from generous support of the Accademia Nazionale dei Lincei in Rome where he enjoyed a long research leave from Italian academic duties. He also acknowledges support from Academic Dean Shauna

Marshall and Dean Nell Newton at Hastings as well as from the staff and colleagues at the Dipartimento di Economia, Cognetti De Martiis at the University of Turin and from the Italian Ministry of University, which contributed to the funding of the research.

He also wishes to thank colleagues at the University Los Andes, Bogota, Colombia; at the Catholic University and San Marcos University, Lima, Peru; at the University of Chile, Santiago, Chile; at the University of Buenos Aires and Torquato di Tella, Buenos Aires, Argentina; at the University of Bamako, Mali; at the University of Havana, and of Santa Clara, Cuba; at the University of Montreal, Canada; at the University of Macau and at the University of Hong Kong, Peoples Republic of China, where he has been fortunate to visit and exchange ideas with too many colleagues to be mentioned, and/or to present drafts at different occasions during the research that led to this book.

Laura Nader benefited from discussions with many colleagues at conferences at the Max Planck Institute in Halle, Germany; at the University of Edinburgh, Scotland; at the University of Ghent in Belgium; and at the World Bank. She thanks Professor Rik Pinxten of Ghent for his early support of this project. She is particularly grateful to Ralph Nader for his early perusal of this work and for his advice on civic fundamentals.

Introduction

> The only truly political action . . . is that which severs the nexus between violence and law.[1]
>
> *[source] Giorgio Agamben*

With all that has been written about imperialism and colonialism, it is remarkable what scant notice is taken of the role of law therein. While theoreticians of Euro-American imperialism profess to recognize the rule of law as keystones of the "civilizing process," its dark side has been neglected. Law has been used to justify, administer, and sanction Western conquest and plunder, resulting in massive global disparities. Thus, we argue, imperial uses – past and present – of the rule of law are behind the current less-than-ideal practices of distributive justice. They are cultural projects that merit explicit theoretical attention because they structurally thwart the use of law to explain the disparity in world wealth.

An ethnocentric configuration of institutions and belief systems has produced a powerful Euro-American use of "rule of law" ideology as key to colonial and imperial projects, whether exercised by British, French, American, Belgian, Dutch, Spanish, Portuguese, German, or Italian colonial interests in pursuit of their enrichment. The general story we seek to convey in this book also concerns the contemporary period and the appropriation by dominant powers of resources and ideas belonging to other peoples, sometimes justified using notions of civilization, development, modernization, democracy, and the rule of law. Our story is about the incremental use of law as a mechanism for constructing and legitimizing plunder. Our intent is to examine the extent of the law's dark side and to explain the mechanics of such imperial uses of it.

Other imperial projects, such as Chinese, Japanese, Islamic, or Soviet conquests, have had and have their own configurations surrounding appropriation, but the key question in our book does not concern these other geographic areas although eventually it might be useful to compare the ideological institutions that govern plunder by peoples of different times and places. What *is* of interest to us in this book are the mechanisms through which the transnational rule of law, as a deeply Western idea, has led incrementally to patterns of global plunder, a process initiated by the expansion of Euro-American society worldwide, and now continued by nations, in particular the USA, and multinational corporate entities independent of explicit political or military colonialism.

Our book traces the evolution of the role of law in practices of what we call plunder, often violent extraction by stronger international political actors victimizing weaker ones, in two apparently separate phases of the history of Euro-American international human relations – colonialism and present-day neo-liberal corporate capitalism. Though discrete, these historical moments share a variety of communalities, patterns of continuity and actors, although important differences cannot be excluded. Because our main intention is to understand the present with the help of the past, we focus on the United States in particular – the current dominant world political power, the likes of which has no precedent.

Rhetoric attendant to the rule of law has flowed throughout Euro-American expansions and with repetitive frequency to camouflage the taking of land, water, minerals, and labor as happened in countless locales to native peoples under colonialism. When legal scholars or practicing lawyers speak of law, they commonly refer to the purposeful functions of the law – a process for facilitating and protecting voluntary arrangements, or as a process for resolving acute social conflicts, or as a process necessary for orderly continuities. But Euro-American law cuts two ways. The nefarious functions of the law are adumbrated in research on European colonialism, on "legal orientalism," on law and development as legal imperialism, or work on the "war on terror" and its transformative effect on the rule of law both in the foreign arena and on the domestic front. Here we build on such a body of work. Using a variety of examples and episodes we contend that throughout Euro-American history, law commonly justifies plunder by hegemonic nations or other powerful actors. The law, as constructed today by means of the World Trade Organization (WTO) agreement, the International Monetary Fund (IMF), and World Bank contexts of conditionality, and the ethnocentric nature of many rights discourses, is a rule of law that justifies looting to the paradoxical point of being itself illegal. At issue is whether the rule of law, operating in the context of colonialism and imperialism, results in disorder rather than order, providing for continuity in oppression rather than interruption of the colonial practice.

The transformation of the rule of law *ideal* into an *imperial* ideology has accompanied the move from a need of social justice and solidarity towards the capitalist requirements of efficiency and competition. To wit, for instance, Argentina in the 1990s,[2] when Wall Street became richer at the expense of the Argentinean people. Other examples of plunder legalized by the imperial rule of law we find in Iraq. As Tariq Ali notes: "Force not law . . . has been used or threatened to impose new laws and treaties,"[3] thereby recognizing the lawlessness inherent in such privatized justice as Paul Bremer's edicts. These are not grounded in legitimating bodies and result in rooting the current hydrocarbon laws, powerful vehicles of the transfer of Iraqi wealth to multinational corporations, assisted by illegal forces of occupation.

Ideas such as the promotion of the "rule of law," a key tenet in American discourse on foreign policy – a major part of the "white man's burden" – have been avoided in public discussion because their positive connotation has always been taken for granted. Today, in the name of democracy and the rule of law, the American public has been persuaded of the moral acceptability of military aggression and occupation of Iraq, utilizing once more George Kennan's "straight power doctrine" to protect both extractive and ideological objectives.

Educated political debate on fundamental civic questions must include a critique of the imperial uses of the rule of law in Iraq and elsewhere. How has American law been transformed into imperial law? How do these changing laws support American political and economic dominance in the world today – a dominance that is problematic for many world citizens who suffer its consequences? To what extent has the rule of law worked in the colonial past and how does it work today as a powerful ideology concealing plunder?[4] Have we reached the point in which such ideology, promoting human rights discourses, notions of democracy, development, and this rule of law, should be exposed for what it is and abandoned? What are the alternatives to this rule of law in the long path of civilization, and when is it illegal?

Law as fictional jurisprudence is a place to start in giving a roadmap of the instances in which we describe the rule of law being fundamentally illegal, since concepts such as *terra mullius* (empty lands that are not empty) have been used to justify plunder since the beginning of European expansion and are still in use today, as we indicate further on (see Chapter 3). This is a clear example of rule of law rhetoric used as a cover, a camouflage, or as propaganda when engaging in lawless or criminal operations. Paul Bremmer's dictates in Iraq, or privatization laws used to transfer the loot to foreign powers, as in Afghanistan and elsewhere (see Chapter 5), are a contemporary example of what happens when force and violence are used to create the law of the oppressor, when ends justify the means. The rule of law can be deemed illegal when it is applied criminally, arbitrarily, and capriciously, victimizing weaker subjects, or when it violates the spirit and the letter of treaties such as the Geneva Convention, aimed at limiting war related plunder, or when those in power purposefully and systematically do not enforce the law or enforce it based on double standards or discriminatorily. We consider the rule of law illegal when without legitimacy it is rammed through impotent legislatures without adequate disclosure, debate, or hearings (see Chapter 7), or when it uses unlawful or deceptive promises to co-opt or buy legislators, as happened when the WTO and NAFTA were enacted. Law can be said to be illegal when produced by legislators elected in faked, imposed or polluted elections, in which only insignificant minorities actually vote or in which voters are forced to participate. These are some of the pathologies of the rule of law that we will expose in this book and that we capture with the idea of plunder as illegal rule of law.

Western countries identify themselves as law-abiding and civilized no matter what their actual history reveals. Such identification is acquired by false knowledge and false comparison with other peoples, those who were said to "lack" the rule of law, such as in China, Japan, India, and in the Islamic world more generally. Similarly today, according to some leading economists, Third World developing countries "lack" the minimal institutional systems necessary for the unfolding of a global market that now serves (as in the past) to further the construction of Western superiority.

We argue in this book that foreign-imposed privatization laws that facilitate unconscionable bargains at the expense of the people are vehicles of plunder, not of legality. The very same policy of corporatization and open markets, imposed today globally by the so-called Washington consensus, was used by Western bankers and the business community in Latin America as the main vehicle to "open the veins" of the continent, to borrow Eduardo Galeano's metaphor, with no solution or continuity between colonial and post-colonial times. It was used in Africa to facilitate the forced transfer of slaves to America, and today to facilitate the extraction of agricultural products, oil, minerals, ideas, and cultural artifacts in the same countries. The policy of violently opening markets for free trade (especially of weapons), used today in Afghanistan and Iraq, was used in China during the nineteenth-century Opium War, in which free trade was interpreted as an obligation to buy drugs from British dealers. The policy of protecting Western industry by means of tariffs and barriers to entry, while at the same time forcing local industries to compete on the open market, was used by the British empire in Bengal, as it is today by the WTO in Asia, Africa, and Latin America. In all these settings the tragic human suffering produced by such plunder is simply ignored. In all these settings law played a major role in legalizing and legitimating such practices of powerful actors against the powerless. Yet, this use of power is scarcely explored in the study of Western law.

The dominant image of the rule of law, we argue, is false historically and in the present, because it does not fully acknowledge its dark side. The false representation starts from the idea that good law (which others "lack") is autonomous, separate from society and its institutions, technical, non-political, non-distributive, and reactive rather than proactive: more succinctly, a technological framework for an "efficient" market. Because of these false representations, good governance that ostensibly characterizes the law's purposes becomes the backbone of naturalized professional arguments that are marshaled to legitimize plunder.

We argue that the rule of law has a bright and a dark side, with the latter progressively conquering new terrain whenever the former is not empowered by a political soul. In the absence of such political life, the rule of law becomes a cold technology, and the dark side can cover the whole picture as law yields to embrace brute violence. The political empowerment of the bright side of law can stem from a variety of places, not necessarily rooted in justice. During the Cold War, for example, there was some incentive to practice a democratic rule of law in its positive functions of order, conflict management, principled and fair decision-making. But the change in the balance of power after the Cold War nourished the law's dark side, removing the political bite to the law. The United States' ruling elite no longer needed to persuade other countries and people of the values of democracy and the virtue of the rule of law which after communism, in its Soviet realization, had collapsed under corruption and illegality. Gradually, incentives for institutional virtues declined in the West. A public shift from justice to profit, from respect to thefts, followed within an atmosphere of silenced political debate, overwhelmed by self-congratulatory rhetoric, such as the end of history, through the 1990s. Later the political silence accompanying plunder was further normalized by talk of patriotism, "detainees," "enemy combatants," and special tribunals reminiscent of earlier nineteenth- and twentieth-century authoritarians including anti-law phases as in "tort reform" or torture policies. Such post-September 11 praxis, as well as its perennial power surrender to corporate actors, takes us a long way from an American model of legality and democracy that, though rhetorical and hypocritical in many ways, has been admired worldwide and arguably contributed to the ending of the Cold War.

Because of the scope of our project, we have selected materials and illustrations that include large parts of the world but are not meant to be comprehensive. In our examples, the uses of the rule of law are discussed in the past and in the present, both domestically and in their international dimension, taking into due consideration the declining role of states as compared to large corporate actors. When large corporate actors dominate states or become knitted with them, law becomes a product of the economy, and what was once "Western" domination is now multinational corporate capitalism. Democracy, rule of law, development, international human rights, and arguments about "lack" are in the present legal landscape a strong part of the rhetoric of legitimization of international corporate extraction.

Contemporary mass cultures operate within a short timespan. Most Western intellectuals do not grasp that it is because of previous expansionist empires that cultures become connected with one another and share a good deal of world history. Worse, many intellectuals do not acknowledge that it is exactly because of the plunder of gold, silver, bioresources, and more that development accelerated in the West, so that underdevelopment is a historically produced victimization of weaker and more enclosed communities and not the disease of lesser people.

Prevailing short-term and short-sighted opportunism must be overcome. Far too many politicized people exist in today's world – as demonstrated by the worldwide opposition to the US invasion of Iraq – for American imperialism to be sustained. A narrative history of the imperial adventure rendered in historical and contemporary legal terms opens up a possibility for a radical rethinking of a model of development defined by Western ideas of progress, development, and efficiency. A vision of a just society necessitates that we eschew an idea of freedom that allows for massive inequality because the rule of law is invariably used to protect the bottom line. Liberation is a better word than freedom. Liberation cannot exist without authentic democracy, and no democracy exists without just distribution of resources. Does the rule of law still have a role in attempting to establish the conditions for liberation?

Perhaps empowering its bright side and fully exposing the dark aspects of the rule of law can transform it into a tool for taking control of a runaway world, fueled by an economic dynamic called neo-liberalism. Perhaps the rule of law cannot be reformed and only revolution can disentangle it from the lethal hug of plunder. In both cases, understanding plunder is a precondition for action. New directions call for a recognition of the configuration that has accompanied the different waves of Euro-American expansions. A reconfiguration would mean, first and foremost, a clear rejection of an ideology of inherent superiority of Western culture that does not recognize that the West is itself part of something much larger. After all, the discovery of agriculture and three great world religions – Christianity, Islam, and Judaism – had their origin in the Middle East. Most importantly, for our purposes we propose a hard-nosed look at what is behind the rule of law as an undisputable value of current corporate-dominated capitalism.

Several outstanding thinkers today, in and out of academia, are suggesting that the problems we are facing are systemic to a several-hundred-year-old system of Euro-American expansion and domination based on extraction and plunder, a system that is now adopted by India and China. Cultural and material destruction has proceeded at an accelerated pace at least since the eighteenth century. The two legitimizing strategies, one motivated by a universal concept of justice, the other by a universal concept of efficiency (the former commonly associated with colonialism and the latter with modern Americanization) are deeply flawed and no longer acceptable. The "lack" argument, where a comparative absence is created that can only be remedied by transferring law from a Western source, is, also, outrageous when seen as yet another imperial move. Similarly outrageous is law as a social and political tool that empowers local elites to interface with the global economy in the face of increasing social inequities. Plunder, we suggest, is an important concept to unify and portray, *as the rule*, distortions in the model of capitalist expansion that are at most acknowledged as exceptions.

Perhaps plunder as the rule rather than the exception allows the reader to get outraged. The Enron scandal, the mutual fund scandal, and other examples portrayed as exceptions (such as torture in Abu Ghraib, Guantánamo Bay, and

Baghram Air Force Base or the use of illegal weapons of mass destruction in Falluja) in fact are the rule of corporate capitalist development; workers are victimized; people lose their savings; innocents are killed; peasants are starved. The distinction between what is legal and what is illegal blurs in a world in which the rule of law is reduced to a dull rhetoric or to Orwellian double-speak. How much more suffering do we need to realize that similar tragedies are the rule and not the exception? How much more time do we need to recognize the civilizing failure of corporate capitalism and the need to organize radical alternatives to its destructive models of development?

Chapter 1, "Plunder and the Rule of Law," attempts an anatomy of plunder and introduces the main thesis and method of the book. It shows the reader the multiple meanings of "rule of law," the hegemonies facilitating Euro-American expansion, the colonial project linked to its imperial present, and how the end of the Cold War equilibrium has facilitated the construction of the current empire of lawlessness. Chapter 2, "Neo-liberalism: Economic Engine of Plunder," begins with a concrete example of plunder in contemporary Argentina, as originated by mighty and respected institutional actors such as Wall Street firms and the International Monetary Fund. It also introduces the idea of structural adjustment, comprehensive development, and conditionally imposed rule of law as germane to plunder. Chapter 3, "Before Neo-liberalism: a Story of Western Plunder," approaches the issue of continuity, tracing the roots of current neo-liberal policies to Euro-American colonialism. Chapter 4, "Plunder of Ideas and the Providers of Legitimacy," begins with a concrete example of plunder – that of ideas, in the form of Western patents and intellectual property rights imposed on resources belonging to weaker peoples. It also introduces lawyers, economists, and anthropologists as providing legitimacy to practices of plunder justified by the rule of law. Chapter 5, "Constructing the Conditions for Plunder," begins with the concrete example of the legally facilitated plunder of oil in Iraq, and discusses a variety of other current geographic and political settings in which rule of law ideology has proved effective in constructing the conditions of interventionist plunder. Chapter 6, "International Imperial Law," develops a theoretical explanation of the various examples thus far provided focusing on the role of the law. It discusses the way in which the Anglo-American conception of the rule of law has become hegemonic, describing the global legal transformations as an unfolding of imperial law. Such transformations, we argue, have prepared the present empire of lawlessness scenario. Chapter 7, "Hegemony and Plunder: Dismantling Legality in the United States," tackles the domestic impact of post Cold War scenarios, addressing transformations of the American rule of law as an ideal justification of plunder. It shows how such transformations, perhaps unavoidable in an imperial setting, have facilitated what we call plunder of liberty, a process of social transformation creating the ideal soil for further corporate plunder. Finally, Chapter 8, "Beyond an Illegal Rule of Law?," attempts to draw some conclusions based upon recognition of the uses of the rule of law in imperial adventures as no longer in any people's self-interest, a central challenge to law's legitimacy in the twenty-first century.

1 | Plunder and the Rule of Law

An Anatomy of Plunder

The expression "rule of law" has gained currency well outside the specialized learning of lawyers, where it displays a long pedigree, having been used at least as far back as the times of Sir Edward Coke in late sixteenth-century England. In recent times, however, it has reached political and cultural spheres, and entered everyday discourse and media language. Pronounced in countless political speeches, it promenades on the agendas of private and public actors, and on the dream-lists of many activists.

Unfortunately, as almost invariably happens to buzzwords used in a wide variety of semantic contexts, the term has incrementally lost clarity and is today interpreted in widely disparate ways. Today the concept is by no means reduced to a technical legal meaning. It is not specific even in lawyer's lingo, let alone in common everyday use. Few of its users seem to mind this lack of precision, which derives from the wide variety of new meanings that the concept has gained through time, space, and different user communities. "Rule of law" is almost never carefully defined as a concept; users of the expression allude to meanings that they assume to be clear and objective but that are not so. Rule of law has thus become part of that dimension of tacit knowledge, described by Polanyi in his classic study of human communication.[1] Naturally, this would be a perfectly innocent and common phenomenon, not worth an inquiry, were it not for the weighty political implications of the phrase in different contexts.[2]

We can begin observing that the connotations of the expression "rule of law" have always been implicitly positive. The nineteenth-century legendary constitutional scholar Albert V. Dicey, for example, argued that the "rule of law" was the defining trait of British liberal constitutional civilization as opposed to the French authoritarian tradition based on administrative law. Today, the concept is inextricably linked to the notion of democracy, thus becoming a powerful, almost undisputable, positively loaded ideal. Who could argue against a society governed under democracy and the rule of law? Indeed it would be like arguing against the law being just, or against a market being efficient. In this book we are not moved by the desire to argue against the rule of law. We only wish to gain a better understanding of this powerful political weapon, to question its almost sacred status, by analyzing it as a Western cultural artefact, closely connected with the diffusion of Western political domination. We will try to disentangle its connection with the ideal of democracy, and on the contrary recognize its close association with another notion, that of "plunder."

Let us clarify, before we continue, what we mean by the term "plunder." The *American Heritage Dictionary* defines "plunder" as "to rob of goods by force, esp. in times of war; pillage," and "plunder" (the noun) as "property stolen by fraud or force." It is the latter definition that especially brings to mind the dark side of the rule of law. We address both looting by force and looting by fraud, both wrapped in the rule of law by illustrious legal practitioners and scholars. We trace the development of the critical supporting role that the rule of law has played in plunder. But what of plunder itself? The term conjures up images of ragged conscripts struggling with chests of gold, centuries ago. In what follows, we will expand what is commonly meant by plunder far beyond these connotations. For part of the supporting role that the rule of law has played is to constrict the very meaning of the word plunder to acts most of us think that we are incapable of committing.

An overly broad definition of plunder would be the inequitable distribution of resources by the strong at the expense of the weak. But take that approach to the problem and narrow it to include notions of legality and illegality. Narrow it to the point where children are starving amidst scenes of catastrophic violence, while thousands of miles away (or only a few miles away if we observe the deprivation of "illegal" uninsured immigrant children in California's Central Valley) the more advanced in age ride in a 3-ton, gas-gulping SUV (sports utility vehicle). Now draw a connection between the two: plunder. Or take a farmer who has no "legal" right to use the types of seeds he and his forebears have planted for centuries and trace a line from those seeds to obscene profits now generated by their new corporate owners: plunder.

Let us begin with tracing the notion of the rule of law to the very origins of the Western legal tradition: the highly symbolic moment in which law and politics divorced, bringing to humankind the miracle of a government of laws and not of men. In a government of laws, we preach, even today, to such countries as China or Cuba, the most powerful ruler must also yield to the rule of law. It was Sir Edward Coke, possibly the most influential common law judge ever, who used the concept of the rule of law (rooted back to the "constitutional" nature of English monarchy as established by the Magna Carta) to foreclose the King's participation in deliberations of the common law courts. According to this early notion, there exists a domain of learning that is specialized and belongs to lawyers. The King (James I, 1603–25), no matter how powerful, was not legitimated by this specialized learning, thus he could not sit as a judge in "his own" courts of law. The case, "Prohibition del Roy" (1608 12 Coke Rep 63), was decided during a very harsh period of English history eventually leading to regicide and the interregnum. During this political struggle, the common law courts (jealous of their jurisdictions) were allied with the barons, sitting in Parliament, themselves long suspicious of every attempt at modernization that the monarchy, beginning with the Tudors (especially Henry VIII), was endeavoring to carry out. Indeed modernization was a threat to the privileges of the landed aristocracy, and the alliance with common law courts successfully protected the Englishman's long established rights to property.[3]

Thus, the birth of the rule of law, whether we place it at the time of the Magna Carta or at that of Sir Edward Coke, had nothing to do with notions of democracy, unless we wish to assert that the English Parliament of the time was a democratic institution! As widely recognized by contemporary historians, the birth of the rule of law was actually the triumph of medieval social structure over modernization. It has only been the subsequent Whig rhetoric of English scholars, accompanied by the narrative of continental Roman Catholic historians aimed at libeling Henry VIII, that has reconstructed this story in a quite opposite way, convincing us of the false notion that progress and civilization were protected by the alliance between Parliament (democracy!) and the common law courts (the rule of law).

Thus, the rule of law, an early tool used by lawyers to claim a special professional status as guardians of a government of laws, was in fact born out of their role as guardians of a given, highly unequal, and certainly non-democratic distribution of property in society. This very same background clearly emerges from the Federalist papers (particularly Nos 10 and 51) where James Madison seeks to justify the need of a constitutional order based on checks and balances as a way to avoid factiousness and the oppression of the majority over a minority. Here again, despite the elected nature of the US Congress, the rule of law is received as a protection of unequal property distribution, favoring the minority of the "haves" against the majority of the "have-nots": "But the most common durable source of factions has been the various and unequal distribution of property. Those who hold and those who are without property have ever formed different interests in society."[4] The protection of the unequal distribution of wealth (to a large extent plundered from Native Americans with the take justified by natural law), is thus at the very root of the founding fathers' worry about the possibility that the majority could actually decide to redistribute property more equitably. The democratic ideal had to be limited by a variety of skillful legal techniques (including federalism and the electoral system) most importantly, once again relying on the professional check of lawyers whose very elite would sit in courts, the institutional guardians of the rule of law.

Because of its long pedigree as a darling of the ruling elite, the rule of law has always been portrayed as a "good thing" and nobody is expected to argue against it in the present dominant political discourse. Of course, one could recall notions of law as a superstructure of the economy – a traditional critique of the very idea of bourgeois legality. Nevertheless, the conception of the law as an autonomous (or at least semi-autonomous) social field is so persuasive that today both Marxist scholars and social observers agree with it. Thus, bereft of any powerful intellectual critique, the rule of law lives today in a comfortable limbo, stretched to fit the needs of every side of the political spectrum as a symbol or an icon rather than as a real-life institutional arrangement with its pros and its cons to be discussed and understood as those of any other cultural artefact.

Recently, Niall Ferguson, an academic historian[5] with remarkable access to the dominant media and public discourse, has offered an example of such legitimizing power of the rule of law by introducing a (moderately) revisionist case for the British empire. One would want to incidentally observe that the very term "loot," a diffused synonym of plunder and pillage, is a Hindu word introduced into the English vocabulary after the spoliation of Bengal. A nostalgic observer, Niall Ferguson argues extensively that the rule of law as a global legacy of the British empire is such a precious asset left to humankind worldwide that the brutal violence used to impose it (including war, plunder, slave trading, massive killings, ethnic cleansing, and genocide) cannot be condemned *tout court*. Similar revisionist arguments, based on broad notions of civilization, can be seen as re-emerging also in France, where a recent statute urges history school-text writers to put colonialism in a more balanced light.

In what follows we examine the rule of law as deployed by European colonial powers in their colonies and trace its evolution and transformations into the reign of the present hegemonic power, the United States. Not surprisingly, the Western rule of law, while defining its legal letter as does a train that lays its own tracks, is very often an instrument of oppression and plunder and thus ironically swells with a spirit of illegality.

Someone inquiring into the ultimate meaning of the popular expression "rule of law" soon realizes that the idea has at least two different aggregates of meaning in the dominant liberal democratic tradition, both of them, to be sure, sharing nothing with plunder. In the first, the rule of law refers to institutions that secure property rights against governmental taking and that guarantee contractual obligations. This is the meaning of rule of law invoked by Western businessmen interested in investing abroad. International institutions such as the World Bank or the International Monetary Fund (IMF) often charge the lack of a rule of law as the main reason for insufficient investment by rich countries in poor ones. The rule of law is thus interpreted as the institutional backbone of the ideal market economy. The synonym "good governance" is also used to convey this meaning. Normative recipes for market liberalization and opening up of local markets to foreign investment (often paving the way to plunder) thus come packaged with the prestigious wrapping of the rule of law.

The second approach relates to a liberal political tradition rooted in "natural law," a school of thought developed by the fifteenth and sixteenth-century Jesuit jurists at Salamanca and later becoming a dominant jurisprudence through Europe (including Great Britain), in the more secular form of "rational law." According to this tradition, society should be governed by the law and not by a human being acting as a ruler (*sub lege, non sub homine*). The law is impersonal, abstract, and fair, because it is applied blindly to anyone in society (hence the time-honored icon of justice as a blinded deity). Rulers might be capricious, arrogant, cruel, partisans – in a word: human. If the law does not restrain them, their government will end in tyranny and corruption. In this tradition, echoed in the Federalist papers, and highly valued among the American founding fathers, a system is effectively governed by the rule of law when its leaders are under its restraint; it lacks the rule of law when authority is so unbounded that the leader can be considered a dictator. The lack of the rule of law, in this second sense, is a worry for international human rights activists and institutions concerned with the consequences of unrestricted, ruthless governments on target populations.

Some conservatives might favor the first meaning, protecting property and contracts, and use the second to gain support for military intervention. The second meaning, providing rights, is a favorite of the moderate left and of many international human rights activists seeking to do good by the use of the law (the "do-gooders"). Perhaps someone located in the so-called "third way" would claim to be a champion of both meanings, which appear to merge in the recent, comprehensive definition of the World Bank: "The rule of law requires transparent legislation, fair laws, predictable enforcement, and accountable governments to maintain order, promote the private sector growth, fight poverty and have legitimacy."[6]

In both perspectives, the rule of law is interpreted as a *negative limit* to the power of intervention of the state. Consequently, on the one hand, the state has to provide and respect the rule of law as a kind of consideration for the concentration of power following sovereignty. On the other hand, the rule of law is conceived as something above the state, a legitimizing factor of the very state itself.[7]

A system can be governed by the rule of law in one or the other sense. There are systems in which property rights are worshipped but that are still governed by ruthless, unrestricted leaders. President Fujimori's Peru or Pinochet's Chile are good recent examples of such arrangements, but many other authoritarian governments presently in office mainly in Africa, Asia, and Latin America that follow the "good governance" prescriptions of the World Bank also fall into this category. Similarly, President Bush's United States, with the present imbalance of power heavily favoring the executive over any other branch of government, today only nicely fits the first definition of the rule of law (see Chapter 7).

In other systems, with good human rights credentials, governments interpret their role as significantly redistributive. Property rights may not be sacred, and a variety of "social theories" may limit their extension or curtail them without compensation. In such settings, quite often, courts and scholars might develop theories that limit the enforcement of contracts in the name of justice and social solidarity. Consequently, they might fit the second but not the first definition of the rule of law. Scandinavian countries, amplifying attitudes shared at one time or another in history by a number of continental legal traditions such as France, Germany, and Italy (or the United States'

New Deal), might offer such a model in Western societies. Perhaps present-day Lesotho or President Salvadore Allende's Chile might offer actual or historical examples in the south.

Western countries have developed a strong identity as being governed by the rule of law, no matter what the actual history or the present situation might be. Such identity is obtained – as is the usual pattern – by comparison with "the other," almost invariably portrayed as "lacking" the rule of law. A recent interesting example is a front page story of the *New York Times* called "Deep flaws and little justice in China's court system."[8] The author describes the case of an innocent Chinese man, framed by prosecutors, sentenced to death, and eventually released because of favorable circumstances. The article implies that such cases would not happen when the Western rule of law is in place. Unfortunately, the reader is never informed that hundreds of similar cases routinely happen in the US criminal justice system, and increasingly the "mistakes" are discovered only after the execution happens.[9] Thus, our self-portrait as governed by the rule of law forecloses understanding for what has been called legal "orientalism."[10]

The lack of rule of law has historically stimulated and justified a complex variety of patterns of interventions of powerful states or economic actors in relative power vacuums for purposes of plunder. The Western conception of the rule of law, serving the expatriate community, international investors, and the desire to organize authoritarian power more effectively, was imposed, with a variety of strategies, upon China and Japan in the late nineteenth and early part of the twentieth century in order to "open up" the Asian market for foreign plunder. Earlier, throughout the American continent, the "lack" of individual ownership, a symbol of the natural law conception of the rule of law, justified the taking of Indian lands deemed vacant by the Western "discovery" principle. Today the rule of law, still an undefined and under-theorized concept, is mightily sponsored by so-called structural adjustment plans (SAPs), the instruments through which the international financial institutions (World Bank and IMF) condition their loans. The lack of rule of law has also justified the relentless illegal bombing (through the North Atlantic Treaty Organization, NATO) of former Yugoslavia by the United States government, with the support of both right-wing and center-leftist European governments. It has again been used, together with a variety of other rationales, in order to attempt justification for the later invasions of Afghanistan and Iraq.

The idea that law is an instrument of oppression and of plunder competes with entire libraries of law and political science which exalt its positive aspects. Because of such imbalances, a historical and comparative perspective is unavoidable for understanding an unfolding of plunder perpetrated by a variety of uses of the rule of law. One of the most historically significant of such interventions is, of course, colonialism, which will serve as a background for our principal goal – an understanding of the current situation as continuity rather than rupture, old vices rather than novel attitudes. The Western world, under current US leadership, having persuaded itself of its superior position (ethnocentrism plus back-up power), largely justified by its form of government, has succeeded in diffusing rule of law ideology as universally valid, behind whose shadow plunder hides, both in domestic and in international matters.

According to a poll of the Pew Global Attitudes Project, today 79 percent of the American people believe that it is a good thing that American ideals and values be spread in the world, and another 60 percent openly believe in the superiority of American culture.[11] While comparative data show significantly lower figures in other Western countries, it is a fact that such attitudes of Western superiority enable an expansionism and imperialism that only a very formalistic vision of law and sovereignty can consider a rupture with the colonial era.

Present-day international interventions, most significantly in Iraq and Afghanistan, led by the United States are no longer openly colonial efforts. They might be called neo-colonial, imperialistic, or simply post-colonial interventions. Although practically all of the European colonial states (most notably Portugal, Spain, Great Britain, France, Germany, and even Italy) regarded themselves as empires, for our purposes, "empire" describes the present phase of multinational capitalist development with the USA as the most important superpower, using the rule of law, when it uses it at all, to pave the way for international corporate domination. Colonialism refers to a discrete historical phase, terminated by formal decolonization, in which Western powers carried out colonial extraction in competition with each other. The substantial continuity between the two phases is found in the imperial uses of the rule of law to achieve and justify what can only be called plunder.

Plunder, Hegemony, and Positional Superiority

Our exploration of how the rule of law is used to justify plunder requires a variety of tools, including the notion of *hegemony*,[12] power reached by a combination of force and consent. Power cannot be maintained long term only by means of brute force. More often it is imposed on groups of individuals who more or less "voluntarily" accept the will of the strong. In international relationships, the role of consumerism in the diffusion and final acceptance of US values in countries such as those of the former Socialist block clearly exemplifies the means by which such consent, the key to hegemony, can be reached.

While force is generally the province of repressive institutions such as the army or the police, consent most often is produced by institutions such as schools, churches, or media as illustrated by the US multibillion dollar effort in the war on drugs.[13] Such institutions are integral to hegemony and at the same time make its component ideology a cross-social-class concept, thus going beyond the narrower Marxist idea of ideology as a class-specific device.[14] Hegemony is hence at least in part reached by a diffusion of power between a plurality of individuals across classes. This diffusion of power becomes a key concept for refuting the idea that power is imposed from the top.[15]

The diffusion of power to build hegemony, however, that in the law accompanied the colonial development of modern Western-style adversarial legal institutions, resulted in the birth of *counter-hegemony*. Close examination of the use of law in colonial times[16] shows that "empowerment" is an unintended consequence of the formal rule of law. Subordinates often welcomed the advent of adversary courts in which to vindicate rights and obtain justice. Women, for example, availed themselves of this new opportunity to subvert patterns of patriarchal domination by using colonial courts. Because of this empowerment potential of the law, colonial rulers often entered into alliances with local patriarchal powers, limiting access to the modernized legal system and acknowledging "traditional" power structures (often invented). These linked ontogenies of hegemony and countervailing power are of crucial importance. In fact, the rule of law displays a double-edged, contradictory nature: it can favor oppression but it can also produce empowerment of the oppressed that leads to counter-hegemony. This is why powerful actors often attempt to tackle counter-hegemony by incorporating harmonious "soft" aspects aimed at disempowering potential resistance from the oppressed by limiting their use of adversary courts. Today, the worldwide alternative dispute resolution (ADR) movement functions as a strong disempowering device, that the dominant discourse makes attractive by the use of a variety of rhetorical practices, such as the need to remedy the "excesses" of litigation, or of promoting the desirability of a more "harmonious" society.[17] Just as in colonial times, tradition, invented or otherwise, served this disempowering function. These are the kind of continuities we explore.

Generalization and the construction of stereotypes for control purposes is one of the most powerful strategies aimed at downplaying the complexity of different social settings, and then justifying their domination and plunder. The "other" is described as simple, primitive, basic, static, lacking the fundamentals, in need of the simplest and obvious things, thus proving a basic incapacity for self-determination. This process, part of a tacit dimension of dominating cultures, can be seen at play both in past colonial times and today. For example, the current Islamic Middle East, composed of more than 25 countries, with a very complex variety of laws, cultures, people, and institutions, is constantly described as the "Arab world" or the "Muslim world," as if these were the same and as if there were no variations within one or the other.[18] Similar unfortunate simplifications are also at play in the exportation of the rule of law.

Export of the law has been described and explained in a variety of ways, for example, imperialistic/colonial rule, or imposition of law by military force, as during military conquest. Napoleon imposed his Civil Code on French-occupied Belgium in the early nineteenth century. Similarly, General MacArthur imposed a variety of legal reforms based on the American government model in post World War II Japan, as a condition of the armistice in the aftermath of Hiroshima. Today, Western-style elections and a variety of other laws governing everyday life are imposed in countries under US occupation, such as Afghanistan or Iraq.

A second model can be described as imposition by bargaining, in the sense that acceptance of law is part of a subtle extortion.[19] Target countries are persuaded to adopt legal structures according to Western standards or face exclusion from international markets. This model describes China, Japan, and Egypt beginning early in the twentieth century, and, indeed, contemporary operations of the World Bank, IMF, the World Trade Organization (WTO), and other Western development agencies (United States Agency for International Development (USAID), European Bank of Reconstructive Development (EBRD), etc.) in the developing and former socialist world. This model of legal imperialism is the least explored by scholars, although it is the most interesting because of the complex individual and institutional motivations in the exercise of power.

A third model, constructed as fully consensual, is diffusion by prestige, a deliberate process of institutional admiration that leads to the reception of law.[20] This third model is considered the most diffused one. It diminishes the direct power dimension and cultivates a stereotype of Western superiority that needs to be fully appreciated. According to this vision, because modernization requires complex legal techniques and institutional arrangements, the receiving legal system, more simple and primitive, cannot cope with the new necessities. It lacks the *culture of the rule of law*, something that can only be imported from the West. Every country that in its legal development has "imported" Western law has thus acknowledged its "legal inferiority" by admiring and thus voluntarily attempting to import Western institutions. Turkey during the time of Ataturk, Ethiopia at the time of Haile Selassie, and Japan during the Meiji restoration are modern examples. The institutional setting of the admiring country is thus downgraded to "pre-modern," rigid and incapable of autonomous evolution. Interestingly, if the transplant "fails," such as with clumsy attempts to impose Western-style regulation on the Russian stock market, or as with many law and development enterprises, let alone elections in troubled war-torn countries, it is the recipient society that receives the blame. Local shortcomings and "lacks" are said to have precluded progress in the development of the rule of law. When the World Bank produces a development report on legal issues, it invariably shows insensitivity for local complexities and suggests radical and universal transplantations of Western notions and institutions. The inevitable failure of such simple-minded strategies, blamed on the recipient, reinforces Western hubris and self-congratulatory attitudes, while radicalizing the recipient countries.

Law, Plunder, and European Expansionism

One could begin with tragic images of poverty, death, and exploitation in the silver mines of Potosi, in what is now Bolivia, where an estimated 8 million enslaved Indians lost their lives, to understand the causes and the lethal consequences of colonial plunder. The human and social costs of "opening the veins" of Latin America[21] have been so high that only today, after half a millennium, has demography given back a majority to natives in Latin America. The obsession of sixteenth-century Spanish conquistadors for gold and silver, tragically satisfied with genocide in the Americas, sets a scene. But the historical set could be as easily placed 200 years later in modern-day Bangladesh in order to immediately refute Western revisionist arguments on the benign nature of the British rule of law as a colonial legacy. Bengal was described by Ibn Battuta, a legendary medieval Arab traveller who had explored most of the world in the fourteenth century, as one of the richest lands that he had ever seen. In 1757, the year of the battle of Plessey (decisive for British domination of the subcontinent), its capital Dacca, a center of cotton trade and textile industry, was as rich, thriving, and big as the city of London. An official inquiry of the House of Lords shows that by 1850 its population had declined from 150,000 to 30,000, that malaria and jungle fever were taking over and that Dacca, "once the Indian Manchester," was becoming small and poor. The city never recovered and it is today one of the most impoverished places in the world. The scene could also be set in western Africa, where hard data of population depletion caused by the slave trade are appalling. According to much of the best historiography, such depletion, in a West African country that has traditionally suffered from population scarcity, is the most significant cause of low development and poverty.

Behind the early colonial efforts of the European powers lay the need to finance the tremendous economic necessity of the newborn centralized systems of government, essential for capitalist development to happen. Without gold, silver, cotton, and human beings coming from faraway lands, it would have been impossible to finance the institutional system that eventually paved the way to industrialization and development.[22] At the beginning of the eighteenth century, the East India Company a quasi-private, pre-colonial agency, handled more than half of British trade, and the fortunes that it generated for its shareholders were beyond imagination.[23]

From the perspective of the powerful, plunder is a rational maximization of utility, the loot being a return for the investment in military and political might. Plunder thus captures a variety of practices, from slave capture and trade, to extraction of gold and resources in faraway "no man's land," that have long been construed as illegal by international and domestic law. Such theft describes activity that is highly objectionable from a moral viewpoint because the pursuit of profit takes place without regard for the interests, rights, and needs of other weaker human beings or groups. Nevertheless, when such practices accompany powerful ideological motivations, they become acceptable as the dominant moral standards of a given time. Thus, the Crusades used religious zeal to justify mass murder and looting in the Arab East. In a manner not dissimilar to how many crusaders justified the need to defend the holy sites, the rule of law shows a continuous record of justification of oppressive practices, as we will see in Native American settings and the use of the concept *terra nullius*, empty land as rationalized by law.

Today, international law bans occupying powers from engaging in plunder, both directly and indirectly in the aftermath of armed conflict, thus seeking to restrain the strong from carrying on its "natural" behavior of abusing the weak. Consider, then, the current war in Iraq. It is still the rule of law, lacking in Saddam Hussein's days, that is used in some circles to justify, according to international law, the current illegal occupation of the country by the USA, Britain, and a few allies. It thus appears that the rule of law, no matter if domestic or international, can both be used to justify plunder and abuse of the weak, and to attempt to limit abuse. Thus, the contemporary pursuit of dominant positions in oil-rich areas in Central Asia and Iraq is camouflaged by the need to export democracy and the rule of law, showing a remarkable pattern of continuity, and only perhaps a different level of ideological sophistication, in the way in which the West dominates the rest. This picture is in need of deeper scrutiny.

One of the most important and dramatic developments of the second half of the twentieth century was decolonization. In 1961, the year of Africa, as many as 17 former colonies gained independence. Today, we recognize that colonial rule was a complex construction of laws, practices, economic relationships, political platforms, and ideologies, with plunder as a central organizing principle.[24] The very construction of the prototypical colonial relationship followed a strategy by which the brutal and violent extraction was to be transformed into legal hegemony by a variety of discursive practices, and of economic embrace aimed at obtaining local "consent." For example, by the second half of the eighteenth century, 90 percent of the military forces occupying India were made up of indigenous mercenaries: *indirect rule*. Because such strategies were more successful than not, it should be no wonder that the local police force is the most common target of attacks in Iraq today.

Yet, few colonial practices, despite the demise of that obsolete model of formal domination, have been effectively abandoned after decolonization, thus telling a story of continuity. Revisionist ideas emerging today in the West are the result of arrogance, cynicism, frustration, or simple lack of understanding of plunder, the single most significant factor producing and sustaining poverty in the world. An impressive pattern of continuity can be found behind formal independence of former colonies, and today a nostalgic colonial rhetoric of modernization and the rule of law is re-emerging.[25] Nobody has put it more clearly than the Tanzanian legal scholar Issa Shivji: "The moral rehabilitation of imperialism was first and foremost ideological which in turn was constructed on neo-liberal economic precepts – free market, privatization, liberalization etc., the so-called Washington consensus. Human rights, NGOs, good governance, multiparty democracy and rule of law were all rolled together. . . ."[26] With the increasing visibility of illegalities, rule of law rhetoric becomes more ubiquitous, as in earlier viable efforts of justifying the take.

The need to justify the international policy of the dominant Western minority in the world population, resulting in increasing social inequality, has produced much social (and individual) denial. This denial, facilitated by international progressive legal instruments such as bans on slavery, aggressive warfare, the arms trade, or genocide, has prospered as a powerful political factor allowing the perpetuation of practically all such officially banned activities, under the ideological umbrella of Western "democratic" ideals of policy-making justified by law. But discontinuity between a past of ruthless violation and plunder (colonialism) and a present-day, international legality respectful of the rights and the independence of all the peoples of the world, is merely superficial. The observer who does not wish to be ensnared by the dominant rhetoric must be highly suspicious of formal legal "success stories," such as decolonization or even the ban on slavery. One can learn from the past, for example, that slavery had been banned well before the formal colonial partition of the African continent that took place at the end of the Berlin Conference in 1889. At the time of the generalized ban on slavery between the 1830s and 1860s (but in England the Commons had already banned slavery by a statute introduced by Lord Wilberforce in 1807), the so-called "dark continent" was already depopulated to a point that has made recovery impossible to this day. Certainly the slave trade was a largely recessive business for Western capitalists, carried out mostly by local African chiefdoms.

The Berlin Conference signed the beginning of the "scramble for Africa." Participating Western powers presented the struggle against the slave trade still carried on by some African chiefs as the single most compelling moral argument for the civilizing mission of colonization. Again, there is a remarkable continuity with the moral argument of the Catholic Spanish conquistadores, seeking to civilize the Maya and Inca people accused of practicing human sacrifice. In light of this history, contemporary human rights activists crusade in good faith against female circumcision or the *burqa* without considering the possibility of their being instruments for the justification of plunder, which thrives in Africa or the Middle East victimizing the very same populations whose women they struggle to liberate.

Today, global public opinion is divided as possibly never before in its interpretation of the present. As is usually the case, the division is largely between the "haves" and the "have-nots," between the winners and the losers, between the included and the excluded, between the north and the south, or between the right and the left. However, the complexity of the international scenario and the multiplicity of the possible narratives make divisions even deeper, cutting across groups and social classes to individual motivations and moral characters. One side believes that the dominant corporate capitalist model of development, also known as the "end of history,"[27] is the best possible path to prosperity and liberation of everybody everywhere. According to this vision, largely the product of cynicism and self-indulgence,[28] but sometimes shared in good faith by some true believers, the solution is only to make the superiority of the capitalist model of development understood by those that are not yet directly benefiting from it. Readers sharing such a vision might reject the notion of plunder that we are articulating, arguing that such a notion is structurally incompatible with the rule of law. Plunder would be an intimate contradiction, an "illegal" rule of law, at most an exceptional pathology that the rule of law would cure rather than produce.

The other side believes that it is precisely because of the current model of corporate capitalist development that the division between the "haves" and the "have-nots" is so dramatic and irremediable. Thus freedom and prosperity for the rich, with their exaggerated patterns of consumption and waste, is possible only by a conscious effort to avoid liberation of the poor and disenfranchised. According to this second vision, the rich and the powerful not only use instruments of governance to maintain and enhance their privileges, they also resort to propaganda to show that everybody will ultimately benefit from the current state of affairs.[29] An anatomy of plunder frames a way to understand whether plunder can be cured by the rule of law. Can the path of development be changed by political practices compatible with legality, or can change happen only outside of the current legal order, by means of revolutionary transformations in the political space? Can a new legal order capable of exorcizing plunder come about? How? These are some questions that can be answered only by carefully dissecting the imperial uses of the rule of law, analyzing them in their historical unfolding of the present.

The rule of law has faithfully served plunder through history, to the point that some trace of Western conceptions of legality can be found at least at a superficial level in almost all the legal systems of the world.[30] The end of the Cold War, however, changed the conditions of international competition post World War II conditions that justified the pursuit of the rule of law as a Western strategy of liberation. The unfolding of an international monopoly of "legally" organized violence that characterized the so-called "end of history" (also known as Pax Americana, the Washington Consensus, or, more simply, empire) has produced new conditions. The perceived strength of the rule of law in the United States made its law highly prestigious and later hegemonic worldwide through the Cold War and its aftermath. The rule of law has thus been capable of hiding its connection with plunder, itself protected by its highly respectable companion. This arrangement, though undeniably hypocritical, can occasionally limit plunder in its brutality, by counter-hegemony or incidental empowerment of weaker social actors, while plunder continues unbounded in the post Cold War scenario.

In the aftermath of September 11, 2001, we witness even more damage to that already quite feeble form of rule of law known as *international legality*. Inaugurating the state of exception as its new companion, with a skillful manipulation of the emotional impact of that act of terror, US President George W. Bush's administrative officials thrust aside international law and ridiculed it as an impotent and expensive bureaucracy. For example, the Guantánamo concentration camp, where large number of innocent prisoners, mostly singled out by race, have been denied basic rights, and the shameless attitude of the US Supreme Court in justifying such horrors, has shown the impotence of international law against imperial power. For those still credulous the substantial irrelevance of the International Court of Justice ruling against the Israeli wall has shown how the imperial exception applies also to faithful US allies. The revelation of a systematic practice of torture in the prison of Abu Ghraib, Iraq, and the reluctant prosecution of minor scapegoats as the only official reaction to it, has possibly inflicted a definitive blow to the US rule of law ideal.[31]

The destruction and occupation of Afghanistan and Iraq by the United States and its few allies, while yielding gigantic economic returns for dominant corporate players, from the promise of oil extraction, to reconstruction contracts, to military supply, to privatization of security, to new fiscal havens, have made the *liaison* between plunder and the rule of law difficult to hide. It thus becomes crucial to dig into assumed moral virtues, to subject to strict scrutiny the liabilities in a model of corporate capitalist development that seems continually more questionable.

Any inquiry into the rule of law is not free of responsibilities. One could argue that because even hypocrisy is evidence of a sense of limit, it is better that plunder and the rule of law entertain a hypocritical connection than to have total brutal lawlessness grounded in the state of exception. Exposing rule of law practices is still a citizen's duty. It is worth illuminating the historical and present relationship between plunder and the rule of law in order to restore legal civilization, and argue for a more radical and revolutionary departure from the present model of "development".

Institutionalizing Plunder: the Colonial Relationship and the Imperial Project

In the colonial relationship, the law sanctions a pattern of subjugation of weaker populations by stronger ones. This relationship, whose origins are old and variable in different geographic areas, painfully and openly continued through the twentieth century, producing strains in the relations between colonial powers that caused, among other factors, the outbreak of World War I. Socialist thinkers in the West, such as Friedrich Engels and Karl Marx analyzed, challenged, and exposed this legal subjugation. It was formally abandoned, at least as a relationship sanctioned by international law, with the decolonization movement in the aftermath of World War II. But it left permanent scars in the collective consciousness of millions of people affected by domination.

The colonial state was created and constructed on the European model as an aggregate of legal rules and institutions of governance. It is thus based on the law and also on a variety of informal discursive practices that legitimize the law. Lawyers are crucial suppliers of such discursive practices, as sometimes are foreign colonial functionaries (or anthropologists) and locals who share with the others a foreign training. One need not assume a mean-spirited motivation in such suppliers of colonial legitimacy, nor the same motivation in each one of them.

As indicated, law has at least a double dimension stemming from the motivation of its users: oppression and empowerment. Colonial powers, often allied with missionaries and anthropologists (as we later indicate), no matter if in good or bad faith, use law for lowering resistance to outright plunder, seeking legitimacy for exploitive activity. They use propaganda and construct law as an aspect of a superior civilization, claiming resources as a matter of right rather than as the fruits of plunder. Resources have to be given up to foreigners in consideration for the development and civilization that foreigners bring to the "underdeveloped beings" inhabiting the colonial setting. Law thus gains the support of Western-educated local elites, and then functions as a device for centralizing power. An alliance between local elites and colonial personnel thus develops early, with law reform and modernization the notions around which such alliances are organized. First and foremost was the social pacification necessary for plunder underwritten by law.

Without legal institutions and stable local organizations, it would have been impossible to secure the advantages of the "first come first served" model of appropriation typical of early colonialism but unsustainable in the longer run. Such early activities were best symbolized by the brutality of the East India Company's extractive practices, criticized as early as 1776 by Adam Smith.[32] The founder of modern economics denounced what he referred to as "the Company that oppresses and dominates Oriental Indies." He denounced that three or four hundred thousand people died every year of starvation just in Bengal (under control of the East India Company from 1757, well before formal British colonization) because of the policies of this private machinery of war and plunder.

Official state colonization, wrapped in the law, and based on the privatization of land and private entitlements to local cronies of the colonial power, was necessary to avoid the permanent scramble between competitive colonial powers that invariably followed the early take of possession. Eventually the colonized elite, sometimes due to international circumstances, sometimes by mobilization of the masses, got rid of the colonial power and established themselves as formally independent states. But independence is a formalistic idea that needs to be appreciated in context. The colonial relationship, in the form of neo-colonialism, remains based on local elites extracting a price for their services as agencies of hegemony. Thus, not only legal colonization but also formal decolonization appears as the outcome of international competition in which the law had an important role to play. This appears, for example, in North America, Oceania, and perhaps South Africa, where European newcomers, after engaging in genocide, established themselves as a new colonized class eventually able to free itself from colonial domination by the former mother country. More often, mostly for demographic reasons (in Latin America and India, for example), a colonial class had to come to terms with local populations.

Colonial models of exploitation developed, exhibiting some degree of cooperation by the local people, a fundamental source of cheap labor necessary for extractive economies (impoverished natives were massively used in mining throughout Spanish Latin America and elsewhere, and natives were staffing the army and most colonial institutions in Imperial India). Alternatively, labor could arrive in the form of slaves harvested in western Africa, as in the plantations of the southern United States, the Caribbean, and Brazil, allowing ships to sail the "triangle" always fully loaded. For example, British ships would leave London, Manchester, or Liverpool for the African West Coast loaded with all sort of artefacts for the African slave trading elites. They would leave packed with slaves bound to plantations; and they would return to Europe loaded with American loot, in the form of metals, guano, wood, cotton, etc. Similar arrangements were in place on the east trade line with some variations, such as those engaged in the forced sale of Indian opium to China. At the height of the British empire, modes of indirect rule through law governed and extracted resources in the interest of London over more than a quarter of the surface of our planet.[33]

A Story of Continuity: Constructing the Empire of Law (lessness)

Around the completion of decolonization, in the core of the Cold War years, it is easy to detect a pattern of continuity beneath an image of separation. New "sovereign" local elites kept ties with former colonial powers, or established new relationships in the bipolar political world, extracting substantial benefits from skillfully playing the Cold War chessboard or even, such as in the case of Nehru's India, profiting from the Sino-Soviet division of the late 1950s. Local lawyers, often trained both in the West and in socialist countries, figured prominently in these new settings. The debate on the benign or oppressive nature of Western rule of law was resolved in favor of the former even by socialists such as Julius Nyerere of Tanzania or by leaders such as Ghandi (himself a lawyer) in India, not to be re-opened again here. Thus, one constant – the recognition of the rule of law as a benign force on the path to development – emerged reinforced in the aftermath of decolonization. Its role in colonial plunder appears underestimated even in the more polemical political rhetoric of the emerging nationalists and "post-colonial" scholars and novelists.

Through the twentieth century, for example, the so-called Monroe Doctrine (1823) kept Latin America solidly under US influence, and the European colonial legacy yielded to a process of American hegemony. In this setting, organizations like the CIA (Central Intelligence Agency) provided the straight power and political brutality, while the first *law and development movement* provided a robust rhetoric of the rule of law and of its lack. These forces, regardless of their very different motivations, ended up supporting fascist dictatorships, invariably favoring plunder by large US corporations, such as that of the notorious United Fruit Company.

Asia was marked by war in Korea and Vietnam and by a fierce competition both within the communist bloc and outside of it. In this turbulent period, Western ideas of legality, a legacy of the nineteenth century that forced open markets by economic and military means, were possibly confined to a very marginal layer of the complex political patchwork. Nevertheless, the anti-law attitude of the Chinese "great leap forward" and of the "cultural revolution," never obtained final regional hegemony, contrasted as they were by Kruschev's legalistic and Brezhnev's bureaucratic vision of socialism. Ironically, by relentless Western propaganda, the lack of the rule of law was eventually cited as responsible for the post Vietnam War horrors in South East Asia, making US rule of law rhetoric successful today even in an area where its violent imperialism appeared with the gloves off.

Warfare, violence, racism, and delicate international Cold War confrontation characterized the situation in the Middle East and more generally in Islamic North Africa. The issue of the relationship between Islam and legal modernization was early on the desks of legal reformers, and its importance was witnessed by the tremendous prestige and influence through the area of the most important legislative products of such efforts: the Egyptian Civil Code of 1949 and the Iraqi Civil Code of 1953. Western notions of rule of law and of statehood have helped subvert the relationship between Islam and government, putting government (the state) in control and politically dividing the community of the faithful. Meanwhile, notions of backwardness, rigidity, and the immutability of Islamic law have been advanced even in the most otherwise respectable legal literature, with the final result of getting rid of those aspects of Islamic law (such as solidarity, and the duty to care for the poor) less friendly to the neo-liberal order.

A setting in which the fundamental unfolding of colonial, post-colonial, and imperial legal continuity appears is the most recently independent region of sub-Saharan Africa. Here, a staggering plurality of legal forms accumulated on top of each other, producing a degree of stratification and of pluralism difficult to find elsewhere. Moreover, it is here that, through the Cold War, the political dimension of the formal legal system was widely acknowledged and was highly symbolic. Constitutional documents succeed each other with the same intensity as coups and revolutions. The international financial institutions and the most powerful Western agencies of development adhered to a "hands off the legal system" policy that is itself an acknowledgment of the political connection between local law and international political competition. Despite some limited US efforts towards modernization in the domain of legal education in the 1960s, law was considered too "political" to be an area of intervention in Africa through the Cold War. But when the Cold War ended, law in Africa started to be constructed as a "merely technical" device whose legitimacy was to be based on economic efficiency measured by the capacity to attract foreign investment. In the new post Cold War scenario, financial support became available for law-related projects of development and a new law and development movement blossomed to facilitate the unfair opening up of markets of intellectual property, raw materials, and cheap labor via elaborate, legally complex trade agreements.

The end of the Cold War weighed heavily on these so-called post-colonial areas. By the early 1990s it became clear that US imperial power was unwilling to share access to Middle Eastern oil or to pay the ongoing rate to local ruling classes or to neo-colonial competitors such as France or other Western countries. The first Gulf War paved the way for the transformation of neo-colonialism, with a plurality of competing actors (France, England, etc.) into a US-dominated monopolistic setting. The United States claimed new imperial status, while the colonial order, rather than being substituted for by independence, liberation, and equality, has given way to an imperial order: the British still own the diamond mines in Sierra Leone; the mines in Bolivia are still run by multinationals fiercely struggling against President Morales' nationalization; oil in Nigeria is under the control of American oil companies.

The high concentration of military power in the hands of the monopolistic superpower seems to have transformed the competitive conditions in which the rule of law was developed in the colonies, as well as those of formal decolonization. Economic and political policy-making is organized around the Bretton Woods institutions (the World Bank and IMF) and is carried on by other non-politically accountable entities such as the WTO or the G8. The use of straight military power that enforces this neo-liberal hegemonic order is increasingly accompanied by a rhetoric of exceptional circumstances (war, terrorism, energy crisis, etc.) rather than by a rhetoric of religion, civilization, or even law – more in the direction of the pre-colonial private plunder of the East India Company than in the direction that fueled the hopes of decolonization.

Significantly, in Africa, as in Latin America, Central Asia, China, and elsewhere, the law became a technological commodity, a mechanism that could be supplied by international development agencies or private firms. Intervention could fix the shortcomings and "lacks," blamed on the colonial (European) and post-colonial (communist) order or simply on caricaturized Islamic or Confucian local obsolete conceptions. Neo-liberal power could then impose, in striking continuity with the colonial order, a version of the rule of law that entrenches rather than restrains, or controls the giant corporate model of economic activity. This order, obtained by a relentless process of corporatization through legal and illegal means, favors the smooth transfer of natural resources at bargain prices from public ownership to the rich oligarchs. Technocrats, mostly economists, substitute in an increasing number of functions – colonial officials, lawyers, anthropologists, and missionaries – in the production of legitimacy. Local elites, once trained in Europe, are trained in the United States.

An American law firm can secure for its corporate clients their vision of the rule of law: a guarantee of the return of the investments in the gigantic pipeline to transfer oil from the Caspian Sea to the Mediterranean. By negotiating contracts and bilateral treaties, the newly created "right of free transfer of oil" can legally be enforced by private militia or by puppet governments. Other law firms specialize in contracts of reconstruction: "Take off the helmet put on the hard hat: reconstructing Iraq and Afghanistan" is the motto of one such large firm in the Washington DC area: plunder and the rule of law.

The last 10 years of the twentieth century were crucial in the refinement of imperialistic and hegemonic aspects of American law. Nobody has put it more clearly than leading international lawyer Richard Falk:

> The logic of hegemonic authority extends beyond the implications of unequal power and influence, to encompass the rather amorphous, yet significant, role of global leadership. Such a hegemonic role in an era of moderated international conflict is premised on military power, but crucially also includes normative reputation as a generally benevolent political actor, a provider of order beneficial to the global public good, and not just action driven by the national interests of the hegemonic power.[34]

The pursuit of "normative reputation" has stood on a simple ideological platform since the time of Woodrow Wilson. A strong emphasis on freedom, democracy, and the rule of law, as deeply rooted American values, has accompanied almost all US foreign interventions, invariably presented as in the service of the public good rather than in the interest of the intervening power. Such an idealized vision, often contrasted with an enemy face of Nazi fascism, communism, oriental despotism, etc., has allotted to the United States significant prestige as a benevolent international ruler, despite horrors such as Hiroshima and Dresden, for which the "Marshall Plan" has been deemed adequate compensation.

To be sure, during the Vietnam War, US prestige dramatically declined worldwide. Nevertheless, the communist totalitarian alternative was enough to make a sufficient number of intellectuals – particularly lawyers – still ready to buy into the benevolent nature of US rule of law, its intimate connection with the capitalist economy, and ultimately with freedom. The present ideological construction of the Islamic world (as represented by Khomeini, Ahmedinejad, or the Taliban) also introduced a racist component, but the substantive charges against the "enemy" have not been changed: the adversity to American values of universal freedom, democracy, rule of law, gender equality, and human rights – a remarkable pattern of continuity. Of course, then as today, such values are presented as inextricably connected with the capitalist model of development, the natural outcome of a genuine pursuit of freedom.[35]

One could say that the nineties were the decade in which US international power and law entered into a more marked phase of hegemony. As we discuss in further chapters, legal and political hegemony implies a consistent effort to Americanize international institutions, promoting an ideological image of democracy and freedom in order to persuade the public of the benign nature of the international leader, sometimes by means of propaganda and manipulation. By the very early part of the new millennium, attempts to rule by "normative reputation" cower under an annual military budget of over $600 billion (2007 figure).

This book will not catalog the many occasions in which the new world order, born after World War II and accomplished after the symbolic fall of the Berlin wall, has been enforced by unprecedented military strengths and violence.[36] For the purposes here we can assume that force is today, as it had been at the time of the Crusades, of Pizarro, and of the British opening up of eastern markets, the most important instrument for imposing the hegemony of Western values, although followed by legal justifications and outright propaganda.[37] Developing and accomplishing unchallenged primacy of physical strength has produced much of the hegemonic position of the United States.[38] Today the United States government spends more on its army than the aggregate nine countries beneath it in the ranking of the top spenders. Nevertheless, in a project of expansionism, force requires ideology to gain some consent both in the camp of the hegemonic power and among the victims. This is where the rule of law plays a crucial role.

Transformations into the rule of law have accompanied significant changes in the way in which the capitalist superpower attempts to rule the world. Plunder prospered even during the most "virtuous" phases, in which the American rule of law was at the peak of its prestige, spontaneously followed and admired worldwide as a possible model of liberation. Nevertheless, the weakening of the bite and of the credibility of the rule of law in more recent times made plunder even more possible, itself being transformed, emboldened, and able to reach new heights through corporate shaping of the law.

In the 1990s, as a result of the fall of the Soviet Union, most Western communist and socialist parties started a major self-critique. A large part of the intellectual elite that during the Vietnam era was critical of US imperialism, quite suddenly discovered the virtues of the "free market," thus weakening intellectual resistance to rampant Reagan/Thatcher capitalism.[39] According to the new, quickly developed, orthodoxy, the political apparatus of the Soviet model simply could not resist processes of internal corruption because the plan was a poor substitute for the market and because freedom and entrepreneurship were sacrificed. When Soviet political failure included all possible alternatives to capitalism, an idealized model of capitalism started to be compared with a historical and contingent realization of socialism. The reach of a time-honored hegemonic strategy consisted in comparing a favorable self-portrait with an essentialized other, a strategy already well developed in a variety of forms of "orientalism" through the colonial era.

Discursive practices are needed because in any society and in any complex aggregate of people, leaving to one side the cynical, there is space for both idealists and the resigned. In different times and spaces the ratio of such people can change, and legal institutions, as with the media or the dominant culture, play a major role in determining their proportions. Passive, disengaged individuals might facilitate hegemony, intervention, and plunder so that this kind of citizenry contributes in creating cynical environments in which plunder triumphs. The early story of the crusaders in the Arab world and their easily triumphant plunder in the late eleventh century has been explained by such subdued and cynical attitudes.

In the next chapters we describe the techniques by which the plunder of resources and people happen – a guide to how a more technically sophisticated life of plunder has evolved, sometimes by use of the rule of law as its fig leaf, sometimes by using power as if it were law.

2 | Neo-liberalism: Economic Engine of Plunder

The Argentinean Bonanza

The construction of a neo-colonial scheme is quite simple: rather than a warship, and an openly discriminatory legal system, it is the mirage of efficiency and an image of rule of law that allows legal plunder. The ideological weapon used by the new local elites and by their Wall Street counterparts, is the desire to build efficient markets governed by the rule of law. This is the unique path to development as conceived by the vulgate of the international financial institutions, also known as the Washington Consensus or neo-liberal policy. As in the recent case of Argentina, freed from Spanish colonial rule by Libertador San Martin as early as 1816, the outcome follows a staggering pattern of continuity in plunder.

The story of neo-liberal plunder in Argentina begins to unfold in the early phase of the global market boom that followed the triumph of Western capitalism in the Cold War. Historically, Argentina has defaulted on its loans four times, two of which were due to global economic crises in 1890 and 1930, long before the World Bank and the International Monetary Fund (IMF) even existed. The first default significant for the neo-liberal story happened in 1982 as a consequence of the last British imperial war, the Falkland-Malvinas War, followed by the fall of General Galtieri's fascist regime of terror (a regime backed by the CIA). Then in January 2002, the Argentine government announced it would default on \$141 billion in public sector debt – the largest default of a sovereign state in history.

The last two defaults opened and closed the 20 years of triumph of the neo-liberal model inaugurated by Prime Minister Thatcher and President Reagan in the early 1980s. The 20 years separating one default from the other are particularly significant for a study on plunder because they have been characterized by: (1) an abundant use of democracy and the rule of law rhetoric in a previously military and traditionally authoritarian state; and (2) a major role performed by the international financial institutions in securing stabilization and alignment of the Argentine model to the dictates of the neo-liberal policy. Interestingly, an unprecedented degree of influence was exercised through this period by Chicago school-style economic doctrines, symbolized by the political fortunes of one darling of the international financial institutions, the University of Chicago trained economist Domingo Cavallo, a long-standing Minister of the Economy who served under several Argentinean presidents.

It was Cavallo's decision, much applauded by the Washington Consensus, to establish a fixed conversion rate of one Argentine peso to one dollar in 1991, thus inaugurating the new, bolder, post-communist season of US hegemony. The result of this "pegged" rate was the surrender of Argentine economic sovereignty to the United States (and thus to the global institutions of corporate capitalism, where the USA retains the lion's share). The reasons for this move were the same as those of the dozen countries (most notably Equador) whose economies are today officially "dollarized" – dire economic recession, high inflation, large fiscal deficit, and widespread bank failures.

Little more than 10 years after Cavallo's bold move, five presidents changed in a few weeks and the peso was finally "freed" from the dollar. A rush to the banks followed the dramatic peso devaluation, where depositors found out those withdrawals were strictly limited, leading to street protests and violent riots from Buenos Aires to Salta. The Argentines had found out that their economy, including the most valuable part of its public sector, and in particular their savings, had been looted. Shortly after that, many small investors in the United States and Europe discovered the same unhappy fate of the savings they had invested in Argentine bonds. In the course of the same 10 years, the big securities firms in Wall Street – prestigious names like Morgan Stanley, First Boston, Goldman Sacks, or Merrill Lynch – reaped nearly $1 billion in fees from underwriting Argentine government bonds. They were packaged as derivatives in a variety of creative forms, with the handsomely compensated help of Wall Street law firms with equally prestigious names.

There have been many perpetrators in the plunder that affected 57 percent of the Argentinean people that are officially poor today, despite living in one of the most naturally wealthy countries in the world. We are not interested here in placing blame or political responsibility. On the contrary, we are interested in understanding the dynamics of plunder, its connection to rule of law ideology, along with the current hegemonic role of American law. In fact, plunder of such magnitude requires impressive professional skills in the domain of law and finance and some political groundwork, an activity carried on by controlling the political process in the United States, the country that after 1991 (because of dollarization) was exercising *de facto* economic sovereignty over Argentina. This is where lawyers and economists become unavoidable actors of global plunder. This is plunder as a motivating force and ideology – and a consequence of global capitalist development rooted in the rule of law.

The basic need behind the neo-liberal policy of development, through the major international financial institutions, is that of sustaining demand for Western-produced commodities and the opening of new unrestricted business opportunities in basic sectors such as communication, healthcare, mineral extraction, etc. In order to reach these objectives, the elites in the targeted countries in Asia, Latin America, or even Africa, often cronies of powerful corporate interests, are lured into unsustainable rates of consumption by a variety of practices aimed at smoothing their process of dismantling and selling off the public sector. Again, there is not much new under the sun; neither in terms of policy nor of the instruments used to pursue them. For example, under Mexican dictator Porfirio Diaz, in power from 1876 to 1910, the policy was "to allow foreign and national entrepreneurs to take advantage of laws designed to free up land, labour and national resources."[1] Diaz's laws are similar in spirit to those of open market restructuring promoted by neo-liberal acolytes, beginning with President de la Madrid (a former honorary President of the Latin American Society of Law and Economics). Such laws "did spur development, but often at the expenses of villages and communities throughout Mexico whose lands the developers absorbed and whose citizens became impoverished workers."[2]

Today one of the most diffused strategies to impose dependency on the third world is that of granting apparently cheap credit to elites so that luxurious consumption of corporate-produced commodities outside of any productive investment naturally follows. Once the country is dramatically indebted, mostly towards private banks or small investors, the IMF intervenes by "negotiating" structural reforms almost invariably benefiting the stronger corporate creditors, leaving small investors in dire straits and the local economy in tragic shape. One could argue that these are the rules of the capitalist game, a survival-of-the-fittest model that naturally advantages the more skillful players. Nevertheless, such a strategy can still be considered plunder, because it is like encouraging an addicted gambler to keep playing on credit in a casino and then taking away his family home where his innocent wife and children live, because he can not pay back what he has lost. And by IMF standards it is all perfectly legal!

Because this book aims at illustrating plunder as a practice featuring a variety of global actors, the example of the Argentine futures market is particularly appropriate because of the sophisticated legal and economic mechanisms at play. In the case of the recent major default of this naturally wealthy country, the losers have been globally located (many in old Europe) although the Argentines took the lion's share of the suffering. The law has both produced and attempted to remedy plunder, confirming the current hegemony of US law.

In order to attempt to understand this remarkably creative form of legalized plunder, we must first briefly familiarize ourselves with the concept of "derivatives." A derivative is a financial instrument whose value derives from that of some other security, like a stock or a bond or from the value of some commodity, currency, or index. Derivatives are legal titles of two kinds: options and forwards. On financial markets it is possible to buy a stock but it is also possible to buy an option on that stock. The "call" option, i.e. the *right* to buy a stock at a future time and price, is a derivative because its value is derived from that of the underlying stock. The "put" option, i.e. the *right* to sell a stock at a future time and price is also a derivative because again its value depends on that of the underlying stock. While options give *rights* to buy or sell, forwards create *obligations* to buy or sell at a future time and price. They are also derivatives.

A practical example might illustrate how this works. Imagine that a new watch is announced for the market. You know its characteristics but still do not know how much it will cost. If you do not want to wait until the watch arrives at the shop, you can buy (say for $100) the right to buy it at $5,000 when it arrives. This is a *call option*. If the watch arrives and costs $6,000 your call option was a good deal because its value is $1000 and you only paid $100. If the watch arrives and costs $4,000, your call option was a bad deal, because you would have been better off saving the $100 dollars of your option and buying the watch at retail value. Remember that options create rights *not* obligations, so when you buy an option for $100, the value of your option increases with the value of the watch but you never risk more than $100.

A different possibility, should you not wish to buy a call option for $100 is to enter into a *forward*. A forward creates a right *and* an obligation. Under the forward, you can oblige yourself to buy the watch for $4,000. In this case, your derivative increases in value together with the value of the watch. If the watch arrives at $6,000 dollars, your forward was a very good idea because it is now worth $2,000. But if the watch arrives at $2,000 then you *must* buy the watch at $4,000, so you have lost $2,000.

This is a very simplified explanation but it is enough to understand that derivatives are, plainly speaking, bets on the future value of the principal.[3] The principal might be such a complex thing as the economy of a country, something whose value is much more difficult to predict than that of a watch. In the real life of financial markets derivatives are packaged as complex combinations of forwards and options linked to staggering varieties of factors. Amongst the factors that get combined to create derivatives may be economic indexes of foreign countries, such as the exchange of their currency, the inflation rate, the rating given by an agency, the yield of government bonds, and so forth. Of course, many such factors are not casual but might be affected by the behaviors and the decisions of the elites governing the economy, both locally and internationally (or plainly American in the case of dollarized economies such as then Argentina or Ecuador). The art of a good investment banker is to package derivatives in a form that is attractive for investors, particularly by legally attempting to hide the real risks involved in betting while marketing the deal as a calculated and limited risk protected by the law.

One could argue that some or even most of such practices are in fact illegal, and that an economy based on the rule of law would not allow plunder to happen. Litigation about the Argentinean scandal is already happening and because of technical mechanisms that we will describe in Chapter 6, plaintiffs suing in the United States are much better off than those suing in Europe or elsewhere, thus once more confirming the hegemony of American law. Nevertheless, plunder maintains an ambiguous relationship with the rule of law, since it is capable of constructing notions of legality and illegality. In other words a fine line divides the legal and the illegal in these complex transactions, and plunder prospers precisely because the line is so thin and variable.

For example, the IMF recklessly provided a façade of respectability to a tremendously irresponsible packaging of the local economy (which was actually quite weak) into an invented "emerging market." It was the IMF that made available, during the Presidency of Carlos Menem, a cash flow conditioned on measures that, short of being structural adjustments, only favored more public wealth transfer from the multitudes to the elites. The IMF significantly contributed to the creation of a decade-long bonanza for the actors of a gambling market of "derivatives" and for a local upper class that, thanks to the one peso/one dollar rate, and to the other pro-rich measures elaborated in Washington, was developing absolutely crazy imported commodity consumption behaviors. This upper economic class, holding substantial deposits and investments in the USA, and sending their children to US elite schools, has convincingly been compared to the *colonial elites* invented by the mother country.[4] It is the elite's US-educated children who are naturally absorbed into the prestigious staff of the international financial institutions, as representatives of the "third world" and therefore demonstrating the diverse and representative hiring policy of the poor countries they serve. Is this legal? Is this plunder? Is this just bad policy? The lines are thin and deserve to be explored.

It would be simplistic to place the whole responsibility on the international financial institutions. Private investment banks and rating agencies deserve their share of responsibility too. To help the reader understand the scam that led to the plunder of the Argentine people (and of global small investors), we offer a concrete example of the "manufacturing" of emerging markets bonds.

Former investment banker and now attorney Frank Partnoy offers a first-hand insider's description of the process by which the big financial business goes "hunting" in "emerging markets."[5] His book is a true mine of information on the way in which very risky gambling on the derivative market is packaged so as to appear risk-free to institutional investors worldwide. It offers a particularly interesting example in a chapter significantly called "Don't cry for me Argentina" describing a sale of worthless Argentine bonds, repackaged to make them attractive. This sale, carried out in a few weeks by a trader in his mid-twenties, produced a $4 million fee to Morgan Stanley, and a large fee to the New York law firm of Cravath, in consideration for a couple of phone calls. Interestingly, in the mid-nineties this kind of transaction was not even considered an exceptionally compensated one in the industry.

In 1992, the Central Bank of Argentina, implementing a "structural adjustment" requirement to consolidate the public debt, issued an enormous $5.5.billion bond. The bonds were called *Bonos de Consolidacion de Deudas*

Provisionales, popularly known as BOCONS. The diffused debt thus consolidated was towards local governments, suppliers, pensioners, retirees, etc. The characteristics of these bonds made them very unattractive. Not only were they coming from a government at high risk, but they also would pay no interest for 6 years. The principal would increase in value each month as a consequence of a mysterious alchemy of several different monthly interest rates. It would be impossible for the holder to know how many bonds he would actually have. Moreover, when after 6 years some interest would actually start being paid, the principal value would start declining in the course of the 48 months necessary to get back, by monthly instalments, the principal and the matured interests. During the 48 months the interest, calculated on the progressively declining amount of the principal, and itself linked to mysterious indexes, would also start decreasing.

If you were an Argentine pensioner, you would find it quite rough to live on zero dollars per month for 6 years, the only certain aspect of this scheme. You might consequently dislike the legal requirement of consolidation attached to the Washington Consensus-generated structural adjustment plan. If you were not someone stuck into it, with some understanding of what actually was issued, you would probably not want to buy in. As a consequence, you would not end up financing the crazy consumption rates of the Argentine ruling elite in times of dire straits. In a word, you would not participate in what, if deemed illegal, would be a conspiracy (Wall Street actors, international financial institutions, local ruling elites) to plunder that beautiful country.

Nevertheless, here is where the legal and economic genius of the Derivative Product Group at Goldman Sachs (and later, Morgan Stanley) entered into the picture. An offshore trust in the Cayman Islands was created where the BOCONS would be deposited. Any payment until the maturity date of 2002 was to be made into the trust. A contract was then signed between the trust and Morgan Stanley by which the investment bank would receive all the BOCONS payments and in consideration of that would pay a flat interest rate to the trust beginning immediately (thus lending money to the trust for 6 years). The trust would then issue "units" paying a large interest rate partially backed by Morgan Stanley and aggressively marketed by Morgan Stanley itself. These simplified BOCONS, re-named "Repackaged Argentina Domestic Security Trust I" would pay interest immediately, would appear not to have a fluctuating principal, and seemed very safe, backed as they were by Morgan Stanley, who would disclose (if at all) only in very tiny obfuscatory print, that they were in fact highly complicated and risky derivatives. Of course the IMF rhetoric, which the Center for Economic and Policy Research has recently exposed for having systematically exaggerated in the last 16 years the future growth in Latin America, had a role in convincing prospective buyers.

Clients flocked to this deal (Morgan Stanley sold $123 million of trust units), and to many others in the "emerging" markets, leaving the pockets of these smart financial engineers full of untouchable fees, with no responsibility for the economic fate of Argentina or the investors in its repackaged BOCONS. These products were derivatives, despite the conscious internal policy of banning the term that, as we are told, even obliged the withdrawal from circulation and reprinting of an earlier more honest prospectus as soon as the bosses of the investment bank realized that the word "derivative," which evokes risk, was mentioned in it. And as with all derivative products betting on a country strangled by international debt, their value was quick to fall.

Of course, as the winners were clear, so have been the losers, not only the investors but also the weak inhabitants of a duped economy. Crucial to this deal were three components: (1) the use of an offshore trust, remote from the (unlikely) controls of the Securities and Exchange Commission (SEC); (2) the "one peso/one dollar" deal, introducing hard currency into an emerging economy and thus making it more attractive; and (3) the generous rhetoric and rating of Argentina as an emerging market, despite the corrupted policy of Menem and the ruling elites.

Once more, while plunder is clear, so appears to be its connection with the rule of law, in the form of a market-friendly, global, legal environment for economic investment. Certainly, many economic actors contributed to the economic disaster that followed this decade of bonanza. Not only international actors, but also much of the ruling class beneficiaries of the structural adjustment programs and of the other neo-liberal measures introduced by the policy of the international financial institutions, which we turn now to.[6]

Neo-Liberalism: an Economic Theory of Simplification and a Spectacular Project

We have described plunder in Argentina as favored by the Washington Consensus or neo-liberal policy. But what is neo-liberalism? What are its roots? Who are the actors implementing its political project? How does neo-liberalism relate to plunder and the rule of law?[7]

Neo-liberalism can be seen as a revolutionary theory accompanied by praxis. Just as the building of socialism in the Soviet Union was the product of a theory (Marxism) and praxis (Leninism), reacting against a deeply grounded political order (Russian czarism), similarly neo-liberalism is the product of theory and praxis reacting against a previous order, the *welfare state*. This simple parallel is sufficient to show how the Reagan/Thatcher revolution, which spawned the neo-liberal praxis, can be seen as a reactionary move. The neo-liberal revolution targeted progressive social and political settings. It has reacted against a frontier of institutional development, the so-called welfare state. It has reacted against the thorough attempt to build, in a complex society, a structure capable of responding at least in part to the needs of its weaker members. Neo-liberal theory blamed inefficiency on the welfare state. Neo-liberal praxis has been grounded in privatization, deregulation, downsizing, outsourcing, and taxation cuts.

Consequently, neo-liberalism can be considered to be more than a revolution, a restoration of a nineteenth-century bourgeois political setting, in a society that for the first three-quarters of the twentieth century had moved worldwide in the direction of more socially concerned models of development. To be sure, theories of "the social" in legal and political thinking began to unfold in the last part of the nineteenth century and became a dominant pattern of legal and political thought by the second decade of the twentieth century.[8] These social models put at the center of the picture the social group (or the state), but to better serve the individual in society: affirmative rights rather than negative liberties. They were mostly developed by French and German legal and political thinkers and by Scandinavian praxis, but spread well beyond the contours of the Western legal tradition, setting the intellectual ground for the welfare state. We can find such theories in Catholic solidarity thinking, in the intellectual imaginary of the Second International, in Egyptian modernization efforts, in Mexican revolutionary rhetoric, in Argentinean Peronism, and, of course, in the social platforms of Teddy Roosevelt and Franklin Delano Roosevelt. These are theories that display a notable component of ambiguity, so that often intellectuals and thinkers of the social wave are functional to bolster authoritarian and even fascist regimes. In Argentina, for example, Peron has been considered the mentor from the Montoneros to the extreme right. Nevertheless, after the horrors of World War II, social theories were purified of their degenerations; they were enriched by a whole new dimension of economic sensitivity by Keynesian economics, and provided an ideal of advanced, progressive society throughout the capitalist bloc.

The political and economic theory of neo-liberalism can be considered the product of conservative economic ideology made accessible to non-economists by epigones of the Austrian school, such as Friedrich Von Hayek. A variety of tenets comprise this critique of the previous order. The welfare state, rather than being seen as one of the most advanced frontiers of human civilization that capitalism could meet, is considered a wasteful bureaucratic organization to be abandoned as rapidly as possible. The state regulation – a system of legislation that organizes the structure of the welfare state, presides over the relationship between the individual and the public organization, and takes care of society by means of regulation of wealth distribution – is challenged as corrupt, captured by special interests. It is exposed as a corrupting factor of a natural, spontaneous, case-law-based legal order, protecting property rights and based on courts as neutral solvers of private conflicts arising in a free market.[9] Exploiting the ambiguous relationship between socialism and the social, political, and economic theories grounding the welfare state, neo-liberalism emphasizes the value of individual freedom and portrays the state, once again, as an inherent Leviathan, the enemy of private property and self-determination. As in the times of Sir Edward Coke, an activist progressive and proactive government attempting to redistribute some public wealth among social classes in the interest of the weaker is presented as a violation of the rule of law.

This simplistic platform, based on notions of sanctity of property, free enterprise, and retribution for risk-taking, has effectively revived notions of "freedom of contract" as a limit to state intervention that courts of law had considered obsolete since the 1930s even in the United States. No intellectual theory can impose itself and mutate into a revolution capable of discarding so many of the previous aspects of civilization – free healthcare, legal aid, well-funded education, and security of employment – without a strong and authoritarian political action capable of transforming it into praxis. Reagan and Thatcher originally provided this political action. It was eventually naturalized as a "structural component" of the free world, making it a bipartisan philosophy, by Clinton and Blair, followed by a variety of European "leftist" governments eager to participate in the triumphs of the "end of history."

Exploiting fear by means of deliberate exaggeration of the Soviet threat, the conquests of the welfare state began to be constructed as "too expensive" and inefficient, particularly during the oil crisis of the mid-1970s. Conservative British Prime Minister Margaret Thatcher and Republican US President Ronald Reagan, backed by the military industry complex, became the champions of massive transfers of public resources from the social welfare system into the repressive *apparati* of the state. Such transfers would allow the West to outspend the Soviets in the rush to stockpile weapons of mass destruction, and at the same time would set the basis for overcoming the state of general economic depression following the oil crises of the seventies. Corruption and a huge military expenditure not only forced the competing Soviet bloc into economic downfall, it also reasserted imperial ideals (the Falkland-Malvinas War), overcame humiliations such as the hostage crisis in Tehran, and, most importantly, created the basis for a new world order under US hegemony (Pax Americana).

The revolution needed praxis to impose itself and, most importantly, needed institutions in order to overcome the risk of being subverted by the next change of parties in power. While both the Tories in the UK and the Reagan political ticket were to remain in power throughout the 1980s, their revolutionary legacy was by no means challenged when the conservative parties had to finally leave office. Both Clinton in the USA and Blair in the UK accepted neo-liberalism as a bipartisan legal and economic recipe, a true economic constitution of the post Cold War international assertion of power known as the Washington Consensus. Why? How? The answer is probably to be found in a thorough revamping and restructuring of the institutions of global financial stability – the IMF and World Bank – that the Anglo-American winners of World War II had created at Bretton Woods in 1944. Such restructuring, transforming international financial institutions into global legislators, was in need of a thorough theoretical transformation of the very idea of law, from a political artefact into a neutral technology. Without such transformation the Bretton Woods institution's intervention into targeted legal systems would have been impossible to legitimize, given the fact that their bylaws expressly forbid political interventions. We will see in the next chapter how lawyers and economists have been eager to provide the intellectual tools for such theoretical transformation.[10]

The radical abandonment of the economic theory that had guided Lord Keynes in his master-minding of the World Bank and the IMF, and the restructuring of these institutions as informal global legislators, has transformed the neo-liberal economic policy into a sort of global economic constitutional order. Some observers indicate the irony that the World Bank and IMF, the brainchildren of Keynes, are now the final obstacles to adopting Keynesian economic policy throughout the world, even in light of obvious failures of neo-liberal models, such as symbolized by the Argentinean default previously discussed. Because of the new global economic constitution, no state today could claim a role in the management of the economy large enough to be able to carry on economic enterprise and to be a major employer. The trend, imposed by the Bretton Woods institutions, is to deregulate, downsize, outsource, and privatize. This irony, that Keynesian policies have been squeezed out of Keynes' Bretton Woods creations, is easy to explain because neo-liberalism is an expansionist economic policy much in need of institutional power in order to be able to open up world markets for corporate plunder. Keynesian policies, because of their state centrism, were either local in nature (building of infrastructure, etc.) or, as models of international development, they required relatively powerful and well-structured states. Hence their emphasis on legal modernization of state apparatuses in the third world, a target that development agencies abandoned well before accomplishing it. Moreover, born out of the Great Depression, the aggregate of complex Keynesian economic policies not only were context-specific but certainly were not overly optimistic on the potentials of unlimited large-scale capitalist expansion.

Neo-liberalism displays a philosophy opposite to that of Keynes. To begin with, while still in its infancy, neo-liberal policies produced a significant collapse of the opposite Keynesian model, so that it unfolded for the best part of its life within a highly optimistic and self-congratulatory vision of the merits of corporate capitalistic expansion. Moreover, neo-liberalism profited from the debacle of Soviet socialism and from the apparent willingness of the Chinese bloc to adapt to Western capitalist standards (Deng Xiaoping's move towards socialist-capitalism in China dates from 1978), which allowed them to survive the pressures of Western-dominated economic competition. Consequently, neo-liberalism is a monopolistic economic policy, in the sense that for the better part of its life it suffered neither competition nor opposition from alternative policies. The radical attempted discrediting of Keynesian economics, mostly pursued by monetarist scholars at the University of Chicago, and the diffused sense that technocratic decision-making was more efficient than the political process, are all factors that explain changes within the intellectual posture and the political function of the Bretton Woods institutions. The legal scenario produced worldwide by the imposition of this global legal and economic philosophy, as it happens, is the ideal environment for plunder.

During the Cold War, proponents of corporate capitalism had to consider the social effects of their economic policies, since they needed the legitimacy that stems from being publicly perceived as more socially desirable than its socialist alternative. In the aftermath of the Cold War, no revolutionary alternative seems to be available for disadvantaged masses in the West, so that their consent to the consumer society, despite its injustice, could be assumed by the new leadership without any need to obtain such consent by welfare policy. An interesting example of such a mirror effect of the Cold War can be found in Finland where the capitalist model, in constant and close comparison with the communist alternative, produced some of the most advanced institutions of welfare ever built, institutions whose dismantling quickly began after the collapse of the Soviet alternative.

In formerly socialist countries, moreover, the rhetoric of "transition" – once used by the party to justify the shortcomings of socialism and presented as a mere transition phase *to* communism – was quite cynically transferred to the opposite camp. Now the poor and oppressed, literally dying of homelessness, disease, and hunger in Moscow and elsewhere, are told by cynical leaders that the suffering needs to happen during the transition to fully fledged capitalism, and that neo-liberal shock policies are aimed at making the transition short. Needless to say, this scenario favors corporate plunder made highly visible worldwide by new Russian gas-, oil-, and other natural resource-rich tycoons, displaying an amount of wealth that is simply plunder *per se*.

Because of these historical accidents, particularly the self-perception of being the best and only possible path, neo-liberalism displays the arrogance typical of ideological monopolies. Double standards that arise in economic policy are the best examples of such arrogance. Developed countries (particularly the USA) maintaining a variety of protectionist policies (e.g. no drug imports from Canada) while preaching open markets, and the law allowing the transnational mobility of goods and assets are good examples.

What is most important to observe is that such high levels of self-confidence and hubris determine a universalistic attitude, which denies context specificity. Neo-liberalism aims at expansion out of its universal claim to offer the best possible model of development. Universalism and double standards are reflected in the unfolding conception of the rule of law. In pursuit of the neo-liberal world, the rule of law is considered as a universal minimal legal system, capable of harsh control of the individual threatening the bottom line of property rights and incapable of limiting corporate actors. A control of the weak was created by the strong, both domestically in the relationship of the state towards individuals, and internationally in the relationship between states. The Bretton Woods institutions, transformed into global legislators by means of the contractual power that they enjoy, became the ideal tools for pursuing such a new wave of global capitalist expansion. They were the ones capable of transformation. Once they themselves transformed, the Reagan/Thatcher revolution morphed into an institutional praxis – naturalized, universalized, and located beyond the reach of opposition parties.

These institutions, by contractually conditioning desperately needed financial aid to domestic law reform, have played a major role in transforming the rule of law into an instrument of plunder in the exclusive interest of large international investors. While the default of Argentina offers a good example, many more will be offered later. Suffice now to think about the global transformation of labor law, dismantling the guarantees and protections of workers in the name of flexibility and full employment; about the progressive dismantling of environmental protection in areas inhabited by weak groups; about the dismantling of the same measures of protection of local small business and farmers that in the capitalist world had guaranteed (and still guarantee) development and sustainability; about very strict enforcement of intellectual property underpinned by big money, stifling the development of local creativity and imposing suffering and death (due to monopoly drug patents).

Keynesian economics, the leading doctrine behind the welfare state, with its strong link with politically supported legislation and regulation, came under attack at the same moment in which a conception of the law as an aggregate of technical and neutral private law rules, to be evaluated in terms of economic efficiency rather than substantial justice, was becoming dominant in the United States. As a consequence of these changes of intellectual paradigm and because the (former) Soviet Union could no longer monitor its areas of political hegemony in the third world, law and institutions became new targets for World Bank and IMF intervention – breaking a long-established taboo against intervening in the law, which was perceived as a key aspect of the political process of recipient countries. The law was now neutral and technical. It could be targeted, modified, and fixed, directly or indirectly, in the same way in which it is possible to intervene to fix a sewer system or a hospital.

Neo-liberal economists and lawyers trained in law and economics became the most powerful advisers of the World Bank and the IMF, in developing their recipes of "good governance." Since dismantling is easier than constructing, such advisers busily showed how easy it is to change complex aggregates of local institutions in favor of market-friendly ones. The concept of law that dominates the economist's discourse is indeed as simple as to be universal. Economists have traditionally been impatient with the complexities that occupy lawyers. To them, legal complexity as an aggregate of a variety of context-specific institutional and political structures is only a source of transaction costs; ideology is "intellectually uninteresting," as a leading Italian-American economist recently told the lawyer amongst us. The law, they believe, should facilitate rather than restrict market transactions. The local political and legal process, in the economists' view being corrupt and unreliable, increases transaction costs by discouraging investments and the efficient allocation of resources. That is, legal and political "distortions" restrict the free flow of resources from whoever values them less to whoever values them more. Therefore, in the view of the Chicago school, where Domingo Cavallo was trained, local institutional settings should be "adjusted" in order to facilitate such flow. Thus the notion of rule of law as a guarantee of investment returns, as discussed earlier. As in the case of the Argentinean futures, the rule of law, manufactured in New York mega firms, guarantees the translocation of resources from the weak to the strong.

In these adjusting exercises, collectively known as *structural adjustment programs* (SAPs), the political process plays no role. Indeed, the strategy is exactly to focus on the "merely technical" nature of the simple changes that are required in order to secure transfers of property to their most efficient users.

It is difficult not to see how such efficient transfers are deeply connected to the initial endowment of resources. Indeed, the "willingness to pay" for a given resource, the yardstick that economists use in order to see whether such a resource is actually in the hands of whoever values it most, is a function of the "capacity to pay" which in turn depends on the amount of resources already available to each of the actors of the transaction. Consequently, the rich are systematically favored when policy is evaluated in terms of efficiency, which explains the enormous increase in the gap between the rich and the poor under neo-liberal globalization. Global neo-liberalism applies the logic of "willingness to pay" to all resources wherever they might be located. Oil, for instance, should be transferred from whoever values it less to whoever values it more at the lowest possible transaction costs. Obviously, the rich countries with their higher consumption rates demonstrate higher willingness to pay. To withhold oil from the market is thus constructed as an inefficient practice, which because of the natural law framework inspiring such economic vision, borders on immorality – an accusation often used against countries in OPEC (Organization of Petroleum Exporting Countries). Similarly, "knowledge" should be transferred to the West, because here it is more valued in economic terms. In the neo-liberal scheme, all resources, knowledge, land, and labor, wherever located, must be available for whoever is willing to pay for them. Any measure to defend local policy-making is condemned as an attempt to close the market, an anathema for neo-liberal policy, "constitutionalized" in the neo-liberal order. As in the "self-enforcing" logic of the World Trade Organization (WTO), any attempt to close the market justifies economic and political retaliation. This is but continuity with past retaliations to "open up" markets such as the Opium War in China, or the British post-colonial wars in South America.

Economic policies underlying structural adjustment are thus promoted as responding to higher universal needs and standards, those of oligarchic efficiency and economic growth, which are defined as constitutionally superior to those local interests that the (local) political process usually attempts to satisfy. The (local) political process is then handed its first priority: the implementation of the "simple" institutional conditions capable of grounding an efficient marketplace for corporate actors. Since such conditions are deemed universal, universal actors such as the Bretton Woods international financial institutions dictate them. SAPs, recently renamed *comprehensive development frameworks*, drafted by such institutions are implemented and enforced by direct (more recently, "participated") economic conditioning, thus reaching the local political process with irresistible power. Being linked to much needed cash, they are poised beyond reach of both government and opposition parties. Indeed, they can only be evaluated and judged by macro-growth and other indices, interpreted by the financial gurus of the IMF and of private rating agencies allied with it.

Such policies are, however, based on highly simplistic but highly interventionist legal formulations. For example one reads in the *World Development Report* produced by the World Bank in 1999:

> Without the protection of human and property rights, and a comprehensive framework of laws, no equitable development is possible. A government must ensure that it has an effective system of property, contract, labor, bankruptcy, commercial codes, personal rights laws, and other elements of a comprehensive legal system. . . .[11]

Nothing is thus beyond the reach of the new global legislators. The World Bank's vision of nothing less than a "comprehensive legal system" cannot be seriously challenged politically by any opposition party with a future claim to be voted into government because it would be politically irresponsible to alienate the international source of economic survival. In this sense, the notion of comprehensive development is capable of making neo-liberalism a constitutional structure intimately connected with the logic of electoral politics. By this strategy, global technical rule-makers claim sovereignty over local politics.

It is important to stress that while this key neo-liberal strategy is more visible and more direct in developing and transitional countries, it is by no means limited to them. Even in contexts traditionally within the center, like Germany for example, the logic of neo-liberalism has not been less influential in determining winning political platforms in the aftermath of the Cold War. Social democrat leader Oskar Lafontaine, for example, reluctant to embrace IMF-dictated structural policies, was defeated by a more "realist" politician, Gerhard Schroeder, precisely because of Lafontaine's lack of international credibility due to his critical positions towards IMF plans. Thus, the Social Democratic Party was able to succeed in office to Kohl's conservative government only by fully acknowledging respect for the prescriptions of the Bretton Woods institutions. A very similar story can be told for Blair's victory within the British Labour Party, and for the transformation of many ambitious political leaders both from the left and from the right who have renounced previous "social platforms" for the dictates of the Washington Consensus. An example from the left can be found in former communists such as former Prime Minister Massimo D'Alema in Italy or Vladimir Putin in Russia. From the right, the best-known example is Spanish former Prime Minister Aznar who repudiated his "social" past as a supporter of fascist dictator Francisco Franco to become a coveted champion of the Washington Consensus.

Neo-liberal policies, precisely because they privilege the universal needs of market order over the local needs of the political constituency, are often unpopular and spark resistance. Despite the empty rhetoric of "equitable development," the losers in neo-liberal globalization processes are the weakest layers of the population, already impoverished farmers forced to buy genetically modified seeds that work only for one cycle, small shopkeepers displaced by the global chains of distribution, blue collar workers forced to accept pay cuts so as to not lose their jobs. Typically, such large numbers of losers are alienated from an electoral political process dominated by the rich and by corporate investments. In the United States, the top 0.25 percent of the population invests more in politics than 80 percent of individual contributions; in this model of democracy, corporate actors outspend by more than 10 times trade unions and other non-profit organizations. In the economic logic of democracy, contributions to the political process are seen as investments so that it is *natural* that their returns favor whoever made such investments. What follows is the irrelevance of the electoral process for whoever cannot afford to invest into it, because the neo-liberal alternative between conservative and third way parties reduces to a minimum the social impact of political change. In this scenario, it is irrational to devote attention to electoral politics, which in turn helps to explain low turnout and the depoliticized attitude of most people.

Again, this is by no means limited to US politics. An inverse relationship between the degree to which neo-liberal policies are implemented and people's participation in the electoral process is easy to detect worldwide. Needless to say, the lonely impotent crowd thus created might occasionally react with violence, particularly in those contexts where what is at stake is making ends meet, such as in the street revolts in Argentina in the aftermath of the freeing of the peso from the dollar. This is why neo-liberalism is very often accompanied by authoritarian rule and a police state, with the most infamous examples in Pinochet's Chile or Fujimori's Peru, just to mention two darlings of the Chicago school. The ruling elites, themselves impotent executors of policies designed elsewhere by the actors of economic globalization (IMF, World Bank, WTO), cannot respond with policy decisions for the needs of the people and consequently respond with the use of violence. Needless to say, the repressive apparatuses of the state – the military, the police, and the penitentiary systems – being the only public resource beneficiaries of the processes that we are discussing, are ready and willing to act, repressing any voice stemming out of the chorus. It is no wonder that in the United States from 1972 to the present, the population of prison inmates (thanks also to the prison privatization process, which created incentives to keep people in prison) has increased from 326,000 to over 2.3 million (2005 figures). It is even less wonder then, beginning at Seattle in 1999, that there have been no meetings of the so-called "free world" leaders (including the thus far failed process of European constitution making) that did not happen behind an iron curtain of police aimed at excluding participation, silencing opposition, and repressing protest.

Direct repression is not the only means by which the few winners of the neo-liberal process deal with dissent from the many losers. Another effective strategy that needs to be appreciated in order to put into some political context the "merely technical" recipes of the neo-liberal globalization process, is aimed at silencing opposition even before it actually emerges. The aggregate of such strategies exploits sentiments of fear and insecurity in order to avoid non-homogeneous behavior. During the Cold War, the fear of communism in Western societies was exploited in this way by means of a variety of ideological practices. Today, the fear of Islamic terrorism plays a similar role. If conjugated with job insecurity, the outcome is the production of docile, fearful individuals willing to stick with the leader no matter what his policies might be. Imposed harmony by means of the alternative dispute resolution (ADR) industry, and the construction of any dissent as unpatriotic, are phenomena that modern Western societies are experiencing today but that in other autocratic contexts, such as Meiji Japan beginning in the nineteenth century, have long been the rule.[12]

Neo-liberalism is thus an aggregate of social, political, economic, legal, and ideological practices, carried out by a variety of actors that respond to what we consider the formidable logic of plunder. The reduction of the public sphere and the large extension of the private sector, to the exclusive advantage of the stronger and corporate actors, is the thrust of such policy. The legal way by which the strategy is implemented in subordinate contexts is the notion of "comprehensive development," which invariably points at the need to develop "good governance and the rule of law" that we have alluded to and shall describe further in the following section.

Structural Adjustment Programs and the Comprehensive Development Framework

One analyst, Vincent Tucker, put it this way:

> Development is the process whereby other peoples are dominated and their destinies are shaped according to an essentially Western way of conceiving and perceiving the world. The development discourse is part of an imperial process whereby other peoples are appropriated and turned into objects. It is an essential part of the process whereby the "developed" countries manage, control and even create the Third World economically, politically, sociologically and culturally. It is a process whereby the lives of some peoples, their plans, their hopes, their imaginations, are shaped by others who frequently share neither their lifestyles, nor their hopes, nor their values. The real nature of this

> process is disguised by a discourse that portrays development as a necessary and desirable process, as human destiny itself.[13]

To be sure, we could substitute the term "colonization" for "development" in the previous quote taken from Tucker, an African scholar. The description would fit both phenomena, thus producing the idea and the mechanisms of continuity that we explore in this book.

Structural adjustment has long been the tool to implement development policies with the stick of conditionality. More recently, structural adjustment, a notion deeply resented by many borrowing countries, has been renamed *comprehensive development* broadening even more the subject matter of non-strictly financial intervention. Conditionality has been also renamed, with another move in the direction of politically correct, *participatory approach*, but it would be difficult to locate actual policy changes. The original idea, advanced by Lord Keynes at Bretton Woods, of worldwide economic stability and ordered growth, under the umbrella of a bank and a fund with a role of intervention to sustain distressed economies was changed only once in the early 1980s into a model of world governance by transnational, unaccountable, law-making political actors.

Once again, in order to understand this evolution, it is necessary to put it in its historical and political context. The rise of the United States as the hegemonic capitalist country in the aftermath of World War II, and the indisputable axis between the United States and Great Britain, which characterizes the contemporary world order, was prepared well before the end of the hostilities. The idea of the USA and UK was to "avoid economic anarchy stemming from competitive devaluation, multiple rates of exchange and other restrictive trade policies. The plan these two nations set in place was designed to introduce international discipline and exchange rate stabilization."[14] At the end of formal negotiations at Bretton Woods, the International Bank for Reconstruction and Development (better known as the World Bank), the International Finance Corporation, and the IMF were established. Participating countries agreed to submit to a degree of international economic discipline, but received guarantees of non-intervention in internal political matters.[15] They actually delegated to the IMF (specifically in charge of assuring exchange rate stability) certain prerogatives of national economic sovereignty. The IMF was created to provide a short-term balance of payment assistance for members who were in difficulties with external payments. The World Bank was empowered to temporarily provide financial help to countries that would have to recover from the devastation of World War II, and to more permanently preside over the economic development of developing nations by granting long-term targeted loans.

Two historical points are in order. First, while developing countries clearly outnumbered industrial nations at Bretton Woods they "did not affect to any degree the negotiations or the outcome, as the terms of the debate has already been set in the bilateral exchanges between the US and the UK."[16] This might possibly be due to the power of the USA and the UK, to the lack of a common vision in developing countries (most of which were at that time still colonies), or simply to the usual problem of effectiveness in participation because of limited resources as it is the case today at the WTO in Geneva.

Second, at their inception, the international financial institutions (and certainly through the crisis of September 1971 when the United States went off the gold standard, leaving virtually all world currencies floated) enjoyed tremendous prestige in the third world, being widely considered agencies of liberation rather than of oppression. Conditionality, structural adjustment, and the fundamentalist pursuit of neo-liberal policy were needed to change this perception, beginning in the late seventies. In a way, the very change of attitude toward these institutions in the third world has resulted from an openly political use of them, pursued in the aftermath of the Reagan/Thatcher revolution and aimed at the systematic plunder of third world resources.

It would be unfair to entirely blame the international financial institutions for this state of affairs. Unquestionably, other actors, including the private banking sector, and the rise to power of the so-called "kleptocracy" through the third world (generals like Suharto, Mobutu, and Noriega who were able to transform public resources into private assets by the use of bribery and violence) bear their share of responsibility. Nevertheless, while one might expect from ruthless weapon or diamond traders, oil adventurers, tyrants, secret services, or even private corporate power structures less than commendable behaviors, it is more difficult to accept the same behavior by actors endowed with the tremendous prestige stemming from the status of international organizations institutionally connected with the United Nations. This, in particular, is because of the *systematic use of the idea of rule of law as a weapon to gain consensus for practices of plunder*.

Once again, the described historical evolution is connected with oil. In 1973, OPEC imposed an enormous oil price increase by limiting supply. The price of oil quadrupled on that occasion and further tripled in the second shock of 1979 when the supply was even further limited. The outcome of the first increase was the sustained price boom of raw commodities, benefiting many third world countries. Moreover, the international financial institutions and the private banking sector were in receipt of a tremendous amount of so-called "petrodollars," so that lending to developing economies became available at relatively low interest rates (an average of 1.3 percent between 1973 and 1980) and with almost no concern for the deleterious effect of such cash flows on very weak economic and institutional systems.

The second increase in oil prices led to a worldwide recession because of policies developed by the Reagan/Thatcher revolution in response to the emergency (and to win the Cold War). This state of affairs was dosed with the so-called "monetarist recipe," mostly justified by the fear of inflation. Monetarist policies included economic austerity measures and a variety of public welfare spending cuts, causing large increases in unemployment and the depression of demand. Industrial economies thus reduced imports of raw materials; interest rates grew dramatically (to an average of 5.9 percent between 1980 and 1986) so that non-OPEC third world countries with an over-reliance on raw material extraction and export were literally thrown into a state of bankruptcy. Stronger economies further profited from the third world's weaker economic positions by imposing terms of trade so unfavorable that balance of payments positions quickly became unbearable. Continued borrowing at much higher interest rates, however, was unavoidable so that a major share of subordinate countries' foreign exchange earnings (themselves reduced by import contraction in rich economies) went towards the servicing of debt. It is not difficult to imagine the fate of social spending – ideologically challenged, together with traditional Keynesian policies, by Chicago monetarists – in poor countries overwhelmed by debts. As usual, weaker social actors suffered most from this state of affairs.

This dramatic scenario, bringing desperation to poor people worldwide, can be understood outside of abstract economic notions by a basic comparison with a household. Imagine a South American family of a father, mother, three children, and two grandparents. The family produces coffee and sells it on the international market. Suddenly, because of international contingencies, the price of coffee increases and the increased earnings, together with the availability of a mortgage at a very low variable rate, persuades the parents to buy a home and move into a more urban setting in which their children can get a better education. Life in the new setting is more expensive because consumption habits become more sophisticated, so the mother, who used to take care of the grandparents, starts working in the family coffee-producing business. A maid is hired to take care of the grandparents and the smaller children. All of a sudden, a crisis reduces coffee consumption and the price drops. Simultaneously, interest rates on the mortgage increase so that there is simply not enough money to make ends meet. The family, to take care of the children and grandparents, now seeks new borrowing. Knowing of an available prestigious state-certified plan, they apply for a loan. After papers are signed, it turns out that the prestigious lending agency, which they relied on to overcome the difficult moment, is itself carrying on usury practices. Now the household is in the lender's hands. The lender, fearful of not being paid back the principal, decides that children should leave school and go to work and the maid should be fired; the grandparents are abandoned alone for most of the day.

Clearly within such a scenario, the lending institution, which for a moment was seen as providing liberation from necessity, is now detested as a predatory agency with its gloves off. The changes come incrementally: the family is disrupted, and the weakest members of it – the old grandparents and the young children – are the ones suffering the most.

This story is an allegory for the consequences of the aftermath of the oil crisis of monetarist economic policies on less developed countries. And indeed, by the mid-1980s, the international financial institutions "came to realize that the prospects for recovery of the full principal and the interest payments were becoming increasingly unlikely due to the deflation of the industrial economies and their lack of supervision of the investment strategies of the borrowing countries, where much of the lending has been used to fund low-productivity projects."[17] Of course, in the hope of eventually recovering the principal, the Bretton Woods institutions, now solidly controlled by Anglo-American conservative governments, continued to lend, this time, however, applying harsh conditions very similar to those that required the kids to be sent to work and dumping the old of our story.

Structural adjustment is essentially the contractual agreement by which developing countries give up economic and legal sovereignty in consideration for financing. Because the desperate need for financing in the third world has long been created by strong economic and political actors, themselves dictating the economic policies of the Bretton Woods institutions, such contractual agreements are affected by an imbalance of power.[18] Consequently, they frame the law to serve the interests of the stronger actors, thereby operating to transform the rule of law into a facilitator of plunder and an instrument of social oppression. Naturally, the rhetoric of the rule of law serves its powerful ideological role and it is by no means abandoned.

Today, the IMF and the World Bank base their lending to underdeveloped economies on certain predetermined conditions. Such conditions, in theory, should enable the adjusting country to change the structure of its economy so that in the long run it can meet the needs of efficient utilization of the factors of production to ensure sustained growth. In practice, this pompous description means that once economic sovereignty is handed over to the international financial institutions, the political economy of a state *must* be restructured along the lines of neo-liberal orthodoxy. This implies that "the role of the State in all its progressive and social welfare functions is being sharply reduced, and the economies themselves have been opened via trade and financial liberalization to the unimpeded forces of world market competition."[19]

With this clear strategy in the developing world, and a similar, though more subtle one for Western economies, the international financial institutions exercise today tremendous political power worldwide, outside of any kind of control except the will of their majority shareholder. One should appreciate, in order to avoid maintaining the discussion at a senseless abstract level, that the international financial institutions – not imagined as outright political actors in the days of their establishment at Bretton Woods in July 1944 – are not structured to function as political institutions. Consequently, and quite naturally, they do not maintain any space for democratic legitimacy. Being organized as hierarchies along the model of the Anglo-American public company, a chief executive officer (CEO) and a board are in charge of strategic decision-making that is then implemented by a hierarchical structure, acting with a variety of advisory boards, as in any other kind of complex economic organization.

Development Frameworks, Plunder, and the Rule of Law

Lending, both for the purpose of development and for the purpose of servicing the debt, is today offered within a context of more or less stringent conditionality. While the harshness of the policies imposed to "structurally adjust," or as it is called today to "comprehensively develop," can vary significantly from place to place depending on a variety of political factors, a number of aspects commonly characterizing World Bank institutional interventions, we submit, fit more or less directly the definition of plunder.

To begin with, all third world countries have been hemmed in on the long road to structural adjustment.[20] Second, those reforms imposed by the international financial institutions on poor countries are reforms that, despite the free market rhetoric, "regulate" capital accumulation at a world level to the benefit of dominant economic and political elites by forcing the opening of weaker markets while keeping the stronger ones highly protected. Third, these plans are grounded in a straightforward version of the so-called orthodox neo-classical view of economics, in particular the undisputed "efficiency of free markets" and private producers, and the benefits of international competition and trade disregarding the power disparities. Fourth, they use domestic law of the indebted countries as a vehicle of enforcement of international obligations and of control of social unrest, thus depriving target countries of a significant amount of sovereignty and illegally intervening in their domestic political choices.

While we do not wish to reproduce here the results of a wealth of scholarship that has analyzed, supported, challenged, or exposed such policies, we need to at least spend a few more words on the economic policy imposed by means of conditionality. This policy uses the law to transform the Bretton Woods institutions from financial stabilizing entities into destabilizing political actors of the contractually imposed neo-liberal world governance project. Behind a faked political neutrality and technocracy serving universal interests, this policy hides a reactionary political platform in pursuit of the interest of the wealthy few countries holding the majority votes at the IMF and World Bank. The World Bank and IMF are connected today with the WTO, the United Nations, and with other international organizations offering an image of general interest while in reality serving the interests of their majority shareholders, no differently than any other private corporate entity motivated by profit. The Washington Consensus has turned the Bretton Woods institutions from Robin Hood into Shylock. To get a realistic picture one should take into consideration the fact that the Washington Consensus tightly connects US and European economic interests through more or less formal and bureaucratic organizations such as the Organization for Economic Cooperation and Development (OECD), North Atlantic Treaty Organization (NATO), or the G8. The fundamental task of this "legal" setting is to open up profitable markets for dominant corporations by means of Western development agencies. While sometimes competing among themselves, powerful development agencies share the target of capitalist global domination by diffusion of the Washington Consensus both by means of rule of law ideology and, not rarely, with the use of tremendous violence.

Finally, and this is an essential caveat to always keep in mind, the description of the formal connection between the institutional actors of the Washington Consensus does not render justice to the very intimate, substantial and ideological bond between the "naturalization process" of neo-liberalism and the transnational corporate actors. Indeed, the same forces are at play, for instance in lobbying the US Congress or the European Commission (thus making law), in selecting and controlling many high-level officials of the Bretton Woods institutions or in determining the electoral successes of a variety of elected politicians (directly affecting domestic political processes). The outcome of such complex dynamics is a radical transformation of the rule of law. Short of limiting the interests of strong actors (political or economic), allowing weak ones to seek the help of the law to assert their rights, as in its traditional and highly positive justification, the rule of law becomes an oppressive agency of plunder oppressing the losers of social processes. The rule of law abandons its aspect of shield for the weak and is transformed into a sword for the strong.

Orthodox neo-classical economic theory (including its perception of the rule of law) is the most powerful legitimizing ally of the Washington Consensus and is offered as "proof" of the sound nature of conditionally imposed SAPs or "participated" comprehensive development frameworks. These plans imposed and strongly supported by the Washington Consensus, are indeed based on the essential economic concept of equilibrium between supply and demand. Corporate free market and free trade (which are not free, rather corporate managed trade) are considered the best methods for achieving an efficient equilibrium. In order to reach such a result, two kinds of reforms are imposed, external ones and internal ones. Such reforms are supported by the empirically starved model of supply and demand used to show how free markets – that is, markets that are allowed to find equilibrium through the unimpaired interaction of supply and demand – will produce the most efficient outcome, not only for a given product (e.g. oil) but, in aggregate, for the economy as a whole.

Internal reforms interpret legislation and state participation in the economy as disruptive to achieving efficient equilibrium because legislation introduces practices limiting free competition. For example, in the labor market, a "minimum wage" requirement keeps salaries above the equilibrium point producing unemployment. By cutting wages, it is demonstrated with graphs, production will shift to more labor-intensive producers thus reducing unemployment (but shouldn't we begin to enforce "maximum wages" for corporate executives given the distortions that obscene distributions of stock options produce on world markets?).

In the neo-classical model, barriers to entry in a given industry particularly threaten the natural reach of an efficient equilibrium point. The assumption being, once more, that competition is the best recipe for efficient equilibrium. Measures to increase efficiency must thus reduce barriers to entry and promote competition. This theory provides a rationale for privatization and liberalization programs. Hence, structural adjustment invariably contains measures to disaggregate the supply side through denationalization, removal of state subsidies, and massive privatization. This, in turn, allows cutting taxes since state-run redistribution for the sake of social justice is itself inefficient, and welfare functions are privatized; therefore the state needs less tax revenue.

The social costs of such policy might be lethal. For example, the privatization of the railway service from Dakar (Senegal) to Bamako (Mali), acquired by a Canadian-based corporation, has caused the closing of a large number of stations around which small local markets and villages had developed over time. This informal economy, crucial for the survival of many people, has consequently collapsed, leaving thousands of starving peasants facing the impossibility of using the train to take their products to larger markets.

External policy reforms are approached too. Here the neo-classical model develops (and also demonstrates with graphs) the so-called "theory of comparative advantage," which "conclusively" demonstrates the superiority of unrestricted, spontaneous free trade. In a nutshell, the idea is that if international trade barriers are abated, each country will end up specializing in its most efficient outputs (e.g. cheap labor, or coffee, or natural beauty, or lumber). Countries will find it cheaper to purchase products on the international market using the revenue from international sales of products that it is better fit to produce. In other words, according to this idea, it is senseless to attempt the production of coffee in Finland. The Finnish would be better off buying coffee in Colombia, while specializing in producing canned herring and cell phones. While the argument seems persuasive, it proves to be so simplistic as to lose any policy potential in the real world, particularly because of the double standards used by developed economies providing an immoral justification of the inhuman exploitation of cheap labor (which is not substantially different from wage slavery) that obliges billions of people to work for salaries that do not afford subsistence. Since history matters, as many new economic paradigms are now ready to acknowledge, one should consider that the path to corporate capitalist development in the West was not only made possible by colonial plunder but also by many protectionist practices protecting early accumulation.

Economies in their infancy simply cannot afford to compete with fully developed ones, so that the opening of third world economies to unrestricted foreign investment results in writing a blank check to transnational corporate predators which simply put out of business all local economic activity. Needless to say, the theory of comparative advantage focuses on selective growth objectives that are given much greater weight than income distribution policies and immorally erases the difference in points of departure. The story of decolonized Latin America "opened up" by British trade shows more than any graph the fundamental equation between market liberalization within an imbalance of power and plunder. The flourishing of "free trade zones" in today's third world is the perfect economic counterpart of the Potosi mines in economic contexts in which the only thing to export is cheap labor.

The aggregate of internal and external reform plans, that is the governance of target markets in their internal functioning and in their degree of "openness" to international competition, imposes a downsizing of the public sector, with consequences faced by the poor.[21]

In order to reach this end result, a sort of neo-liberal paradise in which powerful market actors can turn every individual in the world into a consumer and any unskilled worker into a commodity, development plans indicate five major areas of reform and imperatives:

1. Allow free markets to determine prices.
2. Reduce state control of prices.
3. Divest resources held by the state into the private sector.
4. Reduce the state budget as far as possible.
5. Reform state institutions (courts and bureaucracy) in order to facilitate the private sector (good governance and rule of law).

These five imperatives, accompanied by detailed policy prescriptions such as abolition of minimum wages, ending food subsidies (e.g. Mexican corn), abolition of rent control programs, reduction of labor security standards, contracting out of public services (transportation, education, healthcare pensions, etc.) to the private sector, and transfer of public resources and operations to corporate actors, are typically pursued by SAPs within a two-phase strategy.

A stabilization phase, based on negotiation of a stabilization loan for 12–18 months or an extended fund facility for up to 3 years, is designed to finance an austerity plan. Following this first phase comes a longer term deal, the real structural adjustment loan of the World Bank or the structural adjustment facility of the IMF. The entry into the second phase, usually accompanied by significant inflow of funds from other agencies (European Union or Switzerland as in the case of Benin), is conditional upon radical cuts of government expenditures, downsizing of bureaucracy, ending of subsidies, devaluation, deregulation of exchange rates and price control, and the ending of state monopoly in exports or in the distribution of essential commodities such as rice. All of this is the direct interest of debt repayment.

Only a tiny minority of countries ever reaches this phase because massive unemployment, economic recession, hyperinflation, and social unrest are in most cases the outcomes of what is ironically called the "stabilizing" phase. Usually, private security business thrives in these conditions. Funds are made available to cushion these problems, but more detailed conditionality, further limiting the power of local governments to cope with the situation, is usually attached. Because of this economic vicious circle, the legal system has to be used for its most basic and oppressive function: controlling and repressing victimized people who peacefully resent and resist this legalized exploitive activity. The ensuing economic, legal, and political instability amounts to propitious conditions for what can only be described as "joint ventures for plunder" involving international corporate actors and local oligarchies, aimed at transferring public assets to private corporations often active in private securities and the prison business.[22] Impoverished courts and state institutions, actually overwhelmed by a tremendous new workload following corporatization, can only function as enforcement agencies protecting uneven distribution of property against workers and peasants. They have neither the authority nor the means to challenge the legality of the "adjusted economies," transformed by the Bretton Woods country club into ideal environments of legalized plunder.

3 | Before Neo-liberalism: a Story of Western Plunder

The European Roots of Colonial Plunder

Recent writings about globalization, and the globalization of law in particular, recognize Americanization of the international legal order or at least the presence of a heavy American imprimatur on transnational ideas and practices related to the rule of law. Such recognition, however, is ahistorical for the most part, linking the Americanization of the international rule of law with the rise of contemporary neo-liberal hegemonies.

A more historical view suggests that this process of Americanization did not begin recently, nor did it originate in the United States. Instead it originated with transfers of law and people centuries in the making. In attempting to reconstruct this picture, we will mostly focus on the intellectual and political roots of American imperialism. Because of this focus, most of our attention is given to the English roots, leaving to one side the Portuguese, Spanish, French, and Dutch roots of Western plunder. Influential books such as Blackstone's *Commentaries* (1765)[1] allowed European doctrine and British common law to gain currency early on in the English-speaking Americas. Thus, any story about the Americanization of the transnational rule of law needs to consider its European genealogy and its philosophical underpinnings. Indeed when we speak about the Americanization of the rule of law, it may be more precise to note that it is a Euro-Americanization in both political and economic dimension. Thus the interest of discussing the two, in relationship with each other and in relationship to settings of reception of the rule of law and of plunder therein.

Both Europeans and Americans used law as part of their colonialist and imperialist rule, with colonizing powers imposing their own ideas of law on their colonies. Today the imposition of law is more a result of transnational efforts at homogenization for purposes of capitalist expansion, but law is still the vehicle for legitimizing plunder. The rule of law is undoubtedly one of the more powerful "civilizing" devices used, and plunder, yesterday as today, might well be the most powerful force behind the unfolding of the Western ideology of the rule of law. Most likely its power stems from persuading other societies that they lack the rule of law principle, a strategy often accompanied with the promotion of harmony as another fundamental value of civilization.

Mainstream scholarship blames many contemporary post-colonial settings for the "lack" of rule of law, but at the same time it neglects the history of that rule of law principle in connection to plunder. In this chapter we attempt a re-telling, one that includes the historical dimension in understanding American hegemony through legal ideology in the contemporary world.

The Fundamental Structure of US Law as a Post-colonial Reception

By the early part of the twentieth century, US law had already received from Europe, and digested in a genuinely original way, the fundamental components of its legal structure. The English common law tradition had transmitted to the former colony the ideal of judges as oracles of the law, and of a strong, independent judiciary as the institutional framework in which judges could best perform their role as guardians of property rights. American law has developed the legacy of Sir Edward Coke and expanded it to the point of inventing constitutional adjudications. American judges are not only oracles of the law and the leaders of the professional legal system, they have also the power to declare, in the process of adjudication, political decision-making as unconstitutional.[2] This outstanding extension of judicial power within American law generated the belief (noticed as early as de Tocqueville[3]) that any political problem might be, sooner or later, decided by a court of law within the *neutral* logic of the rule of law. This belief was carried to its outermost extension in the Nuremberg trials, and possibly to its very limit in *Bush* v. *Gore* a case that we discuss further in Chapter 7.

Thus, the colony functioned as a mirror for England, and yet revolutionary America reacted against the colonial power to a large extent because of its intrusion in property rights and interests. A written constitution, the oldest in the West, was a reaction against the unwritten mysteries of the British constitutional system. England was a deeply centralized legal and political system. In contrast, the US legal system became the most decentralized one imagined thus far.

The continental European legal tradition (civil law) also transmitted to the United States some fundamental modes of thought that US law busily incorporated and transformed during the nineteenth and twentieth centuries. French-refined natural law tradition conveyed to the United States the idea of universal individual rights, once again rooted in an absolute ideal of the sanctity of property rights typical of the bourgeois state. These merely "negative" rights, considered as protections of the individual from government, rather than sources of government obligations to provide for the individual, have been enshrined in the US Constitution, influential as they were on a majority of the founding fathers.[4] Not only has the universalistic ideal been carried to the extreme, as witnessed among other things by notions of universal jurisdiction of US courts in the vindication of such rights,[5] but negative rights, in the absence of thick notions of sovereignty and statehood, as developed by the Jacobeans, became a genuine limit to the redistributive activity of the American government. Notions of freedom from government intrusion have guided constitutional adjudication throughout the history of the United States. A strong limit to any proactive government can be seen as the result of these early imports from Europe.

Germany also transmitted to the United States one of its fundamental characteristics: the presence of strong, independent academic institutions as another circuit of professional check on the political process. Only because the law was considered a science, was it natural to argue for its teaching in university settings. Otherwise, law in America could well have remained a practical business, as it continued to be in England until well after the Victorian age. American law schools (professional schools staffed with faculty who regard themselves as academic scholars) are the only ones in the world (Japan is recently following) that offer basic legal education at the graduate school level. Consequently, and paradoxically for a system based on a "professional school," the average American lawyer is exposed to more years of academic training than any other colleague in the world. Moreover, because of this further expansion as compared to academic undergraduate legal education in Europe, and because of the economic strengths of private institutions such as the Ivy League law schools, American academia can well be seen today as the global lawyer's graduate school, in the sense that ambitious lawyers worldwide complete their undergraduate legal education with a graduate degree in the United States.[6]

Thus, at least four traits of present-day "global" notion of the rule of law can be traced back to the US experience: (1) a written constitution; (2) constitutional adjudication; (3) individualistic rhetoric based on negative rights; and (4) legal professionals as "social engineers" active in a highly decentralized system organized to protect property rights.

A Theory of Lack, Yesterday and Today

The imperial side of law has a long history even if we restrain our analysis to America. Indeed, it was present before the American Revolution of 1776. It was already present in doctrinal thinking of the early time of plunder, when British colonists arrived in North America and encountered Native American communities.

The rule of law has justified genocide since the beginning. We need only recall that European doctrines of discovery principle hold that "European explorers' discovery of land in the Americas gave the discovering European nation – and the United States as successor – absolute legal title and ownership of American soil, reducing Indian tribes to being mere tenants."[7] The rule of law, grounded in natural justice, was used to justify and validate land appropriation, and the discovery principle remains to this day one of the most entrenched legal doctrines undergirding US federal Indian policy to the detriment of Native Americans.[8] This in the face of the Declaration of Independence that "all men are created equal."

Validation of appropriation was also inherent in the philosophy of John Locke's *Two Treatises of Government* (1698).[9] Native American properties could be appropriated by command of the Christian God, "As much land as a Man tills, plants, improves, cultivates and can use." Later on, Swiss scholar and statesman Emerich de Vattel was equally explicit in his *Law of Nations* (1797), a work which also gave legal justification for the colonial appropriation of lands:

> The earth belongs to all mankind . . . All men have a natural right to inhabit it . . . All men have an equal right to things which have not yet come into the possession of anyone. When, therefore a Nation finds a country uninhabited

> and without an owner, it may lawfully take possession of it. In connection with the discovery of the New World, it is asked whether a Nation may lawfully occupy any part of a vast territory in which are to be found only wandering tribes whose small number cannot populate the whole country . . . we are not departing from the intentions of nature when we restrict savages within narrower bounds.[10]

Because the United States were born as a nation out of an anti-colonialist revolution, such origins played a role both in erasing from the national consciousness the original internal colonial plunder and in characterizing the style of US imperialism in contrast with European colonialism. Thus, for example, in their early relationship with China, whereas the European countries favored territorial control by physical apprehension (the British in Hong Kong, the Portuguese in Macau), the United States favored one-sided "open door policies" from the nineteenth and early twentieth centuries, quite conscious of their own economic advantage in international expansionist competition with the Europeans. By so doing, the United States could, on the one hand, confirm themselves as anti-colonial champions, by blaming as colonialist the European physical occupation, and on the other hand, they could fully exploit, for the purpose of plunder, the time-honored policy of market liberalization. Within this open door policy, the rule of law, in the form of sanctity of contracts and of property rights security, was crucial to the interests of American investors and was thus "promoted" by the American government through the use of extorted agreements of extraterritoriality and immunity from Chinese jurisdiction. Such self-serving practice was ideologically promoted as offering a "civilizing" model for reform of local law, a condition for the eventual admission of China into the "family of civilized nations," subjects of international law.[11] This episode can be seen as a century-old preview of present admission of China to the World Trade Organization (WTO), though the power ratio seems dramatically changed.

The policy of using forced market liberalization rather than direct colonial control was similarly key to British success throughout Latin America both during Spanish and Portuguese colonization and after San Martin and Bolivar achieved formal independence in the first part of the nineteenth century. In fact, through the era of colonization, official Spanish and Portuguese plunder of raw materials (especially metals) was mostly used to service the debt owned by the Crown to bankers in the city of London. After formal independence, Great Britain waged war, directly or by proxy, on multiple occasions to guarantee the opening of the markets to its companies, allowing continuing plunder of raw materials yielding astronomic profit, and precluding the development of internal markets that could simply not compete with cheaper goods industrially manufactured in Great Britain. The few measures of local governments daring to protect local business in the hope of avoiding the tragic decline of a promising young industry were systematically denounced as contrary to the rule of law, protecting the global rights of the British companies to do business with a guarantee of return.[12] The few local leaders that attempted to resist – by limiting the "sanctity" of exploitive contracts of labor, or those of private "mining rights" acquired at trivial costs from their corrupted political predecessors, or the *latifundio* structure, favoring a local upper class notorious for its extravagant, very expensive, consumption habits – were simply forcibly removed from office, and their legacy officially despised for centuries. Among such leaders, one should at least remember Jose' Artigas from Uruguay, who dared attempting a land reform in 1815; Juan Manuel de Rosas of Argentina, defeated by British and French warships in 1852; or Francisco Solano Lopez of Paraguay, murdered in 1870 after a 5-year heroic war of resistance against Argentina, Uruguay, and Brazil, who waged a proxy war for Anglo-American capital against what was at the time the country that had reached the highest point of independent civilization ever in Latin America.[13]

Open door policy remained the official creed well after the Monroe doctrine (1823) still wrapped in anti-colonial rhetoric, was established, ostensibly to avoid a colonial scramble between European powers in South America. In fact, as we know, the doctrine has served as an effective claim to reduce Latin America to a US backyard, granting to US companies (such as United Fruit) trade monopolies in the region. Clearly, "open doors" never really meant free competition.

An instructive example comes from the recent history of Brazil, where President Gertulio Vargas dared threaten the interests of the US iron industry in 1954, by behaving as a rational economic actor, preferring to sell the metal at much higher prices to the Polish and Czechoslovakian governments rather than at the price that US companies were willing to pay. He was almost literally driven to suicide, as witnessed by his last letter placing the blame of his tragic decision on the international pressures precluding him the possibility to serve the interests of his country. The principal beneficiary of Vargas' death was US Hanna Mining, which could keep exploiting the Pareopeba valley, which contained the richest iron reserves on earth (worth around $200 billion). After all, Hanna Mining lawyers could argue that their client had paid almost $6 million (!) for the control shares of the British firm

St Johns, which had exploited Brazilian mines since the early days. No matter that St Johns had no legal title to transfer over the metal. New titles were created. The exploitation could then continue until 1961, when President Janio Quadros signed a bill annulling the illegal rights of Hanna Mining and restored the Minas Garais to the national reserve to which it belonged. Four days passed and President Quadros was forced to resign by the armed forces. In his dramatic farewell address he blamed the tremendous international pressure for forcing him to go. Vice President Joaho Goulart succeeded in power but, quite unexpectedly, maintained his predecessor's policy. Hanna Mining challenged the Quadros bill in front of the Brazilian judiciary, but its validity was upheld. Next, Brazil explored the possibility of directly shipping and selling iron to Europe (both socialist and capitalist), but this proved too much for US interests even before happening. A coup in March 1964 overthrew Goulart and brought to power Castelo Branco, a murderous dictator and an anti-communist fanatic. By December 1964, Hanna Mining got Castelo Branco to cancel the Quadros bill, and got full power to exploit the mines and even a rich government subsidy to build its own port and a railroad serving it from the mines. US Steel, another big corporation from the north, received similar rights on the Sierra de Los Carajas mines. The dictator said that Brazil lacked the capital to exploit its wealth. Eduardo Galeano reports a few comments:[14]

- *Fortune*: "the revolt that overthrew Goulart last spring arrived like a last minute rescue [for Hanna Mining] by the 1st Cavalry."
- US Ambassador Lincoln Gordon: "the success of the plot might be included with the Marshall Plan proposal, the Berlin blockade, the defeat of communist aggression in Korea and the solution of the Cuban Missile crises as one of the most important moments of change in mid twentieth century world history."
- *The Washington Star*: "Here is a situation in which a good, effective, old style coup by conservative military leaders might well serve the best interests of all the Americas."
- US President Lyndon Johnson (in a message congratulating interim president Ranieri Mazzili): "The American people have watched with anxiety the political and economic difficulties through which your great nation has been passing and have admired the resolute will of the Brazilian community to resolve these difficulties within a framework of constitutional democracy and without civil strife."

While the last comment overwhelms all the others in hypocrisy, what we have here is a chorus, saluting plunder stemming from "open door policy," a double standard version of a free market. The continuity, if one observes present-day conversations on the role of law in economic development, is just too staggering not to be noticed. Modern rule of law, a fundamental guarantee of open markets, is still presented as promoting modernity and rationality, a "civilizing process." The "civilized" still require the guarantee of the law to do business in faraway countries. The rule of law significantly contributes to the *ex post* rationalization of unlimited Western profits amounting to plunder. What has changed, if anything, is only the rationalization and justification policy behind the Western filling up of what amounts to an ideological constructed local "lack."

The same strategy seems to have been used for a very long time to force the Western rule of law upon weaker economic settings, thereby "opening up" the markets for plunder: by the ideological use of the "lack" argument, a comparative need is created that can only be remedied by the unique possibility of transfering law from the dominating Western source (be it German or US law in China, or current "law and economics" as a basis of law reform in South America). Moreover, because the rule of law, endorsed by international law-enforced standards of civilization, is constructed as a socially and politically neutral tool, local oligarchies are empowered with a cross-cultural tool of self-empowerment, becoming capable of interfacing with the global economy (introducing open door reforms) while maintaining traditional social inequalities.

Contemporary examples of cultural property appropriations illustrate this dynamic. Activists like Vandana Shiva note that the principal arguments used today to justify patenting of local collective knowledge are still based on Locke and de Vattel's notions of the rule of law as a protection of property rights and of "lack" in traditional conceptions of knowledge. As a universal instrument, law calls upon this key principle of control – the notion of lack – to legally justify plunder. Indigenes lack modernity and development; they lack the capacity and knowledge that allows full utilization of their environment; they lack law, they lack treaties, they lack a legal culture. More generally, the international legal mainstream has deployed a similar strategy in the years following the establishment of US hegemony in Latin America, with regard to the local civil-law-inherited legal tradition. Latin American states, the successors of European colonial powers, are thus depicted as inept imitators of obsolete European legal style. This attitude does not spare any peripheral legal context; all local legal traits are described as impairments to market-based development.

Today, we hear repeatedly that China lacks law or was and is averse to law. Such statements are often accompanied by arguments as to the difficulty of bringing the rule of law to China. One American lawyer has stated that: "Basically, the bar must be invented as a profession without any guidance from Chinese tradition or China's recent history."[15] Beyond lacking law the Chinese are now charged with ignoring the law they had: in the dominating Western vision, *li*, grounded in 2,500 years of Confucian tradition, is no law but just *social propriety*, while *fa*, its legist's counterpart, also more than 2,000 years old, is considered mere coercion and criminal sanction, itself a primitive instrument, too narrow to qualify as real law. Thus erasure becomes part of the policy of creating the need of neutral professionalized Western law, preferably based on common law notions. The strategy is transcultural. Islamic law, itself a venerable scholarly tradition, is itself described as mere *religion* not really law.[16] As such it is irrational (said Max Weber), immutable, and incapable of providing an efficient framework for economic development. Thus, what has buttressed the hegemonic scope of law is an internal cultural logic, based on lack or emptiness that has had lasting power over centuries of Euro-American dominance, even though perceptions of lack may change, with the change of the hegemonic legal systems.

In the US-dominated context of the rise of economic interpretation of the law, this theory of lack has been rationalized as a lack of efficiency or a lack of "professional" institutions, thus substituting "natural" justice (typical of early civil-law-dominated natural law) with economic efficiency as a new, prestigious, legitimizing ideological tool of plunder.[17]

Nowhere is this dynamic more evident than in examining twentieth-century law and development movements, sponsored by powerful US institutions such as the Ford Foundation and the leading law schools, in a time when US rule of law prestige was at its zenith. Lack remained a central feature. For example, South American countries lacked sophisticated academic legal institutions. Latin American legal culture lacked skills of social engineering, something that could be found only in the US academy, thus justifying transfers of law. James Gardner made this point early on in his pioneering work *Legal Imperialism* (1980).[18] It was a work ahead of its time because in the 1980s Americans did not want to admit that imperialism couched as development aid or progress was what the law and development movement was about:

> The handmaidens of democracy sometimes turned out to be the handmaidens of a dictatorship or authoritarian state. [Ibid., p. 281] . . . [I]t became clear that

> American legal missionaries were engaged in a process that was ethnocentric in origin, character, and implementation, and that law and development service to the Third World was an insignificant measure oriented toward the implicit transfer of American legal models . . . the basic question remains: why are American legal missionaries interested in legal assistance, and in the transfer of American legal models? [*Ibid.*, p. 283]

The strategy of de-politicization of law, presented as a value-neutral technology rather than a political instrument in the hands of local and international power elites, allowed "development work" to be done disregarding the politics of the local context. The law and development work in South America was directed at Brazil's authoritarian state, Allende's socialist Chile, and Colombia's "democracy," and was not much different than today's plans of law reform; World Bank-originated comprehensive development plans (structural adjustments) are aimed at Brazil, Ecuador, and Uruguay's left wing leaning governments and at Colombia's authoritarian administration. It would be impossible to understand such phenomena without taking into consideration that many of such legal missionaries were genuinely moved by justice motives, though they probably forget to ask themselves, as every "neutral" scholar should always do, who was paying their salary.

Recent criticism has followed up on early analysis of law and development and on its current resurrection.[19] The work of US development lawyers who sought to directly transplant American institutions into Brazil, Chile, and elsewhere to promote democracy by legal means illustrates how, 30 years later, there have been massive changes in legal education resulting in the repositioning of faculties of law and the state, the reproduction of knowledge-governing elites, and the making of elite hierarchies, ultimately germane to neo-liberal projects and US domination. This new class of lawyers connects the local and the international, speaking alternatively for one side then the other, all the while dependent on American modes of legitimatization: "the import and export of dominant US expertise is shaped by national agendas and national histories." Thus the cosmopolitan elite deploys the "linguistic and cultural baggage necessary to accede to the new places of privilege in the international (re) production of knowledge and power. These new places are above all the great law schools of the East Coast."[20]

Lawyers and law professors from Latin America acquire social capital in their native countries (because they fill the lack) through US doctorates and legal know-how. Law is central in chronicling American expansionism and in understanding American imperialism since “law and legal institutions provide cover for activities that cannot be spoken about in polite cosmopolitan circles.”[21] We describe such activities as plunder. New legal activities are oriented toward the United States in the service of neo-liberal economics. This discourse shuts out discussions of law in the service of justice. In the service of corporate capitalism, law becomes a structural, economic, or technological component, never a moral or cultural, let alone political, one. Efficiency dominates today, but the discontinuity is only apparent. Plunder is still the motivation and the outcome.

In the contemporary neo-liberal view of the law, less developed economies are seen as lacking something very simple and universal. They lack the simple and universally valid minimal institutional system necessary for the unfolding of an efficient market. In a seminar for senior bankers at the World Bank, Judge Richard Posner of the United States Court of Appeals in Chicago, a leading author in law and economics and one of the protagonists of the triumph of this movement in the American academy, set forth the basic theoretical underpinning of neo-liberal strategy. According to him, three very simple things are needed in order to develop the efficient institutional system necessary to make capitalism work: secure property rights; freedom of contracts; and a system of independent courts as agencies of enforcement and of case law development. At the same seminar, another leading American author, Professor Bernard Black of Texas added that even a system of independent courts might be too complicated to obtain because of the fundamental “lack” of legal professionalism and organization characterizing developing economies. According to this scholar, the World Bank should aim at the creation of a “self-enforcing” legal system, something that does not even require tackling this fundamental and context-specific lack.

Economists have long worked with universal legal models that have never existed in any real legal system. Such models of property, contracts, and enforcement rooted in God or in reason but never in history, have been directly inherited from eighteenth-century natural law thinking as received by Adam Smith, the founding father of the economic profession, and rarely re-discussed by the following mainstream generations of economists.[22] Such ideas are those advanced by natural law thinkers such as de Vattel and Locke, providers of legitimacy for eighteenth-century colonial genocide in America.

The revival of naturalism in the leading American school of economics thus plays an important role: developing countries lack something very simple and universal. This position, emphasized in widely circulated and highly influential documents such as the World Development Reports[23] produced by the World Bank, serves a dual function. To begin with, it emphasizes the inadequacy and lesser quality of peripheral elites, labeling them incapable of creating something as basic and natural as market corporate capitalism. Countries on the periphery are thus intellectually humiliated, creating the psychological conditions for the acceptance of foreign hegemony. Consequently, such elites are in need of training by the main agencies of Western cultural hegemony, the great academic institutions of the United States. Once trained by such institutions, the third world's elites are co-opted as staff of the international financial institutions providing some formal but, practically speaking, very limited diversity. Frantz Fanon, in his classic work,[24] has identified a very similar phenomenon in the tragic French colonial relationship with Algeria.

Today, the Bretton Woods institutions are provided with the means to implement a clear-cut strategy: build a simple and universal rule of law capable of stimulating efficient transfers of property from whoever values them less to whoever values them more. This exercise indicates the tackling of property rights (e.g. that of intellectual property, which needs to be Westernized), of contractual freedoms (e.g. contractual restrictions serving labor security must be banned), and of institutional structures (either by reproducing US-inspired patterns of "adversary legalism," which we call reactive institutions, or in the apparently contradictory exploitation of alternative dispute techniques (ADRs)).

Although the arguments for neo-liberalism spread through a coalition of diverse institutions, law is central. In the field of legal practice, US law firms have been able to define the role of international lawyers operating in the global market of legal services. In discussing the successful transplant of the corporate law firm, it is important to mention that firms are often granted their own extra-legal, pseudo-governmental space by weak governments "outsourcing" their government duties to the private sector.[25] The entrepreneurial style of American lawyers is transforming the Western legal cultures of Europe as well, although traditionally Europeans de-emphasized the use of lawyers as political lobbyists and business negotiators. In the present competitive climate, the French are said to lack competence in procedures and in formal legal requirements. The same thrust would include the "New Europe" and the post-Soviet bloc as sites for new legal imperialism.

Recent scholarship points to American legal logic that has affected the entire system of Japanese law because "the flourishing of economic approaches to law encourage bureaucrats and legal scholars to look more to Common Law notions which has had implications for the structuring of hierarchies within the legal academy." [26] This is not to say that such "universal" or "global" principles are not subject to local interpretations, but at the same time, the successful promotion of the American entrepreneurial style of lawyering worldwide has led to an increase in attention to international law, at least as a strategy of "branding" American law schools. New York University Law School has made international law the centerpiece of its "global law" program, the explicit aim of which is to encourage the "export of American legal ideas and concepts throughout the world indicating a further intensification of 'Americanization' and internationalism within the US itself."[27]

Scholars are now seeking to understand the centrality of law in globalizing processes, and the mechanisms driving the law's diffusion. Depictions of lawyers at the service of power elites reflect reality. What we are assessing here is the role of plunder as a powerful force behind legal diffusion. Yet, reaching the consciousness of the role of plunder in the diffusion of the rule of law should not necessarily play into the hands of inevitability thinking. The rule of law might carry today, as it did in the colonial past, a degree of counter-hegemony.[28]

The possibility of counter-hegemony certainly needs to be considered, in order to attempt an evaluation of the rule of law and of its relationship with plunder. As we will discuss in the next section, it certainly seems that such a possibility has produced yet another level of plunder-driven transformations, both in the past and in the present.

Before Neo-liberalism: Colonial Practices and Harmonious Strategies – Yesterday and Now

As mentioned earlier, adversarial and conciliatory models play important roles in globalization strategies today as they did throughout the construction of colonial legality. In fact, we have traced the classic Western notion of rule of law back to the protection of property interests of the landed aristocracy, within the adversary common law model of adjudication typical of the courts of law at Westminster. Today, an alternative to this idea, based on conciliation and harmony rather than adjudication and conflict, is rapidly expanding both in core Western systems and, as part of law reform packages, is being exported to the developing world. Plunder is not foreign to this remarkable structural change of the rule of law. Consequently we need to trace this story too.

Explorations among the mountain Zapotec of Oaxaca, Mexico and elsewhere[29] first led us to understand the use of harmony ideology in the success of European *non-military* global colonization tactics. Coercive harmony is a mode of cultural control. Soft institutional settings work well for colonization projects, whether during the colonial period, or in the present. Harmony ideologies may be used to suppress people's resistance, by socializing them toward conformity by means of consensus-building mechanisms, by valorizing consensus, cooperation, passivity, and docility, and by silencing people who speak out angrily. The use of coercive harmony is present in the United States and also in international settings. Harmony law models, such as ADR, are thus most likely part of a hegemonic control system that spread throughout the world, along with European political colonization and Christian missionizing during colonialism, an earlier globalization, where fear of resisting violence made extra-legal conflict management appealing.

We have already discussed (Chapter 1) how, whenever modern law could incidentally empower the colonized, an alliance quickly developed between the colonial power and traditional elites to preclude the use of courts. Plunder requires avoidance of counter-hegemony that might stem from the rule of law. Thus understanding the diffusion of American harmony law models – sometimes called ADR, sometimes IDS (international dispute settlement), and sometimes referred to as extra-judicial – is an integral part of a study of plunder. Such informal procedures are found operating outside or even inside ordinary courts, in non-governmental organization (NGOs), in taking care of disputes with the international financial institutions,[30] in peacekeeping strategies, peacemaking, and reconciliation,[31] and in colonizing policies.[32] Informal procedures are also used in the settlement of environmental disputes such as international river disputes,[33] or in business disputes, or most obviously perhaps in the various trade agreements such as GATT (General Agreement on Tariffs and Trade) and NAFTA (North American Free Trade Agreement). These are all examples of how governance operates without following adjudication procedures, regardless of legal implications, and commonly justified by reference to economic or political crises. Yet, their powers and implications for plunder may have been vastly underestimated. ADR, as the rule of law, is usually assumed to be benign, so a hard-nosed look is in order.

Just as adversarial law models are loaded with value assessment in relation to their being part of a path to progress and development, so too are harmony legal models. Indeed, both models play an important role in the diffusion of American values of efficiency and pragmatism, because ADR is presented, domestically as abroad, as a pragmatic advantageous alternative to possible excesses of adversary litigation. In this perspective, the rule of law, once fully developed and professionalized, might experience a growth crisis, sometimes presented as a "litigation explosion," that ADR can cure at low social cost, therefore being an efficient alternative to litigation.

Mainstream thinking deems ADR to be beneficial in less developed countries that, "lacking" a high level of legal professionalism, might find it hard to properly organize a machinery of adversary adjudication. Thus, the World Bank (that actually makes mandatory the use of mediation to solve conflicts with assisted countries) promotes conciliation and mediation of disputes as a pragmatic alternative for development. ADR moreover is often presented as more "culturally sensitive" to the difference of mentality of countries "lacking" the rule of law. The Western mainstream still largely perceives non-Western legal systems as a caricature-like image of the Qadi (Islamic judge) dispensing (expediency-based) justice sitting under a tree, made famous by Max Weber and once used even by US Supreme Court Justice Felix Frankfurter. Thus ADR, with its emphasis on informality and case-specific justice, is deemed congenial to local needs, because it is closer to what is stereotyped as "oriental" mentality.

Even though such "harmony" models have little to do with American ideas of justice and having one's day in court, they are often taken for granted or deemed benign, with little attention to the fact that power disparity is even more pernicious in informal justice than it is in adjudication. We need to remember the pacification role of Christian missionaries and of their rhetoric of social harmony, under conditions of colonial domination or imperialistic conquests, in South America and Africa. There, notions of Christian resignation to a superior will of God have curtailed effective resistance, favoring plunder. Thus harmony ideology like ideologies of efficiency and the rule of law is germane to plunder.

Today, legal reforms worldwide increasingly standardize and ritualize ADRs or IDSs to fit global power strategies in a manner that *erases differences* caused by uneven power or diverse or competing cultural styles. In the process of standardizing ADR, thinking about the conflict becomes narrow and technical, and context shrinks. ADR thus becomes just another technical and professional system of justice, with its specialists and its professionals, only loosing the empowerment factor (for the weaker party) that might come from the potentially counter-hegemonic use of public courts of law. ADR thus becomes a forum of private justice where "Anglo-American law firms in international business transactions, the Uruguay Round of the GATT, and the formation of the World Trade Organization (WTO), . . . credit-rating agencies, and so forth"[34] play a major role. The shift is from public courts to private panels, from formal adjudication to informal or negotiated justice, part of the more generalized movement to privatize everything from prisons to social welfare institutions, thus losing the empowerment and potential counter-hegemony that sometimes comes from the adversary nature of the judicial process. It is then no surprise to find ADR clauses in most standard contracts, with banks, insurance companies, telecoms, and corporate employers eager to offer their own "private justice" to their clients.

A regime of transnational commercial law, a hegemony of neo-liberal concepts of economic relations structured very much in an American corporate style, systematically removes constitutional and institutional protections and access to law, where victims of plunder could possibly complain and maybe occasionally even win. In this arena, international arbitration and the new specialties in conflict resolution are key legal mechanisms of control. Yet, none of these happenings are standing still, and the dialectic between plunder, adjudication, and ADR is variable and in constant flux. There seems to be a trend, as any history of the WTO can attest to. Originally, the WTO seems to have been written in the spirit of legalism; it "called for a vigorous dispute-settlement procedure which contemplated effective use of arbitration . . . and even appeal to the World Court in some circumstances."[35]

Structures governing international trade can change from one decade to another. It is thus instructive to sort out the relevant shifts in dispute resolution since the 1940s, from the rule of law principle, to pragmatism, to independent panels and consensus decisions and from earlier pleas for democratic legal procedures. One can see the jockeying for power by means of preferred disputing mechanisms.[36] Today, the power of the WTO resides in its dispute resolution panels allowing any WTO member country to challenge the domestic laws of any other member. These panels are held in secret, with no right of citizens or subnational authorities like State Attorney Generals to participate, and panel decisions are automatically adopted with no independent appeal, no written record, and selective enforcement. It is no light observation that states are conceding certain of their prerogatives to supranational entities. Even though the shifts from one type of disputing style to another are never total, that they occur at all is worth noting because it indicates how elastic models of dispute resolution, packaged as "rule of law," are.

Global reform trends seem to pursue elastic arrangements in dispute resolution to strengthen the advantage of the stronger bargaining partner. It is imperative to understand the makeup of the "soft" technologies of law such as ADR, and how such soft technologies might fit with plunder. It is, however, also important to understand that the contemporary muddy ideology of the rule of law can embrace both adjudication and ADR, sometimes in apparently contradictory ways. For example, the so-called Washington Consensus urges China to observe international patents or to create a court system to enforce business contracts, while at the same time urges Bangladesh to negotiate with India over the Ganges rather than take their complaints about water rights to the World Court. As Charlene Harrington observed, "Global business and finance seem to be astride a giant contradiction: while they campaign to dismantle legal restraints in one part of the world, the wealthiest societies, they are simultaneously urging poorer nations to adopt mainly ones that will protect private property from political interferences."[37] However, the reality and the variations are even more complex, because the globalization process results in variant power interactions, commonly hidden in the shadow of US inspired law and quite often determined by plunder.[38]

4 | Plunder of Ideas and the Providers of Legitimacy

Hegemony and Legal Consciousness

American legal hegemony can best be seen (and is much more relevant from a political point of view) as a change in legal and political consciousness rather than as a pattern of transplantation of formal legal rules and institutions. Legal reception is a highly creative activity, and transfers of law would be severely misunderstood if approached only as a mechanical import–export exercise of codes or legal institutions. A better approach is to monitor the diffusion of professional ways of thinking about the law, and to address, in colonial or imperial contexts, major intellectual changes in elites. Viewing legal globalization with a state-based lens on the production of norms (e.g. focus on the diffusion of law from France, Germany, and the United States) is not useful for perceiving the nature of the post Cold War legal order. Such perceptions are too strictly connected with territoriality and they fail to understand the mighty role of transnational institutions of global governance (the World Bank, International Monetary Fund (IMF), and World Trade Organization(WTO)) as well as that of transnational corporate actors in the private production of law. Similarly, the colonial project is perhaps best appraised as a relationship – initially and often violently – involving a variety of colonizing actors, both public and private, rather than a discrete relationship between one mother country and one colony. A territorial, state-based perception of the colonial relationship would be too narrow. It would focus on formal institutions and miss the international dimension of both the colonizing effort and of the resisting forces.

Both the colonial relationship and current hegemonic globalization include a persuasive ideological dimension. Subordinates, or at least a significant portion of them, must be persuaded of the superior nature of the dominant order and civilization compared to their own. Without such an ideological component, oppression would be a much more costly exercise. An outright display of physical violence is not a viable long-term strategy. Soft power is much more efficient than hard power, and the establishment of the ideological apparatuses supporting its construction is a crucial aspect of any project of plunder.

While power sometimes uses outright propaganda, professionalism proves more effective in persuading the more educated sectors of the population. Particular professional elites acquire, at the international level, the influence necessary to provide legitimacy to hegemonic power. Their role, most importantly, is to target local intellectuals and public discourse in order to use the prestige of a local influential social class to narrow the costs of physical domination while maintaining foreign control and, ultimately, plunder. Such international and domestic intellectual support allows the imperial project to credibly promise to the local populace, civilization, wealth, development, and liberation. It is an ideological exercise, the province of mainstream ideologues, to render outward plunder invisible and the practices supporting it as acceptable to most because of its benevolent nature.

The function of providing legitimacy is sometimes institutionalized, as in the case of Catholic missions in colonial times. Sometimes, it is more decentralized, as in the case of a much-admired solo scholar lecturing through the world of academic invitations. The non-critical posture of such persons over their own legal and political system might itself function as a powerful ideological justification for the state of subordination because it ultimately provides conservative role models for local elites.

Programs such as the Fulbright grants for lecturing abroad, or a variety of other similar, often commendable, initiatives are examples of what we mean. In this case, to be sure, nothing forbids the traveling lecturer from being critical. Nevertheless, the process of selection and the psychology of the role, make self-critique highly unlikely. In 2005 Professor John Yoo, the author of the notorious torture brief, was Fulbright Professor at the University of Trento, in Italy. It is problematic to ascertain whether Henry Sumner Maine's prestigious views of social progress were congenial to the colonial project because he was expressing them as a colonial official or whether he accepted a post of colonial office because he held such views.

Similarly, it is difficult to establish whether a leading scholar in, say, law and economics becomes influential worldwide because he already holds views that are congenial to the dominant neo-liberal ideology or whether he absorbs such an ideology because such are the expectations of his hosts at economics departments worldwide. Possibly the question is not even interesting. It is though a fact that a vast majority of leading intellectuals at the center hold imperialist (or colonialist) views and because of such views their voices are amplified by the aggregate of institutional factors that might be called the ideological apparatuses of global governance. Such views, prestigious as they are, provide professional legitimacy to the imperial project.

In this chapter we shall therefore provide a discussion of some "providers of legitimacy," a diverse group of intellectuals who help in the construction of a legal consciousness coherent with imperialism. Such intellectuals do not need to share any particular motivation except perhaps some "professional project" dictated by loyalty to their scholarly discipline. As individuals, their motives can be indifferent.

We shall begin our discussion with materials on plunder in the domain of ideas. We will then discuss how legalization of plunder is provided by the development of a shared legal consciousness among intellectual elites developing a variety of self-serving strategies. We shall begin with economists, today operating in the USA in close contact with lawyers and policy-makers, to see how their professional project first colonized American legal thinking and then claimed a global role in the providing of legitimacy to legalized extraction or plunder. In order to discuss continuity we will then turn to anthropologists, in particular those concerned with the law, because of their extraordinarily important role in legitimizing colonial plunder.

Intellectual Property as Plunder of Ideas

The immediate aftermath of the Cold War was opened by the invention of the world wide web protocol on the internet. It is enough to browse the internet once to see its American cultural imprint. The quantitative and qualitative advantage of US-based English language sites is yet further evidence of the very strong cultural hegemony of the United States in this network, the ultimate symbol of globalization and progress. The so-called "digital divide" demonstrates the appalling growth of the difference between rich and poor countries, created and dramatically expanded through the internet by what can be seen as another ideological apparatus of global governance: intellectual property. Information is today perhaps the most important source of wealth. Intellectual property, rooted as it is in an extreme Western individualistic notion of property law, is incompatible with existing modes of property and fundamental communitarian values of many societies. Western intellectual property ideas are expanded worldwide through the internet and enforced by TRIPS (trade-related aspects of intellectual property) agreements, the intellectual property "branch" of the powerful WTO. Intellectual property formalizes the disparity of wealth and power that technology yields, through granting to the global market-dominating minority an advantage seemingly impossible to overcome. The non-territorial nature of intellectual property as symbolized by the internet and the claim of universality and of objectivity of its justification is producing more institutional imperialism.[1]

Global legitimacy of intellectual property is rooted in the notion that individual creativity deserves a prize and that exclusive property rights constitute such a prize. We are back to Locke and to natural law justifications of individual ownership, the same previously discussed line of thinking that granted legitimacy to early genocides and looting in the "vacant" Native Indian lands of North America. Nobody would farm without guarantee of exclusive property on the outcome of his/her labor. Nobody would have incentives to create if there were no intellectual property rules granting a monopoly on the benefits of his/her creativity. Nobody would genetically modify seeds without guarantee that the legal system would help impose such technology on farmers worldwide, forcing them to abandon communitarian practices of seed sharing and swapping.[2] Such eighteenth-century rhetoric, reinforced today by simplistic neo-classical legal and economic models, denies notions of alienation and exploitation and the simple fact that intellectual property rights can very often freeze the *status quo* rather than promoting innovation and change.

The general universalistic individual-centered philosophy propagated by intellectual property rights and by the institutions created to enforce it worldwide (World Intellectual Property Organization, TRIPS),[3] serves the needs of powerful corporate actors. Patents and copyrights are monopolies. In the name of efficiency and innovation, it promotes the notion that ideas, like every other resource, should be placed on the market to become the property of whoever is willing to pay more for them, thus increasing social wealth. This seemingly neutral justification hides the relationship between willingness to pay and capacity to do so, thus naturalizing the continuously increasing advantage of the stronger market actors.[4]

The hegemonic aspects of the intellectual property revolution are very easy to perceive both in their component of power (economic and political pressure to force non-Western countries to accept international intellectual property protection agreements) and in their ideological component, indispensable to reach consent (intellectual property justified as a universal natural law conception and as a modernizing, efficient idea needed for development). Of course, as with all institutions of hegemony, intellectual property uses double standards not only in its intellectual justification but also in its actual use. In the first perspective, it promotes monopoly as efficient, otherwise an anathema for economists. In the second, it is sufficient to compare the generic anti-AIDS drug saga in South Africa (where as many people die of AIDS every week as the victims of the September 11, 2001 events) with the treatment and the respect that the intellectual property of the German-based Bayer pharmaceutical multinational company has been granted by the Bush Administration in the aftermath of the "anthrax crisis" in the fall of 2001.[5] As our readers might recall, the Bush administration had single-handedly allowed generic production of the antidote drug whose patent belonged to Bayer, and the pharmaceutical industry, strong with the weak in South Africa but weak with the strong in America, has immediately shown generosity in disregarding its patents and willingness to cooperate with the American administration.

Our discussion of plunder of ideas has to return once more to the European roots of American law, because our story here is about Euro-American, not Islamic or Asian, appropriation of other people's resources and ideas. The examples we use fall in the intellectual property rights' area, a Western law of copyrights, patents, trademarks, and trade secrets that, by individualizing global knowledge, make it easily appropriable and transferable to whoever is willing (and able) to pay more for it. The basic assumptions that facilitate the function of law as a technique of appropriation become clear when, in transcending national boundaries, such ideas collide with non-Western assumptions, challenging, for example, notions that one cannot patent old ideas in the service of the group rather than the individual. To fully understand contemporary issues about intellectual property, a cross-cultural comparison is useful.

The case of the Kayapo in Brazil has been fully documented. Article 27 of the TRIPS agreement maintains that for an invention to be patented, it must be "non-obvious" (substantially altered from a natural state), useful, and novel, and it must be the product of a specific individual. The Kayapo conception of what constitutes human invention differs radically. The Kayapo consider knowledge to be a product of nature and not of human nature. Next, for the Kayapo, knowledge is not always translated into "useful products." Whereas the TRIPS agreement requires an invention not to have been known, indigenous knowledge is passed down from generation to generation. Any Kayapo can know a cure – it is in the public domain. The final criterion that it be considered the product of a specific individual would not fit the Kayapo context, for their knowledge is communal and difficult to attribute to one particular person and thus consequently more difficult to commercialize. Thus, Western intellectual property rights are not composed of values expressing the full range of human possibility but rather are composed of beliefs reflecting the interests of the Western market-dominating minority and then universalized. Note that exactly the same story could be told for the individualization of property over commonly held cultivable land in western Africa, a super-imposition of Western individualistic conceptions germane to free transferability to whoever will pay most for it. Invariably, individualization and privatization policies, supported by international financial institutions, favor Monsanto and other multinational corporations interested in buying land otherwise not available on the market for experimenting with GMO (genetically modified organisms) technology.

The Kayapo are only one example. The literature is replete with episodes of "fishing expeditions" in which Western scientists in the field observe practices or cultural expressions based on centuries-old local knowledge. Not only scientists, but also "cool hunters," observing juvenile communities to get inspiration from shared ideas of what is cool (tattoos and piercing in the Amazon, or the hip hop symbols of the African-American ghetto such as the hood, would be good examples). They then return home to obtain "new" intellectual property rights for the purpose of global exploitation of these common ideas in the music, fashion, or pharmaceutical industries. Often, once the individual property structure imposes itself on this knowledge, a global market emerges for the raw materials, raising prices and consequently stripping the locals of all possibility of keeping the traditional use, simply because they have no capacity to pay the new "Westernized" price.

The best-known example is the Indian *neem* plant (the village pharmacy), traditionally serving many health purposes. Western scientists "discovered" the active principle and then obtained a patent for oral hygiene use in Florida. Its wide commercial application in the West (for toothpaste) made prices rise to the point of making it unaffordable to its traditional users whose oral hygiene is dramatically declining. In western Africa a very similar story can be told for *karité* butter, now coveted by the Western cosmetics industry (which often pretends to operate within fair trade principles[6]); other examples abound. African scientists, often after long years of study and sacrifice, are faced with a dramatic alternative: either to remain idle and poor, working at best for public institutions and laboratories, lacking all funds because of structural adjustment program (SAP)-mandated cuts in research and education, or to accept working for Western private "fishing expeditions," in air-conditioned, well-equipped laboratories. Such private laboratories "improving" the *karité* butter or other traditional processes and ideas, often the only ones subsidized by Western donor governments, eventually patent their inventions. Of course, in accepting the latter alternative, these scientists give up all claims for their "inventions," many times the fruit of shared communal knowledge of their villages of origin.

Creative and impoverished African singers, whose rhythms now enrich the Western media industry or creators of tattoos, necklaces, and piercing, now copied and commercialized through Western malls, enjoy no returns as the real inventors. These individuals only look for minimal resources to express their creativity, often the product of accumulated local knowledge: recording places, art laboratories, etc. To be able to work and express themselves, they "transfer" to the companies that allow them these minimal facilities the exclusive intellectual property rights, usually of communal origins: plunder.

While the ideological nature of the idea that individual intellectual property stimulates creativity is exposed by such facts, one can observe how Western institutions actively promote the legal instruments of such plunder. For example, the European Union, an important "donor" in Mali, conditions research and other cultural grants to the Malian government to the passage of new, stricter intellectual property law. This conditionality serving the Western industry is shamelessly spelled out in writing, because the development benefits of intellectual property law are now taken for granted.

Solutions to the fundamental tension between individualistic ideas and communal knowledge have been proposed, such as new legal concepts based on a more culturally inclusive depiction of intellectual property that recognizes the collective rights of indigenous people as "collective inventors."[7] Others, more imbedded in the intellectual property/creativity equation, suggest the use of contracts between extractor and extractee, or promote ideas of "creative commons." There has been an explosion of published solutions to these issues (such as James Love's proposal to circumvent the patent system), but it is not our purpose here to examine proposals or to review this literature. Rather, we need to better understand the significance of the current challenge to elucidate the means by which recent trade laws have been legitimized, and why commercial interests do not just take what they want, by persuasion or power, but instead invent legal circumventions.

A powerful ideology has developed around intellectual property, allowing it to become a sophisticated instrument of plunder. Western ideas and conditions are universalized, taken for granted, and naturalized by such ideology, which is mostly produced by the different intellectual elites that we will discuss in the next sections. For example, the natural law notion of "first possession" of vacant spaces, sometimes rendered with the idea of "first come first served" is used, almost unchallenged, in the allocation of "domain names" over the internet. Anybody, by paying a moderate fee, can occupy a free domain name that after occupation can be used, as in any form of individual ownership, only by obtaining his consent. Thus an efficient market of domain names is created, granting to everyone equal possibilities in this new frontier of human wealth. What seems more natural, fair, and efficient to anybody owning a computer, internet access, and $15?

These conditions, however, are neither natural nor universal. It is no surprise that American companies now "own" the domain name "Yanomani.com" or "SouthAfrica.com," thus positioning themselves legally to claim returns on future uses of these names. People and countries, disadvantaged by the digital divide, might have to pay to use their own names in the global space of the internet. Just as the Yanomani people and other general losers of the globalization processes will have to pay for newly patented subsistence necessities which are privately owned, such as genetically modified seeds developed in corporate-owned cultivable land: plunder.

Providing Legitimacy: Law and Economics

Economics is widely perceived today as the "queen of social sciences." It is the only one officially recognized as a "true science" to the point that, among the so-called social sciences, a Nobel Prize is granted only in economics. Liberal guru Sir Karl Popper recognized economics as science, while denying such status to sociology, law, anthropology, or psychology. It is no surprise that within the neo-liberal project, economists have become more and more influential in policy-making, providing "neutrality," "scientific knowledge," "objectivity," and ultimately a powerful intellectual justification for the ban on redistribution of wealth in society. An Austrian economist, Friedrich Von Hayek, can be considered the intellectual mentor of the Reagan/Thatcher revolution.

Although economists can differ much among themselves in political beliefs, they almost unanimously share a faith in positivism. They believe that a descriptive dimension can be distinguished from a prescriptive or normative one. Consequently, they accept political divisions in the world of "ought to be" while their professional project is to describe, explain, and predict the world of the "is." Economists, moreover, consider the "profit motive" (described as utility maximization) as the sole human motivation capable of being an object of "scientific study." They consequently consider even altruism as maximization of individual utility. The altruist is someone who derives selfish utility from being generous. The justice motive is thus reduced to a subform of utility-maximizing behavior.

Universality is an important aspect of the behavioral "laws" that economists describe, so that economics can be considered to be the same in New York, Paris, or Bombay. True, some economists assert that institutions or cognitive biases matter, and have consequently paid more attention to the institutional or even cultural context of their prescriptions.[8] Nevertheless, the sense is still that local fundamental differences do not affect the validity of the "universal laws" according to which markets work. Institutional differences can be tackled in the normative dimension by harmonizing, in order to obtain some universal conditions of efficiency. Alternatively, differences can be "exploited" within a competitive pattern itself aimed at efficiency. Notions of "good governance" and "structural adjustment" share the belief in an evolutionary pattern of development that poor countries should walk in order to reach the "optimal conditions" of market capitalism. What anthropologists believed a century ago and then abandoned is today the common creed of the queen of social sciences.

We do not aim to caricature the work of economists. Their scholarly discipline is highly sophisticated and formalized, so that non-professionals cannot even understand much of their knowledge. Nevertheless, as already described in a previous section, policy prescriptions derived from economists (think of the Chicago Boys in Chile), being ultimately political, must be discussed and criticized in political terms. Even when in good faith, and even when open to the cutting edge of the discipline's developments (paying due attention to institutional and cognitive biases), economists invariable present peripheral countries as so feeble that they are not even able to accomplish very basic recipes for economic success and development.[9] The mainstream economic profession has thus deeply internalized, ultimately because of its utilitarian axiology, both the self-congratulatory attitude of the West and its condescending, humiliating, and often racist attitude towards the rest.

Equally simplistic are the shared perceptions within the economic profession of the reality of the legal system, both in Western settings and *a fortiori* in peripheral countries. Nevertheless, as often happens, short of being understood as a disciplinary limit, simplistic analysis and simple prescriptions are key to the success of a literary genre. Thus economic pundits transmitting such dominant, simple-minded approaches to the general debate through newspapers and other media are relevant here as influential policy-makers and legitimizers of the global "rule of law" as an instrument of plunder. It is the roots of this influential professional dialogue in the United States that interests us in this section.

The encounter of interest between the legal and economics professions happened at the height of the Cold War, when an anti-formalist form of legal reasoning, known as *American legal realism*, intellectually dominated US legal culture. American legal realism can be described as a candid approach, recognizing that the law is mostly the product of the decision-maker's policy decisions, often stemming from his political vision of society. Such an approach was in sharp contrast with previous formalistic ideas of the rule of law as a pre-existing order that the legal interpreter was only supposed to discover by almost mechanically applying to factual situations, relevant statutes, and precedents.[10] In the realist vision, the lawyer was to operate as a social engineer, balancing conflicting interests and thus "creating" the legal framework for future social interaction – a dramatic departure from a "textual" tradition of lawyering that still dominates outside the United States, but still a clear recognition of the "normative" nature of legal reasoning. A leading legal realist, Herman Oliphant, created a successful motto for this American anti-formalist legal approach, by suggesting that lawyers should "Get out of the libraries!" According to this vision lawyers should immerse themselves in the study of social interaction to search for the best possible institutional solutions. The belief, which had long been the entire universe of mainstream Western lawyers, that rules can be "discovered" in previous statutes and precedents, had to be abandoned.

For this purpose, lawyers needed the guidance of other social scientists, such as sociologists, anthropologists, or economists. Karl Llewellyn, for example, another leading legal realist, knocked at the door of anthropologist E. Adamson Hoebel to explore forms of "legal life" outside of libraries.[11] And many other realist lawyers, too, felt that non-lawyers were needed in the law faculties in order to develop non-textual paradigms of thought. Among such non-lawyers appointed to teach in the most prestigious law schools in the 1950s, we find many of the founding fathers of "law and economics," leading Chicago economists such as Aaron Director or Ronald Coase.

Lawyers, to be sure, did not limit themselves to using their guides for an intellectual journey outside of textual reasoning. Not many of them were looking for progressive approaches aimed at challenging the *status quo* of the law. Not many were seeking, with economic tools, better approaches to examine "dark places." In Western countries, dominated by the rhetoric of democracy, when lawyers candidly perform their often-contested role of law-making, acknowledging their own policy platforms, they experience a loss of legitimacy. In a very interesting public recent example, one can use the confirmation hearings of Chief Justice Roberts of the US Supreme Court. This skilled lawyer successfully used the metaphor of the judge as a "neutral umpire," just applying the law as he finds it, thus gaining confirmation by denial of any personal policy platform.

Many American lawyers, particularly those located on the more conservative side of the political spectrum, felt that decades of dominant legal realism required a restructuring of the lawyer's legitimacy as a neutral umpire. The law, they held, needed to be refurbished, reclaiming some objectivity and neutrality if legal scholars and judges were to keep a social role as "hidden law givers" in a politically legitimized representative system of government. Considering law as the policy preference of the last decision-maker, like realists did, exposes the legal profession to a fundamental challenge: if law is as biased as the political preferences of the decision-maker, why should the decision-maker be a professional lawyer rather than a politician, a doctor, or a car dealer?

As we have discussed, in Western jurisprudence, the rule of law – vested as legal science and a specialized form of knowledge – has served the purpose of asserting the special role of lawyers, decision-makers lacking political legitimacy, at least since the time of Sir Edward Coke. If the time-honored metaphor of the lawyer as biologist (appellate cases being his laboratory specimens), discovering a pre-existing legal system and then applying it to facts with a geometric deductive reasoning, no longer could serve the purpose, having been ridiculed by decades of legal realism, "social science" could now do the legitimating trick. And first among social sciences was economics, in whose DNA one finds the denial of any legitimacy of normative discourses such as those typical of lawyers.

Economics could, at the same time, offer a good guide outside the black letter of the law, and a new strong source of legitimacy. After all, economists were dealing with incentives, and incentives meant focusing on the behavior of the recipients of legal precepts – something happening beyond the legal text. Economists, moreover, beginning in the 1950s, applied their "scientific" analysis to the behavior of politicians and other institutional actors. By claiming that politicians are rational maximizers of their chances to be re-elected, they developed an approach known as "public choices," claiming to be able to predict the content of legislation and regulatory activity by focusing on the connection between legislators and special interests. By so doing they were still focusing on something outside the legal text understood as the outcome of the political process. Their worry centered on the production of norms, on law in the making, the processes and the forces determining its content (so-called "rent seeking," studied by Nobel Laureate James Buchanan). While traditionally lawyers were focusing on legal norms and precepts *as they are* (or as they should be), economists were claiming that the focus should be turned on what comes before (public choices) and after (incentive-reactive behavior) the legal precept. The focus should be on *the process* and on the social consequences of its outcome.

As to legitimacy, economics handbooks were full of rhetoric grounded in science and objectivity. The early success of economic reasoning in legal matters can thus be justified by at least two factors: (1) once the focus is on the process, then all would accept that the process should be efficient; and (2) efficiency was claiming objectivity, something essential in a strategy of legitimization. While justice is the domain of subjective feelings, efficiency is the domain of objectivity based only on a few simple, clearly spelled out criteria.[12]

Economists had an agenda too, so the dialogue with lawyers not only served the need to provide legitimacy to the lawyer's role but also would eventually further the political role of the economist by involving them in law-making and legal interpretation. And the agenda was common to conservatives and progressives. The more open-minded of the economists, such as the early Ronald Coase (himself a Nobel Prize recipient), felt that segregation between the two disciplines was absurd. After all, at an earlier stage, law and economics were not even separate domains of knowledge: the founding father of modern economics, Adam Smith, was a professor of law.

It was only positivism, an approach that by the late nineteenth century had conquered both disciplines, that almost paradoxically created a cultural impasse to communication between them. For economists, as we already know, positivism meant the full separation between facts and values, between the "is" and the "ought," between positive and normative discourses.[13] For a long time they simply could not communicate with lawyers, given the constant confusion between these levels of discourse that characterizes how lawyers talk about justice. The few economists, such as Thorstein Veblen or John R. Commons, who attempted to overtake the logic of economic positivism by maintaining a dialogue with lawyers and institutions, themselves focusing on issues of distributions, were accused of socialism and marginalized by the economic orthodoxy.

For lawyers, on the contrary, positivism meant full separation of the domain of law from that of morality, politics, society, and whatever is "outside" of what the authority *poses* as law. Positivism meant, in terms diffused by leading Austrian jurisprude Hans Kelsen (himself, as Hayek and Popper, a refugee in England), a *pure theory* of the law. In this perspective, economists were tainted by their constant policy discourses, something beyond the pure idea of the legal system.[14] Naturally, the pure theory of law, granting legitimacy to the rule of law simply because it is the rule of law, does not second guess its use however oppressive it might be. It thus introduces the idea that the law, once posed and effective, is self-legitimized, can never be "illegal," and can never serve plunder, a term *per se* evoking illegality and not the rule of law.

This separation of legal and economic thinking has extracted a high toll that became very visible when the oil crisis of the 1970s compelled the rethinking of priorities. From the lawyer's side, the welfare state had been constructed with very little attention to the economic effects of its regulations, so that by the time of the oil crisis, sustainability started being questioned, more and more successfully, particularly in England and the United States. On the economist's side, Keynesian policy, so crucial in recovering from the crisis of the 1930s, was developed without considering the legal structure of its implementation, in particular the autonomy and strengths of the legal and bureaucratic structure, capable of defeating, by complex patterns of resistance, any macro-reform.

Consequently, while some economists were eager to better understand the legal picture, hence overcoming the costs of decades of incommunicability, others used the new Chicago creed to attack Keynesian policy because of its emphasis on the role of the state. They also scrutinized the political process within a public choice model, to claim back to "the market" (to the private domain) what Keynesianism had transferred, arguably unsuccessfully, to the public domain level of (redistributive) state intervention in the economy. Public choice theorists monitoring the distortions of the political process (in particular of legislation and regulation) were finding their natural allies in the early work of apologists of the common law tradition, such as Chicago scholar and Reagan appointee to the federal judiciary, Richard Posner. Under this alliance, in the name of efficiency and objectivity, issues of distribution and substantive justice – so crucial to traditional legal analysis and to the realist legacy of the New Deal – were simply left behind.[15] The normative dimension was de-legitimized in the legal discourse that was to become "positive," like that of any other social science.

The economic approach to legal reasoning would not have achieved a global role if it had not been leveraged, beginning in the Reagan years, by a fully fledged political agenda, a real industry capable of flooding with cash any movement giving cultural prestige to deregulation and other reactionary politics of those years. It is sufficient to look at the early, very lukewarm reception of these new ideas in Europe to understand how much lawyers were willing to resist efficiency and privatization in the name of justice and distribution. But the multiplication of academic chairs, endowed research facilities, fellowships, and the like in a prestigious context such as the United States academia (today's global graduate school) was a certain recipe for global success, including its spread to China, India, and elsewhere.

Historically, the way in which a new, politically powerful paradigm of research is able to seize a leading position in a plurality of cultural contexts is often by making previous approaches look obsolete and primitive.[16] This has certainly been the strategy by which the economic approach to the law has been able to seize a global role, by offering an expansive, universalistic model that expresses itself in English (the new lingua franca) and which claims to be the latest natural legal order of the global age.

Within these assumptions, any approach to the law that still considers it a political institution which cannot be understood and described in graphs and numbers is disposed of as obsolete. Any approach that requires something other than a reactive minimal philosophy of governance (Hayek's political theory) has been entirely out of fashion since the fall of the Berlin wall. Any approach claiming a normative and openly value-guided role for lawyers marginalizes them from the much coveted company of social scientists.

For the economic approach, law is supposed to create incentives for market actors. The skilled lawyer and policy-maker is not appreciated if his suggestions require a proactive and expensive activist posture of governments, let alone if he argues for economic redistribution by taxation or other obsolete Keynesian measures. The legal scholar can only count on the natural existence of markets: his role is to produce a correct set of market incentives. The quintessential example of this attitude is the celebrated "self-sufficient" model of corporate reform produced by leading American scholar Bernard Black for the Russian Federation.[17]

Nothing is natural in all of this. As we have seen, the relationship between economists and lawyers has a history and is contingent, politically motivated, and historically driven. It is important to consider this in order to rebuke the narrative of necessity and natural evolution that characterizes so much of the imperial project, which to the contrary is today, as in the colonial past, a *project by design.*

While it would be grossly exaggerated to claim that efficiency reasoning enjoys a dominant role as an approach to legal scholarship worldwide, we can nevertheless see that it is the main intellectual vehicle used to diffuse expansionist and universalistic American legal ideas, including tight notions of intellectual property.[18] The new producers of global law, private and public international institutions of global governance (the WTO, World Bank, IMF, mega law firms, rating agencies etc.), implement policy based on the value of legal efficiency. Moreover, the merger of law and economics has produced the now diffused general understanding of *law as a technology* (a refurbished strategy for its de-politicization), as witnessed by the significant numbers of "centers for the study of law and technology" created by lawyers and economists through the major US law schools, usually funded by large intellectual property law firms.

A very clear bias in favor of the efficiency of common law adjudication promotes courts of law and (quite paradoxically) alternative dispute resolution (ADR) as the most important actors of a reactive legal system, structurally incapable of the redistribution of resources in favor of the weak. Privatizations of every possible domain, including that of ideas, and structural reforms, sustained by the international institutions of global governance, make economic reasoning in the law one of the most important vehicles of diffusion of self-centered American ideology worldwide.

Powerful organizational structures, producing a flood of professional literature, were created to transplant in Europe, Latin America, and elsewhere the idea that the law should be grounded in economic efficiency rather than in social justice. Organizations like the European or Latin American and Caribbean Society of Law and Economics began their operations as early as the late 1980s. Once transplanted outside the USA, economic reasoning in the law displays the high level of ambiguity that actually allows it to flourish. Conservative scholars admire its intellectual elegance and share its political biases. More progressive and liberal scholars see its potential in subverting the highly formalistic and black letter flavor of local conceptions of the law (still based on legal positivism) and claim that the conservative political bias is something that can be left on the other side of the Atlantic Ocean. Because of this de-politicizing force (though former Mexican President de la Madrid served as Honorary President of the Latin American Society of Law and Economics), the economic approach to legal reasoning was able to persuade many "global" legal professionals that issues of distribution were better tackled by taxation than by adjudication and that, as a consequence, efficiency should become the pole star of legal interpretation. Such lawyers were paving the way to a mode of thought subversive of the traditional relationship between law and the market, which emphasized the need of the former to regulate and check the actors of the latter.

Since the 1990s, the relationship between law and the market began to be gradually subverted in US legal theory. The law, it was posed, should be without values, efficient, and serve the function of facilitating rather than constraining transactions. As a consequence of this philosophy, the law should be "market friendly," that is it should limit itself to protecting property rights, freedom of contracts, and enterprise. The law should be adapted to the necessities of the market, domestically and in particular in the so-called "emerging markets" – today's version of the colonial concept of India, symbolized by the India Company – both eastern (Asia) and western (America). Because of this ideological revolution, carried out by leading American scholars and funded by conservative foundations, today it is the corporate dominated market governing the law and not the other way around. Moreover, because of the re-emergence of bold development discourses, efficiency reasoning in the law gets exported by means of forceful practices of imposition (e.g. conditional loans) rather than freely chosen as a prestigious approach to the law by lawyers worldwide. Developing efficient i.e. corporate friendly legal systems in the third world thus becomes a new civilizing mission in which many do-gooders or more cynical actors eagerly engage with generous financial support from a variety of powerful sources. This strategy of de-politicization of the law is necessary for the international financial institutions that, as a consequence, fund it abundantly. In the bylaws of different institutions belonging to the World Bank group, for example, there is an explicit ban of political intervention; through the Cold War this was interpreted as limiting its activity to strictly economic issues, thus not to the law because of its political content. Today, the notion of "comprehensive development," the new World Bank priority, attracts the law (governance as opposed to government), which has been duly de-politicized by its economic transformation, to the core of economic development. Consequently, intervention in developing legal systems is not banned but actually encouraged.[19]

Not surprisingly, in the era of global single thought, with the triumph of transnational corporate actors over the state, the relationship between the law and the market has been reversed. Positivistic notions of the omnipotent sovereign state whose values and priorities, reflected in the law, could be carried out at any price (or without paying any attention to such prices) have withered. The notion of the law as a set of incentives rather than as a pyramid of binding orders, as a carrot rather than a stick, has been critical in unseating state centerism from its dominating jurisprudential status. The idea that market forces produce the law is now accepted. On the one hand, public choice economists "demonstrate" how regulation and legislation are "captured" by the special interests sustaining political campaigns of politicians, described as rational maximizers of their chances to be elected. On the other hand, scholars in law and economics work out all sorts of Darwinian evolutionary theories showing how "investment" in litigation resources produces "returns" in terms of the survival only of the more efficient rules. Seen from this perspective, the law, produced by the legislature or by courts in the process of adjudication, "naturally" favors business interests "investing" in the rule of law. This new concept easily walks the path of saying not only that the law is up for sale, but also that this is "natural" and it should be so.

An economic approach to the law thus locates itself in the conservative mainstream, restating the usual cynically ideological platitudes. What do you expect? The political process is captured and adjudication reflects investments! Once it conquered the mainstream status by marginalizing all openly normative and redistributive arguments, efficiency reasoning has thus transformed the choice for candor, typical of realist jurisprudence, in an even more extreme choice for cynicism. Discourses on distribution and on values have been abandoned. Transformation of an economic approach to the law into an organized and corporate-funded intellectual industry has expelled any distributional worry from the cutting edge of academic and policy discourse. People worried about values, with just distribution of resources, with problems in accepting unconditionally the paradigm of the *homo œconomicus*, are now depicted as bleeding-heart idealists, or naïve first-year law students, simply incapable of understanding the "scientific" logic that explains how things work.

Of course one might question the gain, in terms of legitimacy for the legal profession, in cynically recognizing that the rule of law is up for sale and that whoever can invest more in legal education and law-making (including hiring more expensive lawyers and lobbyists) will "naturally" benefit from the returns on such investments, by winning the case or obtaining a business-friendly legal environment. The rule of law should lose appeal as much from being controlled by political power as by business interests. Nevertheless, only the first distortion, blamed on socialist legality and on other non-Western conceptions, is constructed as *lack* of the rule of law. The second distortion gets constructed by strong corporate actors as the way things should be, in the name of economic efficiency and market expansion and development.

Universalized notions such as intellectual property, thus find in (bad) economic policy, rather than in law, their legitimating force. They are deterritorialized, "naturally" placed beyond the reach of the state whose only role is to enforce it, not to draft its limits and frame its content in order to reflect the needs of the people. Quite often, with the help of skilled lawyers, American corporations transfer their intellectual property, patents, trademarks, and even logos to other entities incorporated in fiscal paradises such as the Cayman Islands or the Bermudas. They subsequently pay royalties for the use of their own intellectual property. They can legally deduct such efficient royalty payments from their taxable income, thus hiding a large share of their revenues: plunder. They can do so because legislators of both parties cynically described as "natural maximizers" of their chances of being re-elected, behave according to the economist's prediction. Efficiency is the powerful factor granting legitimacy to universal constructs such as intellectual property and to their expansion beyond reasonable limits.

To be sure, the rhetoric of property transmits a sense of perpetuity; so temporal limits are implicitly the exception rather than the rule. For example the small online publisher Eldritch Press has attempted to challenge the excessive duration of contemporary copyrights (between 50 and 70 years after the author's death), constantly and incrementally increased in lengths paralleling the increase in power of the entertainment industry. Eldritch's action, aimed at re-conquering some knowledge for the public sphere, was defeated by the powerful Hollywood industry, investing in the political and judicial process according to the predictions of law and economics.[20] First, an investment in lobbying Congress produced the so-called Sonny Bono Copyright Extension Act (also known as the Mickey Mouse Act, because it aimed at taking care of the expiration of copyrights on Mickey Mouse, the *Wizard of Oz* and other valuable property of the Hollywood industry). Second, more investment in litigation (including the hiring of economic consultants) has shielded the act from a constitutional challenge that reached the Supreme Court. Obviously, the pro-entertainment industry decision of the Supreme Court opens fundamental strategic questions on the possibility and realism of using courts of law for progressive purposes. Clearly, exorbitant intellectual property instruments of plunder have powerful allies in high places.

Economic reasoning in the law has reached peripheral countries where a technocratic elite holds power. Today, professional associations of lawyers and economists are active from Latin America to Asia to Oceania. The leading books for lawyers written by American economists are translated into many languages, and examples of the tremendous worldwide influence of their modes of thought are too numerous to be described here. Economists from less developed countries educated in the United States serve locally as consultants and providers of legitimacy and prestige to – often corrupt – powerful elites. Internationally, they occupy positions in financial and policy institutions eager to show openness in their ranks for people from peripheral countries. But these elites, from Asia, Africa, and Latin America think like Westerners, because they have absorbed, in their prestigious academic study, the rhetoric of Western technocratic elitism. They thus serve the Western project of oppression and ultimately plunder by means of "efficient" law, of which intellectual property is but one example.

The story repeats itself. As the Church (as a colonial institution that would educate a local class) and anthropologists (who would provide the necessary degree of intellectual prestige to the colonial project) were facilitating colonial plunder, so today US academic institutions educate local ruling classes; economists provide the degree of intellectual prestige indispensable for carrying out plunder by means of an efficient law serving the needs of innovation and development.

Providing Legitimacy: Lawyers and Anthropologists

Providers of legitimacy are active both at the center and on the periphery. They are present in the current scenario as they were in the colonial past, where perhaps anthropologists – rather than economists – were the most influential intellectual elite determining policy and lawyers' visions of different cultures. Anthropologists moreover have provided crucial information about non-Western cultures; many times they are present when valuable practices, products, and ideas are "discovered," later to become objects of Western intellectual property protection. Also, they may be present as students of cultures in whose land toxic wastes are to be dumped or where oil is discovered. It is important, as a consequence, to examine the role of Anglophone anthropologists from the beginning of the discipline, both at the core and at the periphery. Interestingly, it is often the case that the critical potential of a discipline is obliterated as soon as the discipline gets institutionalized and transformed into an "industry." The unfolding of the anthropological project in the United States and Britain is particularly significant when examining the link between anthropological knowledge and colonial power, thus showing continuities with the current role of economists described in the previous section.

The development of American anthropology corresponds largely to three phases: from the end of the American Civil War to the last decade of the nineteenth century; from the end of the nineteenth century to the onset of World War II; and the military industrial period, roughly covering a 60-year period from World War II to the present.[21] Anthropology reflected the historical events of the times, providing ideological support for state practice. In the nineteenth century, social Darwinist evolutionary theory, proving the survival and ultimate superiority of the fittest social settings (the West), was elaborated primarily by lawyer-anthropologists who were useful to state conquest. In the second period, which was called the liberal reform period, anthropologists' theories stressed human flexibility and plasticity, useful in assimilation policies aimed at erasing different cultures. And in the most recent phase, the military industrial period, anthropologists have responded with uncertainties and equivocations about power.

In spite of anthropological dissenters, the anthropological mainstream, whether evolutionary, liberal, or militarized, has had consequences. Anthropology was the first of the "new" sciences, a science that is both soft and hard, both humanities and science, between nature and culture, the past and the present – and as such could search for new ways to understand the human condition writ large. It could question thinking of inequalities as innate. In other words, it could perform as a critique of accepted premises. As twentieth-century anthropologists moved from the armchair to firsthand fieldwork, often amongst colonized peoples, theories of cultural relativism challenged the predominant evolutionary theories of their day.[22] Throughout the twentieth century anthropologists observed the development of science and technology as measures of worth.[23] Some recognized the ideological nature of beliefs, such as progress. Rapid market globalization has made consideration of alternative knowledge systems inevitable.

The concept of progress has had a powerful hold on both unconscious and conscious thought. To what extent is progress continual and inevitable? How do we define it – as societal or technological progress? These questions are of interest to those who still ponder the directionality of our world and whether technological development should be equated with progress, and who should have the power to decide what constitutes development.[24]

The "anthropological attitude" that values detachment and participation as a mode of rethinking existing assumptions has not changed much in the past 100 years, nor have the social prejudices that it either challenged or underwrote: ethnocentrism, racism, sexism, and the use of inadequate measures of human worth.[25] Factors external to the profession became more visible during the Cold War and merit remembering.[26] Social anthropologists were harassed and attacked for their stance on racial and economic inequalities under the influence of McCarthyism in the USA and similar harassment that happened in England.[27] New technologies also entered the picture; geographic information systems (GIS), while useful to anthropologists, were used to locate sites for bombing the people social anthropologists studied. Some physical anthropologists like Earle Reynolds, who worked on the Atomic Bomb Casualty Commission, became an anti-bomb activist and sailed into a US bomb test zone and later into Vladivostok to protest testing by the former USSR.[28] The mainstream American Anthropological Association did not commend his active role nor did they actively support harassed members. At the same time some anthropologists who worked with the OSS during World War II continued their work when the OSS became the CIA after the war.[29] Anthropologists working during the colonial period were often unaware of the settings that enmeshed them – they studied the colonized not the colonizers. Within a generalized assumption of Western superiority, the discipline as a whole suffered from normative blindness, incapable of seeing the general implications of the data it was unearthing.

In the United States, a classic case of normative blindness is that of Cahokia – "hidden in plain sight," as one archaeologist put it.[30] Cahokia stands as the third largest structure in pre-industrial North America. It is an area of 83 hectares – a city of some 20,000 people in a region of some 50,000 people. Notions of a vanishing "race of savages" implied that America's First Nations never reached a level of civilization comparable to that of the invading conquerors in spite of such evidence. The Manifest Destiny ideology required the downgrading of the inhabitants who competed for land with white settlers. The land that white settlers were after had to have been empty.

In the self-critiques of the 1960s and the 1970s, anthropologists began to consider the conditions under which their knowledge had been acquired: the political and administrative inequality between colonial anthropologists and colonized informants.[31] The exploration of the effects of colonial inequality on ethnographic perspectives became the investigation of the distorting effects of anthropological writing. How could anthropology have studied colonized peoples without studying colonizers and missionaries? How could scientific anthropologists have left so much out of their holistic study: women, children, power, diffusion, and the wider context? Over time anthropological description expanded to include power, history, and comparison. As history and comparison entered, colonialism, past movements of things and ideas, and massive migrations of peoples entered the picture. To understand how power works requires comparison with attention to resistance, capitulation, disintegration, and integration, all on local and global levels. The Cold War raised issues of race, war, genocide, counterinsurgency, natural resources, and the double-edged uses of anthropology. Methodologies were revolutionized by access to military technology. The networks linking the academic with the political setting of the national security state meant that the innocence of anthropology was lost. From this vantage, evolutionary theories, positivist methodologies, and later interpretivism were all flights from facing the implications of power, examining how power is produced, exercised, and with what consequences.

Anthropology has the capacity to generate the kind of introspection that can influence the future role of human beings on earth. Why have anthropologists not been able to do so? Or to put it differently, how have anthropologists, unwittingly perhaps, contributed to a legitimization of plunder in spite of impressive findings?

Self-censorship and silence appear at important junctures. In some cases, silence itself has been justified: silence about colonizers not just because the anthropologist might share implicitly the possibility of "progress," or of the civilizing project, or the helping hand. Anthropologists were silent about nuclear testing both in the United States and in the Pacific either because they were fearful or because they thought that silence was patriotic. In addition, positivism has a de-politicizing influence.

An earlier classic example of censorship is the case of James Mooney's fieldwork among the Native American Sioux.[32] In the 1890s, a self-trained anthropologist, Mooney was funded by the Bureau of American Ethnology (BAE) at the Smithsonian Institution to conduct fieldwork among the Sioux. He was not a social evolutionist who thought of people as savage, barbarians, or civilized. Government-funded research, combined with his independent scholarship, culminated in his extraordinary work, *The Ghost Dance Religion and the Sioux Outbreak of 1890.* In it, Mooney detailed the Ghost Dance "cult" among many Native American tribes in the last decades of the nineteenth century, which culminated in the massacre of over 200 Sioux at Wounded Knee in 1890. He documented the greatest aboriginal revival the country had ever seen, one that promised a return to a time without the white man. With empathy and compassion, Mooney made the connection between religious revivalism and the alienation, cultural decay, tragic conditions, and desperation of a people who had suffered enormous losses – land, people, history – at the hands of the white invaders of their land.

The Smithsonian response as a government agency was censorial and prompted by fear that Mooney's work would alienate the Bureau of Indian Affairs and the US Congress, with which they needed to work. Mooney's superiors at the Smithsonian wished he had avoided making the connections between the Ghost Dance and conditions of misery, and avoided comparisons with European religious movements of revitalization whose longings for a prophet would give them a means for redemption.

Mooney's American Indians were not heathens or barbarians; they were part of the whole human race, including the "civilized" human race. His work spanned a period when evolutionary social theories proving the superiority of the white were not just a question of anthropology but of state politics and religious-political practice. Later on, Mooney was barred from further research on the reservations by the Commissioner of Indian Affairs who did not appreciate the references to religious freedom and scientific truths as justification for his research.[33] His boss at the BAE, John Wesley Powell, held the position of the non-political, detached, unemotional scientist for whom Mooney was a constant headache. It was a period when Indians were depicted as wanderers and beggars unattached to private property, an assertion used to justify government plunder of Indian lands. Ideas that were powerful in the wider society were present in anthropology – social evolutionism, notions of "progress," and assimilation – and all these had consequences for Native Americans, who by the twenty-first century have the choice of making a living by gambling casinos or by using their reservations to receive toxic wastes.

Following the Dawes Allotment Act of 1887, the US Congress struggled to solve claims by Indian nations for breaches of the treaties governing their surrender. Finally, in 1946, the Indian Claims Commission (ICC) was enacted to hear these cases. A progressive movement, beginning with John Collier's 1933 appointment as Superintendent of Indian Affairs, attempted to rectify outstanding legal claims. Opposition to these claims was supported on social scientific as well as legal grounds. The ICC had specified that claims could be advanced by Indian tribes, bands, and nations. Perhaps unbeknownst to the original intentions of the US Congress, there was conjured a class of North American Indians who did not fit any of the three categories listed in the ICC mandate, a society too primitive to meet the criteria of a "band," a society that could be considered unorganized. The United States Department of Justice advanced such an argument. Their expert witness was none other than the distinguished American anthropologist Julian Steward, an evolutionist building on the work of nineteenth-century lawyer-anthropologists.[34]

The Paiute, a Great Basin Shoshone tribe, were part of a claim.[35] The land in question dealt with some 325,000,000 acres of land acquired by the United States government without compensation or treaty agreement. The strategy of the government was to deny title to the Indian plaintiffs on the grounds that they were not organized societies, and therefore could not own lands. Julian Steward's categorization of the Shoshone corresponded precisely with the picture favored by the Department of Justice. Steward's evolutionary logic was a line of reasoning much used in colonial law under the British. This doctrine is expressed in the natural law doctrine of *terra nullius* (mentioned previously) – territory unoccupied that consequently could be freely and legally appropriated by the colonizers. In this light, Steward's social evolutionary theory became a matter of legal and political significance, a theory that legitimized the denial of indigenous rights to collectively hold lands. In the case at hand, the Northern Paiutes were not considered to be an "organized" society, and seen as too primitive to belong to one of the three categories, band, tribe, or nation who could own a territory.

Steward's theories[36] sought to connect environment with cultural development, a schema for evaluating the "level" of a specific society from simple to complex. According to Steward the lowest level of socio-cultural integration was the family level, a situation where each family is independent and self-sufficient. Stuck at the family level (not a band or a tribe, let alone a nation), the Shoshone had not achieved a level of socio-cultural integration that had institutions that could hold title to land, a position favorable to the position advanced by the Department of Justice and consistent with the doctrine of *terra nullius*.

The reputation of Steward's project rested on the presumption that his work was scientific and objective, not ideological or interpretive. Concerns raised recently about Steward's science and objectivity emerge from knowledge that his theoretical model was developed during his stint as an expert witness for the Department of Justice over a 7-year period, suggesting that Steward's theoretical project may have been influenced by his close relationships on one side of a number of litigations. By 1950, Steward supported the view that ownership of property existed only when the form of landholding explicitly fit the characteristics of land ownership defined by American law.

According to contemporary investigations the story does not end there. Steward's position on the doctrine of *terra nullius* is argued in Canada as well. In a 1979 judgment concerning rights of the Inuit of Baker Lake, indigenous parties must demonstrate that they lived in an "organized" society in the pre-settlement period. In spite of the efforts of such as former Judge Thomas Berger of the British Columbia Supreme Court in present-day Canadian cases regarding aboriginal rights, the influence of Stewardian ideas are apparent – an interpretation of fact that one archeologist referred to as "an ideological mechanism in deference of privilege." There can be no doubt that anthropological ideas have had a continuing influence beyond the discipline, legitimizing the premises of colonial legal ideology despite the advocacy of anthropologists and lawyers working to reconfigure native rights.

That the recounting of anthropological history should divorce internal politics from external events is ironic, since anthropological thought, particularly as it was articulated in North America, was born from a Jeffersonian tradition of heightened engagement between the scientist and the outside world. Jefferson was interested in the misnamed "Indians" as well as in the African Americans and Europeans who had come or been brought forcibly to the

New World. In his *Notes on the State of Virginia* in 1785 Jefferson writes: "It is to be lamented . . . that we suffered so many of the Indian tribes already to extinguish . . . without . . . [collecting] the general rudiments at least of the languages they spoke."[37] Under Jefferson's leadership the Philadelphia-based American Philosophical Society became an important repository for such studies, and, by means of government expeditions, a large amount of data was collected during the pre-1840 period. Not all were driven by scientific purpose alone.

Following Jefferson's lead, many of the first ethnologists and anthropologists were compelled to action by the complexities of an expanding frontier, especially as they pertained to the "Indian problem." New and prolonged contact with the "other," as we now refer to less familiar groups, secured a place for these early scientists in government discussions about Indian land settlement and resettlement, water, minerals, and assimilation issues.[38]

Of course, *which* ethnologists were to gain the ears, and ultimately the money, of administrators and politicians at this time depended upon how these ethnologists thought the Indian population should be controlled, and subsequently to which theories they subscribed. Henry Lewis Morgan's version of evolutionism, known as progressive (being grounded in a notion of social progress), was used to justify the continuous resettlement of Indians throughout the end of the nineteenth century and into the twentieth century by the movers and shakers of Teddy Roosevelt's time.[39] Progressive evolutionism was also useful to the supporting institutions of the time, and mainly to the BAE, which was placed under the already established Smithsonian Institution. John Wesley Powell, who founded the BAE in 1879, was determined to use anthropologists' work to further the understanding of the Indian populations and to secure the BAE as the "informational arm of Congress and the American people." The Bureau provided the first permanent government-supported research for anthropological work.[40] Powell underestimated the complexities of the role of anthropologists, something that gave him some problems.[41] He suppressed the work of those BAE scholars who did not agree with Morgan's theories used to justify resettlement and assimilation, beginning a long history in which anthropologists' confrontations with dominant social beliefs would be avoided or guided into muddy waters by other anthropologists or publishers, or government agencies. For example, ethnologist Charles Royce's studies of Indian land cessions in the United States, completed in 1885, passionately argued using non-evolutionary theories for the removal of whites from Indian territory. Powell promised publication but the work lay untouched until 1895.[42] It finally appeared in 1899.

Powell represented the dominant legitimacy-providing vision:

> Despite the pitiably frequent cases of personal and temporary injustices to the weaker race, the general policy has been guided by a deep-grounded recognition of the principles of justice and right on the part of both peoples . . . the justice shown the red man is more richly tempered with mercy today than during any earlier decade.

Royce was an alternate voice:

> For two hundred years, a contest involving their very existence as a people has been maintained against the unscrupulous rapacity of Anglo-Saxon civilization.

Critical anthropologists like Frank G. Speck exposed the policies of Teddy Roosevelt, presiding over the further dismantling of Indian lands at the time, and who was speaking, as an evolutionist, of Indian nomadism.[43] Roosevelt and his friends, perhaps legitimized (though unwillingly) by Morgan's evolutionism and later by Julian Steward, depicted the Indians as "wanderers and beggars" unattached to private property, a thin observation used to justify government plunder. The powerful evolutionists were mainstream spokesmen, and they are still with us today disguised as neo-liberals.

With the emergence of the Red Power movement in the 1960s, new economic developments on Indian reservations appeared, namely gambling and the "employment" of Native Americans as the overseers of toxic waste. Today we readily identify a fine line between coercion and informed consent, and anthropological knowledge when at the service of legalized plunder might make it even more opaque.[44] For example, the institutional elements of federal, state, and reservation politics include the nuclear waste industry, a player that has been out of sight in ethnological reports in the past.

A number of issues appear if one considers anthropologists as providers of legitimacy and consent since Europeans came to the New World. Particular conditions in North America shaped the discipline here:

> A profound difference between the history of our discipline in Europe, on one hand, and in the Western hemisphere on the other, inheres in the simple fact that our subjects of study, our "primitive" peoples, were our neighbors – our

> ill-treated, indeed often persecuted, neighbors. In this instance, as in others, the anthropology we did and have done is conditioned by the history and social complexion of the society from whence we come.[45]

The historical base of American anthropology was at home. For the British, and more generally the European, the historical base was away from home. British anthropologists in Africa were also studying people and resources that were the objects of colonial plunder. Max Gluckman spoke about the judicial process amongst the Barotse – to emphasize their commonalities with European legal systems, specifically Roman-Dutch law – rather than examine more directly the colonial impact on African law. His message was clear: the natives are not "savages."[46] His political need was to assert similarity. It took Martin Chanock, a legal historian, many years later to show that often customary law is invented by missionary and political colonialism, thus challenging the meaning of similarity within a structural imbalance of power.[47] Today everywhere is away from "home," but the intellectual justification of plunder continues and "similarity" in the form of evolutionary "convergence" typical of universalistic notions of legal development and progress, still forgets to consider imbalances of power.[48]

In an essay on indigenous rights to traditional lands, anthropologist Richard Reed narrates the history of the creation of a national park (or reserve) in Paraguay where, at the start, indigenous people were expecting to have access to *their own lands* for traditional purposes and to participate in managing and maintaining the park. The context is one of unequal power. As defined by the Nature Conservancy, "acculturated" indigenous people were excluded. For the indigenous people the Nature Conservancy is another *latifundista* in a long history of outside plantation owners. The future of the forests takes precedence over people. Nevertheless it was the Nature Conservancy that had important Washington connections and had amassed a good deal of money for the negotiation of land purchase. In the larger conflict over resources, the environmental protection agencies have the economic and political weapons to confront powerful corporations and national governments. The new developers are the environmental protection groups. The scramble for land continues, like the plunder of indigenous land for private purpose.

Anthropologists have played many roles in their North American work, yet self-reflection, where it is found, is focused narrowly to the exclusion of a wider range of relations, such as dispossession of land or other resources including knowledge. In sum, anthropological knowledge is produced by individuals with different motives, occupying multiple roles. Such multiplicity can include the roles of scholar, advocate (sometimes for colonizers and sometimes for colonized), negotiator between parties, translator of world views, educator intent on overturning prejudicial views, politician or citizen forming policy, expert witness (as when appearing before the judiciary in court), or silent observer. Anthropology appears to proceed autonomously, even though we have documented the opposite for a long time now. This is part of a professional project, even a strategy, that allows anthropologists as neutral scientists to serve as providers of legitimacy. It is not much different from law or economics.

Projects of recolonization and empire in the new colonies of Afghanistan or Iraq can be understood if approached with the full arsenals of anthropological tools, paying due attention to the fact that such tools have been developed in a century-old tradition where, as we have seen, censorship and bigotry have taken their toll. In carrying on any comparison, one must observe the silence about a large part of the planet often referred to as the Middle or Near East. The Islamic world, in general, and the Arab world, in particular, are a part of the world still among the least known ethnographically, a part of the world about which disinformation and misinformation are rampant. Since World War II, anthropologists even seem predisposed to feed silence and starve critical opinion about the area. Some have suggested that working in the Arab world is not a wise career move for aspiring academics. This is particularly so with reference to scholarship on Palestine. One author explained that the silence is due to the massive expansion of public universities, meaning that intellectuals have been absorbed into the state, with the accompanying inability of public intellectuals to critically assess major political events like the 1991 Gulf War.[49] Another author concluded that anthropology has very little to contribute "in a world in which *realpolitik* rules."[50]

The Arab and Islamic worlds are probably the only regions of the globe suffering from the absence of anthropologists that make connections. Where do we write about the impact of Western economic interests on the Gulf? Where do we write about relations between oil supply nations and Western support of dictatorial regimes? One might think that a study of Israel siphoning water and top soil from south Lebanon over its borders, punctuated by sporadic bombing of power stations, would make a contribution to the anthropology of imperialism. How many anthropologists who document war zones elsewhere include the Arab world? There cannot be serious knowledge about a region of the world about which taboo subjects and myths abound. Peace was the theme of the 2003 national meeting of American anthropologists. Yet there were no panels on Iraq, bare mention of the war, and then only in relation to looting archeological objects. On the other hand, there was some justification of US foreign policy, and nothing was included on this central issue, relevant to peace in the Middle East and Palestine.

A recent plethora of efforts to study Islam have revisited old questions regarding Muslims. Particular to this revisiting is legal orientalism and the followers of Max Weber, the father of legal orientalism. Weber's use of categories or ideal types is reminiscent of Julian Steward's evolutionism. His fourfold taxonomy of legal systems with two dimensions – formal/substantive and rational/irrational – generates four categories. Again there is hierarchy. Continental law fits into the ideal type of formal/rational, while Islamic law features "traditional prescription and arbitrary decision-making, the latter serving as a substitute for a regime of rational rules."[51] While seemingly benign, the scholars who elaborate Weber's typology on the ground carry implications that are anything but benign. Currently, social scientists continue Weber's characterization of the capricious *qadi* (judge), using the metaphor of the bazaar to describe a world of chaos, indicating an Arab lack of appreciation for regularity and space and time. Exploring the injustice born of substantive irrationality makes Western law the evaluative standard, setting the stage for plans of US foreign policy today in Iraq and Afghanistan. American foreign policy will presumably save Eastern countries from irrationality, illegitimacy, and unchanging immortality by an imposition of "modern" Euro-American neo-liberal law. The usurpation will be legalized in this case not by *terra nullius* but by *lex nullius*. The perception that they lack something the civilized world possesses becomes a justification for invasions. And now we have the terrorism ticket. Anthropology's myopia, in spite of its real potential, is generally the guardian of conventionality born of nineteenth-century lawyer-anthropologists. The exceptions are either relegated to the margins, escape by means of abstract epistemologies, or leave the field altogether.[52]

5 | Constructing the Conditions for Plunder

The Plunder of Oil: Iraq and Elsewhere

> Plunder, internal and external, was the most important means of primitive accumulation of capital, an accumulation which, after the Middle Ages, made possible a new historical stage in world economic evolution. As the money economy extended more and more social strata and regions of the world became involved in unequal exchange.[1]
>
> *[source] E. Galeano*

While today plunder does not often need the use of outright direct violence, instead subtly using the law to gain a façade of legitimacy to unfair deals, in some instances it appears more similar to the primitive conditions of its early colonial version and takes the form of an outright war of conquest.

In the present phase of corporate capitalism, the prize of war is not necessarily the direct pillage of local valuable resources. Many times, as in contemporary Afghanistan, the prize of war frees the economy and introduces a rule of law capable of sustaining the needs of corporations. As noticed by such different observers as Adam Smith and Karl Marx, capitalist firms are in constant search of new spaces and use no mercy when it comes to opening them up, often by enlisting the services of nation states.

There is very little new under the sun, including, for example, the Opium War in China (1839–42). In the name of free market, the British government waged war to sustain the right of the East India Company to trade Indian opium for Chinese tea. According to the British, the Chinese authorities had no right to protect their population against drug addiction by making opium trade illegal. Similarly, according to the United States, European governments today, signatory countries of the World Trade Organization (WTO), have no right to protect the health of their population by banning genetically modified seeds produced by Monsanto. The Opium War was similar to many other military campaigns that the British and US governments fought to protect the national business interests represented by companies such as United Fruit (more than bananas) or Union Carbide (gas, oil, and minerals) throughout Latin America. Nobody has better expressed the logic of such wars than US President (and at different times Chief Justice) William H. Taft in 1912: "The whole hemisphere will be ours in fact as, by virtue of our superiority of race, it already is morally. . . ." According to a vision, today part of the Washington Consensus, US foreign policy "may well be made to include active intervention to secure for our merchandise and our capitalist opportunity for profitable investment."[2]

Today, as in the past, ideology in a variety of forms and more or less credibly, is used both *ex ante* and *ex post* to hide plunder, with variable degrees of success. Colonialism also made abundant use of ideology to justify a morally unacceptable practice. Modernization, civilization, development, and harmony have been explained as such. True, the United States, in competition with European powers, has always played an anti-colonialist card, but when it comes to the practice of depriving foreign countries of sovereignty, the difference is not that obvious, while much of the rhetoric and the double talk are shared. For example, Haiti was never "colonized" by the US government but was occupied for more than 20 years, during which racial segregation and forced labor were reintroduced, rebelling workers were killed in the thousands, and even the salaries of the president and ministers were suspended, until they agreed to turn the Banco National into a subsidiary of the New York City Bank.[3] A warning for the governments of Afghanistan and Iraq!

Thus, while the substance in Iraq is re-colonization, the form of ideology is more creative, starting with the intellectual de-legitimization of the obvious reason for the war. "It is about oil," cannot be said in sophisticated intellectual circles if one wishes to avoid being depicted as a simple-minded demagogue. Rebellion against that strategy justifies the title of this section. One finds then a variety of forms by which the war, despite its horrors and ultimately uncivilized nature, is proudly presented as a sort of technology expo. Moreover, the very recent construction of the "state of exception," allows a higher degree of horror to be labeled a rare rotten apple in an otherwise working and ultimately efficient machinery. The spectacular and spectacularized torture perpetrated against Iraqi prisoners is constructed as an exception, thus exorcizing and promoting as comparatively "respectable" the murder of thousands of innocent civilians (according to conservative estimates over 900,000 direct civilian casualties – including those killed by death squads, car bombs, etc. – have resulted from the Iraq War as of March 2006).[4] The public exposition by corporate media of the torture scandal thus paradoxically fosters the idea of an otherwise benign activity in the area. Pundits repeat the nonsense that torture is evil but the murderous "war for democracy and the rule of law" using it does not share the same degree of immorality. The evidence offered is the "constitutional process" and the referendum on the constitution as inherently better than Saddam's regime. The mockery of a trial organized by the occupying forces went against any basic notion of the due process of law, and the following execution of Saddam Hussein and his principal aides added a tragic sense of irony to the role of law propaganda deployed in Iraq.

In the days after the September 11 attacks, Americans rallied patriotically behind President Bush's plans for military retaliation and his exhortation that Americans increase consumer spending for patriotic reasons. However, just a few months later, in the wake of the Enron, WorldCom, and other corporate accounting scandals – which finally produced some loss of faith in the benign nature of corporate capitalism – many Americans began to question whether retaliation was good for American security or whether security was used to cover up different aims. Oil looting became part of that scrutiny.

At first the lens moved to the Californian oil company central to the plan to build a major pipeline across the Caspian Sea region – UNOCAL – whose bid was previously rejected by the Afghani government in favor of European competitors. Such a pipeline would transport oil from the Caspian Sea through Turkmenistan, Afghanistan, and Pakistan out to the Arabian Sea. UNOCAL moved quickly after 9/11 to restart, illustrating the tight connection between business interests and US intervention abroad. Scholars such as Michael Klare[5] thought this connection between business and US foreign policy to be a cause of political transformations – access to resources like oil and gas were now considered a fundamental part of US national security. In fact, it was an old pattern resuscitated. The present President of Afghanistan, picked by the US administration and "democratically elected" in October 2004, formerly worked for UNOCAL.

Since the nineteenth century, oil companies have existed to extract oil and to transport it to a place where it can be sold at a profit. Our concern has to do with the use of public monies to support the oil industry profits by direct subsidies, estimated at $11.9 billion a year, and indirect subsidies, estimated as high as $36.2 billion a year, for the military defense of oil-rich regions spanning from the Persian Gulf to Colombia. Government and business are intertwined in a policy of consumption with the United States representing 4.5 percent of the world's population while consuming 25 percent of its oil. Until recently, when larger states like India and China entered the picture, the stage was Western, with oil the symbol of progress and the production and development of energy resources a means for reinforcing Western positional superiority, supported by the presence of over 700 US military bases in about 130 countries worldwide.

Although industrial societies always depend heavily on oil and gas, and oil production clearly fuels environmental degradation, it now poses a specific threat to the planet dubbed "global warming." The picture is further complicated because in the past national security was maintained by means of extended alliance systems. US power today is associated with a powerful military establishment and unilateralism, which invariably causes the proliferation of what have been described as *resource wars*.[6] Economic rather than political security policies lead to resource protection by industrial states eyeing plunder. Researchers at the World Bank have found that states with significant "potable resources" are "four times more likely to experience war than a country without primary commodities."[7]

Sometimes emotions behind such "potables" unmask talk about security and patriotism. Queen Noor of Jordan[8] tells of a meeting between King Hussein and President Bush, Sr. in Kennebunkport, Maine when the former US Commander in Chief expressed the right of "civilized peoples" to take oil as a right. Speaking about Saddam Hussein, he said, "I will not allow this little dictator to control 25 percent of the civilized world's oil." Of course, for Arabs the key words here are "the civilized world," a label with a long colonial pedigree. Under such circumstances for Americans, national security considerations will always prevail over negotiated settlements that might be perceived as the surrender of vital national interests. When economics overshadows political or ideological conflicts, the incidence of unilateral wars is sure to grow. Note the USA-led attacks on Afghanistan and the two wars on Iraq since 1991.

The direct link between oil and military policy is said to have initially surfaced with the transition from coal to oil for British ships in World War

I and as a result of the oil-driven vehicles for combat, reconnaissance, and logistics. Oil is a vital combat necessity, which after the 1973–74 so-called "Arab oil embargo" further ignited the idea of using force to protect vital oil supplies in peacetime. The link between profit and power became the military–industrial complex noted by President Eisenhower in his farewell address. The rise of the imperial presidency and the Pentagon, and the rise of the warfare state meant that economics and politics collapsed into one.

Americans have been divided by oil – its glut and supposed scarcity, and its leverage over China, India, and Japanese sources. The challenge to the ongoing use of public funds to support and encourage the oil and gas industry moves the debate to a more rational use of taxpayer dollars, towards a transition out of fossil fuels towards cleaner, renewable sources of energy. Others support gas guzzling as patriotic and SUVs became embroiled in the pro and con Iraq War arguments and demonstrations.

Because oil executives and former chief executive officers are so deeply integrated in the Bush administration, it appears to some that under George W. Bush the search for oil is a foreign policy cornerstone. Needless to say, this did not start with Bush. Under Clinton we had Plan Colombia, ostensibly to help protect the Cano-Limon oil pipeline, which ferries oil to the Caribbean coast for Los Angeles-based Occidental Petroleum and other companies. Again the lesson is clear – transnational extraction of natural resources from the third world promotes not economic or political stability, but violence and lawlessness. For no one is this clearer than for indigenous peoples.

Indigenous resistance to oil drilling in Colombia provides a clear example. Indigenous U'wa leader Roberto Perez is plainspoken:[9]

> They say that you can't oppose the exploitation of petroleum. It's a Western way of thinking . . . and the transnational corporations that they impose on us in our own territory, but the development they talk about won't benefit the campesinos, the public sectors. The only ones who will benefit are a few groups that hold economic power . . . If the Colombian people had benefited, we wouldn't see the social injustice that we're living in Colombia . . . These indigenous brothers made a mistake by negotiating because the government never fulfills its promises. We convened with the government on two separate occasions, but while we were talking, they gave the companies the go-ahead to continue their oil explorations activities.

The same complaints appear in Peru, Mexico, and Ecuador. In Peru: "In the midst of the process to protect our rights . . . three million acres of Madre de

Dios were handed over for oil exploration to Mobil, Exxon and Elf." And from Mexico: "Twenty years ago, PEMEX arrived and invaded our lands . . . We arrived before PEMEX. Our documents prove it." And from Ecuador: "We already know what is going on within our territory . . . we don't need any company (ARCO) to tell us. Rather, we need to tell you what is going on."[10]

Venezuela is the third largest supplier of oil to the USA and, along with Colombia and Ecuador, provides the United States with more supplies of oil than does the Persian Gulf. Yet, the overt wars are in the Middle East. At least for the moment an attempted coup rather than war has governed the relationship with President Chavez. Within the "strategic triangle" – from the Persian Gulf in the west to the Caspian Sea in the north and the South China Sea in the east – can be found some of the world's largest concentrations of petroleum, whose control for the future is even more crucial than its extraction in the present. The Persian Gulf itself possesses approximately 65 percent of the world's known petroleum reserves. With all lines blurred between politics and business, it is no surprise that the Iraq War is center stage and, despite the satisfaction granted by President Saddam Hussein's barbarian execution, the end is not in sight.

The Bush administration's belief that imported oil is a national security threat is fed by the Independent Petroleum Association of America with statements like, "Our economy is in the hands of foreign rulers" (La Zeaby 2000) and "Saddam Hussein remains the swing producer, capable of holding the world oil markets as ransom" (Oil Online, March 29, 2000). This was before the 2003 United States invasion of Iraq. Since the invasion there have been proposals and predictions. A former executive at the Chevron Corporation (E.C. Chow 2003) argues against waiting to fund the mega oil projects in Iraq by waiting for existing oil incomes. He prefers that international oil companies invest in exploring new fields, and building new installations. However, he concludes on a ponderous note – such investment can only be forthcoming with a stable (and friendly?) political system in Iraq, a political system that will respect the *rule of law*! But, as Tariq Ali smartly notes, history teaches us: "Force, not law, had always determined relations between the West and the Arab world. And force had been used or threatened to impose new laws and treaties."[11] In this case, past events are the best indicator of what is to come.

Western interest in oil resources in the Middle East began early in the twentieth century. The Anglo-Persian Oil Company was taking oil from Iran before World War I. By the beginnings of World War II, Iraq was also a major oil exporter with concessions having been granted to the Turkish Petroleum Company (later the Iraq Petroleum Company). The awareness of Middle Eastern oil inspired Western powers to help shape the region. In the early days of oil production, the private foreign firms capitalized on the absolute power of ruling families in drawing up concession deals resulting, eventually, in an unequal balance in financial and political strength. Concessions included rights to exploration, production, refining, and export, over wide areas and for long periods, subject to the payment of limited royalties to host governments, and the provision of limited quantities of oil for their use.[12] All the cards were in the hands of the major oil companies. Yosuf Sayigh, a leading Arab economist and oil expert, notes that the combined weight of all these components of power gave the companies the power to colonize, intimidate, and influence the workings of Arab governments in the Gulf, a situation that remained largely unchallenged until the mid-1950s – that is about 30 years after the first agreement was signed.

In the 1950s, with a burgeoning of the pan-Arab nationalist movement, there was pressure for the rights of the producing countries to be recognized as the real owners of the oil resources, and therefore the right to receive more revenue. After the founding of the Organization of the Petroleum Exporting States (OPEC) in the 1960s there was a further challenge to the supremacy of the major oil corporations, producing an era of confrontation particularly between Iraq and the oil companies. In 1972, the Iraq Petroleum Company was nationalized, followed shortly by the nationalization of oil in Libya and Algeria. Arabs regarded the struggle put up by oil companies and their governments as proof of greedy Western exploitation of resources belonging to the Middle East, and from 1973 onward the West began to focus increasing attention on Middle Eastern oil in relation to Western needs. Needless to say the Arab use of the oil weapon in the Arab–Israeli War in October 1973 ultimately failed, leaving the Arab masses without the revolutionary power and without any adequate distribution of oil wealth either. In the Gulf, the interests of the ruling elites were directed preferentially towards the West. The decade after 1973 saw Western companies lined up for lucrative contracts. As is usual, the foreign plunder employed indigenous elites.

The official reason for the 2003 American war in Iraq was to remove Iraq's weapons of mass destruction. When none were found the justification for war shifted to the need to rid Iraq of Saddam Hussein's dictatorship in order to bring democracy and the rule of law to the country and the region. In double talk, aggression becomes liberation, a tactic common to old-style European colonialism.[13] By now the calculations are transparent. The privatization of Iraqi oil wells would help weaken OPEC. Plans to impose privatization on Iraqi oil by means of a pro-American puppet government in Baghdad are well on their way, presented to the world as a successful constitutional process. The installation of a puppet regime in Baghdad may, however, be more difficult than in Kabul, but the foundations of the rule of law have already been prepared by Paul Bremer's edicts, totaling some 500 pages. Certain of these laws, whose spirit governs the following autonomous legislation, are relevant to the process by which plunder is legalized.

The political and economic invasion and now occupation of Iraq by the US military and corporations, with the full backing of the Bush administration, appear as 100 orders enacted by Paul Bremer III, head of the now defunct Coalition Provisional Authority (CPA) before "the handover that wasn't".[14] The Bremer orders gave preference to US corporations in the development of Iraqi economy intended to change Iraq from a centrally planned economy to a market economy. For our purposes here it is important to note that Order no. 39 does not shrink from openly asserting such a goal – economic imprints that seek to establish the basic legal framework for a functioning market economy with reforms in the areas of "Fiscal reform, financial sector reform, trade, legal and regulatory and privatization."

A sampling of some of the most important orders might begin with Order no. 39 allowing for the privatization of Iraq's 200 state-owned enterprises, 100 percent foreign ownership of Iraqi business, "national treatment" of foreign firms, unrestricted tax-free remittance of all profits and other funds, and 40-year ownership licenses. Order no. 40 changes the banking sector from a state-run to a market-driven system by allowing foreign banks to purchase up to 50 percent of Iraqi banks. Order no. 17 grants foreign contractors full immunity from Iraq's laws. Injured parties must be brought to US courts under US laws, as in the time of the US Court for the District of China or similar deals in colonized Egypt. In everyday terms, the Bremer orders deny Iraq the ability to give preference to Iraqi companies or employees in reconstruction. In fact Iraqi state-owned companies are actually prohibited from bidding. Foreign products are allowed to flood the Iraqi market, which has forced local producers out of business. With regard to Iraqi oil, US Executive Order no. 13303 of May 2003 and later reaffirmed, revoked international environmental protections for oil spills or other ecological disasters, granting blanket immunity to US corporations that gain possession or control of Iraqi oil or products.

The Bremer Orders were illegal according to international law since they violated the Hague regulations of 1907 (the companion to the 1949 Geneva conventions, both ratified by the United States). Under international law an occupying nation cannot transform a defeated society into its own likeness. And as if all this was not enough, it turns out that no law or presidential directive has ever established the authority's status. President Bush directly appointed Mr. Bremer. Then United Nations (UN) Secretary-General Kofi Annan summarized the situation (September 21, 2004) with a surprisingly stinging attack on the US decision to go to war without UN approval: "Those who seek to bestow legitimacy must themselves embody it, and those who invoke international law must themselves submit to it . . . we must start from the principle that no one is above the law, and no one should be denied its protection."[15] Nevertheless, by February 2007 the Iraqi cabinet approved a draft oil law that would shift the balance of power in Iraqi oil and gas management from the central government to the regions. It would also include production-sharing agreements with international oil companies that some see as essentially privatizing, a U-turn for Iraq's public sector oil production. Such a draft law, according to Rashid Khalidi, "reverses everything that has happened in the Middle East since 1901."[16]

Again, the continuities with the colonial model of law are striking: "Most legal history of indigenous/colonial contact describes this model: at its simplest level, indigenous people have their lands taken away by colonial law . . . indigenous people were victims of every kind of legal violence, fraud and theft."[17] Nevertheless, the rule of law is today considered by many to be a civilizing legacy of colonialism[18] despite the fact that the much admired *Compilation of the Laws of the Indies*, expressly forbidding the violation of Indian rights, was in place through the time in which the Cerro Rico of Potosi' claimed alone an estimated 8 million lives of exploited Indian miners "protected" by the law. Archbishop Linan y Cysneros, in 1685, denied the genocide, exploiting the ideological connection between freedom and the rule of law as a justification for plunder: "The truth is that they are hiding out to avoid paying tribute, abusing the liberty which they enjoy and which they never had under the Incas."[19] This is the same liberty under the law that the Iraqis, according to the dominant account, never enjoyed under Saddam while enjoying, nevertheless, free education and healthcare.

CHAPTER 5

The New World Order of Plunder

It will be useful to spend a few words on the global political order which has emerged at the end of the Cold War, the current background of plunder. With "enemy number one" defeated, it became almost immediately apparent that socialism was not the only radically incompatible alternative to Western institutional settings. Despite colonial attempts, Islam was never erased as a fundamentally different vision of society, development, and morality. Thus the end of the Cold War confrontation opened a Pandora's box of tensions that decolonization had only superficially repressed. Once again, American foreign policy did not need to change much. Its technological presence[20] was still required by its European allies whose internal political landscape incrementally turned to the right.[21] By the early 1990s the socialists went down in defeat in France, Italy, Spain, and Greece. In Scandinavian countries, the social democratic experiment, justified as it was by the confrontational needs of the Cold War, was facing a tremendous and perhaps irreversible crisis. In Russia, the communists were literally forced to accept a spectacular electoral confrontation, in which they would have no chance to gain the technical skills and foreign aid supplied to their opposition.[22] Notions of the "third way" or "New Labor" emerged as the European political landscape converged with its American counterpart. In the United States, at least compared with the "Great Society" of the 1960s, the differential in class representation between the Democrats and the Republicans was blurred.

President Clinton and Prime Minister Blair became icons of the political establishment and the long wave of the Reagan/Thatcher conservative revolution went well beyond the political platform of the tories and republicans that originated it. A culture of exclusion and of assertion began to characterize Western domestic and foreign policy in the United States and, following its lead, in Europe.[23] As an African commentator put it:

> The Berlin Wall fell. Imperialism rode on the triumphal wave to rehabilitate itself. Douglas Hurd, the then British Secretary of State for Foreign Affairs, heaved a sigh of relief: "We are slowly putting behind us a period of history when the West was unable to express a legitimate interest in the developing world without being accused of neo-colonialism."[24]

By the early part of the new millennium, Russia seemed to have turned from a foe into a fundamentally malleable, economically interconnected, and only occasionally reluctant accomplice, with President Putin sharing an interest in the new wave of oppression of the Islamic world that the new US administration inaugurated. The North Atlantic Treaty Organization (NATO) incrementally and dramatically changed its nature. A NATO summit with President Putin in 2002 set the basis for a new strategic and offensive alliance for the further expansion of the free global market. NATO leaders and their former foe now share a common "enemy," making a bond which is possibly stronger than occasional international policy divergence. The notion of fundamentalist, Islamic-originated terrorist activity, exemplified by Chechnya and Palestinian resistance, has justified the "war on terror," so far carried out against Afghanistan, Iraq, and by Ethiopian proxy in Somalia, and threatened against Iran, Sudan, Syria, Yemen, and North Korea.

NATO strikes in Bosnia, the first Gulf War ("Desert Storm"), the US mission in Somalia ("Restore Hope"), Afghanistan ("Enduring Freedom"), and second Iraq War, the Israeli bombing of Lebanon in 2006, and the 2007 proxy war against Somalia are the most visible instances in which the post Cold War Pax Americana had a chance to prove its strength. Thousands of innocent people were killed while public opinion and media propaganda focused on the redress of international human rights, on liberation from tyranny, and on restoration of the rule of law, which the bombing was supposed to guarantee.[25] Some international law scholars have finally defined actions such as the Bosnia NATO strikes, supported by a number of leftist governments, as illegal.[26] The tragic, Clinton-led Somali adventure that culminated with "Black Hawk down" has been erased and Somalis are denied once more peace and self-determination. While the Clinton administration pursued some façade of international legitimacy, the isolationist and unilateralist policy of the Bush administration made the picture much clearer. International law, once at least accepted and invoked whenever capable of serving the interest of a hegemonic power still seeking some consensus, is now openly ignored and despised by the world's one imperial power and its neo-conservative ideologues, despite some resurrected feeble and almost invariably hypocritical resistance by US Democrats in Congress.[27]

True, the attitude of the USA toward international law has long been hypocritical. For example, in reviewing the Supreme Court's nineteenth-century jurisprudence on the government's foreign affairs, "the Court repeatedly utilized international law as a source of authority for United States governmental action, but it did not recognize it as a source of constraint."[28] Hypocrisy is better than open and shameless isolationism married with unilateral brutality in international relationships. For example, the USA's role in organizing Latin American fascist coups against legitimate leaders, from the assassination of Augusto Cesar Sandino in Nicaragua (1934) to the coup of Fulgencio Batista in Cuba (1952) to the spectacular eliminations of President Arbenz in Guatemala (1954) and of President Allende in Chile (1973), including the very recent and almost silent one against President Aristide in Haiti and the attempted one against President Chavez of Venezuela, is accompanied by some policy of denial. Such denial, while hypocritical and scarcely credible, is, however, to be preferred to a political platform openly arguing in favor of such illegal and immoral actions. Though we may consider hypocritical the recent wave of cases bringing a variety of Latin American fascist defendants to US justice in the name of international law, we still prefer hypocrisy to complete impunity.

In this perspective, the second war on Iraq – while only confirming the earlier deadly effect, especially on Iraqi children, of the Clinton administration's "international law sanctions" and by ignoring open opposition of the UN – is a marked escalation in imperial hubris. We now see the openly oppressive use of the rule of law. Certainly, classic notions of international law, such as the sanctity of borders, could be used to justify the first Iraq War, while notions of humanitarian interventions for the protection of human rights had to be elaborated in support of action in the Balkans and Somalia. By the time of the war in Afghanistan, the rule of law rhetoric was in some quarters void of credibility, so that notions of "regime change" needed to be grounded in a state of exception such as the so-called war on terror or the fear of weapons of mass destruction.[29]

Acts of plunder hide behind the construction of a new foe. Today imperial intervention proceeds, as did the colonial project, to target countries whose legal system impairs full membership into the "family of civilized nations" governed by international law. The systems targeted are characterized by a "radically different" conception of legality, now as in colonial times, described as *lack of rule of law*: Western orientalism.[30] All such interventions target societies in which the Western conception of the rule of law has remained either absent or superficial. They are societies in which democracy and the rule of law, as products of Western civilization/colonization, are deeply foreign to local conditions, and are resented as senseless and useless expensive bowing in front of imperialistic symbolic requests. Islamic law, on the other hand, has been able to claim legitimacy by means of the circuits of legitimization that are typical of non-Western societies.[31] A few words of description will be helpful.

Somalia and Afghanistan have much in common, beyond their strategic geographic proximity to oil. They are both traditionally decentralized societies. Both societies encountered Islam early; both of them have worked out, through the centuries, local interpretations of Islamic law to accommodate an old and established pre-Islamic, highly decentralized, customary law. Both societies have been dramatically affected by colonization and by Cold War confrontation, and both have experienced a more recent process of thorough social penetration of Islam in more radical forms. Each country is internally divided ethnically, but at the same time both have built strong national and fiercely independent identities. Neither values ideas of legitimacy based on majority rule. Rather the principle of unanimity, typical of a politically decentralized society, and of war as a legitimating factor of leadership are strong and fierce factors of resistance against the importation of Western notions of democracy, rule of law, and individual human rights.[32] Their Westernized legal elite has been traditionally weak.

As to Iraq, it falls squarely within regionally common and deeply rooted notions of leadership and legitimacy based on a sometimes hotly contested dialectic with Islam. For the moment it is sufficient to observe that the structure of power and the bases of legitimacy of the legal system of these countries, targeted by Western might, while presented as exceptions worth intervention, are rather the rule. The Western conception of the rule of law – with a dominating corporate media rhetoric and presented as universal – is used as a fundamental structure of government at most by US citizens (301 million people: 4.6 percent of humankind) and by the Europeans (455 million people: 7 percent of humankind). Even if we add Japan (120 million people: 2.1 percent of humankind) to these we can still see that the exception is the West, not the rest. It is no excess of cultural relativism to observe this simple fact. Nor is it foreign to Western notions of equality of treatment under the law to reflect on the one-sided way in which international law is enforced.[33]

Not Only Iraq: Plunder, War, and Legal Ideologies of Intervention

As Iraq shows today, powerful Western countries are always in search of legitimizing strategies for intervention. Such strategies serve the function of lowering the political and military costs of intervention and control, and thus are aimed at transforming power into hegemony by introducing degrees of acceptance of plunder by its victims both domestically and in the target areas.[34] During the Crusades, an intense propaganda, originated by Pope Urban II, depicted Arabs as savages deserving a bath of blood. Similarly, practices such as human sacrifice have been singled out to deny humanity to the Incas, thus justifying Pizarro's savage plunder. Today, in a remarkable pattern of continuity, the "imposition" of the burqa, female circumcision, or other asserted human rights violations are used to construct the justification for another wave of Western plunder. Such discursive strategies are used to tackle the moral issues embedded in plunder. Thus, for example, the looting of Palestinian homes in the aftermath of the "Nakba" (Catastrophe) in 1948 (with 750,000 Palestinians forced to flee in terror) not only has been justified by the passing of laws such as the Israeli Absentee Property Law, but on many occasions also by a discursive practice of denial that the appropriated homes were actually ever inhabited. This is how many Israeli buyers, who might well have been acting in good faith, ended up accepting ownership of stolen Palestinian homes.[35]

Because of intervention for plunder, the formal international legal order based on territoriality and the equality of sovereign states, which originated in the seventeenth century (1648) at the Peace of Westphalia, is in turmoil.[36] The slow path toward the construction of an international legality based on formal decision-making procedures, initiated in San Francisco in 1949 with the foundation of the UN, has been abandoned. The United States' invasion of Iraq, the bloodshed and barbarianism that followed, and new legislation imposed by the rule of law, can only be interpreted as plunder unimpaired by international or national law.[37] Nevertheless, the resistance currently taking place in Iraq, Afghanistan, Somalia, and Palestine against the occupying forces, the UN, the media, and even the non-governmental organizations have opened the general issue of the legitimacy of all interventions.

In order to rise above political criticism, entering into the domain of the necessary and natural, Western interventionism, which is incapable of being asserted by ordinary legal means, has been forced to seek a number of higher justifications, such as human rights protection, so that plunder could be once more sheltered from open discussion and critique.

Comparative observation of a variety of target legal settings, from the point of view of international intervention, allows a further step in the understanding of the nature of the rule of law and its relationship with plunder. International intervention is one of the most impressive political efforts of an imperialist society. As with any comparable political effort it creates tremendous distress on the law. Consequently, intervention is one of those dramatic political and social events like emergencies, turmoil, revolution, or war that can be observed as external pressure on the phenomenon of social organization called the law. Dramatic events act on the social fabric as in the physical world, where, for example, the strain artificially produced by a nuclear accelerator is capable of shaking a static equilibrium that tends to be conservative. In such a turbulent environment, the observer can understand much better the inner structure of the law, detecting aspects such as its relationship with plunder that in peace and equilibrium would be unobservable, or less simply observable, because dormant.

A dormant structural characteristic, nevertheless, is by no means absent. Rather, it is present, silently active, and potentially very dangerous, like a dormant fire in a legal system. The impact of the Yalta agreements that divided up the world's influence between victorious powers after World War II on Yugoslavia, another recent theater of Western intervention, may be a useful illustration. The Yalta agreements, signed by Churchill, Stalin, and Roosevelt in 1944, covered over a long history of tension in the Balkans. But the release of political pressure, following the end of the Cold War, has shown that ethnicity has been an issue all along, and that as a legal issue it was dormant, not resolved. Close observation of the political and legal structure of former Yugoslavia shows a hidden pattern of discrimination, including quotas in employment, uneven distribution of public goods, and disproportionate representation in political and judicial power, favoring northern ethnicities to the disadvantage of poorer Serbian masses, throughout General Tito's time. Such hidden and complex patterns of discrimination, entangled in religious and ethnic divisions, were reflected in the law of former Yugoslavia. Ethnic cleansing policies arguably enacted by the Serbian government in the unfolding of the civil war, can then be interpreted as an explosive retaliation to such discriminations, once the cover was been taken off the Yalta Pandora's box. The tension was dormant, not resolved, during Tito's original model of socialist legality.

In Yugoslavia, the traditional gateway between Islam and Christianity (and between Roman Catholic and Orthodox Christianity), effective centralized secular institutions were established under General Tito's rule.[38] Legitimacy was never based on elections but by leadership within the political party. The Western notion of rule of law, diffused through the area by a complex pattern of classic civil law codification, was hybridized with original notions of socialist legality in the post World War II era. The circuits of power legitimacy in former Yugoslavia were to be found more in notions of military leadership

(Tito's partisans) and of party politics than otherwise. The rise of President Milosevic to power and the pan-Serbian dream cannot be explained outside of a thorough understanding of patterns of legitimization radically different from the Western ideal of electoral democracy and the rule of law. The proverbial complexity of the Balkans and the crucial post-Yalta role of Yugoslavia as a Cold War border (with all the hidden interventions thereby justified) cannot be erased or simplified with a story of human rights violations requiring international intervention. The attempt to adjudicate this story in a court of law, both international and within America, is only further evidence of Western hubris attempting to justify *ex post facto* using a pale version of the rule of law.

Conditions of distress, allowing a better understanding of plunder, are by no means difficult to observe in the real life of the law. In 2002 alone, eight major conflicts formally took steps to some conclusion and others have begun since. In the Democratic Republic of Congo on December 17, 2002 a peace treaty officially concluded the war begun in 1998 that has killed 2.5 million people. On December 3, a ceasefire was signed in Burundi where 300,000 victims are officially accounted for in the war that began in 1993. On April 16, 2002, Ethiopia and Eritrea agreed to a border arbitration to conclude a conflict begun in 1998 that killed at least 100,000 people, and which is now on the verge of re-eruption after the 2007 US–Ethiopian invasion of Somalia. A ceasefire was also signed in Sudan on October 15, 2002, unsuccessfully attempting to end a civil war tragedy (fueled by much Western intervention) begun in 1983 that accounts for about 2 million victims. In January 2002, a peace treaty was signed in Sierra Leone concluding a conflict that since its inception in 1991 has left 50,000 victims. Peace was reached in Angola in April 2002, concluding a South Africa–USA-led war of aggression that since 1975 has left about half a million people killed. A peace treaty, moreover, in the Indonesian province of Aceh, capped a war that since 1976 has left 12,000 victims. A ceasefire was reached in Sri Lanka on February 23, 2002 concluding hostilities begun in 1980 that have killed about 80,000 people. While the prospects of such "peace deals" are almost everywhere unstable and uncertain, the victims and plunder are certain with variations occurring only in computation.

In the years following the collapse of the Soviet Union, war has confirmed itself as an almost endemic condition of humankind. Iraq, Somalia, Bosnia-Herzegovina, Afghanistan, Sierra Leone, Kosovo, the Horn of Africa, Palestine, Liberia, and Lebanon are only some of the best-known places in the world in which the civil population has been recently exposed to the horrors of war. Of course, from political and strategic viewpoints as well as from the perspective of international relevance, these and other conflicts vary dramatically.

Nevertheless, one common aspect of all conflicts worldwide stands out: they have been directly produced, or exacerbated, by influence and interventions aimed to plunder both in the colonial past and in the present international order. Be it in the form of the international arms business, the diamond trade, drug deals, or oil extraction and the building of infrastructures for its transportation (pipelines), interventionist policies are invariably determined by plunder; the rule of law and justice might serve at most the hegemonic function of lowering resistance and avoiding historical responsibility. True, the needs of reconstruction in the aftermath of hostilities offer a rhetorical argument for more "intervention," which sometimes is the province of justice-motivated individuals attempting to restore peace, order, and the rule of law. Nevertheless, even in this case plunder prevails in a variety of forms and is particularly important in the "reconstruction business," often hiring more or less gullible human rights activists to serve this purpose.

Any war leaves scores of people with desperate needs. War does not only destroy infrastructure and technology. Most of the time war also dissolves institutional schemes that have required decades, if not centuries, to be constructed.[39] Conflict dissolves or at least severely damages the legal system, both formal and informal. Nevertheless, to alleviate the suffering and to take care of, at least in part, these dramatic social needs, complex transactions are required.[40] The theory of "lack" – according to which target settings are always presented as lacking something that can only be provided by more civilized countries[41] – here finds very fertile ground. Lack might stimulate intervention, both motivated by justice and by plunder.

In war-torn societies, as elsewhere, social demands require institutional answers. The law is an important aspect of an institutional setting in which troubled societies look for responses to their dramatic needs.[42] While social troubles can be largely similar and dictated by basic needs of the population, institutional responses are by no means universal: on the contrary they appear as extremely context-specific.[43] External forces, colonial and neocolonial, however, tend to generalize and abstract from the understanding of the local context within a strategy that denies both specificity and the sophisticated character of local arrangements.[44] For example, cultural practices as different as Sunnah and Pharaonic female circumcision are classified as human rights violations, graphically described as mutilations, and targeted for eradication with complete disregard not only of very deep local variations and conditions but also of the important legal and social aggregative function they sometimes serve.[45] Local legal arrangements essentialized as human rights violations, such as horrifically depicted practices of female circumcision or the so-called "imposition" of the burqa, are used to justify intervention and war today. Violence prospers in this hypocritical environment in which double standards are used to evaluate the legal civilization of the "other."

Institutional Lacks as Conditions for Plunder: Real or Created?

Legal intervention always follows a top-down approach with intervening legal systems perceiving themselves (and often being perceived by local elites) as providing a superior model, a sophisticated recipe for progress. This approach has been exposed as legal imperialism, but has by no means been abandoned as a consequence of such criticism.[46] We have already mentioned the hegemonic use of "lack," with the emphasis on what the subordinate context lacks (institutions, civilization, human rights, resources, elections, manpower, technology, skills, etc.), in order to legitimize oppressive colonial or neo-colonial practices and plunder.

Recipes and policies of intervention, ostensibly proposed to encourage development or alleviate poverty in weaker countries, obey the same logic. A dramatic example comes from the already mentioned privatization of the Dakar–Bamako railway (see Chapter 2), a high priority in the World Bank policy in the area, justified by the "lack" of adequate transportation and managerial skills, and included in the structural adjustment (now comprehensive development) conditionality for the area. This time-honored railway, one of the earliest constructed in western Africa, has produced over time the development of a substantial number of local markets around the various stations through the long journey. Local products were exchanged with travelers and transported at relatively low price to cities where they could enter the official economy. The new US-operated private company (Savage Co.), which received generous government (Malian and Senegalese) subsidies to manage the railroad according to criteria of economic efficiency, favors transportation of raw materials (mostly cotton) produced in Mali to the port of Dakar and imports arriving in Dakar for the market of Bamako. It has consequently closed many stations throughout the journey, reduced the transportation of passengers, substantially increased prices, and fired workers in the hundreds. This choice has dramatically augmented poverty, produced desperation and even suicides, by literally cutting off these local markets from the economic system. More generally it has cut off the people living in these areas from services such as hospitals that they could only reach by trains that now no longer stop to pick them up. Economic and legal dualism, with an informal sector non-communicant with the formal one, has long been the worry of development economics. The corporatization of the Dakar–Bamako railroad, rather than resolving the "lack" of communication and transportation in Mali, has only made the problem much worse by torpedoing the adaptive informal arrangements that, over time, this railroad (a legacy of French colonialism built with African forced manpower) had produced. The World Bank has proceeded with no consideration of the local circumstances, in total disregard of the informal sector that the railroad contributed to generating, and ironically precluding, contrary to its own policy, communication with the general economy of the country.

Universalism in policy prescription (typical of the international financial institutions, USA and European Union (EU) aid, and mainstream economists and political scientists) denies differences and complexities in the areas of intervention, resulting in the construction of a naturally inferior "other." Such discursive strategies amount to simple-mindedness in view of the tremendous complexity, diversity, and sophistication of local contexts and cultures.[47] For example, the Italian government took responsibility at the Bonn conference of "donor" countries for the reconstruction of war-torn Afghanistan, to draft a code of criminal procedure. A tiny fraction (but still 50 million Euros) of a gigantic post-war budget – 85 percent of which was spent on Western military contracts to fight "terrorism" – has been devoted to another high priority: the development of the rule of law, traditionally "lacking" in Afghanistan.[48] The few Western scholars who have seriously studied the Afghani legal and political system know very well that one thing that Afghanistan does not lack is a legal and political culture. What is lacking is the capacity of Western lawyers to understand logic and principles (by no means informal) different to their own; principles that before the colonial scramble proved tremendously effective for the comparative development of this area, a center of very ancient and impressive civilization. In Afghanistan, as in any decentralized society, the requirement of unanimity creates incentives for individuals from a very young age to develop tremendously sophisticated negotiation and political skills. The enforcement mechanisms of this legal culture of unanimity are those classic to a "face to face," group-centered society, where the Western distinction between civil law and criminal law fails. Thus in this context the imposition of a Westernized code of criminal procedure (Italy was selected because of its early Americanization of its criminal procedure, a display of loyalty and admiration to the imperial power) to bring in the "rule of law" amounts to an arrogant attempt of violent centralization of power to advantage Kabul-based Western-friendly elites. This attempt (which is bound to fail) is being carried on in total disregard of the relationship between decentralization and authentic democracy in Afghanistan and of the function of check on the arbitrary power of centralized government that the traditional legal and institutional arrangements have long provided, in spite of being devastated by continuous and failed attempts of colonial centralization of power. The very same lack of understanding of specific local legal arrangements that produced the failure of the early law and development movement in Latin America and Africa is reproduced by the Italians in Afghanistan, with the added aggravation that almost half a century later nobody can claim good faith.

"Double Standards Policy" and Plunder

War, "barbarian" human rights violations, and "lacks" in the local institutional arrangements are by no means the only conditions legitimizing Western intervention preparatory of plunder. Local political, legal, or economic institutions are often described as "unstable," "distressed," or even "failed" by international decision-makers such as the International Monetary Fund (IMF), the World Bank, the UN, or rating agencies such as Moody's. Also in these circumstances the intervention is selective and does not follow principled patterns. For example, no grounds for international intervention, despite dramatic human rights violations, has been found for Tibet, Palestine, and Chechnya – to mention only a few places where horrific human rights violations happen every day. As for Cuba, to the contrary, a US statute, the Helms-Burton Act, intervenes with sanctions not only against the Cubans but also against any of its trading partners. Here the local judicial policy against US violent infiltration, though occasionally rough, is considered a human rights violation of great severity although carried out by a legitimate government to defend itself in a condition of illegal siege and within a history of attempted attacks, of which the one at the Bahia de Concinos (1962) has been only the most spectacular. One should compare Cuba's judicial policy with that of the USA in the case of the five Cubans currently held in US prisons in dramatic violation of due process, being suspected of infiltrating the Cuban American community in Florida and thus being spies. In Iraq a relentless embargo carried on during the Clinton administration dismantled the Iraqi social and legal structure, including a system of welfare, education, and women's emancipation ranking among the highest not only in the region but worldwide. An estimated 500,000 children died as a result of the Gulf War and US-imposed deprivations during the 10-year period between 1991 and 2001, and at least one American legal scholar considers that intervention to be a genocide according to standards of international law.[49]

To be sure, selectivity is a usual aspect of the double standards that characterize the relationship between hegemonic powers and their subordinated subjects. Economic policy too, such as that championed by the World Trade Organization (WTO), is openly based on a double standard. The United States and rich Western countries fiercely defend their protectionist policies while imposing open policies on weaker countries. These policies amount to an economic intervention aimed at "opening up" markets for trade with consequences of death, waste, and devastation no different from those imposed by colonial plunder. For example, milk powder produced in the United States and subsidized at 137 percent, has been dumped on Jamaica, literally forcing the entire dairy sector of the impoverished island out of business. In the exact same days, the Clinton administration was filing a complaint at the WTO to challenge as illegal EU policies agreed upon in Lomé. These policies were aimed at providing the former colonies with a market in Europe for a guaranteed number of bananas as a "compensation" for past colonial practices. The victory of the USA in the famous WTO banana war has produced catastrophic consequences for this market in the Caribbean.[50] But there are also "pull down" features of the WTO against US and European workers, given the exploitative salaries paid in the peripheral world that inexorably weaken their bargain power with corporate employers. Moreover the EU cannot assume the attitude of a benefactor to the former colonies given the scandalously advantageous conditions that it has provided to itself in the recent economic partnership agreements (EPA) obtaining a new series of free trade agreements that from 2008 will replace the Lomé system of preferential access for ACP (African Caribbean and Pacific) countries. Protectionism is necessary for industrial development, at least at its earlier stages, and the industrially advanced countries all used and still use it. Once more, we can see that the double standard economic policy, typical of current neo-liberal globalization, has a long pedigree in the history of plunder. While we could take many examples, from Africa to Latin America, we will shortly explore the already encountered example of Indian Bengal colonization.

Statutes of 1700 and 1720 protected the English infant textile industry against competition from India, where cotton was produced, manufactured, and colored by a thriving local industry, significantly more advanced than the contemporary European one. The statutes banned imports of cotton tissues from India, Persia, and China. Any cotton imported in contravention was confiscated and re-exported. Moreover, the colonial tax system, by unfairly penalizing the industry in Bengal, finally threw local industry out of business, forcing India to import lower quality products made in England out of the cotton produced in Bengal. While this policy literally starved a whole class of artisans, the Permanent Settlement Act 1793 privatized land, granting it to colonial cronies, thus turning Bengal into an economy of exportation of cash crops. The strategy, acknowledged by the Indian Governor General Lord Bentink, was to produce a local landed class with a deep self-interest in British domination. Writing in 1826 his classic *History of British India*,[51] Horace Wilson fully acknowledges, with realism, what today is denied by historians such as Niall Ferguson: these policies were unavoidable for the development of British capitalism. If they were not put in place, the industrial textile mills of Paisley and Manchester would have stopped their activity, crushed by the higher quality and cheaper prices of Indian textiles. The British industry was created thanks to the sacrifice of the Indian one (as pointed out by no less an observer than Prime Minister Jawaharlal Nehru); this was true not only in the textile industry, as in the mid-eighteenth century the Indian naval industry had been one of the most technologically advanced in the world.

Today, as in the past, these double-standard policies are responsible for massive unemployment, inhuman suffering, death, and social distress, producing a sustained demand for security forces, paramilitary personnel, and prisons in the "developing" world. Because the market can supply "law and order," and due to the abandonment of other services by privatized, structurally adjusted states, a new round of negotiations has attempted to liberalize services (police, prisons, schools, healthcare, etc.) dismantled by the impoverished public sector and now up for grabs by international corporate capital. At the 2003 WTO round of negotiations in Cancun, the double standard in economic policy was finally exposed by third world countries that were able to reject, for the moment at least, a new wave of blatantly discriminatory "opening up" policies. Delegations from the third world simply walked out of the round of negotiations aimed at this liberalization of services (GATS or the General Agreement on Trade of Services), which effectively amounts to a policy of legal and economic intervention presented as market liberalization aimed at plunder.

Poverty: Justification for Intervention and Consequence of Plunder

Serious work inquires into the causes of poverty without blaming poor countries as being incapable of carrying out even the simplest tasks, such as running an efficient railroad or producing a "simple" legal framework necessary for "development." Such a strategy of blame and guilt depresses the locals, reinforces racist attitudes in public opinion (broadly intended) of the hegemonic powers, and eventually weakens resistance to plunder.

Poverty becomes relevant for purposes of intervention in the face of the risk of default by poor nations of the international monetary obligations that created it. Such an attitude toward natural resource-rich countries such as Argentina, Bolivia, or Mexico justifies the conclusion that poverty (just as reconstruction after a war of aggression), justifying "secondary" intervention, has in fact been produced in the first place by economic neo-colonial intervention and plunder. In the creation of these ideal contexts for plunder, the role of the IMF, controlled by the United States, becomes particularly questionable. In Latin America where the Monroe doctrine has given the United States more than a century of advantage over neo-colonial competition, plunder has long been the rule rather than the exception. In the words of the dramatic and beautiful prose opening Eduardo Galeano's masterpiece:[52]

> The division of labor among nations is that some specialize in winning and others in losing. Our part of the World, known today as Latin America was precocious: it had specialized in losing ever since those remote times when Renaissance Europeans ventured across the Ocean and buried their teeth in the throats of Indian civilizations. Centuries passed and Latin America perfected its role. We are no longer in the era of marvels, when facts surpassed fable and imagination was shamed by the trophies of conquest – the loads of gold, the mountains of silver. But our region still works as a menial. It continues to exist

> at the service of others' needs, as a source and reserve of oil and iron, of copper and meat, of fruit and coffee, the raw materials and food destined for rich countries which profit more from consuming them than Latin America does from producing them. We lost; others won. But the winners happen to have won thanks to our loosing, the history of Latin America's underdevelopment is, as someone has said, an integral part of the history of world capitalism's development . . .underdevelopment isn't a stage of development but its consequence.

Wealth maximization (also known as Kaldor-Hicks efficiency), the criterion of economic efficiency used in the evaluation of policy by the international financial institutions, might consider this "division of labor" among nations, which we call plunder, as efficient. (It is the already discussed notion of comparative advantage.) After all, there is a growing middle class in India and China. According to this widely used standard, efficiency is met when the winners make more than the losers; enough to *potentially* (never actually!) compensate them for their losses. Thus international economic intervention by the stronger power can be deemed efficient despite its disastrous worsening, rather than alleviation, of poverty.

In Argentina, for example, deals struck by President Dualde (known as the Gringo) with the IMF included the privatization of the central bank and the abrogation of the law against "economic subversion." This law, abolished with a decree of June 19, 2002, provided the only legal basis on which the judiciary could ascertain the responsibility of private banks in the saga that brought the country to bankruptcy and that left 57 percent of the population in poverty (discussed in Chapter 2).

In Bolivia, the political end of President Gonzalo Sanchez de Lozada (forced into resignation and exile because of a popular insurgency) was caused to a great extent by the popular perception that the privatization of the gas industry, to the multinational corporations Pacific LNG and Sempra, was the president's "personal deal." The Bolivian people have been historically looted of silver, mineral salt, and tin. Their desperate poverty and renewed ethnic awareness under the leadership of President Evo Morales might defeat US-inspired economic interventions resulting in "efficient" extraction of such primary resource as water. Thus, in certain contexts plunder may require a higher degree of sophistication to be effectively carried out today, perhaps with more use of the rule of law and the rhetoric of lack.

In Mexico, the even closer proximity to the United States deserves attention. Indian policy, strictly connected with the issue of poverty, is transformed in connection with economic policy, with significant plunder-driven changes in the law. The successive failures of government development policies had emboldened indigenous groups, because of the wealth sitting under their land, to refuse to be constructed as "marginal" or Indian poor. Ethnicity was claiming a higher rank than economic and social condition, even in a grim reality of encapsulation of indigenous groups by means of free enterprise industries such as tourism, mining, or drilling for oil. In 1990 a new program was launched – the Regional Solidarity Funds for Development of Indigenous Peoples. President Salinas created *Solidaridad*, as it was called, to widen Mexico's national poverty program. Under President Salinas, the development process was to be "democratized." The top-down rural development programs prior to 1990 were replaced by "do-it-yourself" development. In this scenario, *solidarity* meant money for indigenous peoples who devised their own development plans, *provided* they did not define themselves as primarily ethnic or political indigenous organizations.

Meanwhile, according to a 1992 report from the Instituto Nacional Indigenista,[53] a new law "eliminates fifteen former requirements for federal approval of foreign investments and permits new projects within the country without federal authorization." A 1993 Lloyds Report describes the conclusion of the sale of government-controlled industries, a divestiture program started by the Salinas administration in 1988. The report also speaks of major federal objectives, which include the need "to upgrade air and water quality and recover woodlands and tropical forests lost through the abuses of man." Once again, a plan ostensibly favoring development of indigenous resources is in fact a new wave of neo-liberal policy aimed at takeover.

Today, powers external to Mexico are organizing Mexican rural peoples by means of agro-industrialization. There is an increasing role of transnational corporations in Mexican agricultural financing, production, distribution, and marketing, accompanied by an increased use of petrochemicals and other forms of technologies, replacing the autonomous producers who grow crops they themselves consume while also selling any surplus. While managers of transnational agriculture may not yet grab the land, they do take control over cultigens. The dynamics of agrarian issues shifts from the national context in which the farmer is poor and indigenous, to a transnational context in which the farmer is a weak player, or perhaps a migrant farm worker who introduces agro-industrial techniques such as herbicide use into a home village. Besides agro-industrialization there are trade agreements like the North American Free Trade Agreement (NAFTA) and the chain of events leading to poverty are increasingly visible. Since NAFTA took effect 13 years ago, imports of corn to Mexico from the United States have increased over 18-fold according to the US Department of Agriculture. In the United States billions of dollars a year subsidize corn growers, most of it going to agribusiness, resulting in corn prices being pushed down and introduced to Mexico up to 30 percent below the cost of production in the USA. Such actions have endangered the future of Mexican farmers who grow corn. On the Mexico side, NAFTA did away with subsidies and price supports, and, by 2008, the USA will be able to export all corn to Mexico duty-free since NAFTA provides for disappearance by that date of the tariffs for exceeding the quotas (which were 206 percent in 1994). Mexico, self-sufficient in corn for some 5,000 years, now imports a quarter of its corn from the USA. The corn growers of Mexico migrate north to work in the fields of California, Iowa, and other places. Finally, an unforeseen consequence of all this is the loss of ancient varieties of corn. Beyond the tragedy of genetic erosion, bioengineered genes from the American imports have invaded ancient varieties of corn in the state of Oaxaca.[54] With increasing areas of unoccupied land, legislation intervenes enabling foreign acquisition of large tracts of land for agribusiness by means of Mexico's Article 27, which allows the privatization of previously communally held *ejido* land.

In 1992 the Mexican Congress approved dramatic changes to Article 27 of the constitution, ending more than 70 years of national commitment to the indigenous (and peasant) sector. These reforms were part of the movement to adapt the agrarian law to the economic integration with North America promoted on the Mexican side by the Salinas administration. In 1994, a resurgence of independent peasant movements surged in Chiapas.[55] Land seizures followed, and attempts to regain these seizures from private owners pushed the independent peasant movement to ask the government to use its legal right to expropriate the land for purposes of redistribution.[56] Chiapas land distribution is currently at a stalemate.

Through all these (and many other) happenings, the conditions for plunder become normalized. In spite of the deleterious record of NAFTA, Central America can now look forward to the Central American Free Trade Agreement (CAFTA), as well as bilateral agreements with the USA, tempting even otherwise progressive leaders like Tabare Vasquez of Uruguay or Lula of Brazil, whose recent hug with President Bush over corn-produced car diesel fuel has already significantly increased the price of tortillas in Mexico.

6 | International Imperial Law

Reactive Institutions of Imperial Plunder

Thus far we have discussed how plunder flourishes in settings of severe power inequality. The inequitable distribution of resources driven by the strong at the expense of the weak, which constitutes the broad definition of plunder, finds in the rule of law the rhetoric of legitimization. This rhetoric constricts the very meaning of the word plunder, to the point of naturalizing, legalizing, and ultimately denying the outrageous disparity in resource allocation, following many social processes in contexts of power imbalance. Thus the rule of law constructs and denies plunder, granting legitimacy to a highly unfair world order.

It is now time to discuss, with more precision, the dynamics of the diffusion of the rule of law structure and ideology as an instrument to naturalize the historical and current power and wealth disparity. While colonial domination exploited notions of superiority and civilization, of which the rule of law was no small part, current neo-liberal domination deploys the discourse of development. Its aim is to globally structure a model of rule of law obedient to the interests of the powerful to freeze the bottom line and to create the legal framework for incremental expansion of capitalism and consequent further increase in inequality. In this scenario, which we call *imperial rule of law*, the perpetrators of plunder are guaranteed by "reactive institutions" (such as courts of law) against disgorging the ill-gotten profits. Plunder is thus legalized and any possible redistribution of resources favoring the impoverished majority is made impossible. Thus the losers and victims of plunder learn that the only legal redistribution beyond the bottom line of the *status quo* is that allowing, by a free market ideology, the winners even further. This chapter follows the transformation of the Western ideal of the rule of law under the lead of the USA into an imperial rule of law grounded in reactive institutions legalizing plunder and making legal redistribution (redressing the weak) impossible.

In Western conception and mythology of the rule of law, political power, which may favor the masses over the few, is not unlimited. It is subjected to professional checks. Such checks, performed by courts of law and by legal professionalism, serve a variety of functions, most importantly the protection of individual property rights against possible usurpation by the majority in power. Courts of law are the channels through which violations of individual and (to a lesser extent) collective rights can be vindicated against private or public actors. But legal academia also provides a professional check on the political process. It reproduces the legal elite, thus granting to the rule of law the legitimacy and prestige stemming from knowledge. It also performs a critical function, scrutinizing the outcome of the political process from the point of view of its compatibility with the fundamental legal values of society.

As a result of this institutional function, both these agencies of professionalism are themselves entrusted with considerable political power. Naturally, this power, stemming from the main repositories of the rule of law, itself cuts two ways. Courts of law can become instruments of oppression when deferring to political power to such an extent that they give up their function of protecting rights. When Earl Warren (late Chief Justice of the US Supreme Court and an unsurpassed champion of individual rights) was the Republican Governor of California, he ordered all Americans of Japanese descent into concentration camps for fear of their possible role as enemy spies. Such an order, in plain violation of the value of individual responsibility and of non-discrimination on ethnic grounds, was challenged all the way to the US Supreme Court. When the court, in the notorious Korematsu case, ruled the gubernatorial order constitutionally acceptable, it produced an even worse injury to the rule of law by legalizing that oppressive practice.

Among legal academics, there are numerous examples of the betrayal of their critical function – for fear or opportunism – such that it leads one to wonder whether their critical role is the rule or the exception. Robert Cover, a late Yale Law School historian, offers a very sober description of such failures in the face of the horrors of the Fugitive Slave Acts in the mid-nineteenth century.[1] Perhaps the greatest German jurist of the past century, Carl Schmitt, will remain known to posterity as much for his brilliant theories about sovereignty as for being an accomplice to Nazi rule. Again, if the prestige of legal academics is used to legitimize and even to legalize rather than to criticize political horrors such as torture or plunder, the ambiguous nature of the rule of law becomes even more obvious.

The political power of legal professionals, though very significant, is nevertheless different from that of the political branches of government. This difference is usually described by the metaphor of the purse and the sword. While the legislative branch has the purse, deciding on apportionment of public money, and the executive has the sword, presiding over the military and the police, the judiciary (and generally the legal profession) has neither. Because of this lack of purse and sword, the political power of the legal profession ends up being explained by a reactive philosophy. In fact legal professionals are bought and sold. As we have seen, the rule of law is rooted in proprietary protection.[2]

The professional check on the political process intervenes only after rights are violated and only when the "users" of the legal system buy such intervention. Within this conception of the rule of law, courts as reactive institutions cannot carry on any affirmative action. For example, Alexander Bickel, a major figure in US twentieth-century constitutional law, in a famous book significantly called *The Least Dangerous Branch*,[3] argues that courts of law should be guided by "passive virtues," refraining from any activist redistributive intervention. In the few occasions in the history of Western law in which courts (sustained by many academics) attempted the creation of affirmative plans to enforce rights they have mostly been criticized for opening a purse that they were not entitled to use. This was the case for the bussing of children in the process of the integration of public schools in the aftermath of the landmark case *Brown* v. *Board of Education*. It was the case when courts attempted to introduce some standards of humanity in US prisons by "governing" them through judicial injunctions. More generally, when the legal profession approaches potential users of the legal system, rather than passively waiting for clients deprived of their rights to show up in their law offices (or in academic legal clinics), commentators raise more than an eyebrow. In the United States, plaintiff lawyers monitoring rights' violations have been depicted as "ambulance chasers" and in a majority of European countries advertising of lawyers' services is considered "immoral" and forbidden by law.

The institutional posture of courts as non-redistributive, passive, institutional actors is thus guaranteed in the political setup of Western democracies by formal and informal circuits. Executives or legislators, not courts, actively pursue policy by redistributing resources, if and when necessary, by taxation. When such a conception is transferred to the colonial setting, with no political enfranchisement, the result is so-called "colonial *laissez faire*." This basically meant on the one hand the absence of (costly) welfare policy (for colonial subjects) in the colony, and on the other hand a weak system of courts as passive enforcers of rights. The resulting institutional scenario was thus ideal for entrepreneurial colonialists and their local ethnic cronies, who could thrive in business and engage in plunder with no need to pay for the social costs that their activity was imposing on society. While the dialectic between regulatory and reactive institutions of government has produced, over time, the welfare state for all European citizens (and, to a lesser extent, US citizens), no such development can be observed in the colonial periphery, where the weaker individuals of society, the old or invalid, once exploited to the limit, are then left to the care of the informal networks labeled as "primitive."

Globalization and neo-liberalism, while leaving this state of affairs mostly unchanged on the periphery, have produced deep transformations at the center. In particular, on the one hand, the constitutionalization of neo-liberal policies by the international financial institutions has significantly limited the power of the states to redistribute resources, causing the decline of the welfare state at the center. On the other hand, institutions framed on the reactive model, such as World Trade Organization (WTO) panels, *ad hoc* tribunals, and independent authorities, are today the only significant legal actors of the international landscape, making the reactive philosophy and the structural impossibility of redistribution the dominant global attitude in the law.

Meanwhile, US courts of law, building on the tremendous economic power of the United States, have extended their power well beyond traditional jurisdictional limits, becoming the most effective and feared global decision-makers in legal matters. This model for extraterritorial jurisdiction derives from nineteenth-century domination, when the US approach opposed the model of territorial occupation, typical of European powers. For example, in 1906, the United States, resenting European colonialism, created a US district court – by treaty– for the province of China, which was abolished only in 1943. This court, successor to previous extra-territorial courts established in 1844, had exclusive jurisdiction over Americans in China and often stretched its jurisdictional limits quite a bit, falling, however, short from the model of territorial occupation and claim of colonial sovereignty used by traditional European powers.[4] Similarly, Article III of the so-called Platt Amendment approved by the US Senate in 1901, later to be imposed as part of the "independent" Cuban constitution of the same year, emphatically refuses colonization – ironically stating that "The government of Cuba consents that the United States may exercise the right to intervene for the preservation of the Cuban independence, the maintenance of a government adequate for the protection of life, property and individual liberty. . . ."[5]

In the present post-colonial global landscape, this style of legal domination by means of a variety of alternatives to straight colonization is the essence of US legal imperialism, both cultural and judicial. It is the rule rather than the exception it used to be before the formal abolition of colonialism.

The notion of imperial rule of law seeks to explain post Cold War changes in the general process of the Americanization of legal thinking. Imperial rule of law, closely connected to plunder, is now a dominant layer of the worldwide legal system. It is produced, in the interest of international capital, by a variety of institutions, both public and private, all sharing a gap in political legitimacy sometimes called the "democratic deficit."[6] A spectacular process aimed at consent building, for the purpose of hegemonic domination and plunder, shapes the imperial rule of law. Imperial rule of law subordinates local legality worldwide, reproducing on the global scale the same phenomenon of dualism that thus far has characterized the law of developing countries. Thus states are devoid of legal discretion, tied as they are to requirements imposed by the imperial rule of law. What is often left in the province of the state is a demoted level of law-making, producing a local legal system that can only fulfill the increasingly shrinking spaces not occupied by imperial rule of law in conjunction with corporate plunder. Local law then expresses itself in local languages, occupies a local legal profession, and serves as a mere executive agency of imperial legal requirement. Local legal institutions are not strong enough to detect and contest plunder because the imperial rule of law naturalizes and legalizes plunder when carried out by the strong corporate actors served by mega law firms. Plunder is the vehicle, and, in turn, the beneficiary of the imperial rule of law.

Ironically, despite its absolute lack of legitimacy, the imperial rule of law is imposed by means of discursive practices branded as "democracy and the rule of law," and in turn it imposes as a natural necessity the reactive legal philosophy that outlaws the redistribution of wealth based on social solidarity, thus further disempowering local law and accountable political processes.[7] US law, transformed and adapted after the Reagan/Thatcher revolution, occupies the core of the imperial rule of law that facilitates plunder in the process of infiltrating the terrain open after the end of the Cold War. Thus, a study of the imperial rule of law requires a careful discussion of the factors of penetration of US legal consciousness worldwide, and a careful analysis of transformations both in the dominant (center) and in the subordinate (periphery) settings. Factors of resistance need to be fully appreciated as well.

US Rule of Law: Forms of Global Domination

In the aftermath of World War II, there was a dramatic change in the pattern of Western legal development. Leading legal ideas once produced in continental Europe and exported through the colonized world are now, for the first time, produced in a common law jurisdiction: the United States. Clearly, the present world dominance of the United States has been economic, military, and political first, and legal only recently, so that a ready explanation of legal hegemony can be found within a simple conception of law as a product of the economy.[8] Nevertheless, the question of the relationship between legal, political, and economic hegemony is not likely to be explained within a cause-and-effect paradigm. Ultimately, addressing this question is a very important area of basic jurisprudential research because it reveals some general aspects of the rule of law, as a device of global governance, and contextualizes its current relationship with plunder.

In principle, we can distinguish a pattern of legal domination from a hegemonic pattern. In the first, a foreign legal system is imposed on the subjugated nation as a coercive apparatus that asserts political and economic power, sometimes even sovereignty, without an effort to build consent. The idea of hegemony, on the contrary, shows an effort by the dominating legal system to be "admired" by the periphery, thus obtaining a degree of consent by the dominated nation.

In practice the distinction between hegemonic and non-hegemonic legal dominance blurs. Law is a detailed and complex machinery of social control that cannot function without some cooperation from a variety of individuals staffing legal institutions. These individuals are usually part of a professional elite, which either already exists in the dominated nation or is created by external power structures. Such an elite provides the consent to the reception of foreign legal ideas that is necessary for any legal transplantation to occur. Hence the distinction between legal transplants produced by domination and those produced by hegemony seems only a matter of degree and not of structure. For example, even in present-day Iraq, where military domination is the only face of power, the rhetoric of democracy and the rule of law are not entirely absent, even if its credibility is at its nadir. In order to understand the nature of present-day legal hegemony, it is necessary to capture the way in which the law functions to build a degree of consent (or resistance) to the present pattern of international economic and political dominance.

A fundamental cultural construct used to create consent is the rhetoric of democracy and the rule of law which is utilized by the imperial model of *governance*, substituting for state *governments* and triumphant worldwide together with the neo-liberal model of capitalism. The last 20 years of the twentieth century produced a triumph in global governance of reactive, politically unaccountable institutions (such as courts of law) over politically accountable institutions (such as direct administrative apparatuses of government). This decline of political legitimacy in the decision-making process produced an increased rhetoric of the rule of law which poses beyond discussion the model of reactive institutions. Tools employed in this process include a variety of concepts constructed as good *per se*.

Democracy and the rule of law do not stand alone as buzzwords aimed at the production of consent in neo-liberal times. As we have noted, notions of structural adjustment, comprehensive development, good governance, international human rights, and humanitarian intervention perform similar persuasive functions. Such notions, including that of "lack," are currently key elements of a strong rhetoric of legitimization of international corporate power determining the diffusion of oppressive institutions aimed at plunder: the imperial rule of law. These notions are today "naturalized" in the global discursive practice, and are called the "Washington Consensus." Their uncritical use produces a state of denial of the way in which the rule of law, often shielding plunder, is produced and developed by professional "consent-building" elites. The consequences of such denial are the creation of a legal landscape in which the law "naturally" gives up its role of constraining opportunistic behavior of market actors. This process results in the development of rules and institutions based on double standards that are functional for the interests of corporate capital and that dramatically enlarge inequality within society.

For example, it is in the name of *good governance* that former socialist states dismantle participation in the economy by outsourcing services and selling public goods. Such processes, presided over by *ad hoc* legal rules, transfer public resources to a very limited number of powerful economic oligarchs. Similarly, it is in the name of *international human rights* that long-standing cultural practices, or kinship structures, in Africa or the Islamic world are essentialized and targeted for eradication, dismantling group-centered social structures, with the consequent production of social mobility and individualization.

The legal landscape is in transition from one political setting (the local state) to another setting (world governance) in which American-framed reactive institutions, both adversarial (e.g. courts) and harmonious (e.g. IDS-ADR (international dispute settlement-alternative dispute resolution) panels), are asserting themselves as legitimate and legitimating governing bodies, outside of direct political accountability. Imperial rule of law weakens political control by putting the powerful global reactive institutions beyond the reach of the political process; plunder follows the demise of a hard notion of legality.

Imperial rule of law, then, is the product of an alliance between a limited number of powerful political actors (the European Union, the North Atlantic Treaty Organization (NATO), the G8 and other powerful states currently subordinate to the USA), the international financial institutions, a variety of large corporate actors, and even international non-governmental organizations (NGOs) – a game in which a very limited number of powerful players compete or cooperate.[9] Just as in early colonial times the private venture capitalists (the East India Company, Hudson Bay Company, etc.) and European colonial sovereigns were connected in an alliance for plunder, legitimized by a powerful intellectual clique, today the global power elite is connected with transnational business in the global pursuit of plunder. In the age of colonialism such political struggles for international hegemony were mostly carried on with an open use of force and political violence (in such a way that final extensive conflict between superpowers was unavoidable). Whereas, in the current age, political violence wrapped in the imperial rule of law has been centralized into a monopolistic power, the United States, dominating enemies, allies, and global institutions, but being itself dominated – as every Western-style democracy is – by transnational corporate actors.

Globalization of the American Way

The fundamental structure of the current imperial version of the rule of law is directly derived from the United States. Such a highly professionalized system, self-praising for having reached "separation" between law, politics, and religion (but, interestingly, highly praising the integration of law and economics), as we already know, is the result of imports from Europe, and then amplified in the United States.

Another fundamental structure of US law – a direct post-colonial reaction against the highly centralized English system – perfectly adapts to an expansionistic, hegemonic project such as neo-liberalism: its high degree of decentralization. This is possibly the most original aspect of the fundamental structure of US law. No other legal system in the world has developed a federal judicial system as complete, sophisticated, and complex as that of the United States. This is exactly the kind of complexity that introduces tremendous advantages in the US legal landscape for powerful economic actors and their corporate mega law firms in pursuit of plunder. In order to manage a very complex legal system, a strong, organized, and expensive bar is required. Complexity can be twisted in the interest of stronger corporate actors, the only ones that can afford the costs of justice. Plunder not only directly benefits from the complexity of the law (ironically, as it also profits from the simple-mindedness of economic thinking), it can also use complexity to dismantle possible counter-hegemonic uses of the law. Alternative dispute resolution, often a mixed process of mediation, negotiation, and arbitration in which the strong and powerful invariably comes out ahead, becomes generally palatable as a reaction to such complexity. Today, mediation, rather than being perceived as another soft strategy allowing distribution in favor of stronger actors, is presented as a device granting cheaper access to justice and therefore favorable to the weak.[10]

The coexistence of a large number of federal and state courts made issues of jurisdiction and choice of law the primary concern of the American legal profession. These are the same issues that are on the desks of lawyers who have to approach global "transnational" legal problems. Consequently, American attorneys already enjoy a legal culture and discourse that is broader than jurisdictional limits. In this scenario, the theoretical or practical "annexing" of one more jurisdiction, whether located in Afghanistan, Eastern Europe, or Iraq, does not particularly change the US lawyer's strongly functionalist way of reasoning. This is why American lawyers, under World Bank, International Monetary Fund (IMF), or American Bar Association (ABA) sponsorship, can frame a constitution or a bankruptcy code during a week-long stay in some remote corner of the world, with no expertise whatsoever in the local legal system, which simply gets erased. US-trained lawyers can, indeed, more or less intelligently speak of any theoretical legal issues with just a very basic knowledge of the actual law, thus making themselves understandable, and their legal culture appealing, to lawyers of very different backgrounds.

The very structure of the American judicial process, moreover, decentralizes power and privatizes activity, thus creating further advantages for the powerful and wealthy and further adaptability to the landscape of globalization. A large variety of activities within litigation such as "service of process" (the procedure used to give notice of litigation), "discovery" (the gathering of evidence in the hands of the opponent or of a third party), or questioning of witnesses (including experts), which are labeled "official" (and therefore provided and paid for by the state) in European legal systems, are private matters in American law, carried on by attorneys at no cost to the public sector and high cost for the litigants. This aspect of US law certainly trades equality for efficiency, because while a litigant in a civil law country can survive litigation even if represented by less than a brilliant attorney (because it is the judge who takes care of most issues and actively supervises the fundamental fairness of the trial) he needs to find a smart and expensive one in a privatized model such as the American one. Consequently, even this aspect of US legal consciousness much better fits a privatized model such as that of global litigation, which lacks a monopolistic sovereign state to take care of justice, equal opportunities, and imbalances of power.

In transnational litigation, often carried out in front of private arbitration boards or where issues of jurisdiction and choice of law are all-important, attorneys less used to the strategies of an adversarial system cannot survive because there is no such thing as an activist judge carrying on most of the business. Consequently, every litigant must get a really sharp (and expensive) lawyer to get effective representation. The aforementioned powerful combination of adaptive forces makes the structure of American law sufficiently familiar so as not to be excessively feared; sufficiently ambiguous and flexible to be successful in the international legal landscape; and, most importantly, it makes US-trained lawyers much more attuned to the characteristics of the global legal landscape. Moreover, as is always the case, the larger the degree of privatization of the procedure, the greater the advantage for the rich and powerful economic actors that find in the complexities and costs of international litigation the best agency of protection for plunder carried on worldwide.

Another crucial aspect of American hegemony in the global landscape is the equation between democracy and elections, which once more confers a definitive advantage to mighty and wealthy corporate actors. The "winner takes all" principle, which in the United States disenfranchises at least half of its citizens, appears natural and obvious only as long as we compare and oppose it to its absurd opposite, that of minority rule. "But if we think how numerous and various can be the means to give to a group a unitary will, we should ask whether H.S. Maine was not right when claiming that the majority rule is the most artificial between all those available."[11] Majority rule as expressed by elections has institutionalized in the United States – and following its lead in many other countries – the notion of a market for votes that carries as a structural consequence a selection of leadership, mostly determined by media control and the availability of large amounts of money.

The notion of a market for votes, as theorized by conservative, public choice economists such as Nobel Prize winner James Buchanan, inserts a high level of cynicism in political theory. It also institutionalizes at the most basic level the subversion in the relationship between the political process and the corporate dominated market. The political process (and the law stemming from it) is thus no longer considered to be a device to control and limit the market. On the contrary, it is the market that controls and determines the political process and the law. Electoral results are thus visualized as returns on investments, with the consequence that only those who "invest" in politics actually determine the law. Naturally, the big corporate actors are the major political investors, outspending individuals, trade unions, or NGOs in the order of more than ten times. Big political investors, moreover, use bipartisan donation strategies to be sure of the return no matter who gets elected. The result of this perverse circle, theorized as "natural" by public choice economists and political scientists, is that on major issues of general importance candidates from both parties offer very similar visions, so that for most people it seems irrational to pay attention to a political process that is predetermined. This is casually explained away as mere apathy. The "naturalization" of the subverted relationship between the market and the law leads to a highly apathetic citizenry and very limited election turnouts.

Note that the theory that law is a natural "return" for investments is not limited to direct legislation and regulation. In the US model, it is extended to adjudication. In a privatized, adversarial procedural system, the party that invests more in the process (more expensive attorneys, expert witnesses with better resumes, more sophisticated jury selectors, detectives, psychologists, etc.) can expect better returns, increasing its likelihood of winning the case. While this was once seen as a problem of equal opportunity, because the stronger party has more to "invest" than the weaker, it started being theorized as efficient by the law and economics literature beginning as early as the 1970s.[12] Today this cynical vision is offered as the only realist and thus non-naïve one in the dominant academic discourses.

Thus a variety of basic institutional factors favoring the stronger economic actors and providing legal coverage for plunder have been internationalized by the hegemonic domination of US law, making the reactive model expand well beyond its context of production. US law has been able to become the "extreme West" of the Western legal tradition. Its fundamental structure develops as plainly and structurally incompatible with alternative ideas, and is relentlessly combated with them: for example, "socialist legality" or "Islamic jurisprudence," but also with notions of welfare state such as the modern continental European. Countries that embrace or have embraced these alternative positions are located at the "periphery" of the free world and are required by imperial law to dismantle their incompatible legal structures.

Interestingly, even European countries, traditionally located at the center, have been gradually pushed to the periphery in the building process of global governance by a constant erosion of the activist and redistributive roles of their sovereign states. Suffice to think about labor law, where years of civilizing evolution in favor of trade unions and workers are dismantled, in the name of efficiency, by both right-wing and so-called left-wing governments through Europe. The less than full development of decentralized institutions, for example, has been singled out as a "lack," a problematic factor in the European context. The new periphery, quite as much as the traditional one, maintains bastions of resistance, certain traditional factors such as the active involvement of a judge in the search for truth, that are an irritant for an American-inspired global legal consciousness.

In the aftermath of World War II, it became quite apparent that the notion of sovereignty and statehood as developed in the continental European tradition was exposed to a strong structural critique. The notion, enshrined in Hegelian philosophy, that the state was an organ pursuing its own sovereign interest, ontologically different from, and occasionally incompatible with, the aggregate of the individual rights of its subjects, was in many quarters deemed responsible for the trashing of the rule of law in fascist Europe. The notion that the state was nothing other than "the government in office" was typical of the pragmatic Anglo-American tradition. This tradition sees the state pursuing an interest that had to coincide with the aggregate of individual interests expressed by the "winner takes all" electoral process. The individual's vested economic rights, which naturally pre-existed the state, must consequently limit the state's activity. The Anglo-American model could claim to be an alternative, more advanced and "free" vision of sovereignty.

The roots were thus established for the "naturalization" of the corporate American way, and for its fundamental challenge to the hierarchical relationship between the political process and free (market) activity. Such a process of naturalizing the institutional setting of the "free world" began in America with Eisenhower's conservative political platform that defeated President Truman's Fair Deal in 1952. Through the Cold War, the polemic towards socialism reinforced such a vision, challenging activist redistributive policies and government intervention in the economy in favor of the poor. Despite the exception of Lyndon Johnson, determined by needs of social pacification in the Vietnam era, this "naturalization" as a protection of the proprietary bottom line constantly determined American politics. Through its influence, the same anti-redistribution vision determines the present posture of international financial institutions. Beginning with the Nixon administration, over the last 30 years any redistributive policy in the United States has been in favor of the super rich. Today the top 24,000 individuals control as much wealth as 90 million of their lower scale fellow Americans. This tiny minority of the population is in full control of the (efficient) political and judicial processes, not only to keep the *status quo*, but actually for purposes of redistribution in its own favor: plunder, abroad, but also at home.[13]

Despite this and other horrors of discriminating US law (such as the incredible numbers of innocent minorities incarcerated and exploited in corporately managed prisons), local American scholarly productions made the prestige of US law felt by legal professionals worldwide, so that the intellectual leadership of American law became an undisputable fact. The years of the Cold War and the demise of the best in Western legality that has characterized most of the communist regimes in the USSR orbit of influence, has confirmed the perception of the benefits of the three fundamental symbols of the American rule of law: spectacular elections (a sort of expensive advertising spot of democracy), strong independent judiciary (with highly visible interventions in US political life), and free and creative academic critique of the political and judicial processes. None of these representations were characteristic of the Soviet experience (nor of today's China and Cuba, the too different and often forgotten socialist alternatives to the Western end of history). So the imposition of such fundamental characteristics worldwide became the recipe for change in the aftermath of the fall of the USSR.

An Ideological Institution of Global Governance: International Law

Since the Nuremberg trials, Western notions of legality have characterized international law. In the building of Western legal dominance, international law has slowly and incrementally developed from a decentralized system of sovereign nations into a more centralized international system, where the Security Council of the United Nations claimed some steering role. In this process, international law has provided rhetoric capable of justifying the use of force by repressive institutions of global governance. It has also played the role of an ideological institution responsible for the ideas that violence over innocent people can be "legal," that a war of destruction can be "fair," or even that there is such a thing as a "peacekeeping" operation.[14]

The rhetorical device used in the process of repressing deviance and asserting as universal and inevitable Western ways of social organization and economic development, based on individualism and social fragmentation, has been a genuinely legal concept: "international human rights." A doctrine of "limited sovereignty" in the interest of international human rights has threatened the traditional nature of international law as a decentralized system based on territoriality and has advocated the needs of centralization in order to make international law more similar to any other system of Western national law. The International Criminal Court is the most advanced point of this move. The treaty of Rome establishing this court can be seen as the zenith in the post-war process of centralization in international law.

Certainly, the decline and demise of international law, produced by the United States at the opening of the millennium, has been much quicker than its difficult struggle to develop some principle. *Ad hoc* courts such as the one used against the late Yugoslavian President Slobodan Milosevic, let alone that against former Iraqi President Saddam Hussein (even if officially an Iraqi court), are the product of an even more openly ideological use of international law, as an *ex post facto* legitimization of war. An interesting development can thus be spotted.

After formal decolonization, which has been significantly encouraged by notions of self-determination grounded in international law, the US government has inaugurated a soft strategy to weaken the bite of international legality, while constructing an embryo of institutional centralization. In the current phase, as the events of Iraq make abundantly clear, such weakened international legality has proved to be very easy to ignore.

The crucial moment of the first phase, based on strict construction of formal sovereignty of the former colonial states, was the so-called "United for Peace Resolutions" by which the United Nations (UN) General Assembly condemned the Anglo-French attack on Nasser's Egypt that followed the nationalization of the Suez Canal in 1956. Thus, what was certainly a neo-colonial imperialist attack was defeated by genuine measures of international law, grounded on strict notions of internal sovereignty.[15] The second phase, that of soft power, is characterized by a signature of such highly symbolic (although mostly futile) treatises as the Kyoto protocol for greenhouse gas control, and by concomitant enlargement of NATO, with its notorious exemptions of military personnel from legal accountability. The international human rights movement, occupying do-gooders worldwide, has provided international support for NATO's legally exempt carpet-bombing of former Yugoslavia.

In the current phase, symbolized by the re-colonization of Afghanistan and Iraq – when even the previous hypocrisy of wrapping plunder up in the rule of law can be appreciated, nostalgically, as a sense of limit – the centralization of "international government" (the UN Security Council) and even the unlikely counter-hegemonic use of the International Criminal Court are potential competitors to US-dominated imperial rule of law. As a consequence, deemed a possible obstacle to plunder, these institutions have been almost entirely ridiculed by reducing them to irrelevant "advisory boards" (the UN Security Council) or to courts of insignificant jurisdiction (the International Criminal Court, which the USA refuses to join), respectively.

Viewing the process of centralization following the establishment of the United Nations in 1949, today we understand that international law is not natural but positive law; its fundamental sources are treaties and customs that need power to be enforced, as in any other branch of a legal system. Some observers assert today that international law is a worldwide legal system grounded in uniformity and in American-born ideals of law and order. The nature and the reality of international law and its relationship with current plunder seems grounded in contradictions. On the one hand, international codes, international courts, and international jails are already claiming to be generally recognized and established (there is a court in Arusha, Tanzania, to try non-Westerners deemed responsible for Rwanda's genocide, and there is a jail in Bamako, Mali, to detain the condemned). Many commentators already approach international politics as if such an international, centralized legal system was already in place on a general basis. With such a system in place (assuming that it is in place), the transformation of war into police power follows as a matter of course. Hence attempts to exercise state-based sovereignty can always be constructed as deviating from a standard of legality grounded in Western hegemonic visions of international human rights.

The reality of an unacceptable double standard does not matter. Be it an attempt to develop nuclear defense capacity in the Middle East (with the exclusion of a nuclearized Israel), be it defending notions of religious societies incompatible with Western notions of secularism, or be it using violence for the purpose of political assertion, these are activities in violation of international law whenever they are performed by non-imperial sovereigns. The possibility of using the rhetoric of international law, as it "should be," is more than enough for the international imperial order. Many honest, law-abiding individuals in the West, targeted by media propaganda and moderately opposing plunder when they understand its presence, genuinely believe that a United Nations resolution could have turned the re-colonization of Iraq from a brutal, imperial war of conquest into a legitimate, humanitarian operation of minority rights protection and part of a process of peacekeeping and reconstruction. Many of such more or less honest believers (including the US Democrat-led Congress) consider the current attempts at colonization of Afghanistan fundamentally different from those of Iraq because of the UN imprimatur!

The tool used to gain consensus, the doctrine of international human rights, is indeed very powerful. It has been advocated by actors motivated by both profit and justice, and started the process of transformation of the very conception of international law developed after the birth of the modern nation state. Notions of human rights and international humanitarian intervention have subverted the model of full sovereignty in internal affairs, of the state serving the interest of its national community within its national territory, as emerged from the Peace of Westphalia. While the first Iraq War could still use the violation of Kuwait's sovereignty to justify its international legality, already in the following Balkan Wars the fig leaf of borders' sanctity could not be used. Intervention aimed at "regime change," illegal within the established scheme of sovereignty, has thereafter been grounded in the rhetoric of human rights violations, perpetrated by *legal sovereigns* such as Slobodan Milosevic, Mullah Omar, or Saddam Hussein.

Today the indisputable power stemming from international law sovereignty can be asserted only by the imperial sovereign and perhaps by a few others of its most faithful servants, or of its realistically feared potential enemies (such as China); but not by any one else. Territorial sovereignty of the average state is thus dismantled for imperial needs.

International human rights is, however, a problematic notion because it provides a selective justification for intervention in the internal political business of all states that are not culturally aligned with Western or imperial rule of law. In the age of imperial legal order and brutal plunder in which we are living, it would be naïve to expect otherwise from international law.

International law thus has an ambiguous relationship with the imperial rule of law. While one would think that its development and centralization might limit the imperial sovereign and thus establish legality, in fact it establishes double standards and political non-accountability. The process of establishing centralized international institutions ends up reproducing on the global scale attitudes, modes of thought, and even institutional arrangements closely resembling those of the United States without the safety valves of the US Constitution and the Bill of Rights.

International law has incrementally changed from a decentralized system of foreign sovereigns to a progressively more centralized, and non-directly accountable, legal system, ethnocentric in its values and governed by professional elites staffing international courts of law and other bodies of governance. "Legal professionalism," perhaps the core aspect of the US legal experience, and certainly an identity trait of the West, gets reproduced at the international level, as the neutral, objective, and universal way to approach problems of international relevance. By reproducing this model, international law has become a politically impotent institutional system, in which courts of law and other non-politically legitimated decision-makers produce laws that can then be enforced only by an imperial sovereign, which acts selectively. What follows is a non-accountable political system, made up of actors that can only be strong with the weak and weak with the strong. Such a system of international law simply has no power against the imperial sovereign and its allies and only serves the needs (if any) of justifying the exercise of domination against weaker actors and plunder. This is quite the opposite of the rule of law's moral claim to help the weak against the strong, as exemplified by US tort law.

The international legal system has thus reproduced on a global scale a professional legal ideology of neutrality, democracy, and rule of law, claiming a façade of legitimacy to the exercise worldwide of unprecedented US political strength. US domestic doctrines of the separation of power and political questions and sovereign immunity, traditionally allow the executive branch (which holds the sword) a quite extended and undisputable degree of unrestricted power because domestic courts defer to it when political issues cannot be transformed into legal ones. Similarly an international law governed by courts of law (the Nuremberg model) depending on the most powerful national sovereign for their effectiveness, necessarily defers to the desires of that state (currently the USA) and produces the façade of legitimacy for the exercise of imperial sovereignty. For example, the *ad hoc* tribunal that judged the late Yugoslavian President Slobodan Milosevic serves *ex post facto* the function of showing that the use of NATO for purposes of illegal regime change showed good judgment, thus writing the winner's history. Decisions of other international courts, such as the one condemning Israel's wall, on the contrary, because disliked by the imperial power, simply do not play any practical role.

Legal institutions once established might produce counter-hegemony, which explains the reluctance by the US government to support the International Criminal Court. Particularly in more recent times, as a reaction to some limited independence shown by the UN Security Council, the dismantling option (named reform) is gaining currency. The unrestricted concentration of executive power in the United States has been openly asserted, and as a parallel development in international law, "unilateralism" rather than soft power has been professed as the preferred doctrine. Imperial law might not need international law any more, even as a faithful servant.

In recent times, the unilateralist politics of the US executive have suddenly halted the post World War II unfolding of international law and the development of the United Nations as a centralized, international, political decision-making body. Interestingly, US courts have displayed a similar imperialist attitude at the decentralized level. In this process one can observe significant transformations in the traditional posture of American courts, which have recently taken a quite proactive role in asserting themselves as domestic judges of the international sphere. While trends are still contradictory and unclear at this point, it is a fact that plaintiffs in traditionally "non-justiciable" matters flock to the United States, attracted by the hope of seeing their rights finally vindicated (such as in the case of the Indian victims of the Bhopal catastrophe or of those of Latin American torturers or survivors of the Holocaust) – many times attracted by a very proactive American plaintiff's bar. This phenomenon deserves attention because it increases the political responsibility of the American legal profession at the global level, whose role once more cuts both ways.

We need to explore, therefore, the hegemonic consequences of a universal discourse on rights enforced by a strong system of courts.[16] We further dwell on plunder facilitated by the diffusion of the "reactive philosophy" discussed previously in contexts where foreign courts and the legal profession – because of more limited institutional power or economic means, or because of differences in local cultures ("lacks" in the hegemonic jargon) – do not operate as effectively as the American ones.

Holocaust Litigation: Back to the Future

On a Sunday afternoon a few years ago, while hanging out in Berkeley, the lawyer among us (U. Mattei) received a phone call. On the line was a young and very kind woman attorney. After introducing herself as an associate of a large San Francisco law firm, she inquired whether she was talking with someone "who knew something about Italian law." Receiving a positive answer, she asked whether it would be possible to arrange a meeting to discuss the possibility of producing an expert declaration for a "class" suing a prominent Italian insurance company. The "class," she said, consisted of Holocaust survivors. After a brief discussion, it was agreed that papers related to the case would be delivered in Berkeley to be perused before the meeting.

The next day, a courier package arrived with a folder containing the complaint and a few subsequent motions. Reading them was quite an unusual experience for a lawyer trained in continental Europe. The reader of the pleadings, all of a sudden, was plunged back in time and space. It was like reading a social history book, describing some of the atrocities that had affected Europe in the 1930s and 1940s. According to the papers, it was a long tradition of the Jewish community of central Europe to be very averse to risk. Not only were Jewish businessmen traditionally insured, but even low-income, non-business people used insurance schemes to invest a limited amount of money in order to provide their daughters with a dowry in the event of marriage. Because of *ad hoc* legislation, apparently introduced to please the insurance business friendly with the Nazi regime, no money has ever been paid for the events of *christallnacht*, when hundreds of Jewish businesses were systematically attacked and looted by a Nazi mob.

The litigation papers produced a mixed reaction in the reader. On the one hand, the atrocities described in the papers were crying out for some reaction, so one felt good to be on the victim's side. Nevertheless, there were so many things that looked odd! How could a US court adjudicate a case naming foreign defendants for events that happened thousands of miles away from the US borders more than 60 years ago?

It is a shared principle among legal systems that legal actions are subject to what is known as a "statute of limitations." This means that if a legal action does not start within a given period of time after the injury, the action is barred and thus the right to legal relief is lost. This period of time is usually shorter than 10 years, in some rare circumstance it stretches to 20, but never to 60 years! The rationale of the limitation rule is very clear and all students easily understand it. To begin with, plaintiffs should not "sleep on their rights." Secondly, courts are not agencies to adjudicate history. After such a long time, witnesses may be dead, evidence can be lost or destroyed, and memory fades. Perhaps a historian in these circumstances can reconstruct the truth but not a court of law.

Courts are not only considered limited in the timespan of their reach; they are usually constrained by space too. In lawyer's terminology they need to have "jurisdiction." This notion, providing so much headache for law students, is extremely complicated in practice but relatively simple in its rationale and principles. To begin with, courts must have some "contact" with the case they adjudicate. The facts, for example, should have taken place, at least in part, within the territorial limits presided over by a given court. Jurisdiction is also based on notions of fairness towards the defendant. While it is possible to sue a defendant in "his" court, for example in the place where the defendant lives, it is not usually considered fair if the plaintiff can just walk into the court across his street and sue someone living very far away. The defendant, innocent until proven guilty, should not be compelled to travel a long way to defend himself.

In the case against the Italian insurance company, the suit was against a defendant domiciled thousands of miles away, the facts had no contact whatsoever with California, and the event happened a very long time ago. Nevertheless, the fact that the US court might very likely adjudicate the question was clear to both the plaintiffs and to the defendants' American attorneys. How could that be?

The meeting with the attorneys took place within the luxurious law offices of what appeared to be a very prominent law firm specializing in representing plaintiffs in major class actions. For a European lawyer, both the degree of specialization of the American bar and the inordinate profits that a successful plaintiff's bar can make, by settling or winning class actions in the

United States, was an unfamiliar notion. In the waiting room, where coffee was immediately offered, there was a brochure showing the involvement of the relatively recently established firm in all the current spectacular litigations, from asbestos to tobacco.

There was a sense of empowerment sitting there, something that would slowly induce one to forget about the issues of jurisdiction and limitations briefly described above. There was a clear feeling that, in such an efficient organization, matters of justice, substantial or procedural, would sound almost obsolete. Such an organization must be able to attract any possible defendant in the United States. Such an organization, by hiring at handsome hourly rates almost any kind of expert, from foreign lawyers to historians, could almost certainly persuade a judge that the American adversary process could make any kind of truth emerge, no matter how far away and how long ago the facts happened. American courts of law, the venues where such an efficiently organized legal profession would engage in a battle for the "truth," have to be almost naturally the "global" decision-makers. How did we reach that point?

The story of courts of law as hegemonic agencies of the global legal order starts unfolding in post World War II developments, and reaches its final stage in post Cold War jurisprudence. The Holocaust has played a direct role in both these phases.[17] In the immediate aftermath of World War II, the Nuremberg tribunal (which tried and sentenced some Nazi officials for crimes against humanity) planted the seeds of an idea of international legality based on courts of law, within a mode of faith in the judiciary and with an eye toward explaining why continental European legal systems had been unable to organize any resistance against the authoritarian power of the fascist state. While the notion of universal human rights capable of court enforcement is certainly rooted in the Nuremberg trials, the idea that the national system of US courts can provide this role worldwide is a post Cold War development in the United States. Holocaust-related litigation is its central drama.[18]

The insurance litigation discussed at the San Francisco firm was just one of numerous lawsuits filed in US federal and state courts asserting what are now commonly referred to as "Holocaust claims." In these claims for events arising out of World War II, plaintiffs maintain that the wrongs alleged – which include concealed bank accounts, looted assets, looted art, and insurance policy claims – are best adjudicated by US courts because various procedural mechanisms of the US judicial system allow efficient disposition of the claims. The role of the Italian law expert in this case, it turned out, was to provide evidence of this assertion of comparative efficiency by testifying that the Italian legal system could not deliver justice in this case.

Each case turns on stories by still-living plaintiffs about themselves, or their friends and family, being either brutally subjected to Nazi horrors during the war (looted assets and slave labor claims) or unscrupulously denied access to their legal entitlements after the war (insurance and bank deposit claims). Commissions have been authorized and funded (Bergier in Switzerland, Matteoli in France, and Eizenstat in the United States) to pursue the question in less than an adversarial manner. The legal activity relates not only to the European theater of World War II; claims have also been filed in US courts by both US and foreign nationals for forced labor and sexual slavery imposed by the Japanese in the Pacific theater of the war.

The Swallowing of International Law by US Law

To understand the claim of American courts to be the global adjudicators, one should look to American law. Hegemony is ultimately self-assertion of power, so it would be naïve to look at global sources establishing it. The US Constitution, drafted in 1787, reflects the natural law beliefs that dominated eighteenth-century jurisprudence. A primary tenet of that belief was the recognition, preservation, and vindication of individual rights, whether they arose in the United States or abroad. The framers and the first generation to follow them gave substance to that belief in part through the idea that international law could be seen as a system of customary protection of such rights. This was reflected in Article III of the Constitution itself, which has been broadly interpreted to include international law claims based not only upon treaty, but also custom as the province of the federal judiciary. Congress further extended jurisdiction to US federal courts through the passage of a variety of statutes including the so-called Alien Tort Claims Act at the end of the eighteenth century, and widely used today to attract international cases to the USA.

The origins of this act remain somewhat obscure and for almost 200 years it lay practically dormant. But the statute suddenly came to life in the case of *Filartiga* v. *Pena-Irala*, 630 F.2d 876 (2d Cir. 1980), in which the court held that the act complained of – torture of a Paraguayan citizen by a Paraguayan official – violated the "law of nations" and that, according to Article III of the US Constitution, the law of nations was directly incorporated into federal common law. Thus, the embryonic but clear potential for US courts of law to vindicate wrongs committed throughout the world, and thereby protect the natural rights of the individual, was given expression. Such violations of natural rights conflicting with clearly established norms of international law can happen and do happen everywhere in the world, and in theory, then, transform the United States into a forum for all the world's grievances.

Beginning in 1996, the impressive explosion of Holocaust-related litigation provided worldwide visibility to this phenomenon.[19] Indeed, European lawyers representing a large number of Europe-based corporations active in insurance, banking, and industry, or even European state entities (Austria, the Vatican, etc.), sued in the USA, are today involved in one capacity or another in litigation on both coasts of the United States concerning hundreds of claims based on facts of more than a half century ago. Because of the distance in time and space of the Holocaust from the United States, and because of the nature of judicial challenge to actions carried out under shadows of foreign law and politics, the Holocaust litigation is the most extreme and emblematic episode of a worldwide trend in international litigation in which US courts promote themselves as *de facto* judges of world history. How that is possible needs some explanation.

This posture of the US courts is now resented as a major phenomenon of legal imperialism, because of the way in which it imposes American standards not only of substantive law (which are, with respect to these appalling events, in any case largely shared by every nation in the world) but also of procedure and of legal culture. As a paradox, while offering judicial remedies against extreme episodes of historical plunder, US courts play a major role in the construction of the American legal hegemony (globally diffused as the reactive project) that legalizes current plunder.

A variety of technical factors explain why US courts attract both foreign plaintiffs and defendants to litigate in America. Such factors explain much of the way in which the US notion of rule of law has been transformed into a global conception, so they are well worth a brief description.

Even at the earliest stages of litigation, plaintiffs will ask the court to allow them some "discovery." Discovery, in the lawyer's lingo, is the judicially supervised activity through which lawyers can obtain information from their adversarial counterpart. Discovery includes collection of any remotely relevant documents and interrogation by aggressive lawyers of the parties and their witnesses, who are obliged to respond. The stunning reach of US discovery is one of the most important factors explaining the present hegemony of US law in worldwide litigation. American-style discovery, often experienced by defendants as a "fishing expedition," is traditionally much resented outside of the USA because it is intrusive and practically incompatible with the presumption of innocence. In this view, American-style procedure shows the hypocrisy of a system that advertises abroad the presumption of innocence as a fundamental aspect of the rule of law, then leaving defendants (both civil and criminal) in its courts at the mercy of the overwhelming power of their opponents. In such an adversarial model, only wealthy and powerful defendants can effectively defend themselves against prosecutors or powerful plaintiff's firms, by "investing" enough money in legal professionals. However, even if proved innocent, they will never recover such legal expenses, and, if guilty but wealthy, they might outspend the plaintiff and win the case: a "market for justice" highly functional to the legalization of corporate plunder.

This economic factor alone explains why poor foreign defendants (e.g. suspect Latin American or African torturers) almost invariably default in US courts, while wealthy corporations successfully resist. The former cases, highly advertised, contribute to the empowerment of the international human rights movement and NGOs exporting US notions of rule of law, while the latter allows for legalization of plunder. Once again, plunder and the rule of law walk hand in hand in maintaining the hegemonic *status quo* based on the prestige of US judiciary.

From an early stage, US-based international litigation is complicated, time-consuming, and very expensive. For example, in a complex international litigation turning on issues of foreign law, a rather extensive list of expert witnesses might be called. Not only do issues of law have to be addressed by expert declarations, but other factual questions that the court needs to know might also require expensive declarations (e.g. historians, bankers, experts of business practice, and the like, typically have to be hired and compensated). Moreover, attorneys have to absorb, to a great extent, the implications that foreign law might have on the case and be prepared to argue it both in the written briefs and in oral argument in front of the court. Since each point of law is thoroughly briefed – in important cases entailing massive searches through case laws for helpful precedents – a large number of attorneys are typically employed in various capacities who are compensated at rates usually ranging from $200 to $500 per hour. It is no exaggeration to estimate that resisting even an entirely spurious claim involving complex international litigation in the US might cost a defendant not less than $1 million per year. This factor

– the high cost of litigation – in large part explains the high rate of out of court settlements.

Besides discovery, other difficulties exist, so that suits in US courts put high financial burdens and sometimes unfair pressure on defendants who might well be innocent. To begin with, the system of attorney's compensation, at least in tort cases, is very attractive for plaintiffs and their attorneys, as witnessed by the impressive wealth of plaintiffs' firms. Plaintiffs' attorneys are usually compensated on a contingency fee basis, which means that they are only paid in case of victory with a very substantial percentage (usually more than 30%) of the "prize" recovered. Defense attorneys, on the other hand, are typically compensated on an hourly basis, which is less lucrative compared to plaintiff cases ending in a windfall, but constitutes a more certain form of compensation. For the plaintiff, such as the "class" of Holocaust survivors in the San Francisco case, suing in a US court is a "risk-free, no cash advance" enterprise. This would simply be impossible in any other jurisdiction due to restrictions in the availability of contingency fee agreements. Legal systems other than the one in the United States fear the entrepreneurial spirit of attorneys so they try to limit the possibility of attorneys organizing as a "business enterprise" by advancing the costs of litigation in the hope of substantial returns.

Tort law in the United States was also traditionally friendly to plaintiffs, having developed a variety of doctrines to extend liability to defendants. A good example might be the so-called "market share liability," first employed in pharmaceutical class actions. According to such doctrine, in the impossibility of ascertaining which manufacturer created damage, liability should be faced by defendants in percentages corresponding to the different share of business. A second feature attracting plaintiffs is to be sure of the availability of punitive damages, thus making injured individuals and their attorneys hope for a windfall. A third is the employment of the jury to determine liability and damages. Finally, and perhaps most obviously, the vehicle of the class action itself – which allows "representative" plaintiffs to pursue the action on behalf of a "plaintiff class" made of unknown victims of the same injury – is one of the most powerful attractions of a US forum.

Sometimes litigation in the United States is the only vehicle available for vindication of rights. And this is indeed one of the strongest rhetorical reasons for the hegemony of American law in the international context. The class action is a technical device that allows relatively small individual interests, which could never afford the costs of litigation, to aggregate, thus forming a large and structured interest strong enough to attract plaintiff lawyers to litigate the claims. Invariably, the winning strategy to persuade American judges to retain jurisdiction is to show how the interest being litigated as a class action in the USA could never find access to courts anywhere else in the world because of the "lack" of the rule of law abroad. It is important to point out that these aspects of US litigation, familiar even to the general public in the United States, are unique tracts of US law that no other legal system in the world shares. Their aggregate result is to attract major international litigation to the United States and to persuade many American legal professionals that they are the only ones operating in a "real" rule of law system.

At the San Francisco firm, for example, it turned out that the Italian expert needed to declare, under penalty of perjury, that the Italian legal system was in disarray, that "lacking" class actions and a powerful plaintiff's bar it would have been impossible to vindicate the rights of the Holocaust victims, and that, in any event, "lacking" punitive damages, it would have been pointless to pursue the tort action there. Of course, there was on file an entirely opposite declaration by another Italian professor, arguing that an Italian court would be a more convenient forum to dispose of these issues, due to the high level of Italian legal civilization, to the high standards of efficiency of the judicial process there, and to the exceptional development of the rule of law in Italy. As often happens, it was a battle of hired guns, the practical judicial translation of the "market for justice" promoting "efficiency" and celebrated in much economic-legal literature.

Because of the attractive force of the American courts for international litigators, and because of the traditional reluctance of US courts (motivated by the rhetoric of international human rights and by notions of rule of law) to give up jurisdiction in favor of foreign courts, a quite interesting phenomenon can be detected. Concepts and notions that are inherently American become part of the common vocabulary and culture of the international legal practice even amongst lawyers belonging to other jurisdictions, further empowering the American bar at the global level.

For example, when a court, wherever located, is called upon to adjudicate issues happening abroad or having "contacts" with a foreign legal system, the issue arises of which law should then be applied. This very complex area of the law is called "conflicts of law" or "private international law." The idea behind it is that while adjudication happens after the fact, the courts should, however, decide on the lawfulness or unlawfulness of a given activity at the moment in which it was carried out, according to the law governing the place where it happened. A simple example is that while driving on the left side of the street would be a reckless activity in America, it would be perfectly lawful in England. Consequently, should an American court be called upon to adjudicate a car accident involving an American driver vacationing in England, it should consider driving on the left, illegal according to US law, perfectly lawful. Once again, while the rationale is simple, the details of this area of law are of staggering complexity. The choice of substantive law governing litigation is a crucial factor for deciding where to sue because, due to legal diversity, a defendant might be innocent according to one law and guilty according to another. American choice of law rules are considered very advanced, and American lawyers are considered world masters in the field of private international law because the choice of law issue has always been part of the everyday practice of the law in a federal system. The American conflict of law system is based on the fundamental idea that the state legal system, having the more intense contact with the facts at issue, should prevail. It is, however, also very sensitive to the idea that the commonalities between legal systems should be exploited in order to obey a notion of judicial economy. Hence a strong functionalist flavor points at not bothering in belaboring foreign law too much when the results of its application would not be so very different from those that would be reached by the application of US law. Non-US law students do not systematically study this area of the law. The course of conflicts is not mandatory, as it is in American law schools, and many lawyers are unfamiliar with it: more empowerment for US-trained attorneys in the global scenario.

Empowered by these diverse factors, US-style rule of law has been smoothly transformed into an international rule of law, and its practitioners in large US firms quite invariably play central roles in large neo-liberal global ventures amounting to plunder. For example, the Caspian pipeline stretching for thousands of miles through Azerbaijan, Georgia, and Turkey establishes new sovereignty rights to a corporate consortium lead by British Petroleum and shows in action the exceptional global skills of US lawyers in foreseeing any possible future international legal consequence of the deal. The multi-billion dollar deal has been almost entirely negotiated by US law firms representing all the interests involved, including foreign states. By expressly making them waive sovereign immunity, US courts of law have been guaranteed jurisdiction against potential foreign plaintiffs, should any problem arise. The provisions of such an agreement, both in contractual and in treaty form, make it constitutionally impossible for future governments of participant countries to rescind it, while giving power to the oil industry-led consortium to cancel its obligations with only 6 months' notice.

Under this newborn international "right to free flow of oil," a quintessential aspect of sovereignty – that of "taking power of eminent domain" – has been granted to the consortium on a thousands of miles long and 10 miles wide strip of land running from Baku to the Turkish coast. Certainly the exercise of this privatized taking amounts to the legal plunder of the land of local disempowered communities along the route, let alone serious environmental and human rights problems. This legally brokered deal, in pure US law firm style, paved the way to extensive contracts of corporate law enforcement (mercenaries) along the pipeline, a renewed source of business for the gun industry already very much in business in an area in which at least six civil wars have been fueled in preparation of the pipeline project: plunder.[20]

Economic Power and the US Courts as Imperial Agencies

Despite being sometimes depicted, for strategic reasons, as similar to most of the legal systems of the "civilized nations," the truth of the matter is that US law is very different from all others. It is the only system with class actions, with civil juries, with unlimited contingency fees, with a fully fledged double set of courts, with graduate law schools – just to offer a few major peculiarities. It is almost alone in using punitive damages, in the extensive use of the death penalty, and in granting tremendous political power to the Supreme Court. It is nearly alone, sharing this aspect with Somalia, in not ratifying the International Convention on the Rights of Children. The US concept of the rule of law should then be seen as an anomaly in Western law.

Specifically to our point, one should consider that the American complex litigation on international law is so far removed from the standards of most non-American jurisdictions that it is very unlikely that any court in the world would enforce most of the judgments entered in the USA against non-American defendants for facts happening abroad. So why do defendants show up in the United States?

The reason is fundamentally to be found in economic power. Many defendants in the global world have significant assets located in the United States and wish to avail themselves of business opportunities in America. Hence, the jurisdiction of US courts is in some sense "voluntarily" accepted by defendants for economic if not for legal reasons. If Lesotho or Colombia were to use the same legal system as the United States, transnational businesses would not feel that it would be advantageous to defend themselves there.

As discussed above, the reaction to hegemonic practices has the potential to become counter-hegemonic. Indeed, such uses of the legal system in the USA today abound. Unfair labor practices abroad, in sweatshops to which international logo-lords outsource production, as well as environmental issues of global concern are often attracted to the US legal system, thanks to the *pro bono* activity of so many social activist groups. Nevertheless, such commendable activity, certainly motivated by justice, ends up asserting even more strongly the idea that US courts of law are natural and effective adjudicators of world grievances and that they can serve as alternatives to political struggle and revolutionary practices to make a better world. It is very unlikely that an inherently conservative judiciary can make good law for progressive purposes.[21] US courts of law might end up serving as monitoring agencies of governments abroad, arbitrarily keeping them to standards that are much different from those respected at home.[22]

It remains true, nevertheless, that nowhere in the world are courts such effective agencies of rights' enforcement as in the United States. The majority of legal systems tend to use avenues other than private litigation to address issues of public concern. Public law and administrative regulation, proactively enforced by ministries or other administrative departments and agencies, are used, for example, to prevent the diffusion of potentially dangerous products such as drugs or genetically modified organisms, rather than allowing their diffusion on the understanding that damaged individuals have a chance to privately recover damages. In times of internationally imposed neo-liberal politics of privatization, adequate funding of these public agencies by national governments is "structurally forbidden." Consequently, alternative models to the reactive, court-based, private enforcement of individual rights "in the public interest" simply become non-viable. Because courts of law preside over the private sector, privatization of such public concerns as healthcare, pension systems, and transportation enlarge the sphere of the courts. Consequently, the direct proactive administrative activity governed by public law and publicly funded agencies, shrinks in the face of private law and its reactive, economically driven philosophy.

When, in the process of privatization/corporatization, responsibility is transferred from a public administrative system governed by the logic of *ex ante* regulation, to the private system governed by the logic of *ex post* adjudication, the role of courts becomes crucial in the organization of society. If courts are not open and effective to redress injury caused by activity not restricted and monitored *ex ante*, what follows is lawlessness. It is the rule of the stronger market actor who thrives because administrative agencies do not monitor (and perhaps tax) him *ex ante*, nor do courts of law check his activity *ex post* once damage occurs. This is precisely what happens everywhere in the world, where effective pro-plaintiff devices do not exist. For example, Union Carbide was not effectively restricted and monitored before the Bhopal disaster by Indian public law agencies, underfunded and ineffective as they were, thus allowing a gas spill resulting in thousands of victims. Nor was the Indian system of adjudication after the Bhopal events able to award adequate compensation to the victims of the tragedy. Bhopal is only one example of a very common global pattern. Almost everywhere in times of neo-liberal policy are state administrative agencies too weak and underfunded to detect and prevent corporate plunder. Courts of law are too weak and captured by wealthy defendants able to "invest" in litigation, to protect the victims that plunder leaves behind.

The globalization of the US rule of law and its reactive philosophy, granting a central role at the international level to adjudication rather than direct politics or administration, thus makes the periphery (i.e. everywhere other than the USA) the ideal marketplace for plunder by predatory international capital. The administrative apparatus of local states is too dismantled and underfunded to secure responsible behavior of local economic actors, let alone to be effective against international corporate plunder. Local adjudication is likewise ineffective. It follows that international corporate capital is much more careful in its behavior within the United States than abroad. While domestically it can always be sued and faces serious risks to pay high damages, if its abusive activity is carried out abroad, jurisdictional barriers, limited discovery, absence of class actions and punitive damages, and a less aggressive professional legal culture, makes the possibility of being sued remote. Any action pursued will be ineffective unless "mercifully" hosted by US courts. Thus, most transnational litigation almost never reaches the final point of a decision over the substantive issues, what lawyers call the "merits". The real battle is over whether US courts will adjudicate the issue. Plaintiffs, wherever located in the world, will try to bring the action in the United States. Defendants (usually corporate entities) will invest in skillful lawyers to keep the case away from American shores. Once the jurisdictional issue is decided in favor of the plaintiff, settlement is very often reached, because the corporate defendant seeks to avoid an American jury. But if the issue of jurisdiction is decided in favor of corporate defendants (as dramatically witnessed by the Bhopal case) then the plaintiff is left almost entirely at the mercy of the more powerful wrongdoer, who, perhaps, will pay a trivial amount of money to avoid bad publicity stemming from public perception of plunder.

The outcome of this complex dynamic of law and power is that American courts of law decide whether they wish to get involved. They keep the power to intervene, but they do so only selectively, skillfully playing with notions of international "comity" (i.e. respect of foreign jurisdiction) when they do not wish to offer an effective forum for plaintiffs. Thus, US courts are the real sovereigns of the international judicial playing field. Consequently, US attorneys, accustomed to such courts, enjoy a major advantage compared to their foreign counterparts, thus becoming the real masters of international litigation. Not only are they native speakers of the language of transnational practice, they are also native speakers of the legal language. Their skills as domestic US forum shoppers makes them familiar with the kinds of issues that are decisive in international litigation, issues that are much less familiar to their foreign counterparts. This explains, to a large extent, the worldwide diffusion of American law firms capable of offering a "better" (and more expensive) job than their local competitors.

Just as in colonial times, when the Judicial Committee of the Privy Council in London was the court of last resort for all the extension of the British empire, and deciding whether to decide, so today American courts enjoy this role at the worldwide level. Just as in colonial times when British lawyers successfully established practices in the colonies, so today their American successors do so in Europe, Latin America, and Southeast Asia. After the fall of the British empire, for quite a long time and until very recently, the Privy Council maintained jurisdiction over faraway countries such as Australia, Canada, and New Zealand. This was to a major extent due to the prestige that English law was still enjoying for wealthy local elites who studied in London. Just as in colonial times children of local elites would attend the London Inns of Court to obtain a legal education allowing them to return to establish a prestigious local legal practice, so today they flock to the United States, fuelling the business of law degrees and other degrees for foreign attorneys. The parallels continue.

7 Hegemony and Plunder: Dismantling Legality in the United States

Corporate market actors and their political cronies are busy modifying those aspects of American rule of law that may discourage plunder. They pursue extension to the center of the imperial rule of law granting immunity to corporate defendants. This desire to make a "plunder-friendly legal system" explains many recent changes in US law, from tort reform, to the alternative dispute resolution (ADR) industry, to caps to punitive damages, which well-paid ideologues of imperial law advertise as moves towards more "market-friendly law". In a now classic law and economics article published by the prestigious *Harvard Law Review*, two of such conservative ideologues, major figures in the field, made a strong case for the inefficiency of punitive damages against corporations while acknowledging Exxon, defendant in a multi-million dollar litigation for oil pollution in Alaska, for generous financial support![1]

Strategies to Subordinate the Rule of Law to Plunder

Establishing the rule of law always cuts two ways. On the one hand, legal professionals, the agents of the rule of law, might grant legitimacy to plunder. On the other hand, they might serve as important checks empowering subordinates by protecting their rights against plunder. Within the United States, big business struggles to transform the law (creating a so-called market-friendly environment) in order to render the United States a place of low-intensity legal accountability. In order to do so, the corporate actors need to curtail the role of courts as potential limits to plunder. Corporate political action, aimed at hegemony of the imperial rule of law, takes a variety of forms. Some of the political strategies are more subtle and difficult to detect, exploiting the very same need for access to justice motivating the struggle for legal accountability. The already discussed ADR movement, now transformed into an industry, is partially one such anti-law strategy, ultimately limiting rights assertion by plaintiffs against plunder.

Sometimes the anti-law action is more open, such as in much tort law reform – like recently in Texas – where punitive damages and other crucial aspects of the structure of the civil justice system have been curtailed by capturing the political process. Naturally, even in such cases, plunder is not openly a force behind legal change, and the reforms advocated are always accompanied by a variety of ideological strategies. Thus, ideology constructs different "good policy" reasons, rarely supported by good empirical data, such as limiting the "greed" of plaintiffs' attorneys (singled out as a class of economic parasites) or limiting insurance premiums that force doctors to practice "defensive medicine," each part of the all-encompassing notion of creating a "market-friendly" legal system which is actually "plunder-friendly."

While courts of law have no purse and are not therefore agencies of wealth redistribution, which explains their global success as reactive institutions (see Chapter 6), it is a fact that adversary courts of law can vindicate the rights of the weak in front of the strong, hence performing some limited distributional role grounded in notions of justice. Think about courts adjudicating rights of unfairly fired employees, or defending consumers' rights against corporate actors, or finding for accident victims against insurance companies. All these decisions are anathema for corporate actors because, when the remedial tools are effective, they can greatly reduce the profitability of plunder.

The corporate strategies to avoid these potential risks can vary in directness, effectiveness and subtlety. Among such strategies we should at least mention the sponsorship of the academic crusade in favor of efficiency reasoning in adjudication (see Chapter 4), arguing that distributive justice should be the province of taxation rather than adjudication (taxation is then itself reduced for short-term political gain so that, once the military apparatus has been satisfied, there is no money to distribute for welfare purposes). The appointment of business-friendly judges to the bench (often law and economics pundits) would be another one. In the decades of neo-liberalism many such strategies have been smoothly and incrementally intensified, sometimes but never very effectively resisted.

A more radical option, subversive of the established constitutional order, is that of using political cronies in a fully fledged attack on the legitimacy of the judicial branch of government. Such attacks also take a variety of forms. The most obvious is curtailing the jurisdiction or the prestige of courts of law, so that the potential users of the legal system either are denied access or simply do not sue out of hopelessness created by a pattern of reactionary judicial behavior. Both patterns have very established pedigrees in Western legal tradition. The first pattern is endemic to the development of the English legal system, where the sixteenth-century struggle between the Crown and Parliament was often carried on by subtracting jurisdiction from the common law courts, mighty allies of Parliament. The second pattern is well known in the United States, where courts of law, often staffed with reactionary judges, have openly engaged in repressive politics, thus losing prestige. Suffice to think of cases like *Dred Scott* in the antebellum period, in which the Supreme Court denied human subjectivity to slaves; or *Korematsu*, in which the Supreme Court approved the plan and practice of confining Americans of Japanese descent in Californian concentration camps. But even outside of these extreme episodes, the pressure is strong to appoint to the judiciary political cronies of corporate power.

In the common law tradition, where judges are the most powerful professional actors, fully fledged attacks on their role might be less common (in America, the tort reform movement attacks juries and the plaintiff bar rather than judges). However, in other systems where the judiciary is traditionally weaker, attacks on the potentially liberating role of the rule of law are more common, even in recent times. In Italy, for example, former conservative Prime Minister (and frequent criminal defendant) Silvio Berlusconi produced quite a stir by publicly stating that nobody who is not a lunatic could decide to be a judge! More generally, attacks on the judiciary as a communist guild whenever worker's rights have been recognized and business interests adjudicated against, has been a traditional tenet of conservative politics in the last 20 years. And in the United States conservatives de-legitimize judges by calling them "activists".

Plunder is a beneficiary of these practices. Attacking the judiciary, appointing extremist or crony judges, attacking the tort system, imposing ADR, curtailing jurisdiction against powerful defendants, are all practices weakening potential legal checks on plunder.

Plunder as the takeover by corporate actors of the empowerment aspects of the rule of law, manifests itself in a variety of ways. The end of the Cold War equilibrium witnessed a relatively smooth but incremental erosion of the empowering features of the rule of law (ADR, tort reform, packing of courts of law with extremist judges) and of other such aspects that made US law appealing to peripheral jurisdictions in many systems worldwide. Quite suddenly, at the opening of the new millennium, the dismantling of such features of the rule of law providing for consensual US hegemony became more dramatic. It is difficult in the present time to continue seeing the United States judiciary and academia as strong and independent professional checks on a democratic political process characterized by a separation of power and accountability. The judiciary is incrementally more and more deferential to a political process captured by specific lobbies. Judges, often less qualified than had been the tradition in common law, have become incapable of crossing partisan lines in gratitude for their appointments. As a result, the most prestigious branch of the American government has been short-circuited by the post September 11, 2001 spectacular attack on human rights. Also, because of a rhetoric grounded in a state of exception, the legislature surrendered almost the entirety of its power to the executive, simply approving without discussion a variety of legislations that in a few months turned the clock of history back decades, making rule of law exports much more nakedly similar to those in colonial times. Even the conservative American Bar Association (ABA), under the leadership of Michael Greco, today engaged in a world-wide crusade for the rule of law which has enlisted Condoleeca Rice and Hillary Clinton among its testimonials,[2] released its 2006 report finding that the US President's excessive use of signing statements is in violation of the US Constitution, thereby undermining Congress' role in enacting laws.

It is difficult, even for an international public opinion fascinated by the American style worldwide, not to observe these dramatic changes happening in front of the eyes of an almost silent US legal academia. Most US commentators are still busy serving as providers of legitimacy, contributing to a rule of law ideology that depicts horrors such as the concentration camps of Guantánamo (for uncharged people, mostly the victims of random roundups), the irresponsible and extensive use of the death penalty, and the brutish disregard for international law, *at most* as exceptions to an otherwise sound and deservedly admired worldwide US rule of law.

American intellectuals and legal scholars at the opening of the new millennium are themselves experiencing a decline in international prestige. Their ideology of the rule of law, marketed globally without attention to plunder and to what is going on domestically, might well be the product of a good faith attitude often motivated by justice (such as in the international human rights movement). Nevertheless, the simple-mindedness following decades of intellectual leadership, the attitude of always talk and never listen, of always teach and never learn, in a word the high degree of parochialism, has began to extract its toll. US legal models, though leveraged by institutions such as the World Bank, International Monetary Fund, American Bar Association, fail to persuade the cutting edge of international intellectual discourse, because of their apparent cultural and political naïveté.

International scholars capable of first hand observations and not dependent on local biased accounts, today resent the declining role of the legal academy as a powerful independent check on the political process in the United States. To understand the weak critical role of the academy, and more generally in the US intellectual discourse, we need only look at the hundreds of pages devoted in any American book on criminal procedure to the celebration of the procedural guarantees of due process at trial (many opinions or decisions of the Warren Court years). Unfortunately, no attention is ever devoted to the fact that only a very tiny minority of defendants (less than 2 percent) will end up at trial and will therefore enjoy such guarantees. Most others, overwhelmed by the superior power of the prosecutor, and without means to defend themselves, enter into plea bargains thus increasing the prison population of disadvantaged innocents, cheap labor, and prison business opportunity for corporate plunder.[3]

The rule of law, transformed into a pale rhetoric, is by no means an effective shield against corporate plunder and oppression either at home or abroad.

Plunder in High Places: Enron and its Aftermath

The word "plunder" evokes buccaneers, mercenary soldiers, and violent bandits. Arsons, wars, and military assault, are the typical scenery of looting.

Nevertheless, shouting crowds with rudimentary weapons are not a necessary element of plunder. Very different actors, in very high places, can actually be described as engaging or promoting plunder. When this is the case, a dense layer of ideology must be in place to preclude detection and an understanding of plunder and greed for as long as possible. Generally speaking, a thick pattern of ideology is developed around institutions, both economic and legal, facilitating plunder. Only ideology, produced by expensive propaganda and branding, can support corporate plunder for significant amounts of time.

The glittering world of Wall Street, made up of a variety of "prestigious" and wealthy actors (investment bankers, rating agencies, economic consultants, mega law firms, accountants, etc.), performs a similar ideological role, covering up practices of plunder such as those described in the case of the Argentinean default (see Chapter 2) in a previous chapter. Such practices and the ideology of the "efficiency" of high finance and of global markets[4] has left many victims – perhaps not directly killed as in the case of embargoes, drug patent enforcement, pay-or-die healthcare, or corporate mercenary soldiers – damaged by the consequential brutality of plunder behind the respectable appearance of the advanced institutions of corporate capitalism acting within their rule of law.

The victims of such ideologically concealed plunder can be located both at the center and on the periphery of the global world, and of course the amount of suffering is proportional to the weakness of the starting point. The Enron scandal is the tip of an iceberg including WorldCom, Arthur D. Andersen, the Mutual Fund scandal, the stock market bubble and crash of the late 1990s, and even the energy crises produced by privatization and neo-liberal policy, that offers examples of plunder right at the US core, of depleted pension funds, lost jobs, and years of savings of many innocent people gone. These are people who would never have thought that, behind the respectable world of Wall Street, one would find a degree of business ethics similar to that of the buccaneer. The very same law-abiding Americans who believe in the virtues of capitalism have been victimized by their heroes. From our perspective, it is not the scandal itself that is worth attention. Much more interesting is the thick layer of legal ideology that serves the interests of present and future plunder, of the sort that is suffered daily by telecom customers, airline travelers, and mortgage, bank account and insurance policy-holders, costing billions of waiting hours a year and still not getting an answer. Every American today is the victim of corporate plunder.

In the Enron case, the need to find a scapegoat for presenting as exceptional and illegal what is instead the structure of legalized plunder, has been so urgent that criminal prosecution (and its ally "deferred prosecution") has been unprecedented. Of course, with so much public attention, exciting career opportunities for prosecutors are there for the taking. Anyway, even some otherwise untouchable white-collar perpetrators, like Mr. Fastow (those that can afford the millions of dollars necessary for an appropriate criminal defense carried out by $500-plus-an-hour attorneys), have actually found their way to jail. Moreover, Arthur D. Andersen, the most historically prestigious of the big international accounting firms, has disappeared from the industry, having made a business practice of destroying evidence of its involvement in plunder based on white-collar fraud. Consequently, all of its wealthy partners worldwide had to face the hassle of looking for a similar job in one of the former "competitors" of Arthur Andersen. Their success at landing new jobs has been one of the clearest and most interesting examples of *de facto* merger in a situation of oligopoly in global services, where the Big Six simply became the Big Five.

The US Congress, where elected representatives of the defrauded people sit, was quick to pass a statute, the Sarbanes-Oxley Act, praised by the media and the government as evidence of the seriousness used in tackling these incidents. Criminal sanctions have been significantly augmented; restrictions and new disclosures entailing a significant amount of new paperwork have been imposed on any economic actor willing to operate in the United States. Foreign corporations have been targets for particular attention, as if Enron or WorldCom were not icons of the most rampant corporate America. A new institution, the Accounting Profession Oversight Board, displays the same amount of toughness used by Franklin Delano Roosevelt in dealing with the 1929 market crash (creation of the Security and Exchange Commission).

But this tough reaction, grounded in re-establishing the violated rule of law, has been mostly symbolic and aimed at the construction of a "state of exception" so that legalized plunder could prosper. Enron has not been seen as a structural component of financial capitalism, the outcome of an endemic conflict of interest producing a market failure possibly as devastating as externalities or monopoly. On the contrary, it has been portrayed as the rotten apple in a basket of good apples, whose detection and bankruptcy are actual evidence of the fundamentally sound nature of the financial market and of the US rule of law. This theory, advanced among many by conservative guru and appellate Judge Richard Posner, at an invited lecture organized by his fans at the Italian Ministry of the Economy in 2003, was accompanied by other corollaries such as the risks of distortions of the smooth functioning of the market produced by the introduction of criminal sanctions.

Nevertheless, the problem seems to be different. In particular, dishonest practices by corporate entities aimed at plunder are the rule rather than the exception, as denounced by countless reports of consumer advocates, prosecutors, and government. Secondly, the problem is not with the creation of rules on paper but with patterns of enforcement. Today in the USA, the Securities and Exchange Commission (SEC), as for all administrative agencies in times of neo-liberalism, is still underfunded and understaffed, so it is unrealistic to think that it can handle the tremendous workload of a monitoring and control agency in a complex market. Finally, the conflict of interest pervades the controller and not only the controlled. This very serious problem has emerged dramatically during the saga for the election of the first president of the Accounting Profession Oversight Board, where the accounting lobby has been able to torpedo qualified candidates considered too independent. Not much later the Bush administration named as Chairman of SEC William Donaldson, founder of the Wall Street investment bank Donaldson, Lufkin, and Jenrette. Donaldson, former New York Stock Exchange chairman and chief executive officer, was also Nixon's former Undersecretary of State.

Despite rhetoric aimed at showing the seriousness of the intent to reform the financial market in the interest of consumers and investors, after Enron little has really changed in the close relationship between plunder and the rule of law. The same groups that were controlling the game before are still strongly in charge and their action has been as global as one could imagine. Indeed, while some limits to the excesses of greed at home are introduced by the already discussed pro-plaintiff aspects of the US legal system, no such limits are apparent once the game is played abroad, where the legal systems simply are not powerful enough to limit defendant corporations. Interestingly, the rhetoric of the rule of law and of plunder as exception has proved successful. Many European observers, when similar cases emerged overseas (Parmalat in Italy, Vivendi in France), were eager to praise the quick and effective response of the US rule of law, thus making it gain back, at least among the legal elite, some of its fading prestige. All such professionally lucrative European cases are now held in the USA.

CHAPTER 7

Plunder in Even Higher Places: Electoral Politics and Plunder

The American concept of corporate capitalism, allowing for plunder of the sort Enron has demonstrated, as well as the myth of electoral democracy (another key ingredient of worldwide US hegemony) were hit hard at the beginning of the new century. However, just as the rhetoric of the rule of law has shielded capitalism from the ideological consequences of the many Enron-like scandals, that of electoral democracy, another stronghold of corporate plunder, has brilliantly survived a major political scandal: *Bush* v. *Gore*. (531 U.S. 98, 2000)

This first global political crisis of the new millennium already displays a post-modern flavor: the tension between the tiny local and the universal global. Indeed it unfolds in a small, almost unknown, little city: Tallahassee, the capital of the state of Florida. This substantially local drama, with a dispute over the recount of a few ballots, began on November 7 and was concluded on December 12, 2000, by what can be considered a spectacular episode of electoral plunder certified by the Supreme Court of the United States.

The way in which the most powerful global politician was chosen has been described in many quarters as a conspiracy, and it can certainly be seen at least as an unfortunate, organized political scam affected by nepotism and other less than transparent practices. Along with George W. Bush, major roles in this saga were played by his brother Jeb, Governor of Florida; by Jeb's appointee to Florida Secretary of State, Katherine Harris; and by five justices of the US Supreme Court (Chief Justice Rehnquist, and Justices Thomas, Scalia, Kennedy, and O'Connor) either directly appointed by George Bush Senior (father of the candidate) or by his closely connected predecessor.[5]

Much has been written about the process, so only a synopsis follows. It took place in Florida, traditionally a swing state, with its 25 electoral votes determinative in the 2000 presidential election. The vote was unusually close, in part because many poor people, most of color, had been disenfranchised by a variety of strategies often used in US electoral politics and quite widely known by the disillusioned public. Such strategies to target groups perceived as certain voters for the adversary party, started long before the 2000 campaign, and are now well documented in the literature.

From a global perspective, what is striking is the tiny difference, 537 ballots, certified by Harris before the US Supreme Court takeover of the issue with a judicially aggressive move that has no precedent. Some people argue that Gore won in Florida and the fact is that Bush received fewer votes than Gore nationwide, a structural feature of the electoral college based on the "winner takes all" model (another feature of US law exported worldwide). The relevant global effect of this election has been renewed waves of plunder and mayhem. To be sure, we are not arguing here that the election of Albert Gore would have made a significant difference.[6] Most of the state-sponsored terror activities determined to plunder, in blatant disregard of international law and of human suffering, were already well in place under the Clinton administration: from Iraq to the Balkans, from Somalia to Plan Colombia. There has been no substantive shift in US foreign policy, based as it has often been, on CIA infiltration, strategic opportunism, and the interests of the military. The end of the Cold War allowed the USA a monopoly on force; but corporate plunder was not an invention of George W. Bush. That corporate capital selects the highest officials (including the President) of the United States has been a distortion of US politics for quite a while. But certainly the style changed, with the sudden abandoning of a large number of strategies aimed at the consensual nature of hegemony, in favor of a more unilateralist conception of international domination. For our present purpose, what matters are a few discrete points discussed below.

First, the process of electoral plunder implicated the Rehnquist Supreme Court as an activist adjudicator, getting rid of its traditional reactive posture, widely celebrated as "passive virtue." Justices in Washington stepped in, taking the decision out of the hands of the judicial system of Florida, and with no authority to do so whatsoever, decided the case in an openly political manner. By acting as a captured political body, the Supreme Court damaged not only its own reputation but also that of the entire judiciary. One should add at this point that the post *Bush* v. *Gore* jurisprudence has only confirmed this attitude of the court serving powerful interests. For example, in the already discussed[7] decision on the Sonny Bono Extension Act (also known, significantly, as the Mickey Mouse Extension Act) in which the court carried on the business of the Walt Disney Corporation, adjudicating in favor of yet another, unjustified, extension of expired copyrights, the Supreme Court continued ruining the global reputation of the US judiciary as a strong independent body capable of courageous decisions to vindicate rights.

Second, a president elected in such a controversial way *needs* to seek legitimacy outside of traditional electoral politics. As in many contexts, in Africa and elsewhere, characterized by non-electoral rule, *war* becomes such a traditional legitimating feature of a non-elected chief. This explains the haste of declaring the war on terror, possibly more than (or in addition to) any other explanation. The sense of the disruption of the prestige of the American presidency produced by the Supreme Court is perhaps best conveyed in the comics of the Italian political cartoonist Vauro. In Vauro's comics, impoverished "Bosnian observers" land in Tallahassee to monitor the fairness of the American elections!

Third, electoral plunder created a sense of urgency in the opposition camp, and in particular in a large sector of the American left, to defeat the non-legitimate leader no matter which candidate could do so – thus "anybody but Bush." This cynical pragmatism, eventually defeated in the 2004 elections, forecloses detached critical observation of the historical record of the Democratic Party. At least in international politics, nearly everything that Bush did was already a tradition of US imperialism. The idea of preventive war might be an unpleasant rhetoric, but its substance has been there at least since the Monroe doctrine in the early nineteenth century. Some aspects of structural continuity depend only in a very limited way on the personality or the party of the president. The same corporate actors, interested in plunder originated by unrestrained expansion of US-dominated markets throughout the world, are perhaps the only true bipartisan forces in the United States.

It is not difficult, then, to express a judgment on whether aspects of continuity or aspects of change prevail in the present phase of US politics. President Clinton might not have differed in international politics from Bush, but he was more accepted in the countries that were not directly targeted by his militaristic attentions. During his tenure, there was an increase in the hegemonic role of the United States because of his capacity to display soft power. The attitudes of the two administrations towards international law, such as the Kyoto protocol on toxic emissions or the International Criminal Court, have been different in rhetoric. While President Clinton was confident that American legal hegemony would eventually grant control to the US mode of thought (and political values) over the criminal court, the present administration made the fear of counter-hegemony prevail.

The electoral plunder in *Bush* v. *Gore*, and the personality and the economic interests of the present leader and his staff, have provoked the beginning of a rather fast decline in the consensual component of US hegemony, and the Bush administration's attitude towards the United Nations (UN) and international law has contributed to this. From the point of view of international legal scholars, the Supreme Court in *Bush* v. *Gore* lost much of the residual prestige that remained from the glorious days of the Warren Court, a court composition and jurisprudence relentlessly celebrated in academic circles.

President Bush, with the support of roughly 25 percent of the American people, that is, less than 1 percent of the people of the world, has been acting ever since as the global decision-maker for war and peace, deciding for plunder generated by military might. What is striking is that his international politics of terror (shock and awe) has ultimately survived the global legitimacy test *because he was elected*. Despite lessons from twentieth-century Europe and elsewhere, where ruthless dictators have been elected to power, elections – no matter how corrupted or stolen – are still ultimately deemed the only relevant aspect of democracy, as the Iraqi and Afghani peoples are experiencing while daily suffering death and plunder.

Plunder of Liberty: the War on Terror

September 11, 2001 is one of those moments in the history of a constitutional order that qualify as revolutionary. Yale constitutional lawyer and philosopher Bruce Ackerman describes the constitutional history of the United States as a path interrupted by constitution-making "revolutionary moments," such as the Civil War, or the civil rights era. In these moments, the constitutional fabric of a nation changes as an outcome of history, abandoning the previous order and structure for a new one. While Ackerman used this idea to describe constitutional developments in the United States, the story of global plunder also benefits from this analytical insight.

No matter how emotional the events of that dramatic day were for the American people, the reaction of the United States political process has been so violent and furious that, in only a few weeks, the wealth of international sympathy that (at least in the West) had followed the destruction of the twin towers was dissipated. Little reasoned effort has been made to understand the complexity of the reasons that might provoke events of the magnitude and strategic importance of the attacks. Nor has any effort been made to account for different perceptions in different places of the world of the very same tragic events, which might have helped seeing plunder as one of the causes of the international catastrophe in which we are living. Suffice to say that the explanations that are dominant in the Arab world, such as the involvement of the Mossad, or even a self-inflicted wound, have been exorcised and banned from the range of hypotheses, without even considering what might have generated these suppositions.[8]

Perhaps there has been so little time to think because, within a few hours, the Bush administration declared the "war on terror," thus shifting the attention to remote theaters of war. This declaration was articulated in two doctrines, foreign and domestic. In foreign policy, the so-called Bush doctrine of "preventive attack" led the United States to quickly invade first Afghanistan and later Iraq – two countries governed by leaders that used to be allies of the United States in the confrontation with the USSR and Iran, respectively. While, as we know, plunder is prospering in those two countries, seeking a new legitimacy in the re-establishment of democracy and the rule of law, only an unprecedented degree of resistance by US and international public opinion, by a number of powerful governments worldwide, in particular France, Germany, Russia, and China, and a strong pattern of bloody internal resistance, has prevented an attack on other countries included in the "axis of evil" (North Korea, Sudan, Iran, and Syria) singled out by President Bush in a messianic address to the nation.

In domestic policy, the war on terror very quickly turned into what Nat Hentoff (in a book that should become mandatory reading in high schools) has called *The War on the Bill of Rights*.[9] Fundamental domestic changes in the rule of law in light of their negative effect on the international reputation of the United States, are relevant to the way in which current and future plunder might use the rule of law to seek legitimacy. These domestic changes, introduced by such statutes as the Patriot Act, the Homeland Security Act, and a variety of presidential orders, signing statements and enforcing policies following these enactments, constitute a "revolutionary moment" in the global scenario. Structural transformations of the US legal system cause the loss of a significant degree of the institutional appeal that explains at least in part its international hegemony. Because of the leading role that US law has been able to achieve worldwide in the aftermath of World War II, we claim that this domestic revolution in the rule of law is by no means limited to the United States. Internationally, the rule of law is now so intimately connected with imperialism and plunder that it is practically impossible to see it other than as a mere and pale ideology. It is now false conscience.

As discussed earlier, in the aftermath of World War II, the ideological component of US hegemony was mostly grounded in a notion of the rule of law that was called "adversary legalism" or the "reactive model of governance" or, simply, the "judicial way." The judicial way, as a theory and as a praxis of governance, has now been virtually abandoned and transformed into imperial rule of law. Despite its connection with plunder having never been tenuous, the current attitude of the Bush administration seems so despising of any constraining aspect of the rule of law that plunder seems to have entered yet another level, possibly closer to the outright model of brutish extraction for profit of the early colonial phase. Nobody has put it more plainly than Assistant Attorney General Michael Certoff, stating: "When we are talking about preventing acts of war against us, the judicial model does not work."[10]

In declaring the war on terror and in adding that this war will never end until the last terrorist with international connections is inactive, the Bush administration has declared the rule of law dead. The judicial model based on checks and balances and on a division of power, has been substituted for by a model of governance concentrating all significant power in the executive. An "alternative legal system" or a "shadow constitution" capable of excluding judicial supervision on all politically relevant issues has thus been constructed in the post-9/11 US legal system. Students of European legal history recall that, during the Third Reich, courts of law were operative and highly respected in Germany. Legal theory was flourishing. Adolph Hitler used only two tricks in the aftermath of the Reichstag fire. The first was to grant absolute immunity to the Gestapo. The second was to staff the criminal courts (holding jurisdiction on politically sensitive issues) with friends of the regime, granting such judges significant discretionary power in the interpretation of criminal law.

Perhaps the most significant reason for the prestige gained by the common law system (and by US law in particular) through Europe in the aftermath of World War II was its superior capacity to resist violent intrusions of political power on individual rights and freedoms such as those that happened in Germany, Italy, and other continental jurisdictions. Courts of law, strongly supported by fiercely independent legal professionals, have always precluded the advent of tyranny – or at least this has been a perception of the common law tradition widely shared in legal circles.

It is entirely natural, as a consequence of these historical roots, that abandonment of the judicial model would have been a very costly decision in terms of international prestige for the United States. When a country that consumes much more than its fair share of world resources and produces much more than its fair share of worldwide weaponry and pollution, ceases to care about the consent of others, brutally abandoning even the façade of legality produced by the rule of law, we are in front of a revolutionary moment. When the exercise of international power aimed at resource consumption loses consent, we can still see aspects of continuity in plunder, but hegemony has been turned into domination.

The US political system thus becomes an open model of "crony capitalism," disinterested in gaining international consent, and only interested in militarily dominating global markets, favoring a small number of billionaire corporate or individual super rich, who control the executive power in their own interest. In such a system political power obtains significant political, economic, and media kickbacks in exchange for facilitating plunder by lucrative contracts, tax cuts, privatizations, and other policies to open up markets for grabs.

Not surprisingly, such a model of governance, whose traits are today quite apparent in the USA, mirrors colonial practices of domination. It has been documented and studied as a backlash against democracy in such diverse settings as Sierra Leone, Indonesia, the Philippines, Kenya, and Ecuador. Yale law Professor Ami Chua, in her book *World on Fire*, thoroughly documents the results of crony capitalism as tragic for the very same "market dominant" minority profiting from it.

Nobody has put forth the idea of domination without hegemony better than George Kennan, the former ambassador to the Soviet Union. Writing in 1948 (when the pattern of disparity in the United States' favor was much less remarkable than today) he said:

> We have 50 percent of the world's wealth, but only 6.3 percent of its population . . . In this situation we cannot fail to be the object of envy and resentment . . . our real task in the coming period is to devise a pattern of relationships which will allow us to maintain this position of disparity . . . We should cease to talk about the rise of living standards, human rights and democratisation. The day is not far off when we are going to have to deal in straight power concepts. The less we are then hampered by idealistic slogans, the better.[11]

It might take a while for the intellectual elites, including lawyers worldwide, to realize that the election of the US administration in 2000 inaugurated the "straight power" doctrine described by George Kennan. One should recall the major accumulation of political capital generated by the performance of the rule of law against tyranny during World War II – political capital that the Bush administration has recently tried to cash in on (unsuccessfully) to force reluctant European allies into the war of aggression against Iraq.

Moreover, throughout the twentieth century, the rhetoric surrounding the rule of law never ceased to flourish so that detecting the changed relationship between plunder and the rule of law in the new "straight power" era can prove difficult. A high level of hypocrisy accompanied US foreign policy throughout the Cold War, so that events such as the September 11, 1973 bloody coup against democratically elected President Salvador Allende of Chile are accepted in dominant circles as minor deviations, since the CIA's political involvement has always been secretive. In international relations and in pursuit of plunder, hypocrisy is usually more efficient than the cynical honesty of straight power.

It took the Bush administration's outburst of unconstitutional political activity (including legislation) in the aftermath of 9/11 to change the perception of foreigners, both professionals and lay people, about the benevolence of the world hegemonic power. More than a half century after Kennan's cynical prediction, the straight power doctrine was institutionally in place not only in the relationship with foreign states and governments but also in that with foreign individuals living, working, or attempting to travel in the United States. Predictably, though the decline of the *culture* of the rule of law in America has resulted in harsh treatment of foreigners, US citizens have not been exempt from the warping of the US Constitution.

It is worth noticing that there has been no decline in the *rhetoric* of the rule of law when it comes to foreign relations. Bringing democracy and the rule of law is still used as a (less and less credible) justification to keep intruding in foreign affairs, often for the purpose of plunder. The constitution-making spectacle in Afghanistan and Iraq is a cynical farce in front of the killings, the brutal violations of human rights, including torture, perpetrated by the unholy alliance of looting war criminals and mercenaries serving corporate giants pretending to be peacekeepers.

Many observers resent such legal regress. William Schultz, the American executive director of Amnesty International, in a book called *Tainted Legacy: 9/11 and the Ruin of Human Rights* is among them. He tells the story of a 20-year-old man, Cheik Melainine ould Belay, arrested by the Federal Bureau of Investigation (FBI). Cheik was the son of a Mauritanian diplomat; he was in the United States to visit family and friends. For some 40 days he was moved from one secret detention center to another, with no contact with relatives or attorneys. He was treated harshly and humiliated and never told why he was detained. After 40 days he was released and deported. He had one last thing to say: "I used to like the United States. I was going to learn English, but now I don't want to ever speak it again." As Schultz commented "alienating people who had previously looked upon the United States with admiration and respect, who had wanted to emulate our traditions and learn the English language – this was no way to make the world a safer place for Americans. This was no way to conduct the war against terror."

While such practices allowed by post-9/11 legislation might not appear directly related to plunder (though it is difficult not to see plunder of liberty), indeed they are. Because it is the connection between plunder and the rule of law that we are discussing, and because the rule of law is largely the rhetoric of legitimization, its declining credibility in the United States is of major importance. Lacking the legitimization of the rule of law, plunder turns to straight power. Moreover, plunder abroad benefits from a climate of fear at home, and the dismantling of the rule of law as a necessary and exceptional measure given the circumstances, is a powerful vehicle to control public opinion. The practice of detaining hundreds of suspects in secret places incommunicado, with no charges and no access to lawyers or relatives, was called "desaparecidos" (the disappeared) during the time of fascist dictatorships in Latin America. In the USA today, this practice affects mostly foreigners but also American citizens such as Hamdi and Padilla, whose cases have found their way into the judicial system all the way to the Supreme Court. In 2004, the Supreme Court fell short of declaring their detention illegal, thus substantially deferring to the executive, while paying lip service to the inviolability of the rule of law. In 2006, in what looks like an ongoing tournament of responsibility evasion, with no actual practical impact on inmates, the Supreme Court ruled in Hamdan v Rumsfeld (126 S.ct 2749, 2006) that the military commissions established by the Bush administration violated the Uniform Code of Military Justice and Article 3 of the Third Geneva Convention. It also held that Congress could not deprive the Supreme Court of its authority to consider whether special military commissions violated federal law. To rescue the current illegal practices, Congress passed the Military Commissions Act of 2006, which set forth more explicit procedures for the military commissions and sought also to block the courts from considering claims of *habeas corpus* on the basis of the Geneva Conventions. Meanwhile Jose Padilla "reappeared", after three years of secret detention and alleged tortures, to stand trial in the Federal District Court in Miami, having been "added" to the pending prosecution of two other middle eastern suspects of terrorist conspiracy. In August 16, 2007 an ordinary jury instructed to apply an unlimitedly broad and unprecedented motion of criminal conspiracy (965A U.S.C.) found him guilty. Padilla faces up to a life sentence in prison for having "applied" to participate in a training camp, thus being a conspirator in the global Jihad.

The practice of allowing the detainment of "enemy combatants" with no formal charges, in inhuman conditions at the Guantánamo military base, thus appears to be *ex post facto* legalized, despite the fuss and expectations generated by the subsequent intervention of the ordinary courts. The current state of affairs allows, moreover, outright torture in the Diego Garcia naval base, and the outsourcing of torture to friendly secret services such as those of Morocco or Syria. All these practices are widely known and reported and have been legally challenged on a variety of occasions, but are substantially accepted by a US judiciary once more engaged in technicalities to rescue a façade of legality.

A few months and hundreds of American corpses later, the torture debate has been stirred up by the major US television network, CBS, providing images of direct torture perpetrated by US and British soldiers, in the Iraqi prison of Abu Ghraib. While as a first reaction Bush and Blair, true believers in a violence-free war, were expressing their feeling of disgust, Italian comic designer Elle Kappa offered this time the best line, having them describing the events as: "Humanitarian tortures, inflicted not to make the Iraqis too nostalgic of Saddam!" Interestingly, not long after the scandal erupted, at least two constitutional law professors, Alan Dershowitz and John Yoo, from places no less than Harvard and Berkeley, have publicly justified the practice of torture in exceptional circumstances on constitutional grounds: fully persuading then Attorney General Alberto Gonzales.

Nevertheless, as to the legal bases of the above-described plunder of liberty, little can be found, of course, in the constitutional order. Not for torture, to be sure, but not even for indefinite detention, without charges, given the due process of law provision of the US Constitution. However, because the US President is also Commander-in-Chief of the military, he produced in this capacity a sweeping "order" (later substituted by a Military Commissions Act) aimed at the creation of special tribunals staffed with military personnel. In such tribunals, where foreigners suspected of terrorism can be tried, all the landmarks of the celebrated US guarantees in criminal procedure, including *habeas corpus*, have been erased. Hearsay evidence, secret evidence, and evidence obtained by torture are admitted; there is no attorney–client privilege; and a presumption of guilt substitutes for that of innocence, like for blacks in South Africa at the time of apartheid.

The special tribunals themselves, enjoying the power of capital punishment (applied without a genuine guarantee of a jury), have not yet been used. It has proved more efficient, in straight power terms to simply keep "desaparecidos" in secret, and, as to the sentence, to directly kill "enemy combatants" by firing rockets on their cars, on the model provided by former Israeli Prime Minister Sharon and by his successor in office with leaders of political opposition. This happened to the American citizen Kamal Derwish, later labeled a thug and a terrorist but holding a clean record. He was killed in Yemen together with five other individuals, two suspected of being al-Qaeda members. The front page story of the *New York Times* reported "The Bush Administration has prepared a list of terrorist leaders the CIA is authorized to kill, if capture is impractical and civilian casualties can be minimized,"[12] which did not receive much follow up. Actually, the language of "killing" terrorists and enemies was consistently used by democratic presidential nominee John Kerry in the 2004 campaign, with no attempt to explain the legal basis for that quite primitive and disturbing desire to trade blood for votes.

The practice of using military orders to limit access to regular courts of law by suspending *habeas corpus* is not a novelty of the Bush administration. Indeed, President Lincoln did the same during the Civil War. However, after his assassination, the US Supreme Court in the landmark case *Ex parte Milligan* (1866), emphatically declared: "The Constitution of the United States is a law for rulers and people equally in war and in peace, and covers with the shield of its protection all classes of men, at all times and under all circumstances." Today the Bush administration claims that by attaching the magic label "enemy combatant" to a person, or by keeping him or her "offshore," it can do away with the limits imposed by the most ancient and admired constitution in the world (as well as by the Convention on Prisoners of War). Some judges of the Second and Ninth Circuit Courts of Appeals disagree (the Padilla and Guantánamo "offshore" cases, respectively). Some others, of the Fourth Circuit, agree with the administration (the Hamdi case). Sadly, the disagreement is mainly along partisan lines. The Supreme Court has taken over the issue and entered three decisions much acclaimed by the media worldwide as evidence of the continuing vitality of US rule of law. Indeed the rhetoric used by the court has certainly been that of the rule of law. Accordingly, the state of war does not allow a "blank check" to the executive. Justice Antonin Scalia, an icon of reactionary judicial politics and a loyal judicial paladin of President Bush, wrote a harsh dissenting opinion which persuaded many commentators worldwide that the 2004 decision of the Supreme Court had effectively limited the power of the executive, thus defeating the Bush administration.

Nevertheless, if we go beyond the majority rhetoric, we must note that: (1) the court has freed none of the detainees; (2) the court has not labeled the activity of the Bush administration illegal; (3) the court has used a technicality claiming that Padilla had sued the wrong defendant; and (4) the court has deemed sufficient guarantee for Guantánamo prisoners a pale version of due process of law – a review by some ostensibly independent body (which falls well below the standard of independence of an ordinary federal court). These mild decisions have been handed over almost contemporarily with another much acclaimed one, this time more directly related to plunder (of land) in straight power terms. In this decision the Israeli Supreme Court has (also mildly) criticized the Sharon administration's building of a wall, ostensibly to protect Israeli territory from terrorist infiltration and annexing more permanently sizable parts of Palestinian land. The wall was criticized as sometimes excessively penalizing some Palestinian households. Again the media have saluted Justice Barak's decision as evidence of the robustness of the rule of law in Israel. Nevertheless, the language of illegality has again not been used, so that at the end of the day, these decisions only reinforce rather than weaken the oppressive use of the rule of law by participating in the making of an uncritical ideology surrounding it.[13]

The post September 11 praxis is getting rid of most of the reasons for which the American model has been admired worldwide, despite its fundamental aberration in the matter of the death penalty. It has contributed to the transformation of a system prizing itself as the crib of the rule of law into a secretive and authoritarian model of government. Obviously the practice did not come out of nowhere. It has been encouraged by a political climate, sacrificing civil rights for the sake of "security," that has found in the Patriot Act the symbol of the deterioration of the American way toward a police state, closer to a grim reality than many living in it are willing to acknowledge. Ben Franklin's words are alive today: "Those who choose security over liberty deserve neither."[14]

As is well-known worldwide, the climate of a congress writing blank checks off budget to the executive was inaugurated with the vote on the attack over Afghanistan. This was a war of aggression, illegal *per se* under international law and the UN Charter, even if the UN Security Council had authorized it (which of course it did not). Nevertheless, the Congress of the United States granted war power to the president with the only exception being Congresswoman Barbara Lee from Oakland-Berkeley. The vote on the

Patriot Act, a very complex and long statute of some 400-plus provisions, had been equally hasty.

An early bipartisan act granted the government the power to wiretap computers of suspects without a warrant. This legislation, presented by California Senator Dianne Feinstein and Utah Senator Orin Hatch, was passed on September 13, 2001 in 20 minutes with a vote from the floor. The fully fledged Patriot Act was approved on October 25 in the Senate with the only opposition from Russ Feingold, a democrat from Wisconsin. In the House, the bill was passed by 356 to 66. It would make little sense to offer a fully fledged critique of this statute, which can only be defined as a major episode of plunder of liberty. Suffice it to mention a few of the most outrageous provisions of the Department of Homeland Security and the USA Patriot Act that crystallized the war on dissent, affecting libraries, families, foreigners, immigrants, and all Americans, including those who increasingly self-censor.

Under Section 215 of the Patriot Act, the Justice Department and FBI agents can access library user records. The law also makes it illegal for librarians even to inform their users that agents have examined their library records. The American Library Association (ALA) opposed provisions of the act that would make it easier for government agents to examine library records. The Library Research Center at the University of Illinois found that 545 libraries had been approached by law enforcement agencies in the year after 9/11. This included 178 visits by FBI agents.

The concern over records extends beyond libraries. Law enforcement agencies have pressed telecommunications companies to turn over customer records voluntarily, "with the idea that it is unpatriotic if the companies insist too much on legal subpoenas first".[15] Then there are the "sneak and peak" searches of a person's home without notice until days after the search has been completed. Section 213 of the Patriot Act thereby contravenes the common law principles that law enforcement agents must "knock and announce." The act also deprives non-citizens of their due process and First Amendment rights, and expands justification for detention and deportation. So-called "black bag" expeditions, in which officials can secretly break into private homes and offices and seize any items, are now allowed. Only after 3 months, during which time we may have thought that burglars had looted our apartments, will we be informed that the police actually did it. In addition, "carnivore" (now renamed DCS 1000) devices can now secretly be installed in our computers. These devices can read whatever mail we might have sent or even (using the so-called Magic Lantern program) messages that we have written but might not have sent. If we are suspected terrorists, everything we type is recorded.

Under the Patriot Act, non-citizens are being stripped of constitutional protections. The Attorney General now has the authority to detain suspects of "terrorist activity" while their deportation proceedings are still pending. Since 9/11 hundreds of suspects (mainly of Arab and Muslim backgrounds) have been detained. How many is not known, but one report suggests that by 2002 the number of detainees had exceeded 2,000 people and others believe that the figures are more than twice as large.[16] *Where* they are detained is not public information. Access to legal representation is at issue. Terrorism, terrorist organizations, and terrorist activities may be broadly defined and this has led to expanding the class of non-citizens subject to deportation. Nancy Chang of the Center for Constitutional Rights in New York City noted, "The term 'terrorist activity' is commonly understood to be limited to premeditated and politically motivated violence targeted against a civilian population."[17] Under the Patriot Act the term has been stretched beyond recognition, and is retroactively applicable. Furthermore, the immigration service may now detain a non-citizen for as long as 7 days without charge of criminal or immigration violation. Beyond such loose interpretations of the rule of law lies often flagrant disregard of the rule of law by those charged with enforcement.

On top of these aberrations, it is important to note that the definitions in the Patriot Act are so loose as to practically give a blank check to the US government to include anybody on their list of terrorists. A person commits an act of domestic terrorism if, "within the United States, activity is engaged in that involves acts dangerous to human life that violate the laws of the United States or any State and appear to be intended to 1) intimidate or coerce a civilian population; 2) influence the policy of a government by intimidation or coercion; 3) affect the conduct of the government by mass destruction, assassination or kidnapping."

Leaving aside the easy irony that this definition fits the international conduct of the United States, so that one can see clearly how acts of terror, as plunder, are in fact constructed as legal or illegal depending on the perpetrators, the report of the American Civil Liberties Union says it best:

> [T]his overbroad terrorism definition would sweep in people who engage in acts of political protest if those acts were dangerous to human life. People asso-

> ciated with organizations such as Operation Rescue and the Environmental Liberation Front, and the World Trade Organization protesters, have engaged in activities that should subject them to prosecution as terrorists . . . once government decides that conduct is domestic terrorism, law enforcement agents have the authority to charge anyone who provides assistance to that person, even if the assistance is an act as minor as providing lodging. They would have the authority to wiretap the home of anyone who is providing assistance.[18]

It is easy to see that in the case of, for example, Muslim charity, even donating money to an organization, without being aware of its full range of activities or of its record at the US government, might expose one to a high risk of an investigation for terrorism.

There is little to be added for our limited purpose. This is more than enough to explain why once admiring crowds of lawyers and intellectuals worldwide are now beginning to look upon the United States as an uncivilized old West from the perspective of legal culture, despite the professional prestige still enjoyed by the giant New York mega-firms and by the US academy.

For the sake of completeness and fairness, however, one should observe that there are important factors of grassroots resistance, such as the hundreds of American municipalities and local governments that passed resolutions in defence of the First Amendment rights against the plunder of liberty; or civil rights associations relentlessly challenging this state of affairs. About 400 cities, towns, and counties in more than 40 states, and the legislatures of eight states, have passed resolutions to protect the civil liberties of its citizens in the light of the Patriot Act. Unfortunately from the global perspective, what counts more is the spectacle. And the present administration's break with the previous effort to maintain hegemony by consent has been spectacular. All internal resistance has been less than emphasized by most media (themselves overcome by the corporate cronies supporting such authoritarian policies) so that public opinion worldwide does not perceive the degree of internal dissent.[19] Moreover, many American people are apparently not aware of the degree of resistance gathering worldwide or the degree of suffering and plunder inflicted by their government on innocent populations.

Lawyers, as a professional group, do not live in a world completely separated from their social context. It is therefore only natural that their professional perception is at least in part the product of the social perception in general. A loss of faith and a sense of betrayal from the "American model" are now more diffused, even between cultivated European intellectual elites, of which lawyers are a constituent part. Scandals such as Enron, and minimalist remedies such as the Sarbanes-Oxley Act, are themselves exacting a toll on the residual capital of the worldwide prestige of the American rule of law and of the model of capitalism that it is supposed to support. While intellectual resistance is sharp in authors such as Noam Chomsky, Howard Zinn, or Gore Vidal, professional lawyers and anthropologists (with a few limited exceptions) are remarkably absent from the dissenting voices. As professionals they grant legitimacy to stronger political actors, and are not public intellectuals with access to the media.

Plunder Undisrupted: the Discourse of Patriotism

We have singled out the Patriot Act, rather than other equally liberty-subversive post September 11 enactments, as emblematic of the dismissal of the rule of law in the United States, the core context of world power, because plunder was extended to liberty, a deep value of the American imaginary. The very title of this statute reveals a policy aimed at silencing or marginalizing political opposition and creating an environment allowing candid plunder.

Eric Feldman, a University of Pennsylvania scholar, examines in an illuminating recount those "traditional" Japanese strategies used to avoid the assertion of rights and the rule of law in what remains an essentially authoritarian society. He singles out mandatory or practically unavoidable mediation and repressive legislation as the two main features of the Japanese model of social control. Discussing the early twentieth-century situation, he states:

> Enacting repressive legislation was another way to limit both substantive rights and rights assertion. It was facilitated by linking political dissent with lack of patriotism. No concept of loyal opposition existed in Japan; rights asserters therefore opposed the state or at least failed to obey it and could be labelled disloyal.[20]

The United States, despite its pride in adversary rule of law and rights' assertion, has not been immune, from time to time, from similarly authoritarian phases. Some have been noted earlier. From the Alien and Sedition Acts of 1789, to Abraham Lincoln's jailing of dissenters and suspension of *habeas corpus*, to Woodrow Wilson's contempt for the First Amendment in World War I, to the so-called "red scares" of 1920 when J. Edgar Hoover deported hundreds of "radicals" and "Bolsheviks" captured throughout the United States, to Joseph McCarthy's hysteria, the passion for labeling dissent as unpatriotic or un-American has characterized a number of discrete political phases.

Increasingly in the public eye are cases involving American citizens. According to Nancy Chang, the Bush administration's:

> refusal to recognize the distinction between core political speech, which enjoys the full protection of the First Amendment, and the crime of treason, has produced an environment in which those who question the soundness of our government's response to the events of September 11 have been faced with visits from the FBI, death threats, and other adverse consequences.[21]

This prompted Representative Dennis Kucinich of Ohio to observe: "It appears we are being transformed from an information society to an informant society".[22] Nancy Chang has summarized numerous incidents, including cases of civil disobedience being considered as domestic terrorism. Political activists engaged in peaceful protest are risking having their dossiers indexed in a database where they can be accessed by law enforcement agencies. Peaceful protests are being infiltrated; people who attend rallies are interviewed and filmed. In Denver two prominent organizations, the American Friends Service Committee and Amnesty International were spy file targets, for which they are suing.

The US administration ushered in a right-wing notion of patriotism actively promoted by President Bush himself in coordination with the broadcast industry. The need for legitimate dissent was dismissed in favor of "balanced" reporting. Dissident positions are dubbed "offensive, irresponsible, unpatriotic" by government officials. This tactic of silencing favors plunder both domestically and abroad. Domestically, it avoids more discoveries of embarrassing stories, such as Enron, WorldCom, Tyco, etc., when plunder emerges from high places despite its being wrapped in the law and escorted by handsomely compensated corporate lawyers. Silencing thus protects the promoted benign nature of corporate capitalism, triumphant after the fall of Soviet communism and based on democracy and the rule of law, which requires a dissent-free society, thriving in shopping malls and politically disengaged. Abroad, where plunder and murder are now overt in the new colonies of Afghanistan and Iraq, silencing eye-witnesses is crucial. With US corpses piling up, public opinion – despite having been turned into quite a cynical, lonely crowd – might finally reject the fig leafs covering the occupation. Cinematic efforts like *Iraq for Sale* contribute to truth telling.[23]

It has always been difficult to defend freedom of inquiry and freedom of expression in times of war. This is one reason why plunder prospers in wartime. And this is the reason why declaring "war," both real or symbolic, has been such a diffused way to establish a state of exception to the rule of law. Suffice to think about the "war on drugs" – which conveniently fills up more corporatized prisons – or, of course, the "war on terror." Like the Alien and Sedition Laws of 1789, the Patriot Act came into being wrapped in the American flag, and supported by fear for national security. When surges of patriotic discourse and patriotic fever sweep the country, there is an immediate need to identify with government calls for national security. But patriotism may turn violent and ugly, and have lasting consequences long after crises have passed. It might even be the most powerful ally of plunder, when the rule of law loses credibility thus failing to perform as a legitimizing influence.

Dissenters founded the United States. In the nineteenth century, abolitionists were the ones who were willing to criticize the powers of the time for the end of slavery. The suffragettes were dissenters and women today have political rights. In the 1960s the dissenters forced the rethinking of the Vietnam War at the same time as the civil rights movement wanted to finish the job begun in the nineteenth century for equal rights irrespective of color, gender, or class; while the consumer movement fought fraud and hazards and the environmental movement sought to address the slippery slope threatening the future of the planet. But since the 1960s and 1970s, a movement to stifle dissent has permeated US society, whether in schools, hospitals, or the political arena, inaugurating a consensus movement that has turned most Americans today into pacified consumers. It bears repeating: plunder can prosper undisturbed if social opposition is silenced.

Let's get specific. First, in the domain of the *media* – two obvious cases are of Peter Arnett and Geraldo Rivera who both dared to tread beyond the elements of scripted TV. Arnett of the National Broadcasting Corporation and National Geographic was fired for his appearance on Iraqi TV reporting the same arguments of TV pundits, namely that the war was not going as planned because of unexpected resistance. He did not mention that resistance was against plunder and re-colonization. But that was enough. Geraldo Rivera of the conservative network Fox News was accused of endangering the lives of American soldiers by giving away details of a military operation while he was embedded with the troops. In commenting on what he calls "patriotism run amok" after 9/11, CBS news anchor Dan Rather commented, "There has never been an American war, small or large in which access has been so limited as this one."[24] Perhaps the explanation is that there has never been an American war so directly inspired by plunder and so difficult to legitimize as this one. Two newspaper reporters were fired for their criticism of Bush in hiding after 9/11 – Dan Guthrie of the *Grants Pass Daily Courier* in Oregon and Tom Gutting of the *Texas City Sun* – a clear message to journalists that they should watch what they say.

A second salient example of intimidation, in October 2001, included an influential Washington-based organization, the American Council of Trustees and Alumni (ACTA). The ACTA issued a document entitled *Defending Civilization*, a piece about 40 pages long in which more than a hundred allegedly unpatriotic campus incidents were described.[25] In the process they accused more than 40 professors of engaging in what the ACTA called un-American activities. They excerpted, and published out of context, comments indicating an overall unpatriotic academy. The report resembles a blacklist, but of course with the appropriate double talk. On the one hand the report says that professors have a right to speak, yet condemns those who do as "short on patriotism," all too reminiscent of Senator Joseph McCarthy's political witch hunts against suspected communists in the 1950s before the Committee on Un-American Activities.

The red scare, one cartoonist notes, has been replaced by the red, white, and blue scare. Anthropologist Hugh Gusterson, the first professor quoted in the ACTA report, rightly dubs its use of intimidation, scapegoat, and propaganda as control tactics. Gusterson also points out the historical links between war and repression of dissenters. After all, Mark Twain was deemed a traitor for opposing US policy of colonization and plunder in the Philippines at the turn of the last century. Gusterson reminds us that "universities are not adjuncts of the American government . . . and the purpose of the university in America is not to cheerlead for whatever chosen policy of the American government is . . . [but] to pursue knowledge and encourage people to think critically."[26]

A chilling effect inevitably follows prying into American lives while closing the door to government information, and participation in self-censorship isolates the real patriots who are attempting to save some meaning to the rule of law, and with it the Bill of Rights. Today plunder in the United States is carried on accompanied by the full array of legitimizing practices, to finally cut the possible counter-hegemonic uses of the rule of law: from limiting access to courts, to mandatory ADR, to authoritarian legislation, to labeling dissent as unpatriotic and "terrorist."

Fear (and money) has been used to persuade members of Congress to hastily give up their prerogatives of control, giving a blank check to the executive to carry on a permanent war. And even the current democrat majority, while voicing dissent to Iraqi occupation in a symbolic vote, fell short of refusing to refinance the mission for fear of being accused of not standing united with the soldiers or because of shared interests in the flourishing military business. Fear, leading to self-censorship, has been used with the mainstream media – transforming even the most prestigious of them into instruments of propaganda in the hands of corporate capitalists rather than critical voices. And fear probably pervades legal academia, thus explaining why legal education has been carried on as if the trashing of the rule of law has not happened.

It is worth reporting the words of Judith Grant, a University of Southern California professor of law:

> I am now experiencing what American legal scholars call a chilling effect, and I was indeed aware of it as a sort of chill running up my spine – a half second of anxiety, almost subconscious, the moment I heard that the Patriot Act had been passed. I feel that chill again when I realize that now I pause a moment before I write almost anything. I think about how a government official might read my writing if he or she were trying to build a (completely unjustified) case against me. I worried even when I wrote that last sentence, then, I worried about my worry. Might someone in the Justice Department ask: Why would she be worried if she were doing nothing wrong?[27]

If the rule of law has surrendered to the rule of plunder, to lawlessness, what future is there for a civilized world?[28]

8 Beyond an Illegal Rule of Law?

Summing Up: Plunder and the Global Transformation of Law

> To endure the global struggle between the superpowers is bad. To live under total hegemonic domination by one of them is worse.
>
> *F. Castro Ruz*

As we began our exploration of the rule of law in openly colonial settings, we could have randomly chosen from a variety of examples – Spanish, Portuguese, Dutch, English, French, German, Italian – all following a similar model wherein plunder and genocide were the norm. Colonial legal systems grew out of competitive contexts, with a variety of nation states claiming imperial status. The law, once used to justify "original" title to property for the conquerors, developed into a complex tool of domination; but its counter-hegemonic use emerged as well.

Historically, Western capitalism has evolved and spread by means of extractive plunder, which leaves associated social costs where they fall. These "externalities" are perhaps the most traditionally studied market failure. Modern corporate capitalism makes active use of the law not only to protect the distributional bottom line, but also to incrementally redistribute resources to stronger parties. As Karl Polanyi has shown in his study of the great transformations,[1] no institutional structure has been strong enough to resist a distribution of resources that overwhelmingly advantages the stronger individuals in society. The rule of law has never effectively countered this state of affairs. To the contrary, it has been responsible for enforcing the disparity favoring the "haves" over the "have-nots," because the protection of private property has been at the origins of Western law, whether in the USA (Federalist papers), England (Sir Edward Coke), or ancient Roman law (legal professionalism). Ruling elites in Europe and the USA have imposed and still impose the social costs of their own development on weaker people, at home and abroad, and the rule of law effectively and elegantly serves this practice. Westerners would not be comparatively rich today if we had not fueled our development with plunder, a gigantic arc of legalized externality production. Many super-rich Americans would not be so had they not captured the fiscal system, the law, and public discourse to their advantage – making the middle class and the poor at home, let alone abroad, pay for their obscene consumption habits.

The ideological construction of the rule of law protecting private property as a desirable aspect of human civilization *per se* has been very successful. Indeed so successful, that today even the dominated masses almost everywhere in the world would consider the imposition of a 90% tax rate on each dollar of earning, after a certain limit (no matter what limit!), to be a radical socialist platform, ignorant of the fact that this was the case under the Eisenhower administration in the 1950s USA.[2]

Unfortunately, the rule of law, as it is conceived today, is an effective limit on any challenge to the *status quo*. This is because it confers a degree of ethical respectability and moral acceptability to the selfish resistance by the strong and rich to disgorge, to the poor and weak, part of their unfair share of global resources accumulated by plunder. Rule of law rhetoric precludes many from understanding that, in the structure of capitalist development, *the rich are rich because the poor are poor* and that a radical redistribution of resources and a dramatic break in the institutional structure that allows this suicidal model of development is probably necessary at this point for the defense of our planet. The rich, not the poor, have unsustainable consumption habits. The rich, not the poor, are leading our planet to destruction.

The essence of the rule of law thus seems to be about protecting the "haves" against the "have-nots," by foreclosing "internationally respectable" governments from siding with the poor rather than with the rich. It is difficult not to see the rule of law as the most powerful component of the dominant rhetoric which singles out generous experiments in dramatically difficult circumstances, such as those generated by the blockade against Cuba, for attack under a false light.[3] Even worse, imperial powers employ such rhetoric to legitimize violent attacks on these social experiments, such as the successful ones against Arbenz in Guatemala (1954) and Allende in Chile (1973) and (dozens documented) against Fidel Castro in Cuba. Indeed, justification for such violent political intervention has been, yesterday as today, the protection of "US interests," eager to maintain the rule of law serving as the prestigious guarantee of conditions for plunder.

Nevertheless, we have also seen that the last round of formal decolonization, mostly involving African states, was the product of a harsh new competition during the Cold War as well as stemming from counter-hegemonic empowerment, itself grounded in the rule of law. As the law formally justifies plunder and favors the robber barons of our day, those seeking to redress the inequalities inherent in empire also wrested the law to serve their causes. Notions of democracy, liberation, equality, and fair distribution then emerged from within the dialectic between socialism and capitalism in the aftermath of World War II.

As noted in earlier chapters, the rise of the American age in the twentieth century has resulted from the development of the rule of law into a mighty and original institution, a model capable of persuading the world of its comparative advantages. The rule of law has been able to serve as a robust institutional framework for corporate capitalist expansion, allowing markets to grow and to globalize their reach. The tension between markets and democracy, between the "haves" advantaged by the former and the "have-nots" who should benefit from the latter, nevertheless required attention because, for a time, socialism was out there as a practicable alternative.

The attempt, in the West, to smooth the harsh consequences of market inequalities in order to dampen revolutionary desires, as well as potentially effective counter-hegemonic uses of the law, involved building institutions capable of some redistribution in favor of the poor: the welfare state and its logic of spending for the social good. This institutional model, based on an activist state, developed in Europe more than in the United States – in proportion to physical and intellectual proximity to the socialist alternative in the East. Even in the USA, not only government-sponsored welfare programs but also activist courts played a legendary role in an attempt at integrating the victimized black minority, the loser in the social resource distribution generated by plunder, offering racial integration for abandonment of revolutionary dreams. The international political and cultural prestige that accumulated with the spectacular role of the Warren Court (world famous for desegregation cases) was useful well after the demise of the welfare state, in order to illustrate the benevolence of the American judicial way. This benevolence is still taken for granted today, despite the fact that, over the last 20 years, discriminatory incarceration, legalized by the courts, has been the persistent response to racial and economic disadvantage in the USA. Data on social inequalities produced by plunder are appalling not only internationally – where countries victimized by former or actual colonization *de jure* or *de facto* are structurally prevented from recovering damages – but also domestically in the USA, where being poor is possibly worse than it is anywhere else in the Western world.[4]

In the USA, the top winners in the game known as corporate capitalism are about 24,000 super-rich Americans. They could easily fit into a small stadium. They control as much wealth as 90 million of their fellow Americans, or the equivalent of everybody living from and including Iowa to the West Coast. Data from 2005 show that the top 300,000 Americans declared an aggregate income higher than that of the bottom 150 million. The top 0.1 percent has more than the bottom 50 percent. Under the imperial rule of law, while the top 24,000 prosper and get richer, 50 million Americans live in deep poverty and the bulk of the middle class is stalled or sliding backwards. The only redistribution by taxation that has worked, beginning with the Nixon administration and continuing to the present, is that favoring this class of super-rich, engaged as they are in plunder under the rule of law. The retreat of the state from the social sphere facilitated big business and produced a renewal of the early conditions of colonial plundering worldwide. Can the law be used to disgorge the loot by displaying some counter-hegemonic potential, or is it bound to remain in the domain of the problem rather than of the solution?

It is impossible to give this question a clear-cut answer. To judge aspects of the rule of law to be illegal in a fundamental sense requires indigenous legal standards separate from nation state and modern globalized legal structures. We return to this inherent conflict shortly, but first consider the dimensions of the problem at hand. Plunder is such a pervasive aspect of the history of global capitalism that the ill-gotten gains that should be disgorged defy imagination. Some years ago economist E. Mandel attempted some accounting. He added only a few factors: the value of gold and silver pillaged in Latin America until 1660, that of the loot lifted by the Dutch East India Company in Indonesia between 1650 and 1780, what was taken by the French through the slave trade, and the returns of over 50 years of British plunder in India. The amount exceeded the total investment in all European enterprises operated by steam in 1800.[5] While these figures sustain the historical conclusion that capitalism developed *through plunder*, litigating such wrongs would be difficult to imagine even in US courts which, as we know (see Chapter 6), are not reluctant to adjudicate history.[6] Recognizing the power of plunder, however, and its close connection to the rule of law, could at least free observers from the dominant rhetoric of the winners. Capital entails no mystery. We can trace the plunder. The mystery is how its brutality, enabled by law, makes this vision of civilization look like utopia in the current phase of narrow thought.

Over the course of 20 years, the fundamental characteristics of the US rule of law have ceased to be seen as comprising merely one possible legal path, capable of coexisting with alternative legal arrangements deserving respect, understanding, and recognition. Instead, models foreign to US cultural imprinting have been abandoned, starved, or stymied because of the irresistible force of US legal expansionism, grounded in a "market-friendly" philosophy that is business prone or plunder-friendly. The monopoly of reactive institutions in administering the global rule of law has proven too weak to offer any effective counterbalance to plunder, both domestic and international, whether wrapped in expensive legal clothing or in naked, straight military power.

The development of an oppressive, imperial rule of law in the US-dominated world, exacerbated by illegal carpet-bombing, torture, and genocide, generates a cry for some substantial alternatives. These cannot stem from the outcome of an electoral process that pertains to the tiny yet market-dominant minority of American consumers, nor from courts of law which form part of the problem. Corporate capital pollutes the electoral process, rendering it unresponsive to a wide range of political preferences. The judicial process, itself, as we have documented, is similarly constrained. Countervailing forces, whereby the rule of law can take on new meaning, would have to reassert a political process capable of reigning in the economic dynamic, from the primacy of the profit motive to the primacy of the justice motive.[7]

Regardless of attempts by international financial institutions to present the rule of law as an apolitical technology that can be imported or exported, we need to recognize that the law (no matter its local style and form) is part of the intimate political and social structure of any society. In most of Latin America, long decades of US hegemony under the Monroe doctrine allowed for the oppression of most of the population within nation state legal systems that facilitated crony capitalism in the interest of foreign plunder. In Africa and Asia, the Cold War chess game produced both liberation and oppression. Everywhere, efforts to develop the rule of law have been gigantic failures, being clumsy Western-centric attempts by justice-motivated professors to intervene in the political process without sufficient power, money, or legitimacy. The powerful many times mentioned institutions of international governance have always been acutely aware of the political nature of the law, but only after the fall of the Berlin wall did they dare violate their own charters against intervening politically by constructing law as a mere component of an economic system of capitalism. Depoliticizing the law, transforming it into a neutral component of the economic system, was made necessary because the internal bylaws of the Bretton Woods institutions preclude political intervention.[8]

In contrast to these preclusions we have seen a whole series of World Bank and International Monetary Fund (IMF) initiatives wrapped in rule of law rhetoric that, pressing for "market-friendly" legal development, continue to preside over unrestricted corporate plunder. For example, of the 125 million people living in natural resource-rich Nigeria, more than 70 percent live today below the subsistence level. The average income of the country is less than a dollar a day. These figures did not change after the discovery of oil (unlike the early successes of distributing oil money to Iraqi citizens under Iraqi state-owned oil), which was plundered by Western capital and its local cronies. According to the dominant concept of the rule of law, not only is this social dynamic of ruthless exploitation perfectly legal, but it is actually encouraged by all the policies of privatization and "structural adjustment" or, as it has recently been re-named, "comprehensive development."

Yet, there has been a vision, at least since the nineteenth century, that law rather than brute force should predominate, thus inserting the rule of law within a conundrum of contradiction. Nevertheless, though plunder has from the start been codified into the rule of law and has provided perhaps the most powerful impetus for the development of nation state law, the law is not exclusively bound as an instrument of plunder. What tension exists between law as an instrument of justice and one of plunder, however, pulls heavily towards the latter. The Cold War readjusted that tension for a brief time in favor of more equitable legal mechanisms, as did some periods of de-colonialism or a few successful revolutionary moments. The problem we now face globally, with the enormous complexity and efficacy of modern legal instruments at the service of plunder, is, as always, how to redress this imbalance. A society governed by dialogue not war (cold or hot) must redress this state of affairs, pursuing, before it is too late, a more just global society and a renewed conception of the rule of law grounded in social justice. A whole series of initiatives can begin to reorient the march of law and to expose those legal growths that comprise the vast bulk of the rule of law (such as those imposed by the international financial institutions) that we must now regard as fundamentally illegal in spirit and practice, being contrary – in their net impact – to social justice, to the basic needs of the people, and for the planet. These initiatives – whose realization requires a cultural if not a political revolution at the center and in the periphery – span the gamut from strengthened small shareholder and stakeholder rights, to assigning responsibility for externalized costs derived from diminishing the quality of the environment, to labor law and tax reform. Legal regimes underpinning common goods serving the common interest, and legal enforcement for the universal right to free education, healthcare, decent housing, and clean water can be financed with the money disgorged by the ill-gotten corporate and individual profits derived from plunder. Taken together, these reforms might produce a renewed idea of legality, grounded in people's needs, and resistant to self-interested "professionalism," imperialism, and de-politicization.

Imperial Rule of Law or the People's Rule of Law?

In local democracies, which anthropologists have discovered on every continent, people exercise evolving local law traditions upon recognizing an injustice. In aggregate, local law traditions provide perhaps the most powerful framework we have for judging the illegalities inherent in the Euro-American – now imperial – rule of law. As the world has grown smaller, with people able to communicate instantly worldwide, local law is increasingly exercised in cosmopolitan contexts. Large numbers of people everywhere now have access to the internet, which can provide an interface between local law traditions and global concerns. In the Sierra Madre of Oaxaca, Mexican citizens at town meetings decided not to allow international mining companies access to mining opportunities because their reputation for polluting the environment, in addition to plunder, in New Guinea, Canada, Ecuador, and Peru, had preceded them. In the interests of health and safety, town citizens in a Connecticut town in the USA voted not to allow waste reprocessing plants to locate, also because their reputation of corporate irresponsibility had preceded them: dumping is a basic externalized cost. In the northern Italian Susa valley, people have vigorously resisted a 35 mile tunnel through the Alps to allow the transit of high-speed trains. Tunnel construction, decided on by the Italian and French governments with a subsidy from the European Union without consulting the people affected by it, will release asbestos fibers into local air, thus presenting a significant cancer risk for the local population. Similar struggles have erupted in Vicenza in 2007 where the Italian government, again without engaging in local discussions, has promised the US government a major enlargement of the military base Del Mulin. Because of alleged NATO (North Atlantic Treaty Organization) obligations, the government has not even dared to ask the USA what kind of weapons of mass destruction might be kept there. In both of these cases, people directly affected by these projects, which were justified – if at all – only at an abstract level, protested to the abridgement of local decision-making in matters pertaining to the use of their land.

The Shias in south Lebanon had to abandon the traditional use of their legal system based on mediation in the solution of conflicts over land (including waste disposal) and water in dealing with the 1982 Israeli invasion and years of plunder of top soil and water that followed. In this case, local law traditions failed to stop plunder by the Israelis, and so Hezbollah emerged to defend south Lebanon from continued expropriation and kidnapping. Resistance by the Shias to plunder has been labeled as terrorism by the international corporate media. Similarly, in Palestine, efforts to use local standards of ownership fail to stem Israeli occupation of the West Bank. In China, local rule of law clashes with water polluters; in Africa over rights to traditional medicine cures; in Bolivia over who owns the water – Bechtel or Bolivian citizens; and in Iraq over who owns and controls the oil. In Chiapas, Mexico, locals have organized in autonomous communities to reclaim their autonomy in decision-making over land use, among other issues. The Kayapo in Brazil resorted to frameworks of customary rule of law to reclaim intellectual property rights; efforts resonating with clashes in India over local rights versus commercial rights to the neem tree (considered the village pharmacy), and local laws governing access to water in their fights with Coca-Cola. In Argentina, workers wrested state law to re-open closed factories. A grounded sense of justice and fairness fuels the exercise of local law. Such efforts may seem inconsequential in comparison to massive extractions enabled by imperial uses of the rule of law, but they form the core of a different ideal of what is and should be legal.

Critics have argued that globalization in recent times is a neo-imperialist force that has left billions of people worse off now than they were 20 years ago. In the United States recent data show that this is so for 80 percent of the people even if, as a nation, the US still consumes, per capita, much more than their fair share of resources in this planet. Americans consume and pollute almost double the amount of the second most active consumers in the world, the Western Europeans.[9]

The spectacle of this wastefully cruel and unfair distribution of economic resources was brought to world attention with the emergence in December 1994 of the Zapatista movement in rural Chiapas, Mexico where previously, by 1992, the state (succumbing to international pressures) had radically changed land and labor law and had privatized state enterprises. At stake were human and natural resources and possibly oil resources. The Zapatistas moved from a *faux* armed uprising to create autonomous municipalities as a model of democratic government and initiated an international network – a People's Global Action (PGA) – for mutual support purposes, indicating that their problems also had a global spread. This international network included not only indigenous groups, but direct action groups and labor unions, in a search of new possibilities (including novel legal tools) to deal with economic inequities. As one anthropologist put it, we are reminded that the little guy still exists, though he may be left out of dominant accounts like IMF and World Bank reports.

As prescriptions from the top move from optimistic forecast to grim reality, we would do well to respect new possibilities, transformative elements often created by those on the receiving end of externalities. But the response comes in the form of re-branding, so that today, after some mumbled apology, the structural adjustment plans, without any significant change in substance, have been renamed comprehensive development approaches. They are still imposed on conditionality and simply attempt to offer a new respectability to the sad rhetoric of development.

In Argentina, resistance to forced adoption of US-style economic laws became the *asambleas barreales* – a network of alternative institutions that occupied and ran worker-managed factories. As we noted in Chapter 2, many Argentineans suffered from an imperial rule of law that tramples upon labor, local economies, consumers, and the environment. Prescriptions from the top that slavishly follow an ideology of the superiority of so-called "free" markets that violate countries' economic and political sovereignty, seem immune to the consequences of their actions. Thus Argentinean workers sought their own solutions, in their case through a counter-hegemonic use of state law.

An example of local law innovation comes from Mexico. In August 2006, the anthropologist among us (L. Nader) embarked on a field trip to the Sierra Madre in Oaxaca to interview older residents on the changes they perceived since the Papaloapan Commission had built roads into the area during the development fantasies of the 1960s. In the 1960s roads were being built presumably to connect mountain villages with the state capital so that their considerable surplus agricultural produce would find its way out and into the state, national, and global markets. As indicated earlier, the North American Free Trade Agreement (NAFTA) allowed US produce to compete with local produce. Instead of sending produce *to* the outside, what we found were mountain villages swamped with produce *from* the outside – foodstuffs such as corn, beans, eggs, and junk food, as well as machines, computers, and commercial music. We also found agricultural lands in disuse. Young people had emigrated from what were only 40 years earlier self-contained, self-sufficient communities, and were now sending remittances home, which people could use to buy global goods imported into the region. Older people who had been supporters of "progress" felt a deep betrayal. Development was not supposed to mean loss of autonomy and increased dependence.

Oaxaca is one of the poorest states in Mexico, and probably the state with the most diversity in indigenous peoples and languages. During the summer of 2006, and during the annual demands of the teachers' union for wage increases and state improvement of schools, the Popular Assembly of the Peoples of Oaxaca (APPO) was formed. Hundreds of organizations, with varying issues, came together from areas of community development, cooperative production, health and social services, human rights, women's rights, indigenous rights, and political action labor unions. They were united by the goal of removing Governor Ulysses Ruiz from office for allegedly embezzling or misusing state resources and using violence in response to the teachers' demands. Although these groups were operating within a non-violent philosophy, between May and December 2006 the region was in turmoil. People began to contemplate their relations with the state based on indigenous Oaxacan understanding of collective responsibility and customary law – when the group conflicts with individual wants "as a basis not just for 'oppositional politics,' but rather for the juridical refounding of a new state form."[10]

The network against bio-piracy, formed of local nodes, has another form and purpose – an international bulwark against the misappropriation of traditional knowledge. As discussed, the interactions of Western law with radically different systems of law challenge a number of basic assumptions in the rule of law that allow for legalizing the taking of old or local knowledge and royalties through intellectual property law. For example, in 2000 and 2002 two patents were granted in the United States for "maca," a high-altitude Andean plant used by the indigenous people in Peru and known as "natural Viagra." A working group was set up by peasant farmers (*campesinos*) and scientists to study maca-related patents that have been registered in the United States, and to investigate ways of challenging the patents. The Andean-Amazon initiative for the Prevention of Bio-piracy extends beyond South America's Andean and Amazon regions to include partner institutions in Brazil, Colombia, Ecuador, and Venezuela. While there are still controversial issues related to who should benefit from the commercialization of native knowledge, the core issue is simply plunder in the form of theft or piracy. At World Trade Organization (WTO) talks, India is pushing for a system that would control how corporations, scientists, and others can use old knowledge – native plants and animals, the neem tree (its bark, trunk, fruit, and seeds), herbs, tea, and even yoga positions – in relation to Euro-American intellectual property law.[11] Researchers from Venezuela to India are developing classified databases of plants and animals that have commercial potential as medicines and foods. Some countries, such as Costa Rica and the Philippines, force companies to pay millions of dollars for the right to "bio-prospect" in their jungles. How this will conclude is unknown, but one thing we do know is that recognition of plunder in relation to centuries-old knowledge is widespread. The imperial rule of law by means of the WTO agreement on trade-related aspects of intellectual property (TRIPS) might eventually be changed by people's rule of law, grounded in social justice rather than the corporate definition of economic efficiency, although how is not yet clear.

Cass Sunstein summarized the effects that collective, copyright-free projects known as "open sources" (such as the well-known encyclopedia Wikipedia) might have in alleviating widespread problems:

> Open-source projects, some of which are emerging in medicine and bio-technology, dispense with the protection of intellectual property law so that numerous users can contribute to improvements. In the domain of health, open-source bio-technology projects such as Bioforge.net might end up saving numerous lives, especially but not only in poor countries. Well-funded projects claiming the protection of intellectual property law will often do much worse than cheaper ones that benefit from widespread collaboration.[12]

The open-source movement encourages widespread, rapid development efforts by making it possible to collect and harness the collective IQ of thousands of individuals. Open-source projects have begun to blunt the tendency of intellectual property laws to create monopolistic conditions for plunder and may lead to significant reforms of those laws, given the competition created when collective knowledge can be amassed for the common good.

Few battles over resources approach the urgency of those concerned with potable water. The plunder of water resources, encouraged by imperial law, often happens with the complicity of official state law. There have been protests denouncing World Bank-endorsed privatization of water, and major river diversions have also mobilized local peoples. Overexploitation of ground water is a critical part of the problem of scarce water resources. The case of Coca-Cola in India is an example of local versus state law. In this case, *panchayat* or village councils in Kerela (southern India) authorized the use of high-powered electric pumps to extract millions of liters of pure water. The company drilled more water than it had been authorized to drill and the level of the water table fell drastically. In addition, Coca-Cola polluted what little water it had not stolen from the community by returning waste water to the aquifer, thus contaminating the remaining water. Women organized to protest about the depletion of the ground water and later a local doctor declared that what water there was available was unfit for consumption. The role of state law and local law gyrated. The village *panchayat* withdrew the operating license for the company, but the loss of the license did not cost Coca-Cola the support of state government. The activity of the women protesters, however, sparked national and international solidarity. Kerela's chief minister ordered the closure of the plant, and in December of 2003 Justice Balakrishnana Mair ordered Coca-Cola to cease the now illegal extraction of ground water in Plachimada. His legal reasoning was important in the making of a people's rule of law:

> Our legal system, based on English common law, includes the public-trust doctrine as part of its jurisprudence . . . the state is the trustee of all natural resources . . . The public at large is the beneficiary . . . so although there is no law specifically regulating the extraction of groundwater, the panchayat and the state are required to prevent any overexploitation of underground reserves. . . .

Accordingly, the court gave Coca-Cola a month to cease water extraction; and it ordered the *panchayat* and the state to ensure that this demand was met. The struggle over Coca-Cola spread to other areas where both Coca-Cola and Pepsi were extracting ground water, with Indian public authorities responding to demonstrations by resorting to violence.[13]

A technique being used in China is what one scholar refers to as *rightful resistance*, where aggrieved individuals and groups unable to use local law against large companies or state institutions turn to established principles to anchor their defiance when protesting for their rights.[14] In China, there is movement through legal means wherever possible. Environmental protests and labor unrests – by one count more than 200 protests a day – and the increasing use of legal systems, national or cosmopolitan, suggests a growing sense of justice rooted in rights assertion against the increase of brutal, state-backed capitalist practices. Although legal reform has largely been driven by the modernization movement germane to capitalist-friendly imperial rule of law, it is clear that use of law is double edged. Damage from pollution, in the Yangtze river, for example, can take precedence over more abstract notions of progress.

In one case a village doctor rallied farmers against a chemical plant dumping pollutants into a nearby river.[15] While the government has sent different messages as to how to deal with pollution issues, it has given awards to environmental activists as well as publicizing the problem itself. Activists know each other and share information, often via the internet, but they have not yet been successful at the local level where water pollution often means fewer fish and slime coating the rivers. In Xipeng, a doctor began a letter-writing campaign along with local farmers inspired by the Hollywood movie *Erin Brockovich*. The Center for Assistance to Pollution Victims in Beijing helped the villagers bring a lawsuit against the factory. Although the settlements were paltry, the village doctor, who was trained by the government to help people far from centers of medicine, concludes that he is doing just what he is supposed to do: protecting public health.

So here is an example of locals being influenced by an American movie about a para-legal who helped a Californian town's residents to win millions in damages from toxic chemicals in their water. The Chinese doctor was also influenced by his mission as a barefoot doctor, trained under the communist regime prior to the economic boom in post-1978 China. And while the USA has decried China's absence of rule of law for years, this challenge illustrates the flexibility and potential for growth held in local law traditions.

The gulf between theory and practice is even clearer with regard to official seizure of peasant land in China. In Shiqiao, the local activists read national land laws and concluded that the laws protected their land-use contracts.[16] The problem of eminent domain – whose use in favor of corporate development has attracted attention in the United States, especially since the Supreme Court decision in the Kelo v. New London case (545 U.S. 469, 2005) has blatantly favored strong corporate interests against small individual owners – is a problem in China as well. In principle, the power of taking private property from an individual, exercising what is known as the *eminent domain* power of a public authority, is limited to cases in which property is taken for *public* uses such as building a hospital or a public road. In the United States an incremental erosion of the public use requirement, sponsored by the diffusion of economic reasoning in the law, has reached the point in the mentioned Supreme Court case in which transfers of ownership from one private owner to another private owner may be justified if the latter, by his *private* use, promises a *public* benefit in the form of a trickle down effect for the community, for example by creating jobs or even higher tax revenues. Such a development strikes a hard blow to the fundamental principle of legal civilization, according to which big interests and small interests are entitled to equal protection in the eyes of the law. This plunder-friendly legal evolution of the law of takings is welcomed by many peripheral countries or emerging markets such as China or India where local governments routinely expropriate land from peasants to transfer it to multinational corporations promising to bring development to the population through their industrial sites. Where this "efficiency driven" (we now say plunder driven) evolution of the law happens, local people strive for justice. When thousands of Chinese farmers were outraged by the confiscation of farmlands,[17] villagers pursued national rule of law rhetoric and won significant concessions.

In the face of farmer rebellions, official China declared the usual priority, attempting to curtail potentially counter-hegemonic uses of the rule of law: "harmonious society." We now know, from comparative observations of colonial settings (see Chapter 4) what this means as a policy: "Harmonious society means nobody opposes me. No different ideas, Chinese don't believe in these slogans anymore."[18] For the government it could mean taking responsibility for farmers' complaints, legal or otherwise, or simply marketing harmony as a cover-up for systems that keep the poor from creating their own wealth. Sadly the government reaction to expropriated farmers' complaints can be much harsher. In a variety of settings, the peasants' struggle against injustice has been tackled with oppressive violence, offering yet new business opportunities for the corporate security business already profiting from plunder almost everywhere when the sense of injustice is defeated and the law is not available to restore it.

For example on March 14, 2007, Nandigram, a village in East Midnapur, West Bengal, was bathed in the blood of poor people, among whom were women and children, when 3000 strongly armed policemen and goons sent by the ruling CPI-M (Communist Party of India – Marxist) surrounded the villages and fired aimlessly at the protesting people. The number of the killed is unknown, anywhere from 14 to 100 according to the different sources. Nandigram had been a focal point of struggle in West Bengal for the previous 2 months, after the chief Minister Buddhadeb Bhattacharya announced that thousands of acres of agricultural land would be grabbed by the government for the purpose of building a chemical hub and a special economic zone owned by Salim, an Indonesian businessman. Unfortunately Nandigram is not an exception in West Bengal, where there is an ongoing attempt on the part of the government to forcibly acquire fertile agricultural land from the peasants. In Singur, in the Hooghly District, nearly 1000 acres of land are being taken from the peasants to allow Ratan Tata to build a small motor vehicle factory. Plunder is hard to resist and the official colors of the parties in power are irrelevant for the people desperately struggling for their rule of law.[19]

Adding to this people's rule of law mix, non-governmental organizations (NGOs) enter the fray. To be sure, sometimes global NGOs are functional to the plunder of sovereignty of weaker states and participate in the process of de-politicizing law leading to the triumph of the imperial rule of law. Their alliances may nevertheless vary. In 2005 Greenpeace launched a global campaign in China for the first time.[20] The targets of their battle were companies using toxic substances in their products, one of the principal modern externalities. To call attention to the problem of illegal dumping, Greenpeace activists collected electronic waste from China's largest e-waste dumping ground and erected a statue at the Eighth International High Tech Expo. Simultaneously, Greenpeace activists delivered a truckload of electronic waste back to Hewlett Packard's European headquarters in Geneva, Switzerland. In 2000, China legally banned the import of e-waste. Yet, enormous amounts of e-waste still end up in China, where workers break it apart so that the metal can be resold and recycled. This recycling results in serious health hazards for the workers and for above and underground waters. China is not the only site of such violations; Thailand, India, the Philippines, Mexico, let alone Somalia which is a global toxic dump, and most likely other places, all face the same health hazards. The goal is compliance with the people's rule of law, grounded in a social sense of justice and responsibility, which alone can give life to the law. This means that companies should take complete responsibility for their products as the full environmental costs of electronic devices begin to emerge as the life cycle of the product is tracked.

Externalities mobilize locals who carry with them notions of justice and injustice, and often survival. They may be indigenous peoples, democracy groups, or single-issue movements. In the above examples, local law is outside the purview of state or cosmopolitan law. It might involve alliances, or exploit counter-hegemony, but it remains a different force not grounded, as is the imperial rule of law, in the needs of corporate capitalist development masked as efficiency. People violated in their sense of justice or threatened in chances of survival (which is often the same thing) are inventing, through networks and groups, legal and pre-legal ways of dealing with life-harming problems and ultimately with issues of resource distribution. Their efforts are legitimized by social necessity. Innovative legal restructuring may be what will allow us to pass this planet on to our grandchildren.

The Future of Plunder

> [A] new basis for security and prosperity can be established for all . . . The right to a job; The right to earn enough to provide adequate food and clothing and recreation . . . The right to adequate medical care and the opportunity to achieve and enjoy good health; The right to adequate protection from the economic fears of old age, sickness, accident, and unemployment; The right to a good education.
>
> *F.D. Roosevelt*

> [A] government does nothing as well or as economically as the private sector of the economy . . . those who would trade our freedom for security have embarked on this downward course . . .
>
> *R. Reagan*

The capitalist welfare state that originated during European-led colonialism, spread only minimally beyond Europe. Its US version, captured by Roosevelt's statement quoted above, has traditionally been co-terminous with high peaks of global plunder and violence. Referring to the 1934 Treaty of Commercial Reciprocity, signed between "democratic" Cuba and the United States, which observers considered even more unequal than the one signed in 1902, a scholar commented: "In 1934 began the time in which it was attempted more violently and viciously to quench Cuban popular and revolutionary movements, while the doors were open wide to US monopolies so that they could plunder the people and the nation's resources."[21] One might recall another peak of global brutality and of domestic welfare conquests, President Johnson's Great Society during the Vietnam War, and make connections between the two tendencies.

At the same time, the welfare state has produced a remarkable vision of inclusion in the aftermath of decolonization. The European "social way" was mostly developed in Germany, Scandinavian countries, Holland, France, Switzerland, and Japan in the aftermath of World War II. Ideally, positive aspects of the social model include the following: the stabilizing intervention of the state; the strong role of trade unions in the creation of a secure and stable marketplace; a public sector of welfare assistance capable of limiting the costs of social exclusion; a strong system of public education and scientific research that does not penalize areas of knowledge incapable of attracting private investment; and a conception of the corporation as a durable relational institution that the state has created and will protect, in consideration for the protection that such institutions offer its citizens.

In the United States, the welfare state was radically challenged and diminished in the aftermath of the oil crisis of the 1970s. During the Reagan/Thatcher era, a neo-liberal imperial rule of law became one that does not compel powerful market actors to internalize their costs. The "victory" of the American-led West in the Cold War produced the perception that global developments can be governed outside of a competitive equilibrium in the almost exclusive interest of plunder – a victory that did not even require the domestic pacifying effects of welfare to market imperialist campaigns of aggression abroad.

Corporate control over political institutions, in the USA and abroad, is part of what we have described as plunder or what the Franklin Delano Roosevelt Administration regarded as fascism in 1938. As a result of these transformations, today, of the 200 strongest economies in the world, only 99 are states, the majority being politically unaccountable, profit-motivated global corporations.[22] Moreover we have discussed developments by which the most important role of global legislators is carried out by the politically unaccountable and corporate-governed international financial institutions.

Recent studies devoted to the Bhopal catastrophe demonstrate in a dramatic way the incredibly complex aggregate of interests and "technical problems" that make it impossible for reactive institutions to succeed in the internalization of social costs in the global setting, in the absence of genuine political accountability and legitimacy. For example, the estimated cost of remediation for ecological damage produced by Texaco in Ecuador in the process of oil plunder is in excess of $5 billion. This is alone half of the country's foreign debt. The question, even considering only a tiny fraction of the value of historical plunder in this brutally exploited Andean country, rises naturally: Who owes money to whom? Yet local courts are ill-equipped to compel companies to pay for the ecological damage, while the international financial institutions bully governments to service their debt. Promoting reactive institutions as the sole conception of the rule of law is thus a strategy to allow corporate plunder, undermining the very features of the legal system capable of confronting externalities rather than grounding them in an economic model both efficient and socially just.

Plunder is not always resented or resisted. In contexts of lesser desperation, or of more impotent ones, notions of seductiveness and appeal due to intrinsic characters of the neo-American model – a story of risk-taking, gambling, and glittering lifestyle – are needed to explain the success of neoliberalism as a practice of plunder. Ideological propaganda is possibly the only notion capable of explaining how the American economic model can provide an example to be admired worldwide – a model which leaves 50 million people in deep poverty and millions more in near poverty (Census Bureau data 2006, 12.7 percent of the US population) and one homeless person every other day dying in the streets of one of its wealthiest cities (San Francisco, 2002–3).

According to Gui Debord, at the end of the Cold War the "integrated spectacle" in which we are living – the synthesis of corporate capitalism and Soviet-style communism – makes it possible for apparent opposites to live in the same body: highly dramatic economic adventures in which the spirit of freedom gets exalted, coexisting with highly dramatic and spectacular exercises of repression, in which the forces of the all-mighty empire become the object of cult. Under these conditions, resistance, short of being an organized counter-hegemonic force, is a random aggregate of political and philosophical thinking, of political action, and of protest, rooted in radically critical and revolutionary political activity that is difficult to be seen as a "project."

What should we do if we are persuaded that the rule of plunder subjugates the rule of law and transforms it into instruments of injustice? What are the first steps to rid our world of the empire of lawlessness? Can people take law into their hands to escape barbarism? How can countries refusing to "go along" organize and propose viable and credible institutional alternatives?

Since the strike movement of 1995, France became the first capitalist nation to reject the American economic model. The French refused to begin to dismantle their welfare state. A group of intellectuals under the acronym MAUSS (Mouvement Anti-Utilitariste dans les Sciences Sociales) questioned the philosophical underpinnings of "the free market," the very foundations of global neo-liberalism. By the mid-1990s MAUSS had become a network of scholars – sociologists, economists, historians, anthropologists, and philosophers (not lawyers!) from Europe, North Africa, and the Middle East. Their answer to calls for France to adopt the American model and to dismantle its welfare state, was to promulgate an economic idea originally proposed by American revolutionary Tom Paine: the *guaranteed national income* (Richard M. Nixon advanced a similar idea as president!). Reform of welfare policy need not begin by taking away social benefits, but could reframe what a state owes its citizens. Power is being refigured, in this case by scholars alert to the historical transformations and possibilities in deconstructing economic principles that have been normalized and enshrined by the imperial rule of law.

The global outrage and resistance to the tobacco industry reveals an effective counter-hegemonic use of law. By 1995, 33 of 35 Asian countries had tobacco laws on their books. By May 2004, nearly 170 countries have signed the Framework Convention on Tobacco Control (FCTC), a demonstration that "working together, the nations of the world can protect people from a reckless and lethal corporate practice." The 200 member Network for Accountability of Tobacco Transnational (NATT) also worked to maintain key provisions of the Tobacco Control Bill: "This is a historic moment in the movement challenging irresponsible and dangerous corporate actions around the world, . . . it is no longer business as usual for Big Tobacco."[23] While there is a difference between signing treaties and implementing them, there may be something to build upon here given that the outrage has focused on advertisements marketing to female emancipation and teenage children.

The preceding examples point to a new form of international scholar and citizen activism. The additive effect might in the long run cause people to be able to differentiate between the light and dark sides of the rule of law, between the seedlings that start with local law traditions and then grow and spread, as was exhibited with global outrage at the US's unilateral attack on Iraq. If more widely recognized for what it is, plunder may become the target of public opinion and legal challenges. Lifting plunder from below the radar screen is a potential mobilizing force, although there is no guarantee without persistence, networking, imagination, and recognition of the difficulties inherent in deconstructing the imperial rule of law, in some places still considered to be a social good.

Exaggeration has often been seen as a key to public relations success with regard to fundamental aspects of Western law: judges challenging political power and rewriting the history of their country and of the world; rights enforced without frontiers; lawyers portrayed as living success stories; scholars engaged in highly creative intellectual exercises with little restraint from the actual technicalities of the law; electoral processes organized as time-circumscribed displays of personality cults (the so-called "color revolution" which is Americanizing many former socialist countries proves the seductiveness of this spectacular model); glittering and highly photogenic police cars; highly visible assertion of the institutional power of life and death; the law portrayed in movies, bestsellers, and TV shows. All of these are aspects of the law "going pop." Thus, what becomes advertised is not so much real and binding nitty-gritty American law, but rather its spectacular aspects. If, however, you are a victim of land plunder, polluted drinking water, or loss of state oil revenues, if you have lost a job or savings, or are the poor target of a fishing expedition aimed at filling up privatized jails – that is where the spectacular hits the ground and the user of law grasps the difference between the light and dark sides of the rule of law. Can we resist the empire of lawlessness with a one-day protest or with a well-articulated suit in a US court of law? It seems unlikely.

The strategy is to develop tools that expose the variety of Western colonial strategies used to deny history, and to develop a critique of ethnocentrism both conscious and unconscious. Did Cicero not remind us: "Freedom is participation in power"? A vision that capitalizes on historical experience offers ideas based on whatever deserves to be saved in the name of justice, wherever it comes from in time and space. Realized Western capitalism and realized European socialism must be compared on an equal footing. Neither, with only few exceptions, have been success stories over time. We need, as Margaret Mead noted shortly before her death, "a philosophy for our own time."

In discussing the continuities between colonialism and neo-liberalism we have offered abundant evidence that capitalism has enough strength and its actors the capacity to deploy an impressive aggregate of effective strategies to overcome difficult moments created by temporary triumphs of legality. Given the fact that, ultimately, the law in action is about politics and power, possibly more than about efficiency or justice, we need to acknowledge the impossibility of significantly transforming the imperial rule of law into a rule of law of the people outside of a fundamental restructuring of the political field. Such an attempt, however, needs to demystify many taboos, one being the *per se* desirability of the historical experience hitherto known as rule of law. There is a renewed need to tell the historical truth, not only to powerful institutions but also to the people, to prove that truth is always revolutionary and might, if politically organized, pierce the thick veil of lies that shelters Western plunder and historical brutality. Western spectacular and imperialist ideas of democracy and of the rule of law should be rejected. What over time should emerge is a very simple notion, today hidden in plain sight by a centuries-old dominant ideological tale: in a world of scarce resources there is a limit to private accumulation to be respected, and the rich (countries, corporations, or, ultimately, individuals) cannot be rich beyond that limit without being responsible for the poor being poor. Trespassing over that substantive limit amounts to plunder, regardless of whether the rule of law, by protecting the bottom line and all externalized costs, enforces such disparities. On this planet, resources are scarce but, if the rich were legally forced to respect the limits of decency, there would be more than sufficient resources for all to live well. Nobody would admire and respect someone who, at a lunch buffet for seven, obscenely ate 90 percent of the food, leaving the other guests to share an amount insufficient for one. In a world history of capitalism in which the rule of law has reproduced that arrangement on the large scale, admiring the rich and the powerful and the instruments used to secure such an unfair arrangement seems indeed paradoxical. People have to be free to build their own economies.

There is nothing inevitable about the present arrangements and their dominant and taken-for-granted certainties. Indeed, it may be that the present legal and political hegemonies suffer from lack: the lack of world culture and of global political realism.

Notes to Text

Introduction

1 Giorgio Agamben, *The State of Exception*, (trans. Kevin Atiell), Chicago: University of Chicago Press, 2005.
2 Discussed in Chapter 2.
3 See Tariq Ali, *Bush in Babylon: the Recolonization of Iraq*, New York: Verso, 2003, p. 177.
4 An interesting examination of this question can be found in W.J. Mommsen & J.A. De Moor (eds), *European Expansion and Law – the Encounter of European and Indigenous Law in 19th- and 20th-Century Africa and Asia*, Gordonsville: Berg Publishers, 1992.

Chapter 1

1 Michael Polanyi, *The Tacit Dimension*, Magnolia: Peter Smith Publisher, 1983.
2 For power implications of vague meanings, or what he calls "plasticwords," see Uwe Porsken, *Plastikworther. Die Sprache einer internationalen Diktatur*, Stuttgart: Klett-Cotta, 1989. For a similar observation on the rule of law as a vague notion, see G. Ajani, "Navigatori e giuristi. A proposito del trapianto de nozioni vaghe," in *Io comparo, tu compari egli compara: che cosa, come, perché* (Valentina Bertorello, ed.), Milan: Giuffre', 2003, pp. 3–18.
3 See D. Lindsay Keir, *The Constitutional History of Modern Britain 1485–1937*, London: Adam & Charles Black, 1947.

4 James Madison, "The Federalist No. 10: The utility of the Union as a safeguard against domestic faction and insurrection," *Daily Advertiser* Thursday November 22, 1787.

5 Niall Ferguson, *Empire: How Britain Made the Modern World*, New York: Penguin Books, 2004.

6 See World Bank, *Initiatives in Legal and Judicial Reform*, Washington, DC: The World Bank, 2004, p. 4.

7 At a later stage we will discuss the implications of doctrinal notions developed in a historical phase of hard political state sovereignty. These doctrines were then used in the current phase of imperial "soft" corporate sovereignty, in which the state is governed by economic forces, as opposed to governing them. See Chapter 6.

8 *The New York Times* September 21, 2005, CLV "Deep flaws and little justice in China's court system," article by Joseph Kahan.

9 See data offered by the New York-based "Innocence Project," a non-profit-based legal clinic which only handles cases where post-conviction DNA testing of evidence can yield conclusive proof of innocence. See http://www.innocenceproject.org/.

10 T. Ruskola, *Legal Orientalism*, Michigan Law Review 101, No. 1, October 2002, p. 179.

11 Cited in J. Rifkin, *The European Dream: How Europe's Vision of the Future is Quietly Eclipsing the American Dream*, New York: Penguin, 2004.

12 Hegemony has been a key concept in Gramsci's reflections. It has been developed, outside of any systematic effort, throughout his work. See Antonio Gramsci, *Quaderni Dal Carcere*, Istituto Gramsci, a cura di V. Gerratana, Torino: Einaudi, 1975. English translation by Q. Hoare & G. Nowell Smith (eds) *Selections from the Prison Notebooks of Antonio Gramsci*, New York: International Publishers, 1971. A good selection of Gramsci's work can be found in D. Forgacs (ed.) *An Antonio Gramsci Reader: Selected Writings, 1916–1935*, New York: Schocken Books, 1988.

13 See Louis Althusser, *Lo Stato ed i suoi apparati*, Rome: Editori Riuniti, 1997.

14 See Louis Althusser, *Lenin and Philosophy and Other Essays* (F. Jameston, ed.), London: NLB Press, 1972. See also the fully fledged overtaking of ideology as a class-specific device in L. Althusser & E. Balibar, *Reading Capital*, Verso Classics Series, London: Verso, 1997.

15 We here mostly refer to Michel Foucault, *Archaeology of Knowledge*, New York: Harper & Row, 1972. The basic notions approached in the text, however, have been developed through Foucault's massive scholarly production. A classic English language selection is in P. Rabinow (ed.) *The Foucault Reader*, New York: Pantheon, 1984.

16 M. Chanock, *Law, Custom, and Social Order: the Colonial Experience in Malawi and Zambia*, Cambridge, UK: Cambridge University Press, 1985.

17 See Laura Nader, *Harmony Ideology*, Stanford, CA: Stanford University Press, 1990. ADR can be justified both as dictated by the needs of efficiency and by a return to tradition. See also Laura Nader, *The Life of the Law*, Berkeley, CA: University of California Press, 2002.

18 Unfortunately such racist stereotyping has also contaminated products aimed at being critical, such as the recent, award-winning, hit movie *Fahrenheit 911* by Michael Moore.

19 Also recently described as "context of conditionality." See Sally Falk Moore, "An international legal regime and the context of conditionality" in *Transnational Legal Processes* (M. Likosky, ed.), London: Macmillan Publishers, 2002, p. 33.

20 This is the classic theory of Alan Watson, *Legal Transplants: an Approach to Comparative Law*, Athens, GA: University of Georgia Press, 1974. On the notion of prestige, see also Rodolfo Sacco, "Legal formants: a dynamic approach to comparative law, Part 1," *American Journal of Comparative Law* 39, 1991, p. 1; and, more critically, Elisabetta Grande, *Imitazione e Diritto*, Torino: Giappichelli, 2001.

21 See Eduardo Galeano, *Open Veins of Latin America: Five Centuries of the Pillage of a Continent* (trans. Cedric Belfrage), New York: Monthly Review Press, 1973 (reprinted 1997).

22 Similarly, without protectionist strategies, it would have been impossible for the emerging industrial effort to unfold and develop in the Industrial Revolution. A classic economic history, focusing on the institutional setting but almost neglecting plunder, is Douglass North & Robert Paul Thomas, *The Rise of the Western World: a New Economic History*, New York: Cambridge University Press, 1973.

23 See E. Wolf, *Europe and the People Without History*, Berkeley, CA: University of California Press, 1982.

24 See Frantz Fanon, *The Wretched of the Earth*, New York: Grove Press, 1965.

25 See Niall Ferguson, note 5.

26 Issa G. Shivji, "Law's empire and the empire of lawlessness: beyond the Anglo-American law," *Law, Social Justice and Global Development* (electronic law journal), 2003:http://www2.warwick.ac.uk/fac/soc/law/elj/lgd/2003-1/shivjiz/shivjiz.rtf.

27 From the bestseller by conservative, London School of Economics, political scientist Francis Fukuyama, *The End of History and the Last Man*, New York: Avon Books, 1992.

28 See Thomas Friedman, *The Lexus and the Olive Tree: Understanding Globalization*, New York: Anchor Books, 1999.

29 Ellen Hertz & Laura Nader, "On Thomas L. Friedman's The Lexus and The Olive Tree," in *Why America's Top Pundits are Wrong about the World* (Catherine Besteman & Hugh Gusterson, eds), Berkeley, CA: University of California Press, 2005, pp. 121–37.

30 See Rudolf B. Schlesinger, Hans W. Baade, Peter H. Herzog & Edward M. Wise, *Comparative Law*, New York: Foundation Press, 1998, p. 283.

31 See discussion in Chapter 5.
32 A. Smith, *The Wealth of Nations*, New York: Bantam Classics, 2003.
33 How this control through law operates has been described in M. Chanock, see note 16.
34 Richard Falk, “Re-framing the legal agenda of world order in the course of a turbulent century,” in *Transnational Legal Processes* (Michael Likosky, ed.), New York: Cambridge University Press, 2002. Available at: http://www.wws.princeton.edu/~rfalk/papers/in.
35 The construction of a new confrontation, substituting Cold War with Islamism, is the political “contribution” of Samuel P. Huntington, “The clash of civilizations?,” *Foreign Affairs Journal* 72, 1993, p. 22. Michel Foucault expounds on a similar idea from a post-structuralist perspective in *Politics, Philosophy, Culture and other Writings*, New York: Routledge, Chapman & Hall, 1990.
36 See, at least, A.M. Weisburd, *The Use of Force: the Practice of States since World War II*, Philadelphia: Pennsylvania State University Press, 1997.
37 For an extreme position on the right, see E.N. Luttwak, “Give war a chance,” *Foreign Affairs*, 78, 1999, p. 4.
38 See J.S. Nye, *Bound to Lead: the Changing Nature of American Power*, New York: Basic Books, 1990.
39 The shift of leftist paradigms to notions compatible with the official dogma of neo-liberalism is usually associated with Tony Blair’s New Labour. The intellectual rationalization of this evolution is the successful volume of A. Giddens, *The Third Way: the Renewal of Social Democracy*, London: Polity Press, 1998. But the consequences of refusal to adapt to the new post-Cold War economic policy are best appreciated by considering the forced resignation of German Chancellor Oskar Lafontaine in 1998, substituted by the “new leftist” paradigm of Chancellor Schroeder from the same party. See R. Falk, note 34.

Chapter 2

1 G.A. Collier, *Basta! Land and the Zapatista Rebellion in Chiapas*, Oakland, CA: Food First, 1994.
2 Id.
3 Interestingly, they have been exempted from laws forbidding gambling. See William Cronon, *Nature’s Metropolis: Chicago and the Great West*, New York: W.W. Norton & Co., 1991.
4 This aspect is thoroughly discussed in Yves Dezalay & Brian Garth, *The Internationalization of Palace Wars: Lawyers, Economists and the Contest to Transform Latin American States*, Chicago Series in Law and Society, Chicago: University of Chicago Press, 2002.

5 Frank Partnoy, *FIASCO: the Inside Story of a Wall Street Trader*, New York: Penguin Books, 1998.

6 Among such actors, one should mention at least the greedy industrialists who, after exporting hard currency to the United States, abandoned their companies overnight, only to return later with the police to reclaim them from the worker's cooperatives that restored the productive process. Such workers, like the Trabajadores Desocupados de la Matanza, are struggling to resist, physically and legally, another looting expedition. They are the heroes of a different model of development struggling for justice to take the form of a fair distribution of resources in the "emerging" economies. By successfully carrying on the business abandoned by their former masters, outside of a hierarchical model but within a cooperative effort, they are living evidence that plunder might not be the only force behind economic *thriving* and that once exposed it can be resisted. One should watch the documentary movie *The Take* (2002) by Naomi Klein and Avi Lewis.

7 See, for a recent account, David Harvey, *A Brief History of Neoliberalism*, Oxford: Oxford University Press, 2005.

8 See Duncan Kennedy, "Two globalizations of law and legal thought 1850–1968," *Suffolk Law Review* 36, 2003, p. 631.

9 See Richard Posner, *Economic Analysis of Law*, New York: Little, Brown & Co., 1986, for a restatement of this position as championed by the law and economics movement in the USA.

10 See Chapter 3 and A. Santos, "The World Bank's uses of the 'rule of law' promise," in *The New Law and Economic Development: a Critical Appraisal* (D.M. Trubeck & A. Santos), Cambridge, UK: Cambridge University Press, 2006, p. 253.

11 See World Bank, *World Development Report 1999: Entering the 21st Century*, Washington, DC: World Bank, 1999.

12 See Eric Feldman, *The Ritual of Rights in Japan*, New York: Cambridge University Press, 2000.

13 Vincent Tucker, "The myth of development: a critique of Eurocentric discourse," in *Critical Development Theory: Contributions to a New Paradigm* (R. Munck & D. O'Hearn, eds), London: Zed Books, 1999. See also S. Latouche, *Sopravvivere allo sviluppo*, Torino: Bollati Boringhieri, 2005.

14 Giles Mohan, Ed Brown, Bob Milward & Alfred B. Zack-Williams, *Structural Adjustment. Theory, Practice and Impact*, London: Routledge, 2000.

15 See, for example, Article IV, 3b of the articles of agreement that funded the IMF, available at www.imf.org, as well as Article IV, sec. 10 of the agreement establishing the International Bank of Reconstruction and Development termed "political activity prohibited," available at http://siteresources.worldbank.org/ibrd/.

16 T. Ferguson, *The Third World and Decision Making in the International Monetary Fund: the Quest for Full and Effective Participation*, London: Pinter Publishers, 1988, p. 26.
17 Bob Milward, "What is structural adjustment?," in G. Mohan et al., 2000, p. 26, see note 14.
18 The best description of SAPs available is the movie by Stephanie Black, *Life+Debt* (2001), discussing SAP and neo-liberal policy in Jamaica.
19 J.L. Dietz, "Debt, international corporations and economic change in Latin America and the Caribbean," *Latin American Perspectives* 55, 1987, p. 509.
20 Typically, decolonization left many new free countries in desperate need of cash because of colonialist withdrawal. This is where the IMF's short-term, full interest loans come into the picture. The oil crisis of the 1970s produced defaults and a second round of conditional loans.
21 Bob Milward, "What is structural adjustment?," in G. Mohan et al., 2000, p. 33, see note 14.
22 See Elisabetta Grande, *Il terzo strike*, Palermo: Sellerio, 2007.

Chapter 3

1 William Blackstone, *Commentaries on the Laws of England*, (1765), Facsimile of the first edition. Chicago, University of Chicago Press, 1979.
2 See *Marbury* v. *Madison*, 5 US 137 (1803).
3 See A. de Tocqueville, *Democracy in America* (R.D. Heffner, ed.), New York: Signet Classics, 2001.
4 For a recent, fascinating discussion of their credo and ideology, see Joseph J. Ellis, *Founding Brothers: the Revolutionary Generation*, New York: Random House Publishers, First Vintage Books Edition, 2002.
5 Id.
6 See W. Wiegand, "The reception of American law in Europe," *American Journal of Comparative Law* 39, 1991, p. 229.
7 David Wilkins, *American Indian Sovereignty and the U.S. Supreme Court: the Masking Justice*, Austin: University of Texas Press, 1997.
8 Laura Nader & Jay Ou, "Idealization and power: legality and tradition in Native American law," *Oklahoma City University Law Review* 23, 1998, p. 13.
9 John Locke, *Two Treatises of Government*, London, 1698.
10 Emmerich de Vattel, *The Law of Nations*, London: G.G. & J. Robinson, 1797 (reprinted 2005 by Clarke, NJ: Law Book Exchange Ltd).
11 Teemu Ruskola. "Law's empire: the legal construction of 'America' in the 'District of China'," available at: http://papers.ssrn.com/sol3/papers.cfm?abstract_id=440641.

12 There is a classic discussion in Eduardo Galeano, *Open Veins of Latin America: Five Centuries of the Pillage of a Continent* (trans. Cedric Belfrage), New York: Monthly Review Press, 1973 (reprinted 1997).

13 These and many more episodes are discussed in Eduardo Galeano, see note 12.

14 Id.

15 Stanley B. Lubman, *Bird in a Cage: Legal Reform in China After Mao*, Stanford: Stanford University Press, 1999, p. 198.

16 R. David, *Les Grands Systèmes de Droit Contemporaine*, Paris, 1966. English translation by R. David & E.C. Brierley, *Major Legal Systems in the World Today. An Introduction to the Comparative Study of Law*, 2nd edn., London: Stevens, 1978.

17 Particularly significant here is the recent World Bank-sponsored literature of law and finance devoted to "legal origins." Such a brand of scholarship, mostly carried on at the prestigious Economics Department at Harvard, tracks the main cause of underdevelopment to formalistic civilian legal origins. See R. La Porta, F. Lopez de Silanes, A. Schleifer & R. Vishny, "The quality of government," *Journal of Law Economics and Organization* 25, 1997, p. 1, and R. La Porta, F. Lopez de Silanes, A. Schleifer & R. Vishny, "Law and finance," *Journal of Political Economy* 106, 1998, p. 6.

18 James Gardner, *Legal Imperialism: American Lawyers and Foreign Aid in Latin America*, Madison, WI: University of Wisconsin Press, 1980.

19 Y. Dezalay & B. Garth, *The Internationalization of Palace Wars: Lawyers, Economists, and the Contest to Transform Latin American States*, Chicago: University of Chicago Press, 2002.

20 Y. Dezalay & B. Garth, *Dealing in Virtue*, Chicago: University of Chicago Press, 1996, p. 199.

21 Y. Dezalay & B. Garth, see note 20, p. 267.

22 The point is demonstrated in Ugo Mattei, *Comparative Law and Economics*, Ann Arbor: University of Michigan Press, 1997.

23 Such documents, stating policy priorities in a variety of fields, are published each year by Oxford University Press.

24 Franz Fanon, *The Wretched of the Earth*, New York: Grove Press, 1965.

25 What Aihwa Ong refers to as "graduated sovereignty;" see A. Ong, *Flexible Citizenship: the Cultural Logic of Transnationality*, Durham, NC: Duke University Press, 1999.

26 A. Riles, *The Transnational Appeal of Formalism: the Case of Japan's Netting Law*, available at: http://papers.ssrn.com/sol3/papers.cfm?abstract_id=162588.

27 F. Cownie (ed.) *The Law School – Global Issues, Local Questions*, Aldershot, UK: Ashgate Publishing, 1999.

28 It is instructive to recall that Native American groups in the United States persevered over the nineteenth and twentieth centuries until the moment came, with the Red Movement of the 1960s, when they could force implementation

of treaty rights. The Lakota Sioux, for example, formulated an ideology of treaty rights that forced recognition of their sovereignty and distinctness as part of their legal claim for the return of the Black Hills in North Dakota. By use of the empowerment aspect of the rule of law, a transnational effort, the sweatshop movement would be an example in which activists made use of American law in dealing with unfair labor practices abroad. We will discuss more examples in Chapter 8.

29 Laura Nader, *Harmony Ideology*, Stanford: Stanford University Press, 1990.

30 M. Goodale. "Legal ethnohistory in rural Bolivia: documentary culture and social history in the norte de Potosí," *Ethnohistory* 49 (3), 2002, pp. 583–609.

31 R. Wilson, "Reconciliation and revenge in post-Apartheid South Africa," *Current Anthropology* 41, 2002, pp. 157–85.

32 S. Merry, *Colonizing Hawaii: the Cultural Power of Law*, Princeton, NJ: Princeton University Press, 1999.

33 Laura Nader. *The Life of the Law*, Berkeley, CA: University of California Press, 2002.

34 S. Sassen, *Globalization and its Discontents*, New York: New York University Press, 1995. See also Laura Nader, "The globalization of law: ADR as 'soft' technology," in *Proceedings of the 93rd Annual Meeting, American Society of International Law on Violence, Money, Power and Culture: Reviewing the Internationalist Legacy*, March 24–27, 1999.

35 J. Jackson, *The World Trading System: Law and Policy of International Economic Relations*, Cambridge, MA: MIT Press, 1989.

36 K. Dam, *GATT: Law and International Economic Organization*, Chicago: University of Chicago Press, 1970.

37 Charlene Harrington, *Shadow Justice: the Ideology and Institutionalization of Alternatives to Court*, Westport, CT: Greenwood Press, 1985.

38 W. Greider, *The Manic Logic of Global Capitalism*, New York: Simon & Schuster, 1997, p. 34.

Chapter 4

1 See the discussion of jurisdictional activism in US courts in Chapter 5.

2 For an excellent article concerned with these notions see Keith Aoki, "Neocolonialism, anticommons property and biopiracy in the (not-so-brave) new world order of international intellectual property protection," *Indiana Journal of Global Legal Studies* 6, 1998, p. 11.

3 See Michael Blakeney, *Trade Related Aspects of Intellectual Property Rights: a Concise Guide to the TRIPs Agreement*, London: Sweet & Maxwell, 1996.

4 Territorial notions of statehood and sovereignty (of Kuwait), such as those proclaimed and defended for the last time by the first war against Iraq (and such as those that have been forgotten by NATO during the Bosnia strikes) are certainly weakened by the universalistic non-territorial philosophy that justifies intellectual property as a prize for (technological) creativity. Why should territorial Gulf and African States own the oil that happens to be within their territorial borders? Why should oil worldwide not be allocated as a prize for the skills in extracting and use it as a source of energy? Shouldn't state territorial sovereignty yield to global needs of humankind as interpreted by the global economy?

5 One can notice that the major South African defeat of imperialistic notions of intellectual property happened within a "group-oriented" cultural model, in which individualistic ideology is less capable of persuasion. See K. Brown, "Globalization and cultural conflict in developing countries: the South African example," *Indiana Journal of Global Legal Studies* 7, 1999, p. 225.

6 An important documentary movie *Le beurre et le prix du beurre* was presented at the 2007 Festpaco in Ouagadougo to expose the scam of faked "fair market practices" by the cosmetic industry.

7 See Darrell A. Posey & Graham Dutfield, *Beyond Intelluctual Property: Toward Traditional Resource Rights for Indigenous Peoples and Local Communities*, Ottawa: International Development Research Centre, 1996.

8 See Douglass North, *Institutions, Institutional Change and Economic Development*, Cambridge, MA: Cambridge University Press, 1990.

9 Hernando De Soto is the best-known representative of this simplistic line of thinking.

10 For appraisals of the realist hegemony in US law, see Grant Gilmore, *The Ages of American Law*, New Haven, CT: Yale University Press, 1977; and Bruce Ackerman, *Reconstructing American Law*, Boston: Harvard University Press, 1984.

11 See Laura Nader, *The Life of the Law*, Berkeley, CA: University of California Press, 2002.

12 For elaboration, see Ugo Mattei, *Comparative Law and Economics*, Ann Arbor, MI: University of Michigan Press, 1997.

13 See Avery Katz, "Positivism and the separation of law and economics," *Michigan Law Review* 94, 1996, p. 2229.

14 Hans Kelsen, *The Pure Theory of Law* (trans. Knight), Berkeley, CA: University of California Press, 1967; and *General Theory of Law and State* (trans. Wedberg), New York: Russell & Russell, 1961.

15 See Kenneth Boulding, "In praise of inefficiency," speech to the National Trustee Workship of the Association of Governing Boards. Available at: *AGB Reports* Jan–Feb, 1978, pp. 44–8.

16 That happened to the French exegetic methodology, considered obsolete by the much more elegant and "scientific" German approach, dominant until World

War II. That was possibly the case of Franco-German inspired "social approach" to law, advertised as a step forward in civilization compared to the previous extremes of individualism and social Darwinism.

17 See Bernard Black & Reinier Kraakman, "A self-enforcing model of corporate law," *Harvard Law Review* 109, 1996, p. 1911.

18 It is very important to mention that cutting-edge pure economists are today challenging the idea of intellectual property, seeing it as a monopoly over rent, as such an enemy to innovation. See, for example, work by Michele Boldrin & David Levine, *The Case Against Intellectual Property*, London: Centre for Economic Policy Research, 2002; and Michele Boldrin & David Levine "Intellectual property: do we need it? – the case to xxxx intellectual property," *American Council Review* 92, 2002, p. 209.

19 See Luca Pes, *Law and Development*, Ph.D. Dissertation, University of Turin, 2007; and A. Santos & D.M. Trubek, *The New Law and Economic Development; a Critical Appraisal*, New York: Cambridge University Press, 2006.

20 See *Eldred* v. *Ashcroft*, 537 US 186 (2003), a challenge to the Sonny Bono Copyright Extension Act.

21 On the three phases of American anthropology, see E. Wolf, "American Anthropologists and American Society," in *Reinventing Anthropology* (D. Hymes, ed.), New York: Vintage Books, 1972, pp. 251–63.

22 On moving anthropology from the armchair to the field see F. Boas, *Introduction to the Handbook of American Indian Languages, Part I*, Seattle: Shorey Book Store, 1971; F. Boas, *The Shaping of American Anthropology, 1883–1911: a Franz Boas Reader*, New York: Basic Books, 1974; B. Malinowski, *Coral Gardens and their Magic: a Study of the Methods of Tilling the Soil and of Agricultural Rites in the Trobriand Islands*, New York: Dover Publications, 1978; and G. Stocking, *Observers Observed: Essays on Anthropological Fieldwork*, Madison, WI: University of Wisconsin Press, 1983.

23 For more on the ideological basis of science and technology, and on Western, non-Western, and intermingled ways of knowing, see H. Gusterson, *Nuclear Rites: a Weapons Laboratory at the End of the Cold War*, Berkeley, CA: University of California Press, 1996; R. Gonzalez, *Zapotec Science: Farming and Food in the Northern Sierra of Oaxaca*, Austin: University of Texas Press, 2001; Laura Nader (ed.), *Naked Science: Anthropological Inquiries into Boundaries, Power, and Knowledge*, New York: Routledge, 1996; and S. Traweek, *BeamTimes and Lifetimes: the World of High Energy Physicists*, Cambridge, MA: Harvard University Press, 1988.

24 On the notion of progress and an anthropological critique, urging that progress be considered an object to be analyzed rather than being taken for granted, see the foundational A. Kroeber, *Anthropology: Race, Language, Culture, Psychology, Prehistory*, New York: Harcourt Brace, 1948.

25 For more on the history of anthropology, see E. Leach, "Glimpses of the unmentionable in the history of British social anthropology," *Annual Review of Anthropology* 13, 1984, pp. 1–24.

26 For a British insider's perspective on British anthropology, see A. Kuper, *Anthropology and Anthropologists: the Modern British School*, London: Routledge & Kegan, 1983; and more broadly, A. Kuper, *Culture: the Anthropologists' Account*, Cambridge, MA: Harvard University Press, 1999.

27 On McCarthy-era anthropology, see D. Price, *Threatening Anthropology: McCarthyism and the FBI's surveillance of Activist Anthropologists*, Durham, NC: Duke University Press, 2004. See also D. Price, "Gregory Bateson and the OSS," *Human Organization* 57 (4), 1998, pp. 379–84; and L. Nader, 1999, "The phantom factor: impact of the Cold War on anthropology," in *The Cold War and the University: Toward an Intellectual History of the Postwar Years* (N. Chomsky, ed.), New York: The New Press, 1997, pp. 107–45.

28 For the story of Earle's work, see E. Reynolds, *The Forbidden Voyage*, New York: D. McKay Co., 1961.

29 For an exemplar of anthropologists' work produced as contributions to the war effort, see R. Benedict, *The Chrysanthemum and the Sword: Patterns of Japanese Culture*, Boston: Houghton Miflin, 1946. For an ethnography produced after World War II on a fieldwork site in which the anthropologist was simultaneously working for British military intelligence, see E. Leach, *Political Systems of Highland Burma*, Cambridge, MA: Harvard University Press, 1954.

30 On normative blindness and Cahokia, see R. Silverberg, *Mound Builders of Ancient America: the Archeology of a Myth*, Greenwich, CT: New York Graphic Society, 1968.

31 The rallying cry to anthropologists for autocritique was sounded by L. Nader, "Up the anthropologist: perspectives gained from studying up," in *Reinventing Anthropology* (D. Hymes, ed.), New York: Vintage Books, 1972, pp. 284–311.

32 The extraordinary work of Mooney is still setting standards for research and extraordinary perspective now, over a century after publication. See J. Mooney, *The Ghost Dance Religion and the Sioux Outbreak of 1890*, Chicago: University of Chicago Press, 1896.

33 For the story of Mooney, his research, and the consequences for the people he studied and him personally, see L.G. Moses, *The Indian Man: a Biography of James Mooney*, Urbana, IL: University of Illinois Press, 1984.

34 The history of some of anthropology's relationship, and sometime complicity, with the North American genocide is recounted in N. Scheper-Hughes, "Coming to our senses: anthropology and genocide," in *Critical Reflections, Section V: Anthropology and the Study of Genocide in Annihilating Difference*, A.L. Hinton (ed.), Berkeley, CA: University of California Press, 2002, pp. 348–81.

35 Specifically note documentation in M. Pinkoski & M. Asch, "Anthropology and indigenous rights in Canada and the United States: implications in Steward's theoretical project," in *Hunter-Gatherers in History, Archaeology, and Anthropology* (A. Barnard, ed.), Oxford: Berg Publishers, 2004, pp. 187–200. For a recent update read Jerry Reynolds, "Bush signs Western Shoshone legislation," in *Indian Country Today*, July 9, 2004, about "one of the largest ongoing seizures of Indian lands in modern times."

36 J. Steward, *The Theory of Cultural Change: the Methodology of Multilinear Evolution*, Urbana, IL: University of Illinois Press, 1955.

37 Quoted in J. Mark, *Four Anthropologists: an American Science and its Early Years*, New York: Science History Publications, 2005.

38 Edward Said, *Orientalism*, New York: Pantheon, 1978.

39 Henry Lewis Morgan's "progressive evolutionism" is expounded by his biographer, C. Resek in *Louis Henry Morgan: American Scholar*, Chicago: University of Chicago Press, 1960.

40 For background on John Wesley Powell and the creation of the Bureau of American Ethnology in the Smithsonian Institution in 1879, see Curtis Hinsley, "Anthropology as science and politics: the dilemma of the Bureau of American Ethnology, 1874," in *The Uses of Anthropology* (W. Goldschmidt, ed.), Washington, DC: American Anthropological Association, 1979, pp. 11–27.

41 Powell appears to have been uneasy with the work of a number of ethnologists. These included Frank Hamilton Cushing, who called into question the ethics of condoning the living conditions on Zuni reservations, and the already mentioned James Mooney, victim of censorship because of his activist role. Cushing's commentary on Zuni living conditions and/or Powell's uneasiness is covered in A. Tozzer, *Social Origins and Social Continuities*, New York: Macmillan, 1931.

42 Charles Royce, "Indian land cessions in the United States," in *Eighteenth Annual Report of the Bureau of American Ethnology to the Secretary of the Smithsonian Institution 1896–97* (J.W. Powell, ed.), 1899, pp. 521–997.

43 For more on Speck's criticisms see H.A. Feit, "The construction of Algonquin hunting territories: private property as moral lesson, policy advocacy, and ethnographic error," in *Colonial Situations: Essays in the Contextualization of Ethnographic Knowledge* (G.W. Stocking, ed.), Madison, WI: University of Wisconsin Press, 1993.

44 With the emergence of the Red Power movement in the 1960s, new economic developments on Indian reservations appeared, namely gambling and the "employment" of Native Americans as the overseers of toxic waste. Today we readily identify a fine line between coercion and informed consent, and anthropological knowledge when in the service of legalized plunder might make it even more opaque. For example, the institutional elements of federal, state, and reservation politics include the nuclear waste industry, a player that has been out

of sight in ethnological reports in the past. The exploration of a relationship between anthropology and plunder is undertaken in J. Ou, "Native Americans and the monitored retrievable storage plan for nuclear wastes: late capitalism, negotiation, and controlling processes," in *Essays on Controlling Processes* (L. Nader, ed.), Berkeley, CA: Kroeber Anthropological Society Papers, 1996. See also Winona LaDuke, *All Our Relations: Native Struggle for Land and* Life, Boston: South End Press, 1999; and Thomas R. Berger, *A Long and Terrible Shadow: White Values, Native Rights in the Americas*, Vancouver: Douglas & McIntyre, 1991.

45 S. Mintz, *Sweetness and Power: the Place of Sugar in Modern History*, New York: Penguin, 1986.

46 Max Gluckman's work emphasizing the similarities of legal systems in Africa and Europe, as an implicit basis for claiming commensurability and equality between Africans and Europeans, is found *inter alia* in M. Gluckman, *The Judicial Process among the Barotse of Northern Rhodesia*, Glencoe, IL: Free Press, 1955; and M. Gluckman, *The Ideas in Barotse Jurisprudence*, New Haven, CT: Yale University Press, 1965.

47 M. Chanock, *Law, Custom, and Social Order: the Colonial Experience in Malawi and Zambia*, Cambridge, UK: Cambridge University Press, 1985 describes customary law as the product of missionary and political colonialism.

48 See Ugo Mattei & Luca Pes, "Civil law and common law. Towards convergence?" in *Oxford Handbook of Law and Politics* (K.E. Whittington, R.D. Kelemen & G.A. Caldeira, eds), 2008 (in press).

49 Patrick Wilcken, *Anthropologists, the Intellectuals and the Gulf War*, Cambridge, UK: Prickly Pear, 1994.

50 For a rather defeatist *realpolitik* view of anthropology's potential contributions, see Z. Mir-Hosseini, quoted in P. Wilcken, note 50.

51 See M. Weber, *Economy and Society: an Outline of Interpretive Sociology*, Berkeley: CA: University of California Press, 1968, p. 1041.

52 For notable exceptions, see L. Nader, note 27, and R. Gonzalez, *Anthropologists in the Public Sphere: Speaking out on War, Peace, and American Power*, Austin, TX: University of Texas, 2004.

Chapter 5

1 Eduardo Galeano, *Open Veins of Latin America: Five Centuries of the Pillage of a Continent* (trans. Cedric Belfrage), New York: Monthly Review Press, 1973 (reprinted 1997), p. 28. See also N. Klein, "Bomb before you burp: the economics of war," *Seattle Journal for Social Justice* Spring/Summer, 2004; and Lewis Lapham, "Lionhearts," *Harper's Magazine* September, 2006 for an incisive

analysis of the Iraq war as an economic success – “the transformation of a godforsaken desert into a defense contractor’s Garden of Eden.”

2 Eduardo Galeano, see note 1, p. 107.
3 Eduardo Galeano, see note 1, p. 108.
4 See Institute for Policy Studies and Foreign Policy in Focus, *A Failed “Transition.” The Mounting Costs of the Iraq War*, available at: www.fpif.org/papers/0409iraqtrans.html.
5 M. Klare, *Resource Wars: The New Landscape of Global Conflict*, New York: Holt, 2002.
6 M. Klare, *Blood and Oil: The Dangers and Consequences of America’s Flowing Petroleum Dependency*, New York: Metropolitan Books and Holt, 2004.
7 Paul Collier & Anke Hoeffler, “Justice-seeking and loot-seeking in war,” unpublished paper, World Bank, February 17, 1999, p. 15.
8 Queen Noor, *Leap of Faith: Memoirs of an Unexpected Life*, New York: Miramax Books, 2003.
9 Rainforest Action Network, *Drilling to the Ends of the Earth: Voices from the Old Frontier*, San Francisco: Rain Forest Action Network, 1998, p. 20. Patricia Urteaga-Crovetto, *Identities and Hydrocarbons: Territorial Claims in the Southwestern Peruvian Amazon*, Ph.D. dissertation, Berkeley, CA: University of California, 2005. Suzanne Sawyer, *Crude Chronicles – Indigenous Politics, Multinational Oil, and Neoliberalism in Ecuador*, Durham, NC: Duke University Press, 2004.
10 Id.
11 Tariq Ali, *Bush in Babylon: the Recolonization of Iraq*, London: Verso, 2003, p. 134.
12 Gerard Butt, “Oil and Gas in the UAE,” in *United Arab Emirates: A New Perspective* (Peter Hellyer, Ibrahim Al-Abed, eds), UAE: Trident Press, 231–48. Also Rashid Khalidi, *Western Footprints and America’s Perilous Path in the Middle East*. Boston: Beacon Press, 2004.
13 Refer to Napoleon via Al-Jabarti, *Al-Jabarti’s Chronicles of the First Seven Months of the French Occupation of Egypt, June–December 1798* (trans. S. Moreh), Leiden, the Netherlands: E.J. Brill, 1975.
14 Antonia Juhasz, “Foreign policy in focus,” *FPIF Policy Report* July, 2004. See also A. Juhasz, “Whose oil is it, anyway?” *New York Times* March 13, 2007.
15 Kofi Annan, British Columbia news, September 21, 2004.
16 David R. Francis, *Why Iraq’s new oil law won’t last*. Christian Science Monitor, March 5, 2007.
17 Sydney Harring, *White Man’s Law: Native People in Nineteenth Century Canadian Jurisprudence*, Toronto: University of Toronto Press, 1998, p. 10. The same author, speaking about the First Nations in Canada puts it even more bluntly: “Canadian law, to be blunt, is often illegal. There is for example a substantial literature on the legal construction of treaty language that requires that such a

language be construed liberally in favor of the tribes . . . the First nations. Legal history is repleted with examples of illegality in Canada's treatment of Indians" (ibid., p. 275).

18 W.J. Mommsen & J. A. De Moor (eds), *European Expansion and Law. The Encounter of European and Indigenous Law in the 19th and 20th Century*, Oxford: Berg Press, 1992.

19 Cited in Eduardo Galeano, see note 1, p. 39.

20 This mental framework is reflected by "realist" paradigms in international law. For an illuminating discussion, see Richard Falk, "Re-framing the legal agenda of world order in the course of a turbulent century," in *Transnational Legal Processes* (Michael Likosky, ed.), New York: Cambridge University Press, 2002. Available at: http://www.wws.princeton.edu/~rfalk/papers/in.

21 See J. Gray, "The passing of social democracy," in *The Global Transformations Reader* (David Held & Anthony McGrew, eds), Cambridge, UK: Polity Press, 2000, p. 328.

22 Communist candidate Ziuganov's chances of victory were tackled by international advisors with the creation of a nationalist leader, General Lebed.

23 See L. Bosniak, "Critical reflections on 'citizenship' as a progressive aspiration," in *Labour Law in an Era of Globalization: Transformative Practices and Possibilites, Part V*, Oxford: Oxford University Press, 2002. See also C. Joppke, "Sovereignty and citizenship in a world of migration," in M. Likosky (ed.), *Transnational Legal Processes*, New York: Cambridge University Press, 2002. Available at: http://www.wws.princeton.edu/~rfalk/papers/in.

24 Issa G. Shivji, "Law's empire and the empire of lawlessness: beyond the Anglo-American law," *Law, Social Justice and Global Development* (electronic law journal), 2003:http://www2.warwick.ac.uk/fac/soc/law/elj/lgd/2003-1/shivjiz/shivjiz.rtf.

25 See S.D. Murphy, *Humanitarian Intervention: the United Nations in an Evolving World Order*, Philadelphia: University of Pennsylvania Press, 1996.

26 Despite the fact that illegality is the rule rather than the exception, given the tight language of the UN charter outlawing aggressive war was always considered utopian and unrealistic. For examples of utopian literature see M. Mills & J. Real, *The Abolition of War*, New York: Macmillan, 1963; G. Clark & L.B. Sohn, *World Peace Through World Law: Two Alternative Plans*, 3rd edn, Cambridge, MA: Harvard University Press, 1966; Richard Falk, *A Study of Future Worlds*, New York: Free Press, 1975.

27 See J. Goldsmith & R. Posner, *The Limits of International Law*, Oxford: Oxford University Press, 2005. For an articulate critique see P. Schiff-Berman, Book review, *Texas Law Review* 84, p. 1265.

28 See S.H. Cleveland, "Powers inherent in sovereignty: Indians, aliens, territories and the nineteenth century origins of the plenary power over foreign affairs," *Texas Law Review* 81, 2002, p. 1.

29 See discussion on Paul Bremer's orders *infra*.

30 For a taxonomy of legal systems based on a distinction between rule of professional law, rule of political law, and rule of traditional law, see Ugo Mattei, "Three patterns of law: taxonomy and change in the world's legal systems," *American Journal of Comparative Law* 45, 1997, p. 5.

31 Islamic law has been a successful provider of "public goods" such as security, charity, and education in many places where the Western notion of state simply failed.

32 More parallels can be found in Ugo Mattei, "Foreign inspired courts as agencies of peace in troubled societies, a plea for realism and for creativity," *Global Jurist Topic* 2 (1), Article 2202, available at: http//www.bepress.com/gj/topics/vol2/iss1/art1. See also Anna Simons "The Somalia trap," *Washington Post* August 15, 1993.

33 For a critique of such an attitude see Noam Chomsky, *The New Military Humanism: Lessons from Kosovo*, Monroe, ME: Common Courage Press, 1999. See also Richard Falk, "Re-framing the legal agenda of world order in the course of a turbulent century," in *Transnational Legal Processes* (Michael Likosky, ed.), New York: Cambridge University Press, 2002, available at: http://www.wws.princeton.edu/~rfalk/papers/in. On the dangers for a role of international leadership of such a double standard in international law, see T.L. Knutsen, *The Rise and Fall of World Orders*, Manchester: Manchester University Press/St. Martins, 1999.

34 See William I. Robinson, *Promoting Polyarchy: Globalisation, US Intervention and Hegemony*, Cambridge, UK: Cambridge University Press, 1996.

35 See George E. Bisharat, "Right of return to a Palestinian home," *San Francisco Chronicle* Section D, May 18, 2003; and G. Bisharat, "Land, law and legitimacy in Israel and the Occupied Territories," *American University Law Review* 43, 1994, p. 467.

36 See Ugo Mattei, "A Theory of Imperial Law. A study on US Hegemony and the Latin Resistance," *Indiana Journal of Global Legal Studies* 10, 2003, p. 383; *Global Jurist Frontiers*, available at: www.bepress.com. See also M. Goodale, "Empires of law, discipline and resistance within the transnational system," in *Social and Legal Studies*, 14(4), 2005, pp. 553–83.

37 Tariq Ali, see note 11, p. 134.

38 For a very instructive comparative discussion, see G.A. Benacchio, *La Circolazione die Modelli tra gli Slavi del Sud (Sloveni, Croati, Serbie)*, Padova: Cedam, 1995.

39 See Douglass North, *Institutions, Institutional Change and Economic Development*, Cambridge, MA: Cambridge University Press, 1990.

40 It suffices to think about: (1) the distribution of international aid; (2) issues stemming from the return home of displaced populations; (3) issues of caring for the many orphans to be placed into private or public care; (4) issues of retribution; and (5) issues of outright pacification of internal turmoil or even handling war crimes, etc.

41 See Laura Nader, "The Americanization of international law," in *Mobile People, Mobile Law: Expanding Legal Relations in a Contracting World (Law, Justice and Power)* (F. von Benda-Beckmann, K. von Benda-Beckmann, & A. Griffiths, eds), London: Ashgate, 2005, pp. 199–213.

42 A user's theory of law is advanced in Laura Nader, *The Life of the Law*, Berkeley, CA: University of California Press, 2002.

43 It would be a mistake to assume that "the law" can reach similar levels of effectiveness and can be used as a panacea; this is a mistake behind much policy of "intervention" both during and in the aftermath of strain and suffering.

44 See Laura Nader & Elisabetta Grande, "Current illusions and delusions about conflict management," *Law and Social Inquiry* 27 (3), 2002, pp. 573–94.

45 See Elisabetta Grande, "Hegemonic human rights and African resistance. The issue of female circumcision in a broader comparative perspective," *Global Jurist Frontiers* 4 (2), 2004. Available at: http://www.bepress.com/cgi/viewcontent.cgi?article=1145&context=gj.

46 See James A. Gardner, *Legal Imperialism: American Lawyers and Foreign Aid in Latin America*, Madison, WI: University of Wisconsin Press, 1980. See also L. Nader, "Law and the theory of lack," in *Hastings International and Comparative Law Review* 28 (2), 2005, pp. 191–204.

47 Laura Nader & Elisabetta Grande, see note 44.

48 Faiz Ahmed, "Judicial reform in Afghanistan: a case study in the new criminal procedure code," *Hastings International and Comparative Law Review* 29 (1), 2005, pp. 93–134.

49 See G. Bisharat, "Sanctions as genocide," *Transnational Law and Contemporary Problems* 11, 2001, pp. 379–425; and G.E. Bisharat, "Right of return to a Palestinian home," *San Francisco Chronicle* Section D, May 18, 2003. See also Barbara Nimri Aziz, *Swimming Up the Tigris: Real Life Encounters with Iraq*, Gainesville, FL: University Press of Florida (2007).

50 See Stephanie Black's film *Life+Debt* (2001) discussing structural adjustment programs and neo-liberal policy in Jamaica.

51 James Mill (ed.), *Classics of British Historical Literature*, Chicago: University of Chicago Press, 1976.

52 Eduardo Galeano, see note 1.

53 Instituto Nacional Indigenista, *Perspectives for the Development of Indian Peoples of Mexico*, Mexico, DF: Caligrato Digital, 1992.

54 David Quist & Ignacio Chapella, "Transgenic DNA introgressed into traditional maize landacres in Oaxaca, Mexico," *Nature Magazine* 414, 2001. Available at: http://www.botanischergarten.ch/debate/QuistChapelaNature011129.pdf.

55 G.A. Collier, *Basta! Land and the Zapatista Rebellion in Chiapas*, Oakland, CA: Food First Books, 1994.

56 Laura Randall (ed.), *Changing Structure of Mexico: Political, Social, and Economic Prospects*, Columbia University Seminar Series, Armonk, NY: M.E. Sharpe, 1996.

Chapter 6

1 Robert Cover, *Justice Accused: Anti-Slavery and the Judicial Process*, New Haven, CT: Yale University Press, 1975.
2 James W. Ely, *The Guardian of Every Other Right: a Constitutional History of Property Rights (Bicentennial Essays on the Bill of Rights)*, Oxford: Oxford University Press, 1997.
3 A. Bickel, *The Least Dangerous Branch*. The Supreme Court at the Bar of Politics, 2nd edn, New Haven: Yale University Press, 1986.
4 See T. Ruskola, "Law's empire: the legal construction of 'America' in the 'District of China'." Available at: http://papers.ssrn.com/sol3/papers.cfm?abstract_id=440641.
5 Olga Miranda Bravo, *Inconvenient Neighbors. The Guantanamo Base and the US Cuban Relationship*, Habana: Jose Marti' Press, 2001.
6 See Alfred Aman, *The Democracy Deficit*, New York: New York University Press, 2006.
7 We will not discuss here the kind of redistribution (in favor of the winners) that is fostered by economic globalization and by its violent restructuring of capitalism. The best recent discussion available of this different kind of redistribution is William K. Tabb, *The Amoral Elephant: Globalization and the Struggle for Social Justice in the Twenty-First Century*, New York: Monthly Review Press, 2001. Every deep transformation in processes of production through history implies redistribution of wealth across social classes in favor of the winners. See the classic Karl Polanyi, *The Great Transformation: the Political and Economic Origins of Our Time*, New York: Beacon Press, by arrangement with Rinehart: Schwerin, 1944. In this chapter, however, we will talk of redistribution in the sense of redistribution favoring social solidarity and therefore aimed at more equality.
8 See Karl Marx, *Capital: a Critique of Political Economy* (J.M. Cohen, ed.), London: Penguin Classics, 1992.
9 See Susan George, *Remettre l'OMC a sa Place*, Paris : Mille et Une Nuits, 2001.
10 See most recent data in Ugo Mattei, "Access to justice. A renewed global issue?" in *General Reports to the XVII Congress of the International Academy of Comparative Law* (Katharina Boele-Woelki & Sjef Van Erp, eds), Utrecht: Eleven International Publishing-Bruylant, 2007, p. 383.
11 See Edoardo Ruffini, *La Ragione dei piu': ricerche sulla storia del principio maggiortario*, Bologna: Il Mulino, 1977; and H. Sumner Maine, *Etudes sur l'histoire des Institutions Primitives*, Paris: Ernest Thorin ed., 1880.

12 See Paul H. Rubin, *Why was the Common Law Efficient?* Emory Law and Economics Research Paper No. 04-06. Available at SSRN: http://ssrn.com/abstract=498645 or DOI: 10.2139/ssrn.498645.
13 See David Cay Johnston, *Perfectly Legal: the Covert Campaign to Rig Our Tax System to Benefit the Super Rich – and Cheat Everybody Else*, New York: Penguin Group, Portfolio hardcover, 2003.
14 See M. Walzer, *Just and Unjust Wars: a Moral Argument with Historical Illustrations*, New York: Basic Books, 1998. For delivering the imaginary view of an agonizing, just decision-maker, see also J. Moore, *Hard Choices: Moral Dilemmas in Humanitarian Interventions*, Lanham, MD: Rowman & Littlefield, 1998.
15 One should note that United for Peace Resolutions are available exactly to overcome vetoes at the Security Council. They have never been used thereafter.
16 See, generally, C.N. Tate & T. Vallinder (eds), *The Global Expansion of Judicial Power*, New York: New York University Press, 1995.
17 See Michael J. Bazyler, *Holocaust Justice*, New York: New York University Press, 2003.
18 The following section is based on a paper by Ugo Mattei & Jeffrey Lena, "U.S. jurisdiction over conflicts arising outside of the United States: some hegemonic implications," *Hastings International and Comparative Law Review* 381, 2001, p. 24; and *Global Jurist Topics*, 2001, available at: www.bepress.com.
19 See Michael J. Bazyler, "Nuremberg in America: litigating the Holocaust in United States courts," *University of Richmond Law Review* 34, 2000, p. 1. This mega-article of some 283 pages details the various Holocaust cases, albeit decisively from the plaintiff's perspective.
20 See A. Reyes, "Protecting the Freedom of Transit of Petroleum: Transnational Lawyers Making (Un)International Law in the Caspian", in *Berkeley Journal of International Law*, 24, 2007, pp. 842–80.
21 This question is addressed *infra*, Chapter 7.
22 The US record in respect to human rights is very poor from the European perspective. The death penalty and the Guantánamo cages are the icon of these double standards. Moreover, the Florida recount saga makes it difficult for US observers to press for fair elections worldwide.

Chapter 7

1 See A. Mitchell Polinsky-Steven Shavell, "Punitive damages. An economic analysis," *Harvard Law Review* 111, 1998, p. 869.
2 See *Berkeley Journal International Law*.
3 See Elisabetta Grande, *Il terzo strike. La prigione in America*, Palermo: Sellerio, 2007.

4 For the sophisticated clothing in the making of such ideology, see R. La Porta, C. Pop Eleches, F. Lopez de Silanes, & A. Schleifer, *The Guarantees of Freedom*, Cambridge, MA: Harvard University Institute of Economic Research, 2002.

5 One of which, Ronald Reagan, was his boss, and the other, Richard Nixon, had appointed Bush Senior to head the CIA.

6 Actually, in the 2000 presidential campaign, during the debate on foreign policy, Gore displayed even more arrogant views than his opponent, by claiming that America had a duty to show to the world the right way (its own) by forcing democracy, the rule of law, and human rights to the rest of the world.

7 See *supra*, Chapter 6, note 7.

8 The first thorough analysis offering a critical key to understand the hatred of American corporations as a "market-dominating" minority controlling much more than their fair share of global resources is due to Ami Chua, *World on Fire: How Exporting Free Market Democracy Breeds Ethnic Hatred and Global Instability*, New York: Anchor Books, 2003. The "self-inflicted" theory is now gaining currency in the USA and the State Department is trying to counter it. See too "US reports seek to counter conspiracy theories about 9/11," *New York Times* September 2, 2006, p. A11.

9 Nat Hentoff, *The War on the Bill of Rights*, New York: Seven Stories Press, 2003.

10 Cited in Nat Hentoff, see note 9, p. 97.

11 Cited in W.I. Robinson, *Promoting Polyarchy. Globalization, U.S. Intervention and Hegemony*, Cambridge, UK: Cambridge University Press, 1996.

12 James Risen & David Johnston, "Threats and responses: hunt for Al Qaeda; Bush has widened authority of CIA to kill terrorists," *New York Times*, December 14, 2002, p. A1.

13 Interestingly, the only court to have used the language of illegality is the impotent International Law Tribunal of the Hague condemning the wall as illegal.

14 The use of politically ideological titles for statutes used to be typical of the Soviet style legislation. It might be worth noting that the USA Patriot Act means Uniting and Strengthening America by Providing Appropriate Tools Required to Intercept and Obstruct Terrorism Act. This covergence is noted by T. Varady, "Notes on Ideological Precepts as Formants of Private Law in Central-Eastern European Countries" in *Opening up European Law*, (M. Bussani, U. Mattei, eds), Durham: Carolina Academic Press, 2007, p. 132.

15 Nancy Chang, *Silencing Political Dissent: How Post-September 11 Anti-Terrorism Measures Threaten our Civil Liberties*, New York: Seven Stories Press, 2002, p. 50.

16 See www.aclu.org/safeandfree/ for reports and updates. For a recent plea not to surrender to the logic of exception by a mainstream liberal political philosopher and lawyer, see Bruce Ackerman, *Before the Next Attack: Preserving Civil Liberties in an Age of Terrorism*, New Haven: Yale University Press, 2006.

17 Updates on the 277 efforts of more resolutions pending nationwide as of September 2007 can be found in the website of the Bill of Rights Defense Committee, www.bordc.org
18 See David Cole, *Enemy aliens*, New York: The New Press, 2003. See also David Cole, "Profiles in legal courage," *The Nation* December 20, 2004, pp. 28–9; and David Cole & James Dempsey, *Terrorism and the Constitution: Sacrificing Civil Liberties in the Name of National Security*, New York: New Press, 2006.
19 N. Chang, see note 15, p. 62.
20 See E. Feldman, *The Ritual of Rights in Japan*, Cambridge, UK: Cambridge University Press, 2002.
21 Robert Greenwald, *Iraq for Sale*, RYKO, 2006.
22 N. Chang, see note 15, p. 94.
23 See www.goatca.org/publications/reports/defciv.pdf. "Defending Civilization: How Our Universities Are Failing America and What Can be Done About It."
24 N. Chang, see note 15, p. 97.
25 See R. Gonzalez, *Anthropologists in the Public Sphere: Speaking out on War, Peace, and American Power*, Austin, TX: University of Texas, 2004, p. 262. See also R. Gonzalez, *Zapotec Science: Farming and Food in the Northern Sierra of Oaxaca*, Austin, TX: University of Texas Press, 2001.
26 See R. Gonzalez, 2004, note 25, p. 248.
27 Cited in N. Hentoff, see note 9, p. 135.
28 See Philippe Sands' *Lawless World – America and the Making and Breaking of Global Rules from FDR's Atlantic Charter to George W. Bush's Illegal War*, New York: Viking Publishers, 2005.

Chapter 8

1 Karl Polanyi, *The Great Transformation*, New York: Ferrar & Rinehart, 1944.
2 See D.C. Johnston, *Perfectly Legal: the Covert Campaign to Rig our Tax System to Benefit the Super Rich – and Cheat Everyone Else*, New York: David Cay, Portfolio, 2003. Also Russell Mokhiber and Robert Weissman, *On the Rampage: Corporate Power and the Destruction of Democracy*. Monroe, ME: Common Courage Press, 2005.
3 On the legality of the current international regime concerning Cuba, see Olga Miranda Bravo, *Undesirable Neighbors. The U.S. Naval Base at Guantanamo*, Habana: Editorial Jose' Marti, 2001. The book contains a very instructive discussion of the history of Spanish and US legal plunder in the island, which culminated in the peace treaty of Paris in 1898 and the imposition of the Platt Amendment (February 27, 1901) to the Cuban "independent" constitution.

4 Elisabetta Grande, *Il terzo strike*, Palermo: Sellerio, 2007; and Loïc Wacquant, *Punir les pauvres: le nuveau gouvernement de l'insecurite sociale*, Marseille, France: Agone, 2004 (*Punishing the poor, the new government of social insecurity*, unpublished manuscript, 2005) have shown how incarceration is used in the USA as a poverty management strategy.

5 E. Mandel, *Marxist Economic Theory*, Vol. 2, New York: Monthly Review Press, 1968, p. 443.

6 See in Chapter 6 the discussion on Holocaust litigation where US courts attempted to adjudicate World War II European events.

7 An attempt, although local, that shows the necessity of a new "constitutional start" to defeat plunder, is taking place in Ecuador where President Correa has called a referendum (April 15, 2007) to allow a constitutional convention for a total break with a past of neo-liberalism that, beginning in the 1980s, reached its peak in the full "dollarization" of the economy in 2000.

8 See for example Article IV sec 10 of the Agreement of the Institution of the International Bank of Reconstruction and Development (one of five institutions that constitute the World Bank Group). It is titled "Political Activity Prohibited" and it reads: "The bank and its officers shall not interfere in the political affairs of any member; nor shall they be influenced in their decisions by the political character of the member or members concerned. Only economic considerations should be relevant to their decisions, and these considerations shall be weighed impartially in order to achieve the purposes stated in Article I." Similar provisions can be found in the bylaws of the International Development Association another member of the World Bank Group. See http//siter-sources.worldbank.org for a discussion pointing at the variety of strategies used to depoliticize the discourse on development in order to reach the law. See also Luca Pes, *Law and development*, Ph.D. Dissertation, University of Turin, 2007, p. 170.

9 Aggregate comparative data are offered by the *Energy Information Administration.* The international ones are updated to 2004 and show per capita U.S. consumption at 342.7 against 146.5 of Europe, 50.8 Latin America, 15.7 Africa, 38.5 Asia and Oceania with a world average of 70.1. Unit is one million BTU/person. See www.eia.doe.gov/emeu/international/energy/consumption.html

10 Deborah Poole, "Political autonomy and cultural diversity," *Anthropology News* 48 (3), 2007, p. 10. In 1995–98 the Law of Indigenous Rights was created, a platform for the "recognition of cultural identities, languages, customs and rights." Although the law has been little implemented, the important exception is the right to elect municipal authorities following traditional *usos y costumbres* (uses and customs), meaning that self-declared "autonomous municipalities" are able to determine their own future over land, territory, and resources. Autonomous communities have a long history in Mexico; each Indian community was to

be a self-contained economic unit, a policy of the Spanish crown to address relative power of the Crown, the colonists, and the Indians.

11 Refer to Vandana Shiva, *Biopiracy – the Plunder of Nature and Knowledge*, Boston: South End Press, 1997.

12 Cass R. Sunstein, "A brave new Wikiworld," *Washington Post* February 24, 2007, p. A19. Cass Sunstein is also author of *Infotopia: How Many Minds Produce Knowledge*, Oxford: Oxford University Press, 2006.

13 Vandana Shiva, "India: soft drinks, hard case," *Le Monde Diplomatique* March, 2005.

14 Kevin O'Brien, "Rightful resistance," *World Politics* 49 (October), 1996, p. 31. See also Nicholas D. Kristof, "Rumblings from China," *New York Times* July 2, 2006, p. 11.

15 Shai Oster & Mei Fong, "In booming China, a doctor battles a polluting factory," *Wall Street Journal* July 19, 2006.

16 Joseph Kahn, "When Chinese sue the state, cases are often smothered," *New York Times* December 28, 2005, p. A1.

17 Edward Cody, "Officials held hostage by farmers in China," *Washington Post* November 10, 2006, p. A26; and Edward Cody, "One riot breaks ground in China," *Washington Post* June 28, 2006, p. A14.

18 Maureen Fan, "China's party leadership declares new priority: 'harmonious society'," *Washington Post* October 12, 2006, p. A18.

19 See Supryo Mukherjee, *Nandigram: the Brutal Massacre of Peasants at the Hands of the Left Front Government*, available at: www.marxist.com/india-nandigram-massacre-paesants.

20 "Greenpeace slams high-tech firms for 'e-waste' in China," Kyodo News Services, Japan, *Economic Newzwire* May 23, 2005.

21 See O.M. Bravo, note 3, p. 88.

22 See Noreena Hertz, *Silent Takeover, Global Capitalism and the Death of Democracy*, London: Arrow Books, 2001.

23 David Graeber, "Give it away," *InTheseTimes.com* August 21, 2000. See also D. Graeber *Fragments of an Anarchist Anthropology*, Chicago: Prickly Paradigm Press (distributed by University of Chicago Press), 2004, p. 105.

Selected Further Reading

This brief bibliography contains the essential literary sources of our work. It is compiled following the organization of the materials in the book. Sources are mentioned the first time in which they become relevant. Many of such works are, however, relevant in a variety of places.

Chapter 1

An Anatomy of Plunder

On the history of the rule of law from the early origins of the expression, the best treatment remains T.F.T. Plucknett, *A Concise History of the Common Law*, Boston: Little, Brown & Co., 1956, p. 48.

As to different theoretical conceptions, including Marxism and different variants of naturalism, one can consult C.J. Friedrich, *The Philosophy of Law in Historical Perspective*, 2nd edn, Chicago: University of Chicago Press, 1963.

A recent discussion of the rule of law as a positive legacy of the British empire and a useful description of its extension can be found in Niall Ferguson, *Empire. The Rise and Demise of the British World and the Lessons for Global Power*, New York: Basic Books, 2003, pp. 359–64. For a critical approach, M. Mann, "Torchbearers upon the Path of Progress: Britain's Ideology of a Moral and Material Progress in India: An Introductory Essay," in *Colonialism as Civilizing Mission: Cultural Ideology in British India* (H. Fisher-Tine & M. Mann, eds), London, Wimbledon: 2004, pp. 1–26. A recent important work on the use of law in the early colonization of Latin America, with particular attention to the scholarly debate in sixteenth and seventeenth century European legal scholarship on its legitimacy is Aldo Andrea Cassi, *Ultramar. L'invenzione europea del nuovo mondo*, Roma, Bari: Laterza 2007.

The fundamental discussion of colonial policy in Latin America remains Eduardo Galeano, *Open Veins of Latin America: Five Centuries of the Pillage of a Continent* (trans. Cedric Belfrage), New York: Monthly Review Press, 1997 (originally published in Spanish in Mexico City, 1971).

Interesting background information on the most recent US-led military interventions in weak contexts can be found in A. Rashid, *Taliban: Militant Islam, Oil and Fundamentalism in Central Asia*, New Haven: Yale University Press, 2000; and Tariq Ali, *Bush in Babylon: the Recolonization of Iraq*, New York, Verso, 2003, p. 134.

As to the notion of empire as used in the present work, see M. Hardt & A. Negri, *Empire*, Cambridge, MA: Harvard University Press, 2001. For the notion of imperialism the classic remains V.I. Lenin, *L' Imperialismo fase suprema del capitalismo*, Naples: La Città del Sole, 2001 (first published in St Petersburg in 1916; English translation: *Imperialism: the Highest State of Capitalism*, New York: International Publishers, 1939).

Plunder, Hegemony, and Positional Superiority

On hegemony the seminal work is Antonio Gramsci, *Selections from Prison Notebooks*, New York: International Publishers, 1971. See also S. Gill (ed.), *Gramsci, Historical Materialism and International Relations*, Cambridge, UK: Cambridge University Press, 1993; and R.W. Cox, *Production, Power and World Order: Social Forces in the Making of History*, New York: Columbia University Press, 1987.

On the notion of apparatuses, originally developed for the state and adapted in our work to global governance, see L. Althusser, *Sur La Reproduction*, Paris: Press Universitaire de France, 1975.

Diffusion of power is a concept explored by M. Foucault in a variety of writings, mostly in M. Foucault, "On Governmentality" (lectures at the College de France) and *The Archeology of Knowledge and the Discourse on Language*, New York: Pantheon, 1982. Harmony as a disempowering rhetoric argument is discovered by L. Nader, *Harmony Ideology. Justice and Control in a Zapotec Mountain Village*, Stanford, CA: Stanford University Press, 1990.

On legal transplants the literature is very extensive. The classic is A. Watson, *Legal Transplants. An Approach to Comparative Law*, Athens, GA: University of Georgia Press, 1974. See also R. Sacco, *La Comparaison Juridique au service de la Conaissance du droit*, Paris: Press Universitaire de France, 1992. More nuanced is E. Grande *Imitazione e diritto. Ipotesi sulla circolazione dei modelli*, Torino: Giappichelli, 2000.

For a critique of the World Bank approach to legal systems see Ugo Mattei, "Legal pluralism, legal change and economic development," in *New Law for New States* (L. Favali, E. Grande, & M. Guadagni, eds.), Politica del Diritto in Eritrea, Torino: L' Harmattan Italia, 1998; and Laura Nader, "Promise or plunder? A past and future look at law and development," in *World Bank Legal Review: Law, Equity and Development* (Rudolf V. van Puymbroeck, ed.), Rotterdam, New York: Martinus Nijhoff Publishers, 2006, 89–111.

Law, Plunder, and European Expansionism

On the economic structure of extraction, the foundational works remain Andre Gunder Frank, *World Accumulation 1492–1789*, New York: Monthly Review Press, 1978; and Andre Gunder Frank, "The development of underdevelopment," *Monthly Review* 18, 1966, p. 17. See also Immanuel Wallerstein, *The Modern World System: Capitalist Agriculture and the Origins of the European World Economy in the Sixteenth Century*, New York: Academic Press, 1974. Another classic is J.C. Mariategui, *Siete Ensayos de Interpretacion de la Realidad Peruana*, 18th edn, Lima: 1970 (originally published in 1928). See also C. Furtado, *The Economic Development of Latin America: a Survey from Colonial Times to the Cuban Revolution*, Cambridge, UK: Cambridge University Press, 1970. One can also consult H. Zinn, *A People's History of the United States*, New York: Perennial Library, 1980, pp. 1–23, for further data.

On the crusades and their ideology, two different perspectives are offered by Thomas Asbridge, *The First Crusade. A New History*, Oxford: Oxford University Press, 2004; and by A. Maalouf, *The Crusades Through Arab Eyes* (English translation), London: Al Saqui Books, 1984.

On plunder in India, see Krishan Saini, "A case of aborted economic growth: India 1860–1913," *Journal of Asian History* 89, 1971, p. 5. See also Peter Harnetty, *Imperialism and Free Trade: Lancashire and India in the Mid Nineteenth Century*, Vancouver: University of British Columbia Press, 1972. On the East India Company see, Ramkrishna Mukerjee, *The Rise and Fall of the East India Company: a Sociological Appraisal*, New York: Monthly Review Press, 1978.

An interesting critical discussion on decolonization is offered by Ania Loomba, *Colonialism–Postcolonialism*, London: Routledge, 1998. The classic remains Frantz Fanon, *The Wretched of the Earth*, New York: Grove Press, 1965. See also for early, now classic post-colonial critiques, A. Abdel-Malek, *Civilizations and Social Theory*. Vol. 1 *Social Dialectics*, Albany: State University of New York Press, 1972; E.W. Said, *Orientalism*, New York: Vintage, 1978. On neo-colonialism, see Amin Samir, *Neo-colonialism in West Africa*, Harmondsworth, UK: Penguin Books, 1973.

For a realist theory of international relationships that remains the most significant legacy of Cold War equilibrium, see H.J. Morgenthau, *Politics Among Nations*, New York: Knopf Publishing, 1960. One should also read, in the same mood, H. Kissinger, *Diplomacy*, New York: Simon & Shuster, 1994. On the Cold War, the literature is very extensive. One interested in gathering the essentials should read at least J.L. Gaddis, *We Now Know: Rethinking Cold War History*, Oxford: Clarendon Press, 1997; and B. Bongiovanni, *Storia della Guerra Fredda*, Bari: Laterza, 2001. See also I. Clark,

Globalization and Fragmentation: International Relations in the Twentieth Century, Oxford: Oxford University Press, 1997; J. Baylis & S. Smith, *The Globalization of World Politics: An Introduction to International Relations*, Oxford: Oxford University Press, 2001.

The literature on post Cold War transformations in the global power structure is extensive. Much of it has focused on the unprecedented military strengths of the USA accompanied by its declining prestige. One should read at least I. Wallerstein, *The Decline of American Power*, New York: The New Press, 2003; L. Panitch & S. Gindin, *Global Capitalism and American Empire*, London: Merlin Press, 2003; and M. Mann, *Incoherent Empire*, London: Verso Books, 2003.

Institutionalizing Plunder: the Colonial Relationship and the Imperial Project

Some essential historical context is offered by E. Hobsbawn, *The Age of Empire 1875–1914*, New York: Pantheon Books, 1987; and P. Kennedy, *The Rise and Fall of the Great Powers: Economic Change and Military Conflict from 1500 to 2000*, New York: Vintage, 1987. For essential economic context, see Giovanni Arrighi, *The Long Twentieth Century: Money, Power and the Origins of Our Times*, London: Verso Books, 1994.

For a discussion of the worldwide expansion of Western institutions, see B. Badie, *L' état importé: L' occidentalization de l' ordre politique*, Paris: Artheme Fayard, 1992 (English translation: *The Imported State*, Stanford, CA: Stanford University Press, 2000). See also D.K. Fieldhouse, *The Colonial Empires: a Comparative Survey from the Eighteenth Century*, New York: Delacorte Press, 1967; A.J.H. Latham, *The International Economy and the Underdeveloped World: 1865–1914*, London: Croom Helm, 1978; and Frederic Mauro, *L' Expansion Europeenne (1600–1870)*, Paris: Presse Universitaire de France, 1967.

On decolonization within the Cold War, see G.P. Calchi Novati, *Decolonizzazione e terzo mondo*, Bari: Laterza, 1979.

Interesting anthropological case studies focusing on elites and legal modernization as an ideological tool of domination are given in M. Chanock, *Law, Custom and Social Order: the Colonial Experience in Malawi and Zambia*, Cambridge, UK: Cambridge University Press, 1985; and S. Engle Merry, *Colonizing Hawaii: the Cultural Power of Law*, Princeton, NJ: Princeton University Press, 2000. For a broad historical discussion, see L. Benton, *Law and Colonial Cultures: Legal Regimes in World History 1400–1900*, Cambridge, UK: Cambridge University Press, 2002. On the relationship between colonial elites and local populations the classic remains Frantz Fanon, *Black Skin White Mask*, NewYork: Grove Press, 1962. On Latin American post-colonial elites, see Y. Dezalay & B. Garth, *The Internationalization of Palace Wars. Lawyers, Economists and the Contest to Transform Latin American States*, Chicago: University of Chicago

Press, 2002. On elite theory, the classic is G. Mosca, *The Ruling Class* (English translation), New York: McGraw Hill, 1939. On elites in the USA the must read is still C. Wright Mills, *The Power Elite*, Oxford: Oxford University Press, 1956.

A Story of Continuity: Constructing the Empire of Laws (lessness)

For a broad and informed discussion of US foreign policy in a variety of contexts (including Haiti, the Philippines, Nicaragua, Chile, and South Africa) one should read W.I. Robinson, *Promoting Polyarchy: Globalization, U.S. Intervention and Hegemony*, Cambridge, UK: Cambridge University Press, 1996. On Middle Eastern policies, see T. Ali', *The Clash of Fundamentalisms*, London: Verso Books, 2001. On Africa, see at least M. Mamdani, *Citizen and Subject: Contemporary Africa and the Legacy of Late Colonialism*, Princeton, NJ: Princeton University Press, 1996; and A. Jimale Ahmed (ed.), *The Invention of Somalia*, Lawrenceville, GA: Red Sea Press, 1995.

On (failed) attempts of legal modernization in such complex scenarios the classic is still J. Gardner, *Legal Imperialism*, Madison, WI: University of Wisconsin Press, 1980. For a more recent economics-driven form of technocratic intervention see E. Buscaglia, W. Ratliffe, & R. Cooter, *Law and Economics of Development*, Greenwich, CT: Jay Press, 2001. More recently and critically M. Trubek & A. Santos (eds), *The New Law and Economic Development. A Critical Appraisal*, New York: Cambridge University Press, 2006.

On very recent trends of US domination outside of the Cold War balances, see R.A. Falk, *The Declining World Order*, New York: Routledge, 2004. See also W. Easterly, *The White Man's Burden*, New York: Penguin Press, 2006.

Chapter 2

The Argentinean Bonanza

A basic discussion of development economics is given in J. Brasseul, *Introduction à l'Economie du Development*, Paris: Armand Colin, 1993. A broad introduction and a critical overview of current economic policy is due to Michel Chossudowsky, *The Globalization of Poverty and the New World Order*, Montreal, Quebec, Canada: Global Research Publications, 2nd edn, 2003. (One might also want to take a look at the website www.globalresearch.ca) A well-known, relatively easy, introduction to financial instruments is given in J. Hull, *Options, Futures and other Derivative Securities*, 5th edn, Upper Saddle River, NJ: Prentice Hall, 2002; and A. Steinherr, *Derivatives: the Wild Beast of Finance*, Chichester, UK: Wiley Publishing, 1998.

Some background data on Argentina are available in L. Bethell (ed.), *Argentina Since Independence*, Cambridge, UK: Cambridge University Press, 1993; and L. Bethell (ed.),

Ideas and Ideologies in Twentieth Century Latin America, Cambridge, UK: Cambridge University Press, 1996. Interesting comparative data are available in J. Dominguez (ed.), *Technopolis: Freeing Politics and Markets in Latin America in the 1990s*, University Park, PA: Penn State University Press, 1997. A study on the most famous example of the role of the so-called Chicago boys in Latin America is J.G. Valdez, *Pinochet's Economists: the Chicago School in Chile*, Cambridge, UK: Cambridge University Press 1995. Most recently see N. Klein, *The Shock Doctrine: The Rise of Disaster Capitalism*, New York, Metropolitan Books, 2007.

For more on Argentina's IMF program and its effects, see, generally, M. Mussa, *Argentina and the Fund: From Triumph to Tragedy*, Washington, DC: Institute for International Economics, 2002. For a detailed summary of many economic analyses of the Argentine crisis resulting from its IMF program, see M.A. Buscaglia, *The Economics and Politics of Argentina's Debacle 5*, available at: http://www.iae.edu.ar/mbuscaglia (October 15, 2002). For a more theoretical explanation of the crisis, see also S. Galiani, D. Heymann & M. Tommasi, *Missed Expectations: the Argentine Convertibility*, available at: http://www.udesa.edu.ar/deptodeeconomia/workp/doc55.pdf (November 2002).

For an analysis of the effect of its IMF program on Argentina's adherence to its international legal obligations with respect to human rights, see J. Morgan-Foster, "The relationship of IMF structural adjustment programs to economic, social, and cultural rights: the Argentine case revisited," *Michigan Journal of International Law* 24, 2003, p. 577. For a prematurely felicitous view of the outcome of the process, see S.E. Hendrix, "Advancing toward privatization, education reform, popular participation, and decentralization: Bolivia's innovation in legal and economic reform, 1993–1997," *14 Arizona Journal of International and Comparative Law* 14, 1997, p. 679. For more general ecological analysis see Herman E. Daly & John B. Cobb Jr., *For the Common Good: Redirecting the Economy Toward Community*, Boston: Beacon Press, 1994.

Neo-Liberalism: an Economic Theory of Simplification and a Spectacular Project

Among the many critical discussions of neo-liberal policies, one of the most interesting is W.K. Tabb, *Unequal Partners*, New York: The New Press, 2002. Equally important is N. Hertz, *The Silent Takeover: Global Capitalism and the Death of Democracy*, London: Arrow Books, 2001. See also P. Bourdieu, "Neo-liberalism. The utopia (becoming reality) of unlimited exploitation," in *Acts of Resistance: Against the Tyranny of the Market* (trans. Richard Nice), New York: The New Press, 1998. A mainstream discussion by one of the "neo-liberal" gurus is H. De Soto, *The Mystery of Capital*, New York: Basic Books, 2000. An interesting discussion showing continuity between neo-liberalism and American capitalism and discussing the fundamental traits of social capitalism is given in M. Albert, *Capitalisme contre Capitalisme*, Paris: Seuil Publishers, 1991. For insightful descriptions of the current institutional transformations in law and society which quickly became classic in their respective academic environments, S. Sassen, *Globalization and its Discontents*, New York: Columbia University Press, 1996 and M.R. Ferrarese, *Le istituzioni della globalizzazione. Diritto e diritti nella societa' transnazionale*, Bologna: Il Mulino, 2000.

A discussion of social theories in legal thinking as an early globalized phenomenon is now available, see Duncan Kennedy, "Two globalizations of law and legal thought," *Suffolk Law Review* 36, 2003, p. 631.

The ideological platform of neo-liberalism is developed by F. Von Hayek, *Law, Legislation and Liberty*, Vol. 2: *The Mirage of Social Justice*, Chicago: University of Chicago Press, 1973. Much of its economic policy is still based on Walt Whitman Rostow, *The Stages of Economic Growth: A Non Communist Manifesto*, Cambridge, UK: Cambridge University Press, 1960.

American courts, in a mood known as social Darwinism, have performed in a way coherent with these dictates through the so-called Lochner era before the triumph of Roosevelt's social policy. See M. Horwitz, *The Transformation of American Law 1870–1960*, Oxford: Oxford University Press, 1992.

On Keynesianism, the best discussion is still M. Blaug, *Economic Theory in Retrospect*, Cambridge, UK: Cambridge University Press, 1997.

On the origins and transformations of the Bretton Woods institutions, see A. Walters, *Do We Need the IMF and the World Bank?* London: Institute of Economic Affairs, 1994. See also K. Danaher (ed.), *Fifty Years is Enough, the Case Against the World Bank and the International Monetary Fund*, Boston: South End Press, 1994; and F. Castro, *Capitalism in Crisis. Globalization and World Politics Today* (D. Deutshmann, ed.), Melbourne: Ocean Press, 2000. See also for an attempt to systematically study the social consequences of dominant policy Z. Baumann, *Globalization: the Human Consequences*, New York: Columbia University Press, 1998.

On recent post-cold war political changes in Europe, see J.J. Linz & A. Stepan, *L' Europa post-comunista*, Bologna: Il Mulino, 2000.

Structural Adjustment Programs and the Comprehensive Development Framework

The best comprehensive study on structural adjustment is G. Mohan, E. Brown, B. Milward, & A.B. Zack Williams, *Structural Adjustment. Theory: Practice and Impact*, London: Routledge, 2000. See also M. Kahler, *The Politics of International Debt*, Ithaca, NY: Cornell University Press, 1986; and S. Haggard & R. Kaufman (eds), *The Politics of Economic Adjustment. International Constraints, Distributive Conflicts and the State*, Princeton, NJ: Princeton University Press, 1992.

On the oil crisis, OPEC, and the flood of petro-dollars see D. Yergin, *The Prize: the Epic Quest for Oil, Money and Power*, New York: Free Press, 1991, p. 633.

The manifesto of so-called monetary policy is given in the famous piece by M. Friedman, *A Theoretical Framework for Monetary Analysis*, Ann Arbor, MI: University Microfilms International, 1971. See also, by the same author, in a broader context, *Capitalism and Freedom*, Chicago: University of Chicago Press, 1962.

A discussion of the impact of World Bank and IMF policies as responsible for the 1997 Asian crisis and of much disruption in the third world, by a former chief economist of the World Bank, is given in J. Stiglitz, *Globalization and its Discontents*, New York: W.W. Norton & Co., 2003. See also S. George & F. Sabelli, *Faith and Credit: the World Bank Secular Empire*, Boulder, CO: Westview Press, 1994. Other important critiques include A. Atkinson, *The Economic Consequences of Rolling Back the Welfare State*, Cambridge, MA: MIT Press, 1999; and R.M. Solow, *Work and Welfare*, Princeton, NJ: Princeton University Press, 1998. There is not much legal work on the impact of these policies. An important exception showing the extraordinary adaptability of the so called "informal" sector is A.M. Tripp, *Changing the Rules: the Politics of Liberalization and the Urban Informal Economy in Tanzania*, Berkeley, CA: University of California Press, 1997. On the perverse effects of cutting taxation on rights there are critics even from the mainstream, see S. Holmes & C. Sunstein, *The Cost of Rights: Why Liberty Depends on Taxes*, New York: W.W. Norton & Co., 1999. On the relationship between globalization and social inequality, see L. Gallino, *Globalizzazione e disuguaglianze*, Roma-Bari: Laterza, 2000. On the social disruption produced by economic globalization policies and consequent migration, see A. Dal Lago, *Non-persone. L'esclusione dei migranti in una societa' globale*, Milano: Feltrinelli, 2000.

Development Frameworks, Plunder, and the Rule of Law

Recent movies have documented how structural adjustment programs actually work and most importantly the consequences that they produce. For Argentina, see A. Lewis & N. Klein, *The Take* (2004); for Jamaica, see C. White, *Life+Debt* (2001); and for Mali, see P. Quaregna, *le bon éleve* (2006). An early important critique is C. Payer, *The World Bank. A Critical Analysis*, New York: Monthly Review Press, 1982.

Chapter 3

The European Roots of Colonial Plunder

On the "Americanization" of law one should read the special issue of *Archives du Philosophie du Droit*, 2001, devoted to "Le probleme de l'americanization du droit."

An extensive discussion can be found in Ugo Mattei, "A theory of imperial law: a study on U.S. hegemony and the Latin resistance," *Indiana Journal of Global Legal Studies* 10, 2003, p. 383. Also see Laura Nader, "The Americanization of international law," in *Mobile People, Mobile Law* (F. von Benda-Beckmann, K. von Benda-Beckmann, & A. Griffiths, eds), London: Ashgate (2005). Important background materials can be found in M. Likosky (ed.), *Transnational Legal Processes. Globalization and Power Disparities*, Cambridge: Cambridge University Press, 2002.

An indispensable perspective, clearly distinguishing "contexts of production" from "contexts of reception" of law, focusing both on pre- and post-Americanization is given by D. Lopez Medina, *Teoria impura del derecho*, Bogota: Ediciones Universidad de los Andes, 2004. Some important economic background of US economic primacy is offered by D. North, *The Economic Growth of the United States 1790–1860*, Englewood Cliffs, NJ: Prentice Hall, 1961. For more on Western expansion, see J.H. Parry, *The Establishment of the European Hegemony, 1415–1715, Trade and Exploration in the Age of the Renaissance*, 3rd edn, New York: Harper & Row, 1966; and Carlo M. Cipolla, *European Culture and Overseas Expansion*, Harmondsworth, UK: Penguin Books, 1970. S. Latouche, *L'Occidentalisation du monde. Essai sur la signification, la portee et les limits de l'uniformisation planetaire*, Paris: La Decouverte, 1989.

The Fundamental Structure of US Law as a Post-colonial Reception

On the fundamental "producers" of law in the Western legal tradition, the classic remains J.P. Dawson, *The Oracles of the Law*, Ann Arbor, MI: University of Michigan Press, 1968. The sources of law are a traditional topic of comparative inquiry; see R.B. Schlesinger, H.W. Baade, P.E. Herzog, & E. Wise, *Comparative Law: Cases, Text, Materials*, 6th edn, New York: Foundation Press, 1998. For a concise introduction to the discipline, dated though still influential, see R. David, *Les Grands Systèmes de Droit Contemporaine*, Paris: 1966 (English translation: R. David & E.C. Brierley, *Major Legal Systems in the World Today. An Introduction to the Comparative Study of Law*, 2nd edn, London: Stevens, 1978).

For a discussion of the fundamental structure of English law, see R.C.A. White, *The English Legal System in Action*, Oxford: Oxford University Press, 1999. On the US system, see K. Llewellyn, *The Bramble Bush. On Our Law and Its Processes*, New York: Oceana Publications, 1981. For a classic short history of US law, see G. Gilmore, *The Ages of American Law*, New Haven, CT: Yale University Press, 1983. A short and very influential introduction to the civil law is given in J.H. Merryman, *The Civil Law Tradition*, Stanford, CA: Stanford University Press, 1985. Also relevant is J. Seligman *The High Citadel – the Influence of Harvard Law School*, Boston: Houghton-Mifflin, 1978.

A Theory of Lack, Yesterday and Today

On individualistic property law as a fundamental institution of Western capitalism, one can only refer to basic introductory reading. See R.C. Ellickson, C.M. Rose, & B.A. Ackerman, *Perspectives on Property Law*, 2nd edn, Boston: Little, Brown & Co., 1995. For a classic historical perspective, see C.B. Macpherson, *The Political Theory of Possessive Individualism: Hobbes to Locke*, Oxford: Clarendon Press, 1962. A discussion on the past and present value of natural law theory of property is contained in Chapter 2 of Ugo Mattei, *Comparative Law and Economics*, Ann Arbor, MI: University of Michigan Press, 1997. For a classic critique, see P.J. Proudhon, *Qu'est-ce que la proprieté*, Paris: Marcel Rivière, 1926. See also F. Engels, *The Origin of the Family, Private Property and the State* (English translation), New York: International Publishers, 1972.

On Western perceptions of Chinese law as "lacking," see T. Ruskola, "Legal orientalism," *Michigan Law Review* 101, 2002, p. 179. For a political and economic background, see Michael Greenberg, *British Trade and the Opening of China, 1800–42*, Cambridge, UK: Cambridge University Press, 1951. On Latin American law downgraded as a mere bad copy of the European tradition, see J. Esquirol, "The fictions of Latin American law, Part 1," *Utah Law Review* 2, 1997, p. 425. For a political and economic background, see D.C.M. Platt, *Latin America and British Trade, 1806–1914*, New York: Harper & Row, 1973. On similar attitudes towards Japan, see E. Feldman, *The Ritual of Rights in Japan*, Cambridge, UK: Cambridge University Press, 2002. On American natives "lacking" property law, see J. Carillo (ed.), *Readings in American Indian Law*, Philadelphia: Temple University Press, 1998.

Before Neo-liberalism: Colonial Practices and Harmonious Strategies – Yesterday and Now

On adversarial conceptions of law as a typical American feature, see R.A. Kagan, *Adversarial Legalism: the American Way of Law*, Cambridge, MA: Harvard University Press, 2001. For a critique of its supposedly neutral implications, see D. Kennedy, *A Critique of Adjudication: Fin de Siecle*, Cambridge, MA: Harvard University Press, 2001. On harmonious practices in a variety of contexts including the USA, see Laura Nader, *The Life of the Law*, Berkeley, CA: University of California Press, 2002. For a critique of soft law ideology, see A. Di Robilant, "A genealogy of soft law," *American Journal of Comparative Law* 54, 2006, p. 499. On the practical impact of World Trade Organization policies, see S. Anderson (ed.), *Views from the South. The Effects of Globalization and the WTO on Third World Countries*, Oakland, CA: Food First Books, 2000.

Chapter 4

Hegemony and Legal Consciousness

On post-modern changes in legal consciousness, see De Sousa Santos, *Toward a New Common Sense*, 2nd edn, London: Butterworths, 2002; and W. Twining, *Globalization and Legal Theory*, Evanston, Illinois: North Western University Press, 2000. On the demise of state-centrist approaches, see S. Cassese, *La crisi dello stato*, Bari: Laterza, 2002 and S. Strange, *The Retreat of the State: The Diffusion of Power in World Economy*, Cambridge: Cambridge University Press, 1996. On current uses of propaganda, see E.S. Herman & N. Chomsky, *Manufacturing Consent*, New York: Random House, 1998; T.H. Qualter, *Opinion Control in Democracies*, London: Macmillan, 1985; and T.L. McPhail, *Electronic Colonialism: The Future of International Broadcasting and Communication*, Beverly Hills, CA–London: Sage Publications, 1981. On professionalism, see M. Sarfatti Larson, *The Rise of Professionalism*, Berkeley, CA: University of California Press, 1977. On the role of intellectuals, see A. Gramsci, *Gli intellettuali e l'organizzazione della cultura (a cura di Valentino Gerratana)*, Rome: Editori Riuniti, 1975. Fundamental background reading is D. Harvey, *The Condition of Postmodernity*, Cambridge, UK: Blackwell Publishing, 1990. See also M. Castells, *The Information Age*. Vol. 1, *The Rise of the Network Society*, Oxford: Blackwell, 1996; and P. Virilio, *La Bombe Informatique*, Paris: Editions Galilee, 1998.

Intellectual Property as Plunder of Ideas

The debate on intellectual property is very rich but usually technical and narrow. For the traditional economic justification, see R. Cooter & T. Ulen, *Law and Economics*, 3rd edn, Reading, UK: Addison Wesley, 2000, p. 126. One should now read, for the critical mainstream, L. Lessig, *Free Culture*, New York: Penguin Press, 2004. An important critique of the critical mainstream is given by A. Chandler, "The new, new property," *Texas Law Review* 81, 2003, p. 715. An interesting collection of data and thoughts is provided in "Sovereignty and the globalization of intellectual property," *Indiana Journal of Global Legal Studies* 6, 1998. For a critique on the claim of originality of ideas, see G. Debord, *La Societé du Spectacle*, Paris : Gallimard, 1992. On his work, see S. Home (ed.), *What is Situationism? A Reader*, San Francisco: A.K Press, 1996. On different recent resisting theories and practices, see K. Lasn, *Culture Jam*, New York: Quill, 2000. For a history of the development of Linux and open-source platforms, see L. Torvalds & D. Diamond, *Just for Fun: the Story of an Accidental Revolutionary*, New York: Collins, 2001; and G. Moody, *Rebel Code: the Inside Story of Linux and the Open Source Revolution*, New York: Perseus Books Group, 2001.

Providing Legitimacy: Law and Economics

This section is based on Ugo Mattei, "The rise and fall of law and economics. An essay for Judge Guido Calabresi," in *Maryland Law Review* 64, 2005, p. 220. How an economist (and world leader in law and economics) sees the role of his discipline in social sciences can be learned by reading R. Cooter, "Law and the imperialism of economics," *UCLA Law Review* 29, 1982, p. 1260. A more critical approach is D.N. McCloskey, *The Rhetoric of Economics*, Madison: University of Wisconsin Press, 1985. Important background information on lawyers as a social group is provided by R.L. Abel & P.S.C. Lewis, *Lawyers in Society*, Berkeley, CA: University of California Press, 1988.

For mechanisms of elite reproduction, see D. Kennedy, *American Law Schools and the Reproduction of Hierarchy: a Polemic Against the System*, New York: New York University Press, 2004. A thorough historical discussion of the relationship between law and economic power can be found in M.E. Tigar & M.R. Levy, *Law and the Rise of Capitalism*, New York: Monthly Review Press, 2000. For a discussion of the role of the legal elite in the making of the global legal order, see Y. Dezalay & B.G. Garth, *Dealing in Virtue*, Chicago: University of Chicago Press, 1996.

For some instructive background of the mechanisms of corporate capitalism, see James O'Connor, *The Corporations and the State: Essays in the Theory of Capitalism and Imperialism*, New York: Harper & Row, 1974; and Charles E. Lindblom, *Politics and Markets: the World's Political Economic Systems*, New York: Basic Books, 1977.

Providing Legitimacy: Lawyers and Anthropologists

For more on the history of anthropology, see E. Leach, "Glimpses of the unmentionable in the history of British social anthropology," *Annual Review of Anthropology* 13, 1984, pp. 1–24; and Laura Nader, *Sleepwalking through the History of Anthropology. Anthropologists on Home Ground, Essays in Honor of William Curtis Sturtevant.* W. Merrill, I. Goddards eds, Smithsonian Contributions to Anthropology No. 44, Washington D.C.: Smithsonian Institution Press, 2002.

For a British insider's perspective on British anthropology, see A. Kuper, *Anthropology and Anthropologists: the Modern British School*, London: Routledge & Kegan, 1983; and, more broadly, A. Kuper, *Culture: the Anthropologists' Account*, Boston: Harvard University Press, 1999.

On moving anthropology from the armchair to the field, see: F. Boas, *Introduction to the Handbook of American Indian Languages*, Part I, Seattle, WA: Shorey Book Store, 1971; F. Boas, *The Shaping of American Anthropology, 1883–1911*, A Franz Boas Reader, New York: Basic Books, 1974; and G. Stocking, *Observers Observed: Essays on Anthropological Fieldwork*, Madison, WI: University of Wisconsin Press, 1983.

For more on the ideological basis of science and technology, and on Western, non-Western, and intermingled ways of knowing, see: H. Gusterson, *Nuclear Rites: a Weapons Laboratory at the End of the Cold War*, Berkeley, CA: University of California Press, 1996; R. Gonzalez, *Zapotec Science: Farming and Food in the Northern Sierra of Oaxaca*, Austin, TX: University of Texas Press, 2001; Laura Nader (ed.), *Naked Science: Anthropological Inquiries into Boundaries, Power, and Knowledge*, New York: Routledge, 1996; and S. Traweek, *Beam-Times and Lifetimes: the World of High Energy Physicists*, Cambridge, MA: Harvard University Press, 1988.

On the notion of progress and an anthropological critique, urging that progress be considered an object to be analyzed rather than taken for granted, see the foundational A. Kroeber, *Anthropology: Race, Language, Culture, Psychology, Pre-History*, New York: Harcourt Brace, 1948.

On McCarthy-era anthropology, see Laura Nader, "The phantom factor – impact of the Cold War on anthropology," in *The Cold War and the University: Toward an Intellectual History of the Postwar Years* (N. Chomsky, ed.), New York: The New Press, 1997; and D. Price, *Threatening Anthropology: McCarthyism and the FBI's Surveillance of Activist Anthropologists*, Durham, NC: Duke University Press, 2004. See also D. Price "Gregory Bateson and the OSS," *Human Organization* 57 (4), 1998, pp. 379–84. For the story of the anthropologist referred to in the text, see E. Reynolds, *The Forbidden Voyage*, New York: D. McKay Co., 1961, p. 60.

For an exemplar of anthropologists' work produced as a contribution to the war effort, see R. Benedict, *The Chrysanthemum and the Sword: Patterns of Japanese Culture*, Boston: Houghton Miflin, 1946. For an ethnography produced after World War II on a fieldwork site in which the anthropologist was simultaneously working for British military intelligence, see E. Leach, *Political Systems of Highland Burma*, Cambridge, MA: Harvard University Press, 1954. To examine the anthropological work of those who worked for the OSS during World War II, see D. Price, "Anthropologists as spies," *The Nation* 271 (16), 2000, pp. 24–7. Franz Boas' article that ignited the censorship reaction was "Scientists as spies," *The Nation* 21 (3), 2005.

The history of some of anthropology's relationship, and sometime complicity, with the North American genocide is recounted in N. Scheper-Hughes, "Coming to our senses: anthropology and genocide," in *Critical Reflections: Anthropology and the Study of Genocide*, Section V, *Annihilating Difference: Anthropology and Genocide* (A.L. Hinton, ed.), Berkeley, CA, pp. 348–81: University of California Press, 2002. See also L. Foerstel & A. Gilliam (eds), *Confronting the Margaret Mead Legacy: Scholarship, Empire, and the South Pacific*, Philadelphia: Temple University Press, 1992.

Max Gluckman's work emphasizing the similarities of legal systems in Africa and Europe, as an implicited basis for claiming commensurability and equality between Africans and Europeans, is found *inter alia* in M. Gluckman, *The Judicial Process Among the Barotse of Northern Rhodesia*, Glencoe, IL: Free Press, 1955; and M. Gluckman,

"The reasonable man in Barotse law" (BBC Third Programme Broadcasts), *Journal of African Administration* 1968: 7 (2), pp. 51–5; (7) 3, pp. 126–31; 8 (2), pp. 101–5; and 8 (3), pp. 151–6 (reprinted in A. Dundes (ed.), *Every Man His Way*, Englewood Cliffs, NJ: Prentice Hall, 1968).

The groundbreaking work explicating the process of creating an "other" is E. Said, *Orientalism*, New York: Pantheon, 1978. Henry Lewis Morgan's "progressive evolutionism" is expounded by his biographer, C. Resek in *Louis Henry Morgan: American Scholar*, Chicago: University of Chicago Press, 1960. See also G. Stocking, Jr., *Race, Culture, and Evolution: Essays in the History of Anthropology*, New York: The Free Press, 1968, pp. xvii and 380; and J. Kenyatta, *Facing Mount Kenya*, London: Heinemann, 1979 (with a preface by B. Malinowski). For a French perspective, see Jean Copans (ed.) *Anthropologie et imperialisme*, Paris: Francois Maspero, 1975.

Chapter 5

The Plunder of Oil: Iraq and Elsewhere

See: P. Chatterjee, *Iraq Inc. A Profitable Occupation*, New York: Seven Stories Press, 2004; J. Martinkus, *Travels in American Iraq*, Melbourne: Black, Inc., 2004; M. Ruppert, *Crossing the Rubicon: the Decline of American Empire at the End of the Age of Oil*, Gabriola Island, Canada: New Society Publishers, 2004; M. Klare, *Resource War. Blood and Oil*, New York: Holt, 2004; and S. Coll, *Ghost Wars: the Secret History of CIA, Afghanistan and Bin Laden from the Soviet Invasion to September 10 2001*, New York: Penguin, 2004. A recent short historical discussion showing some numbers of the profits obtained from plunder by US Corporations thus far in Iraq is given in Louis H. Lapham, "Lionhearts," *Harper's Magazine*, Notebook September, 2006. See also N. Klein, "Bomb before you buy: the economics of war," *Seattle Journal for Social Justice* 2, 2004, p. 331.

The New World Order of Plunder

On the end of the Cold War and some of its suggested causes, see J.L. Gaddis, *The United States and the End of the Cold War: Implications, Reconsiderations, Provocations*, Oxford: Oxford University Press, 1992. The political premises of the so-called "end of history", also known as Pax Americana, have been discussed as early as 1973 by R. Aron, *La Republique Imperiale: Les Etas Unis dans le Monde*, Paris : Callman Levi, 1973. On the influential idea of the "third way" see A. Giddens, *Beyond Left and Right: the Future of Radical Politics*, Cambridge, UK: Polity Press, 1994. A similarly successful (and similarly conservative) intellectual manifesto is F. Fukuyama, *The End of History and the Last Man*, New York: Free Press, 1992.

The end of the Cold War has transformed the left not only in Europe but elsewhere too. For a less sorrowful perspective on Latin America, see Jorge G. Castaneda, *Utopia Unarmed: the Latin American Left After the Cold War*, New York: Vintage Books, 1994. The new enemy has been quickly found in Islam; see S. Huntington, *The Clash of Civilization and the Remaking of the World Order*, New York: Simon & Shuster, 1996. An interesting recent discussion is to be found in M. Mamdani, *Good Muslim, Bad Muslim: America, The Cold War and the Roots of Terror*, New York: Pantheon Books, 2004. On US policy in Latin America one should read T. Halperin-Donghi, *The Contemporary History of Latin America* (English translation), Durham, UK: Duke University Press, 1993; while on the role of war in post Cold War foreign policy it is mandatory to read L. Lapham, *Theater of War*, New Press: New York, 2002.

Not Only Iraq: Plunder, War, and Legal Ideologies of Intervention

In general, for a brilliant re-telling of recent history, discussing motives behind military intervention, see Jacques R. Pauwels, *De mythe van de "geode oorlog": Amerika en de Tweede Wereldoorlog*, Antwerpen: EPO, 2000 (English translation: *The Myth of the Good War*, Toronto: James Lorimer & Co., 2002). See also R. Gilpin, *War and Change in World Politics*, Cambridge: Cambridge University Press, 1981; P. Delmas, *Le bel avenir de la guerre*, Paris: Gallimard, 1995; G. Chiesa, *La guerra infinita*, Milano: Feltrinelli, 2002; C. Galli, *La guerra globale*, Roma-Bari: Laterza, 2002. See also M. Finnemore, *The Purpose of Intervention: Changing Beliefs About the Use of Force*, Ithaca, NY: Cornell University Press, 2003. For a sophisticated discussion on the role of legitimacy, see T.M. Franck, *The Power of Legitimacy Among Nations*, New York: Oxford University Press, 1990. See also G. Gong, *The Standard of "Civilization" in International Society*, Oxford: Clarendon Press, 1984. See also D. Zolo, *Cosmopolis. La Prospettiva del Governo Mondiale*, Milano: Feltrinelli, 1995.

For some discussion of troubled contexts, see E. Carlton, *Massacres: an Historical Perspective*, London: Pinter Publishing Co., 1994; and I. Wallimann & M.N. Dobkowsky (eds) *Genocide and the Modern Age: Etiology and Case Studies of Mass Death*, Westport, MA: Greenwood, 1987. On US knowledge and inaction in the face of historical genocides, see S. Power, *"A Problem from Hell": America and the Age of Genocide*, New York: Basic Books, 2002. On economic intervention, see J.M. Nelson (ed.), *Economic Crisis and Policy Choice: the Politics of Adjustment in the Third World*, Princeton, NJ: Princeton University Press, 1990. See also J. Keegan, *A History of Warfare*, New York: Vintage Books, 1993.

Institutional Lacks as Conditions for Plunder: Real or Created?

In general, on historical episodes of legal intervention, see I. Wallerstein, *European Universalism. The Rhetoric of Power*, New York: The New Press, 2006 pointing at the debate between sixteenth century scholars De Las Casas and Sepulveda on the legitimacy of the conquistadores' power over the natives as the canon of current debate. See L. Hanke, *All Mankind is One: A Study on the Disputation Between Bartolome' de Las Casas and Juan Gines de Sepulveda in 1550 on the Intellectual and Religious Capacity of the American Indians*, De Kalb: Northern Illinois University Press, 1974. On recent legal intervention to bring the rule of law in Afghanistan, see Faiz Ahmed, "Judicial reform in Afghanistan: a case study in the New Criminal Procedure Code," *Hastings International and Comparative Law Review* 29, 2005, p. 93. For a discussion of the informal legal system of Mali, see A. Keita, "Au Detour des Pratiques Foncieres a Bancoumana: Quelques Observations sur le Droit Malien" *Global Jurist Frontiers* 2003, Vol. 3, Issue 1. For a critical appraisal of the de-politicizing consequences of humanitarian intervention, see M. Pandolfi, "Contract of Mutual (In) difference. Governance and the Humanitarian Apparatus in Contemporary Albania and Kosovo, *Indiana Journal of Global Legal Studies* 10, 2003, pp. 369–81.

"Double Standards Policy" and Plunder

A variety of interventionist practices of US foreign policy and a variety of rationales developed since the ages of the Monroe doctrine are discussed in Naom Chomsky, *Hegemony or Survival: America's Quest for Global Dominance*, New York: Holt, 2003. See also Z. Brzezinski, *The Grand Chessboard: American Primacy and its Geographic Imperatives*, New York: Basic Books, 1997.

Among international human rights experts attempting to show cultural sensitiveness, see J. Donelly, *Universal Human Rights in Theory and Practice*, 2nd edn, Ithaca, NY: Cornell University Press, 2003; and C. Eberhard, *Droits de l'homme et dialogue interculturel*, Paris: Editions des Ecrivains, 2002. For a more critical approach, see A. Gambino, *L' imperialismo dei diritti umani: Caos e giustizia nella società globale*, Rome: Editori Riuniti, 2001. See also M. Ignatieff, *Human Rights as Politics and Idolatry*, Princeton: Princeton University Press, 2001. On the World Trade Organization and its structure of exclusion, see S. George, *Remettre l'OMC a ca place*, Paris: Librerie Artheme Fayard, 2001.

For an insightful analysis of one case of imposition of sanctions, their effects on a population, and an argument for extending existing international law to address the sanctions' effects, see G. Bisharat, "Sanctions as genocide," *Transnational Law and Contemporary Problems* 11, 2001, p. 379. On Cuba, see Clifford L. Staten, *The History of Cuba*, New York: Palgrave McMillan, 2003.

Some historical roots of present practices are discussed in J.E. Thomson, *Mercenaries, Pirates and Sovereigns: State Building and Extra-Territorial Violence in Early Modern Europe*, Princeton, NJ: Princeton University Press, 1994. On mercenaries today, see P.W. Singer, *Corporate Warriors: the Rise of the Privatized Military Industry*, Ithaca, NY: Cornell University Press, 2003. On British mercantilism, see Murry G.

Lawson, *A Study on English Mercantilism 1700–1775*, Toronto: University of Toronto Press, 1943.

Poverty: Justification for Intervention and Consequences of Plunder

An economic discussion on poverty showing the approach of the economic mainstream can be found in M.J. Trebilcock, "What makes poor countries poor? The role of institutional capital in economic development," in *The Law and Economics of Development* (E. Buscaglia, W. Ratliff, & R. Cooter, eds), Greenwich, CT: Jai Press, 1997. In general, on poverty, see P. Dasgupta, *An Inquiry into Well Being and Destitution*, New York: Oxford University Press, 1993. On some of its causes, see George L. Beckford, *Persistent Poverty: Underdevelopment in Plantation Economies on the Third World*, New York: Oxford University Press, 1972. See also A. Sen, *Poverty and Inequality*, (G. Grusky & R. Kanbur, eds), Stanford: Stanford University Press, 2006.

For a background on Bolivia's privatization in the natural gas sector, mass popular reaction, and Gonzalo Sanchez de Lozada's exit from the presidency, see the powerful account of M. McFarland Sánchez-Moreno & T. Higgins, "No recourse: transnational corporations and the protection of economic, social, and cultural rights in Bolivia," *Fordham International Law Journal* 27, 2004, p. 1663. For spot reporting on Lozada's exit, see R. Lindsay, "Rural activists back new leader, for now Bolivian President faces demands that toppled predecessor," *Boston Globe* October 29, 2003, p. A8. Fore some of the extractive practices and their consequences in Latin American countries, see: Peter J. Bakewell, *Silver Mining and Society in Colonial Mexico: Zacatecas, 1546–1700*; D.A. Breading, *Miners and Merchants in Bourbon Mexico 1768–1810*, Cambridge, UK: Cambridge University Press, 1971; and Stanley J. Stein-Barbara Stein, *The Colonial Heritage of Latin America*, Oxford: Oxford University Press, 1970.

Chapter 6

Reactive Institutions of Imperial Plunder

This section is based on Ugo Mattei, "A theory of imperial law: a study on US hegemony and the Latin resistance," *Indiana Journal of Global Legal Studies* 10, 2003, p. 383; and *Global Jurist Frontiers* 2002 (available at: www.bepress.com).

On the so-called "passive virtues" of the courts of law as non-democratically legitimized agencies, see A. Bickel, *The Least Dangerous Branch: the Supreme Court at the Bar of Politics*, New Haven, CT: Yale University Press, 1986. Another classic discussion is B. Cardozo, *The Nature of the Judicial Process*, New Haven, CT: Yale University Press, 1921.

On dualism, see I.M.D. Little, *Economic Development: Theory, Policy and International Relations*, New York: Basic Books, 1982. On rule of law and development as undisputable goods, see F. Garcia Amador, *The Emerging International Law of Development: a New Dimension of International Economic Law*, New York: Oceana Books, 1990.

US Rule of Law: Forms of Global Domination

On the role of courts as mighty political actors in US law, the classic is still A. De Tocqueville, *Democratie en Amerique* (1835), Paris: Les Editions Gaillimard, 1992 (English translation: *Democracy in America*, R.D. Heffne (ed.), New York: Signet Classics, 2001). On European legal expansionism in general, see W.J. Mommsen & J.A. De Moor, *European Expansion and Law: the Encounter of European and Indigenous Law in 19th and 20th century Africa and Asia*, Herndon, VA: Berg Publications, 1992. On global changes in notions of legality, see also G. Teubner (ed.) *Global Law Without a State*, Sudbury, MA: Dartmouth Publishing, 1997. See also D. Zolo, "The Lords of Peace: From the Holy Alliance to the New International Criminal Tribunal," in *Global Democracy* (B. Holden, ed.), London: Routledge, 2000.

Globalization of the American Way

On decentralization as a peculiarly original structure of US models of adjudication, see H. Hart & Sacks, *The Legal Process: Basic Problems in the Making and Application of Law*, Tent Ed., Cambridge, Massachusetts, 1958 (reprinted, New York, 1994). A particularly readable discussion is J. Resnick, *Processes of the Law: Understanding Courts and Their Alternatives*, New York: Foundation Press, 2004. For an inevitable discussion from the efficiency perspective, see N. Komesar, *Imperfect Alternatives: Choosing Institutions in Law, Economics, and Public Policy*, Chicago: University of Chicago Press 1996.

On the market for votes, see J. Buchanan & G. Tullock, *The Calculus of Consent: Logical Foundations of Constitutional Democracy*, Indianapolis: Liberty Fund, 1962. On the efficiency of the common law process, see R. Posner, *Economic Analysis of Law*, 5th edn, New York: Aspen Publishers, 1998, p. 271. On the impact on distribution of the structure of litigation, see M. Galanter, "Why the "haves" come out ahead: speculations on the limits of legal change," *Law and Society Review* 95, 1972, p. 9.

An Ideological Institution of Global Governance: International Law

See in general *Human Rights: An Agenda for the Next Century* (L. Henkin & J. Hargrove, eds), Washington: ASIL, 1994; S.R. Ratner & J.S. Abrams, *Accountability for Human Rights Atrocities in International Law: Beyond the Nuremberg Legacy*, Oxford: Clarendon Press, 1997; and W.A. Schabas, *An Introduction to the International Criminal Court*, Cambridge, UK: Cambridge University Press, 2001. See also A. Cassese, *International Law*, Oxford: Oxford University Press, 2001. For more critical visions see D. Zolo, *La giustizia dei vincitori. Da Norimberga a Baghdad*, Roma-Bari: Laterza, 2005; David Kennedy, *The Dark Side of Virtue*, Princeton: Princeton University Press, 2005. On sovereignty, see S. Krasner, *Sovereignity: Organized Hypocrisy*, Princeton, NJ: Princeton University Press, 1999, which has rapidly become a classic. On soft strategies of imperial leadership, see J. Nye, *Bound to Lead: the Changing Nature of American Power*, New York: Basic Books, 1991. On the use of similar rhetoric in the current liberal US academic mainstream, see A.M. Slaughter, *A New World Order*, Princeton: Princeton University Press, 2004.

Holocaust Litigation: Back to the Future

For a detailed discussion, see M. Bazyler, *Holocaust Justice*, New York: New York University Press, 2003. See also, for the direct experience of a master of comparative law, R.B. Schlesinger, *Memoir*, Trento: Università degli Studi, 1999. For an accessible comparative discussion of the intricacies of the law of jurisdiction, see M. Reimann, *Jurisdiction: a Guide to the Jungle*, New York: Transnational Press, 2001. For a discussion of some relevant structures of US procedures, see O. Chase, "American 'exceptionalism' and comparative procedure," *American Journal of Comparative Law* 50, 2002, p. 277.

The Swallowing of International Law by US Law

See, for a variety of materials, J. Paul "Symposium, holding multinational corporations responsible under international law," *Hastings International and Comparative Law Review* 24, 2001, p. 285. For a documentary movie discussing corporate capitalism, see M. Achbar, J. Abbott, & J. Bakan, *The Corporation* (2004).

On US tort law the most balanced and informed discussion is still J. Fleming, *The American Tort Process*, Oxford: Clarendon Press, 1990. For another view, see also P.H. Schuck (ed.), *Tort Law and the Public Interest*, New York, W.W. Norton & Co., 1991.

For an interesting comparative discussion of the main "differences" in civil procedure between the US approach and other traditions, see R.B. Schlesinger, H.W. Baade, P.E. Herzog, & E. Wise, *Comparative Law*, 6th edn, New York: Foundation Press, 1998. For a comparative discussion on the legal profession focusing on US peculiarities, see J. Barcelo & R. Crampton (eds) *Lawyer's Values and*

Ideals, Dordrecht: Kluwer, 1999. For a discussion of US choice of law, see E. Scoles, P. Hay, P. Borchers, & S. Symeonides, *Conflict of Laws*, 3rd edn, St. Paul, MN: West Publishing Company, 2000.

Economic Power and the US Courts as Imperial Agencies

On private attorneys in the public interest, the classic is still M. Cappelletti, "Governmental and private advocates for the public interest in civil litigation," *Michigan Legal Review* 75, 1975, p. 794. On US economic hegemony in a variety of sectors generally, see D. Held & A. McGrew, *The Global Transformations Reader*, Cambridge, UK: Polity Press, 2000. On remedial shortcomings in the global world, see M. Galanter, "Law's elusive promise. Learning from Bophal," in *Transnational Legal Processes. Globalization and Power Disparities* (M. Likosky, ed.), London: Butterworth: 2002. Also see Russell Mokhiber & Robert Weissman, *On the Rampage: Corporate Power and the Destruction of Democracy*, Monroe, ME: Common Courage Press, 2005.

Chapter 7

Strategies to Subordinate the Rule of Law to Plunder

On potential counter-hegemonic use of the law the best read is still J. Harr, *A Civil Action*, New York, Vintage Books, 1995. See, generally, Laura Nader (ed.) *No Access to Law: Alternatives to the American Judicial System*, New York: Academic Press, 1980; R. Nader & W.J. Smith, *No Contest: Corporate Lawyers and the Perversion of Justice in America*, New York: Random House, 1996; and O. Fiss, "Against settlement," *Yale Law Journal* 93, 1984, p. 1073.

On the "need" of tort reform, see S. Sugarman, *Doing Away with Personal Injury Law: New Compensation Mechanisms for Victims, Consumers and Business*, Westport, CT: Quorum Books, 1989; compare it with M. Galanter, "News from nowhere: the debased debate on civil justice," *Denver University Law Review* 71, 1993, p. 77. On the post-modern turn of US legal academies, see S.M. Feldman, *American Legal Thought from Premodernism to Postmodernism: an Intellectual Voyage*, New York: Oxford University Press, 2000.

Plunder in High Places: Enron and its Aftermath

For some indispensable context, M. Roe, *Strong Managers, Weak Owners: the Political Roots of American Corporate Finance*, Princeton, NJ: Princeton University Press, 1994; and L. Loss, *Fundamentals of Securities Regulation*, Boston: Little, Brown & Co.,

1983. Note "The good, the bad, and their corporate codes of ethics: Enron, Sarbanes Oxley and the problem of legislating good behaviour," *Harvard Law Review* 116, 2003, p. 2123; and S. Strange, *Casino Capitalism*, Oxford: Blackwell Publishing, 1986. For a discussion on the changing position of gatekeepers during the 1990s and an attempt to explain their failure, see John C. Coffee, Jr., "What caused Enron? A capsule social and economic history of the 1990s," *Cornell Law Review* 89, 2004, p. 269. For an evaluation of Congress' intervention to cure the problem through the Sarbanes-Oxley Act, see especially p. 303 ff. Compare also John C. Coffee, Jr., "Understanding Enron: 'it's about the gatekeepers, stupid'," *Business Lawyer* 57, 2002, p. 1403. For a criticism of how the act has gone too far in requiring auditing committees composed entirely of independent (?) directors, at least in listed companies, see Roberta Romano, "The Sarbanes-Oxley Act and the making of quack corporate governance," *Yale Law Journal* 114, 2005, p. 1521.

Plunder in Even Higher Places: Electoral Politics and Plunder

On *Bush* v. *Gore* the literature is quite extensive. Because of the quite extremely conservative politics of the author, the most instructive read is A. Dershowitz, *Supreme Injustice: How the High Court Hijacked Election 2000*, New York: Oxford University Press, 2001. See also, for further documentation, E.J. Dionne & W. Bristol (eds), *Bush v. Gore: the Court Cases and the Commentary*, Washington, DC: Brookings Press, 2001. In general on a variety of unfair strategies, undermining the credibility of the US electoral model, see J. Fund, *Stealing Elections: How Voter Fraud Threatens Our Democracy*, San Francisco: Encounter Books, 2004. On US prestige-building strategies, see O. Zunz, *Why the American Century?*, Chicago: University of Chicago Press, 1998. For a description of its decline, see I. Krastev, "The anti-American century?," *Journal of Democracy* 15, 2004, p. 5.

Plunder of Liberty: the War on Terror

On post September 11, 2001 foreign policy doctrines, see R. Falk, *The Great Terror War*, Northampton, MA: Oliver Brench Press, 2003. See also N. Deller, A. Machijani, & J. Burrough, *Rule of Power or Rule of Law?*, New York: Apex Press, 2003. On internal transformations, see D. Cole & J. Dempsey, *Terrorism and the Constitution*, New York: The New Press, 2002; and William Shultz, *Tainted Legacy: 9/11 and the Ruin of Human Rights*, New York: Thunder Marks Press, 2003. See also A. Dal Lago, *Polizia globale. Guerra e conflitti dopo l' 11 settembre*, Verona: Ombre Corte, 2003.

For the North Americans as a market-dominating minority and for notions of crony capitalism, see Ami Chua, *World on Fire: How Exporting Free Market Democracy Breeds Ethnic Hatred and Global Instability*, New York: Anchor Books, 2003.

Plunder Undisrupted: the Discourse of Patriotism

The slogan "fair and balanced" was appropriated, without intentional satire, by the Fox Network News division; see www.foxnews.com. For a critique of Fox News, focusing on its claims to be "fair and balanced," see Robert Greenwald's film *Outfoxed: Rupert Murdoch's War on Journalism* (2004). See also the website www.outfoxed.org. The United States' legal culture is the result of a dialogic process where opposition frequently crosses the line from dissent into struggle. Familiarity with opposition literature is central to understanding the contemporary constitutional framework, legal structure, and political culture that resulted.

For formative dissent during the earlier colonial period, see William Penn (1644–1718), *Some Fruits of Solitude in Reflections and Maxims: Relating to the Conduct of Human Life*, San Francisco: Edwin & Robert Grabhorn, 1926; William Penn, *No Cross, No Crown*, Wallingford, PA: Pendle Hill, 1944; and A. Murphy (ed.) *The Political Writings of William Penn*, Indianapolis: Liberty Fund, 2002. For another colonial dissenter's struggles with colonists over religious liberty, relations between Native Americans and colonists, and greater autonomy from the British government, see Roger Williams' (1604–1683) exemplary tracts, including *The Bloudy Tenet of Persecution for Cause of Conscience Discussed And Mr. Cotton's Letter Examined And Answered*, London: Kessinger Publications, 2004 (printed for the Society of J. Haddon, 1848) or Roger William's *Christenings Make Not Christians*, Providence, RI, S.S. Rider, 1881. His guide to learning Native Americans' language and culture, and a call to end extermination, is given in *A Key into the Language of America*, Detroit: Wayne State University Press, 1973. The body of Williams' work and thoughts had a profound influence on the organization of local governance of the colonies, and of protestant congregations across New England. See J. Samuel & L. Caldwell (eds) *The Complete Writings of Roger Williams*, New York: Russell & Russell, 1963; and *The Correspondence of Roger Williams*, Providence, RI: Brown University Press, 1988 (published for the Historical Society of Rhode Island).

For constitutive dissent during the revolution, see Thomas Paine (1737–1809), *Common Sense and Other Writings*, New York: Modern Library, 2003; and Thomas Paine, *Rights of Man*, New York: Penguin, 1984. For active dissent that became the foundations of the American Constitution, see Thomas Jefferson (1743–1826), *Notes on the State of Virginia*, New York: Penguin, 1999; Thomas Jefferson, *Light and Liberty: Reflections on the Pursuit of Happiness*, New York: Modern Library, 2004; Thomas Jefferson, *Political Writings*, Cambridge, UK: Cambridge University Press, 1999; and J. Morton *Republic of Letters: the Correspondence between Thomas Jefferson and James Madison*, 1767–1826, New York: W.W. Norton & Co., 1995.

In the early years of the United States' nation-building, much dissent focused on the enslavement of Africans and the genocide and plunder of Native Americans. Regarding opposition to the seizure of Native American lands, and in particular against the forced removal of the Cherokee nation from Georgia to Oklahoma, see Jeremiah Evarts, in F.P. Prucha (ed.), *Cherokee Removal: The "William Penn" Essays and Other Writings*, Knoxville, TN: University of Tennessee Press, 1981, pp. 191–2. For dissent aimed at the abolition of slavery, see D. Greene (ed.) *Lucretia Mott: Her Complete Speeches and Sermons*, New York: Edwin Mellen Press, 1980. See also P.E. Eppinger, "Messiahs of every age: a theological basis of nineteenth-century social reform," *Quaker Theology: a Progressive Journal and Forum for Discussion and Study* Spring/Summer, 2004, p. 10.

The call to conscience that roused Mott and other abolitionists extended beyond a single issue and inspired an engagement of government and American citizenship more thoroughly. In the expansion from abolition to freedom of conscience and broader questions implicating other civil liberties, Mott was joined by the Massachusetts transcendentalists Henry David Thoreau (1817–1862) and Ralph Waldo Emerson. See: H.D. Thoreau, *Civil Disobedience, and Other Essays*, New York: Dover, 1993; H.D. Thoreau, *Walden, and Resistance to Civil Government*, New York: Norton, 1991; and H.D. Thoreau *A Plea for Captain John Brown*, Boston: D.R. Godine, 1969. More generally, see W. Glick (ed.) *The Higher Law: Thoreau on Civil Disobedience and Reform*, Princeton, NJ: Princeton University Press, 2004; and *The Essays of Henry D. Thoreau*, New York: North Point Press, 2002. For his mentor, Emerson, see D. Robinson (ed.) *The Political Emerson: Essential Writings on Politics and Social Reform*, Boston: Beacon Press, 2004; *Emerson's Anti-Slavery Writings*, New Haven, CT: Yale University Press, 1995; and *Representative Men*, New York: Marsilio, 1995. See also W.E. Bridges, *Spokesmen for the Self: Emerson, Thoreau, Whitman*, Scranton, PA: Chandler Publishing Co., 1971.

Industrialization and legal change favoring the new interstate corporations over individual workers and plaintiffs inspired fresh dissent after the Civil War. The opposition made the most of new forms of distribution resulting from the print press and accompanying new genres. Political cartoonist Thomas Nast (1840–1902) harnessed the emerging power of widely available popular newspapers to attack abuses of democratic process. See T. Nast, *How Some Men get their Boots Cleaned at Other People's Expense*, New York: Harper, 1900; and T. Nast, *Thomas Nast, Political Cartoonist*, Athens, GA: University of Georgia Press, 1967. See also M. Keller, *The Art and Politics of Thomas Nast*, New York: Oxford University Press, 1968. Novelists like Theodore Dreiser (1871–1945) and Sinclair Lewis (1885–1951) also raised consciousness and aroused action against the new corporations taking advantage of workers and consumers unused to face-to-faceless forms of organization. See T. Dreiser, *An American Tragedy*, New York: Library of America, 2003 (distributed to the trade by Penguin Putnam); and T. Dreiser, *Sister Carrie*, New York: Oxford University Press, 1998. See, too, S. Lewis, *Babbitt*, New York: Modern Library, 2002; and S. Lewis, *Main Street*, New York: New American Library, 1980 (originally published c. 1920). See also J. London, *Letters from Jack London*, New York: Odyssey, 1965, containing unpublished correspondence between Jack London and Sinclair Lewis. John Steinbeck (1902–1968) carried the tradition of dissent through novel and short story through the Great Depression with *The Grapes of Wrath*, New York: Penguin Books, 1997, and *Cannery Row*, New York: Penguin Books, 2002.

For post World War II examples of dissent that have shaped constitutional law and the political culture of the United States, see, for example, Thurgood Marshall (the lead lawyer for the NAACP in the *Brown* v. *Topeka Board of Education* school desegregation case, who himself became a Supreme Court Justice) in T. Marshall, *Supreme Justice: Speeches and Writings*, Philadelphia: University of Pennsylvania Press, 2003. See also: M.L. King, *A Call to Conscience: the Landmark Speeches of Dr. Martin Luther King, Jr.*, New York: IPM, 2001; W.S. Coffin, *The Heart is a Little to the Left: Essays on Public Morality*, Hanover, NH: University Press of New England for Dartmouth College, 1999; R. Nader, *Crashing the Party: Taking on the Corporate Government in an Age of Surrender*, New York: Thomas Dunn Books/St. Martin's Press, 2002; and R. Nader, *The Good Fight: Declare Your Independence and Close the Democracy Gap*, New York: Regan Books, 2004.

On patriotism, see R.A. Falk, *Declining World Order*, New York: Routledge, p. 215 ff; and R. Corey, *Fear: the History of a Political Idea*, Oxford University Press, 2004. On war and its impact on political legitimacy in the USA, see A.M. Schlesinger, Jr., *War and the American Presidency*, New York: W.W. Norton & Co., 2004.

Peter Arnett was fired from his employer, National Geographic "Explorer," and from the network for which he was filing reports from Baghdad, NBC, in March 2003 because of an interview he gave to state-controlled Iraqi television characterizing the US-led coalition's war plans as inadequate. Accounts of Arnett's dismissal may be found in J. Rutenberg, "A nation at war: the NBC correspondent Arnett is dismissed by NBC after remarks on Iraqi TV," *New York Times* April 1, 2003, p. B14; and Xinhua, *Full Text of the Human Rights Record of the U.S. in 2003*, Beijing: Xinhua News Agency, February 29, 2004. At his network's instigation, Geraldo Rivera of Fox News was withdrawn from his deployment with the 101st Airborne Division as an embedded journalist after drawing a map in the sand of his location (meaning, the location of the troops with which he was embedded) and describing the maneuvers they planned to undertake. In a broadcast apology, Rivera said that he had "voluntarily withdrawn" back to Kuwait to "review the situation," quoted in "Rivera apologizes for report," *The Philadelphia Daily News* April 8, 2003, p. 6.

For documentary film coverage on media censorship and self-censorship on the Bush administration's preparations and initiation of war in Iraq, see D. Schechter (director), *WMD: Weapons of Mass Deception* (2004). For a thorough report on non-embedded Western reporters killed in Iraq by US-led coalition forces, see P. Wilson, "Iraq inquest," *The Australian* April 8, 2004, p. 20, which is composed of excerpts from his book, P. Wilson, *A Long Drive Through a Short War: Reporting on the Iraq War*, Sydney: Hardie Grant Books, 2004.

Chapter 8

Summing Up: Plunder and the Global Transformation of Law

Important economic background is given in the monumental work of I. Wallerstein, *The Modern World-System*, 3 Volumes, New York: Academic Press, 1974–89; D. Harvey, *The Limits to Capital*, London: Verso, 1999; and Rosa Luxemburg, *Die Akkumulation Des Kapitals. Ein Beitrag zur Okonomishen Erklarung des Imperialismus*, Berlin: Vereinigung Internationaler Verlags-Anstalten, 1922. See also, for sociological background, G. Arrighi & B. Silver, *Chaos and Governance in the Modern World System*, Minneapolis: University of Minnesota Press, 1999. The benevolent face of the imperial power is described in E.H. Berman, *The Influence of the Carnegie, Ford and Rockefeller Foundations on American Foreign Policy: the Ideology of Philanthropy*, Albany, NY: State University of New York Press, 1983. See also, more recently, J. Newhouse, *Imperial America: the Bush Assault on World Order*, New York: Vintage Books, 2003. See also Fritz Sternberg, *Der Imperialismus*, Berlin: Malik, 1926 and J. Newhouse, *Imperial America: the Bush Assault on World Order*, New York: Vintage Books, 2003; see also I. Mortellaro, *I signori della guerra. La NATO verso il XXI secolo*, Roma: Manifestolibri, 1999.

The fundamental treatment of world capitalist development through plunder remains Eric R. Wolf, *Europe and the People Without History*, Berkeley, CA: University of California Press, 1982. See also William Woodruff, *The Impact of Western Man: a Study of Europe's Role in the World Economy, 1760–1960*, London: Macmillan, 1966.

For some economic background of the contemporary situation, see A. Saunders & I. Walter, *Universal Capitalism: the Changing Balance of Public and Private Power*, Oxford: Oxford University Press, 1994. For some sociological background, see I. Wallerstein, *The Essential Wallerstein*, New York: New Press, 2000, in particular p. 71 ff. For a perhaps too optimistic image of Europe, see J. Rifkin, *The European Dream*, New York: Penguin, 2004.

Notions of freedom and electoral democracy have been used to cover quite opposite practices for a while. See T. Carothers, *In the Name of Democracy: U.S. Policy Toward Latin America in the Reagan Years*, Berkeley, CA: University of California Press, 1991. The impact of the World Bank's non-redistributive policy is often exposed, for example see C. Caufield, *Masters of Illusion: the World Bank and the Poverty of Nations*, New York: Holt, 1996. On the notion of state of exception, see G. Agamben, *Homo Sacer: Sovereign Power and Bare Life*, Stanford, CA: Stanford University Press, 1998.

Imperial Rule of Law or the People's Rule of Law?

For references to the collision between the imperial rule of law and local law traditions, daily news reports from major newspapers in and outside of the United States are a good source as they usually report events or public reactions to crises related to water shortages, pollution, intellectual property, and more. For an overview and references related to interactions between rule of law impositions and the local law, see Laura Nader, "Promise or plunder? A past and future look at law and development," In Rudolf V. van Puymbroeck (ed.), *World Bank Legal Review: Law and Justice for Development*, Rotterdam-New York: Kluwer Law International, 2006. Also published in *Global Jurist Frontier*, www.benpress.com.

The Future of Plunder

Some understanding of the present cynical age is offered by F. Jameson, *Postmodernism, Or, the Cultural Logic of Late Capitalism*, Durham, NC: Duke University Press, 1992. For a survey of issues related to globalization see D. Zolo, *Globalizzazione. Una mappa dei problemi*, Roma-Bari: Laterza, 2004. Other important readings are: C. Johnson, *The Sorrow of Empire. Militarism, Secrecy and the End of the Republic (The American Empire Project)*, New York: Owl Books, 2004; D. Harvey, *The New Imperialism*, Oxford: Clarendon Press, 2003; M. Hardt & A. Negri, *Multitude. War and Democracy in the Age of Empire*, Cambridge, MA: Harvard University Press, 2004; and R. Unger, *What Should the Left Propose*, London: Verso, 2006.

On situationism, a full bibliography is collected in *Internazionale Situazionista 1958–69*, Turin: Nautilus, 1994. A selective bibliography of its English language production is given in S. Home (ed.) *What is Situationism? A Reader*, San Francisco: AK Press, 1993.

On popular images of the law, see R.K. Sherwin, *When Law Goes Pop: the Vanishing Line Between Law and Popular Culture*, Chicago: University of Chicago Press, 2000.

On spectacular aspects of the US social and political system, see R.H. Frank & P.J. Cook, *The Winner Takes All Society: Why the Few at the Top Get So Much More Than the Rest of Us*, New York: Free Press, 1995.

On the use of diffused violence, see M. Foucault, *Discipline and Punish: the Birth of the Prison*, New York: Vintage Books, 1994. See also Barrington Moore, *Injustice: the Social Bases of Obedience and Revolt*, White Plains, NY: M.E. Sharpe, 1978; and *Victories! Winning Campaigns* in *Multinational Monitor*, Vol. 25, Nos. 1 & 2, Jan/Feb 2004 and *The People vs. Corporate Power: a Quarter Century Retrospective* in *Multinational Monitor*, Vol. 28, Nos. 7 & 8, Jul/Aug 2005.

For more critiques of current corporate capitalism and a variety of suggestions, see K. Danaher (ed.), *Democratizing the Global Economy. The Battle Against the World Bank and the IMF*, Monroe, ME: Common Courage Press, 2001.

Documentary Film Resources

These sources are of particular utility for teaching a college course on Plunder or as materials for theoretical discussion of the issues raised in the book.

Africa. Who is to blame?
2005 DVD 48′
by Emily Buchanan

Angola, le pétrole et la misère
2006 DVD 30′
by Richard Klug

Un baril à hauts risques
2005 DVD 52′
by Emmanuel Amara

Commanding Heights: the Battle for the World Economy (1/3 The Battle of Ideas)
2003 DVD 120′
by Daniel Yergin, Greg Barker, William Cran

Commanding Heights: the Battle for the World Economy (2/3 The Agony of Reform)
2003 DVD 120′
by Daniel Yergin, Greg Barker, William Cran

Commanding Heights: the Battle for the World Economy (3/3 The New Rules of the Game)
2003 DVD 120′
by Daniel Yergin, Greg Barker, William Cran

Bhopal, le procès qui n'a pas eu lieu
2004 DVD 57′
by Ilan Ziv

Black gold. The history of oil
1998 DVD 50′
by Michael Rogers

Le Bon Elève: le Mali et Nous
Italy - 2006 DVD 55′ - Blaq out
by Elisabetta Grande, Ugo Mattei, Luca Pes, Paolo Quaregna

The Cola Conquest
1998 DVD 153′
by Irene Lilienheim Angelico

The Corporation
2003 DVD 144′
by Mark Achbar, Jennifer Abbott, Joel Bakan

Darwin's nightmare
France – 2004 DVD 107′– Mille et une Productions
by Hubert Sauper

Davos, Porto Allegre et autres batailles
2003 DVD 102′
by Vincent Glenn

Djourou, une corde à ton cou
2004 DVD 64′
by Olivier Zuchuat

Duel pétrolier en Afrique
2005 DVD 43′
by Helmut Grosse

Enron. The smartest guys in the room
2005 DVD 110′
by Alex Gibney

L'épopée de l'or noir (1/4 L'âge d'or des majors)
2004 DVD 53′
by Jean-Pierre Beaurenaut et Yves Billon

L'épopée de l'or noir (2/4 Le nationalisme pétrolier)
2004 DVD 54′
by Jean-Pierre Beaurenaut et Yves Billon

L'épopée de l'or noir (3/4 L'arme du pétrole)
2004 DVD 54′
by Jean-Pierre Beaurenaut et Yves Billon

L'épopée de l'or noir (4/4 Le déclin pétrolier)
2004 DVD 52′
by Jean-Pierre Beaurenaut et Yves Billon

Esmeraldas et le pétrole. Une histoire explosive
2006 DVD 44′
by Marc Juan

Le fabuleux voyage d'un baril de pétrole
2006 DVD 43′
by Mouhcine El Ghomri

2013 la fin du pétrole
2005 DVD 48′
by Stéphane Meunier

La guerre des cotons
2005 DVD 52′
by Jean-Michel Rodrigo

Guerre de l'eau à El Alto
DVD 27′
by Stéphen Riethauser, Jean-Jacques Fontaine, Dominique De Weck

La guerre du coton
2005 DVD 51′
by Bernard Robert-Charrue

Un "homme intègre" à l'OMC
2003 DVD 50′
by John Paul Lepers

The industrial revolution
2000 DVD 87′

Iraq for Sale. The War Profiteers
2006 DVD 75′
by Robert Greenwald

Irak, à qui profite le pétrole ?
2004 DVD 40′
by Robert Mugnerot et Serge Gordey

Jenin Jenin
2001 DVD 54′
by Iyad Samudi e Mohammed Bakri
Palestinian Occupied Territories

Life and Debt
USA – 2001 86′ DVD – A non-profit Tuff Gong Production
by Stephanie Black

Little Injustices. Laura Nader Looks at the Law
1981 VHS 59′
by Terry Rockfeller

Les maux de la faim
2003 DVD 55′
by Jihan El Tahri

Memoria del Saqueo / Mêmoire d'un saccage
2004 DVD 114′
by Fernando Solanas

Nos amis de la banque
1998 DVD 84′
by Peter Chappell

Pas assez de volume: notes sur l'OMC
2004 DVD 152′
by Vincent Glenn

Les pirates du vivant
2005 DVD 58′
un film écrit et réalisé par Marie-Monique Robin

Pollution à vendre
2003 DVD 50′
by Yves Billy

Power trip
2004 DVD 85′
by Paul Devlin

Le profit et rien d'autre
2001 DVD 57′
by Raoul Peck

Roger & Me
1989 DVD 87′
by Michael Moore

Le beurre et l'argent du beurre
2006 DVD 62′
by Jaques Sarazin, Philippe Baqué, Alidou Badini

Les routes du coton
2005 DVD 83′
by Erik Orsenna, Joël Calmettes

Le scandale Enron
2005 DVD 56′
by Emanuel Amara, Ariel Wizman

Surplus: terrorized into being consumers
Sweden/Italy – 2003 DVD 52′ – Atmo
by Erik Gandini

The Take / La Prise
2004 DVD 97′
by Avi Lewis, Naomi Klein

Tchad : main basse sur l'or noir
2005 DVD 53′
by Nicolas Jaillard

What is wrong with Africa
2005 DVD 41′

The Yes Men
2003 DVD 83′
by Chris Smith, Dan Ollman, Sarah Price

Wal Mart. The High Cost of Low Price
USA 2005 DVD 98′
by Robert Greenwald

Zones de convergence (G8 Evian 2003)
2003 DVD

Produced by Luca Pes, Phd candidate, anthropology department LSE

Index

Page numbers suffixed with 'n' refer to Notes section.

Abu Ghraib 7, 25, 113, 185
Ackerman, Bruce 179, 249
Afghanistan 19, 25, 31, 122, 123, 124, 126, 145, 180, 187
  Bonn Conference 129
  colonization and re-colonization 16–17, 109–14, 151–2
  decentralization in 129–30
  "Enduring Freedom" 121
  see also Taliban
Africa 21, 22, 23, 29–30, 78, 87, 108
  artists 87
  Dakar-Bamako railway 61, 128–9
  documentaries 266, 270
  karité butter 87
  legal pluralism 29
  North 29, 214
Agamben, Giorgio 1
  see also state of exception
Ahmadinejad, Mahmoud 32
agriculture 5, 7, 51, 62, 135–6, 210
  see also genetically modified organisms
aid *see* financial instruments
AIDS 85
Algeria 75, 117
Ali, Tariq 3, 116
Alien Tort Claims Act 158
Allende, Salvadore 16, 73, 122, 183, 198
Alternative Dispute Resolution (ADR) 18, 75, 77–80, 95, 144, 168–71, 194, 219n
American Anthropological Association 101
American Bar Association 145, 171
American Civil Liberties Union (ACLU) 189
American Council of Trustees and Alumni (ACTA) 194
American Indians *see* Native Americans
American Library Association 188
American Philosophical Society 106
Amnesty International 183, 192
Angola 126, 266
Annan, Kofi 119
anthropological attitude 101
anthropologists 26, 90, 99–110, 194, 202, 204, 214
  multiple roles 108
  silence on certain topics 109, 191
  see also Gluckman, Max; Mead, Margaret; Reynolds, Earle; Steward, Julian
Arabs 19, 21, 34, 109, 110, 114–15, 116–17, 124, 179, 189
  nationalist movement 117
Arbenz Guzmán, Jacobo 122, 198
Argentina 35–42, 43, 52, 134, 203, 204
Aristide, Jean-Bertrand 122
arms trade 23, 25, 55, 127
Arnett, Peter 193, 263
Arthur Andersen 173–4
Artigas, José 69
Asia 16, 26, 29, 85, 96, 200, 214
  Caspian Sea 31, 113, 116, 163
  Central 22, 31, 241
  Southeast 29, 167
  see also Middle East; Persian Gulf
Atlantic Ritchfield Company (ARCO) 116

Australia 167
Austria 44, 88, 159
Azerbaijan 163
Aznar, José 51

Baghram Air Force Base 8
Bangladesh 20, 80
  Dacca 21
  see also Bengal
Barak, Aharon 187
Barotse 108
Batista, Fulgencio 122
Bayer Pharmaceuticals 85
Bechtel Corporation 203
Belgium 19
Bengal 13, 20, 27, 132, 209–10
Benin 63
Bentink, William 132
Berger, Judge Thomas 105
Bergier Commission 158
Berlin Conference 23
Berlusconi, Silvio 170
Bickel, Alexander 139
Black, Bernard 74, 95
Blackstone, William 64
Blair, Tony 44, 45, 51, 120, 185, 220n
Bolivia 20, 30, 62, 119, 134, 203
Bonn Conference *see* Afghanistan
Bosnia 121, 126, 177
Branco, Castelo 70
Brazil 28, 69–70, 73, 136, 203, 206
  see also Kayapo
Bremer, Paul, edicts of 3, 4, 118–19
Bretton Woods institutions 30, 45–6, 47, 50, 51, 57–8, 59–60, 63, 75, 201
  guarantees of non-intervention 55
  history 54–5
  influence of US and UK over 59–60
  lack of influence from developing nations 55, 57
  see also debt; international financial institutions
Brezhnev, Leonid 29
Britain 22–3, 30, 51, 120
  Henry VIII 12
  history
    of colonialism and imperialism 20–1, 28, 35, 50, 64–9, 111–12, 132, 199
    common law courts 12, 170
    common law tradition 64, 65, 72, 76, 94, 170, 207
    Privy Council, London 167
  King James I 12
  Prohibition del Roy 12
  see also Blair, Tony; Coke, Sir Edward; East India Company; Reagan/Thatcher revolution; rule of law, Euro-Americanization of
British Petroleum (BP) 163
Brown v. Board of Education 139
Buchanan, James 92, 147
Bureau of American Ethnology (BAE) 103, 106, 228
Bureau of Indian Affairs (BIA) 103, 104
Burundi 126
Bush, George H.W. 114, 176
Bush, George W. 15, 25, 85, 113, 115–16, 118–19, 121, 180, 181, 183, 184, 186, 192, 194
  "anybody but" 178
  see also Bush v. Gore
Bush, Jeb 176
Bush v. Gore 65, 176–9

Cahokia 102
California 11, 136, 138, 156, 170, 208
Canada 47, 105, 167, 202, 230–1n
capitalism *see* corporate capitalism
Castro Ruz, Fidel 196, 198
Catholicism 12, 23, 43, 82, 99, 125
  see also Urban II, Pope; the Vatican
Cavallo, Domingo 36, 49
Cayman Islands 41, 98
  see also corporate capitalism tax havens
Center for Economic and Policy Research 42
Central American Free Trade Agreement (CAFTA) 136
Central Intelligence Agency (CIA) 29, 35, 59, 101, 183, 186, 236n
Caribbean 28, 95, 115, 131
Certoff, Michael 181
Chang, Nancy 189, 192
Chanock, Martin 108
Chavez, Hugo 116, 122
Chechnya 121, 130
Chevron 116
Chicago school economics 36, 46, 49, 52, 91, 93–4
Chile 15, 16, 52, 73, 89, 122, 183, 198
China 5, 7, 16, 28, 29, 46, 50, 68, 71, 72, 80, 111, 116, 118, 134, 140, 149, 203, 208–9, 210
  Confucian tradition 31, 72
  Erin Brockovich 208
  opium 5, 28, 50, 111
  rightful resistance 208
  US jurisdiction in 140
  Yangtze river 208

Chomsky, Noam 191
Christianity 7, 67, 77, 78, 99, 125
  see also Catholicism; Jesuits
Chua, Ami 182
Churchill, Winston 125
Cicero, Marcus Tullius 215
civilizing process 1, 4, 8, 14, 23, 26, 44, 65, 68, 71, 82, 96, 102, 103, 104–7, 110, 112, 114, 119, 122, 127–8, 129, 148, 164, 190, 195, 197, 200, 225–6n
  see also lack; racism
civil rights movement 193
Clinton, Bill 44–5, 115, 120–2, 131, 177, 178
Coase, Ronald 91, 92
Coca-Cola 203, 207
Coke, Sir Edward 10, 12, 44, 65, 91, 197
Coalition Provisional Authority 118
Cold War 5–6, 28, 29, 46–7, 53, 56, 90, 97, 101–2
  Post- 5–6, 24, 30, 33, 45, 51, 83, 119–21, 125–6, 141, 192, 200
  see also McCarthyism
Colombia 73, 115, 116, 177, 206
colonialism 20–3, 26–8, 64–6, 67–9, 74, 101, 105, 112
  decolonization 22, 26–8, 30–1, 62, 120, 150, 198, 222n
  definition 17
  neo-colonialism 17, 27, 30, 35, 120, 127
  see also legitimacy, providers of
Commons, John R. 93
communism 47, 51, 120, 194, 210, 213
Congo, Democratic Republic of 126
contractors, reconstruction 25, 31, 118, 127
control 19, 37, 47, 59, 68, 71, 77–9, 82, 142, 144, 147, 175, 178, 182, 191, 194
  through fear 44, 53, 56, 103, 122, 138, 183, 193, 195
  see also civilizing process; harmony ideology; hegemony; inevitability thinking; propaganda; rule of law, uses of
corporate capitalism 2, 24–5, 30, 36, 46–7, 50, 55, 62, 63, 75, 113, 143, 175, 182, 196, 199–200, 211, 213
  tax havens 25, 98
  see also development, opening markets; neo-liberalism
corporations
  business ethics 173
  deferred prosecution 174
  and elections 51–2
  influence over governments 60, 181, 200, 212; *see also* elites, local
  mutual fund scandal 7–8, 173
  Sarbanes-Oxley Act 174, 191
courts *see* rule of law; United States
Cover, Robert 138
crusades 21, 32, 34, 124
Cuba 122, 130–1, 149, 197–8, 211
  and Helms-Burton Act sanctions 130
  and Platt Amendment 141, 237n
Czechoslovakia 69

Dakar-Bamako railway *see* Mali
D'Alema, Massimo 51
Debord, Gui 213
debt 37–8, 40–1, 42, 56–9, 63, 213
  see also international financial institutions
democracy 23, 32, 36, 58, 73, 91, 113, 122–3, 140, 143, 146, 153, 182, 192, 202
  lack of participation 33, 52
  participation 211–16
  social democracy 51, 120, 220n
  see also elections
Deng Xiaoping 46
Dershowitz, Alan 185
Derwish, Kamal 186
development 6, 20, 26–7, 30, 35–42, 46, 50, 71–3, 87, 114–15, 120, 128, 130, 133, 142, 197, 201, 204–5, 208
  meaning of 53–4, 112
  opening markets for corporations 4–5, 47, 59, 69–71, 131–2
  see also lack; Mexico, *Solidaridad*; neo-liberalism; privatization; property rights
Diaz, Porfiro 37
Dicey, Albert V. 11
Director, Aaron 91
documentary films 192, 266–71
Donaldson, William 175
double standards policy 61, 71, 85, 128, 130–2, 143, 152–3, 235n
Dred Scott v. Sandford 170
Duhalde, Eduardo 134

East India Company 21, 27, 31, 111, 144, 199
Economic Partnership Agreements (EPA) 131
economics 37, 60, 92
  Austrian school 44
  derivatives 36, 38–40, 42
  efficiency in 30, 49, 59, 72, 148, 215
  equilibrium 60–1
  extractive 16, 27–8, 56, 114–16, 196
  as source of legitimacy 60–1, 92
  theory of comparative advantage 61–2
  wealth maximization (Kaldor-Hicks) 134

economics (*cont'd*)
see also Chicago school economics, Keynesian economics; law and economics; rule of law, efficiency in; universalism; welfare state
economists
as advisers 48, 99
positivism of 88–9, 93
role in plunder 37
view of legal process 49, 74, 85, 92
see also law and economics; Smith, Adam
Ecuador 39, 115–16, 212, 238n
Egypt 19, 29, 43, 118, 151
civil code 29
Eisenhower, Dwight D. 115, 149, 197
Eizenstat, Stuart 158
Eldritch Press 98–9
elections 4, 20, 60, 120, 125, 146, 176–9, 200, 235n
alienation from 51–2
export 32
as investments 147–8
as spectacle 149, 215
see also Bush v. Gore
elites, local 7, 27, 28, 31, 35, 37, 52, 73, 75, 77, 82, 99, 117, 128, 130, 140, 167
energy 30, 114, 115, 173, 225n
nuclear 101, 103, 152
see also Native Americans and toxic waste; oil
Engels, Frederick 26
Enron 7–8, 113, 172–5, 190, 192, 267, 270
environment 48, 77, 108, 114, 118, 165, 192, 202, 208, 210
Kyoto Protocol 151, 178
see also water
Eritrea 126
Ethiopia 20, 121, 126
ethnocentrism 1, 3, 17, 73, 101, 153, 215
see also civilizing process; lack; positional superiority, western; racism
Euro-America 1–2, 53, 59, 64–80, 110, 148, 202
see also positional superiority, Western
Europe 36, 44, 59, 64–70, 102, 112, 140–1, 175, 197, 212
anthropology in 107–8
colonialism by 26–9, 77
contrasted with US legal system 75, 120, 139, 146
"lack" in 148
see also Holocaust litigation
European Union 63, 87, 129, 131, 144, 202
evolutionary theories 20, 89, 95, 97, 100, 101–10
exchange rates 36, 42, 54, 55
executive power 15, 139–40, 153–4, 171, 181, 184, 188, 195
Exxon 116, 168

Falluja 8
Falk, Richard 31
Falkland-Malvinas War 35, 45
Fanon, Franz 75
fascism 32, 43, 51, 70, 121–2, 157
Fastow, Andrew 174
Federal Bureau of Investigation (FBI) 183, 188, 192
Federalist papers 12, 14, 197
Feingold, Russell 188
Feinstein, Dianne 188
Feldman, Eric 191
Ferguson, Niall 13, 132
Filartiga v. Pena-Irala 158
financial instruments 38–42, 48
BOCONS 41–2
see also debt; international financial institutions
Finland 47, 61
First Boston *see* Wall Street
Florida 86, 131, 177
Ford Foundation 109
France 14, 17, 19, 43, 66, 75, 129, 151, 180, 199, 202, 212, 213–14, 225–6n
Franco, Francisco 51
Frankfurter, Justice Felix 78
Franklin, Benjamin 178
"free market" 59–60, 62, 71, 204, 214
see also Reagan/Thatcher revolution; regulation
free trade 5, 60–2, 111–12
see also development, opening markets; General Agreement on Tariffs and Trade; North American Free Trade Agreement; regulation
Fujimori, Alberto 15, 52
Fulbright grants 82

Galeano, Eduardo 4, 70, 133
Galtieri, Leopoldo 35
Gardner, James 72
gender equality 32
female circumcision 23, 124, 127–8
burqa 23, 124, 128
women 18, 23, 131, 193, 205, 207, 209
General Agreement on Tariffs and Trade (GATT) 77, 79
genetically modified organisms 51, 86, 88, 112, 165

Geneva Convention 4, 55, 119, 184
genocide 13, 20, 23, 67, 74, 84, 119, 131, 151, 200
  see also violence
Geographic Information Systems (GIS) 101
Georgia 163
Germany 43, 51, 66, 71, 81, 85, 139, 181, 212, 225–6n
Gandhi, Mahatma 28
globalization 64, 76–7, 81–2, 144–7
  consequences 49, 51–3, 88, 101, 181, 203
  see also development; neo-liberalism
Gluckman, Max 159
Goldman Sachs *see* Wall Street
Gonzales, Alberto 185
"good governance" 14, 15, 48, 53, 62, 89, 143–4
Gordon, Lincoln 70
Gore, Albert 236n
  see also Bush v. Gore
Goulart, Joaho 70
Grant, Judith 195
Greco, Michael 171
Greece 120
Greenpeace 210
Group of Eight (G8) 30, 59, 144, 271
Guantanamo Bay 25, 171, 185, 186, 187, 235n
Guatemala 122, 198
Gulf War 30, 121, 131, 225n
Gusterson, Hugh 194
Guthrie, Dan 194
Gutting, Tom 194

Haiti 112, 122
Hamdan v. Rumsfeld 184
Hamdi, Yaser 184, 186
Hanna Mining 69–70
harmony ideology 53, 65, 76, 77, 78, 112, 209
  see also Alternative Dispute Resolution
Harrington, Charlene 80
Harris, Katherine 176
Hatch, Orin 188
von Hayek, Friedrich 44, 89, 93, 94
Hegel, Georg Wilhelm Friedrich 148
hegemony 25, 27, 30–3, 36–7, 82, 83–5, 178, 196
  and consumerism 18
  and counter-hegemony 7–9, 25, 145, 151, 154, 165, 194, 198–9, 204, 209, 211, 213–14
  legal 142–3, 158, 169
  meaning of 17–18
  normative reputation 31–2
  see also elites, local; harmony ideology; lack; United States as empire

Hentoff, Nat 180
Hewlett Packard 210
Hezbollah 203
Hitler, Adolph 181
Hoebel, E. Adamson 91
Holland 212
Holocaust 154, 155–62
  litigation 155–8
  see also Nuremberg trials
Homeland Security Act 180
Hoover, J. Edgar 191
Hudson Bay Company 144
human rights 14–15, 23, 32, 50, 66, 121–8, 130, 144, 150–2, 157, 160, 162, 164, 172, 182–3, 205, 235n
Hussein, Saddam 22, 113, 114, 116, 117, 119, 150, 185
Hussein ibn Talal, King 114

Ibn Battuta, Abu Abdullah Muhammad 21
imperialism 6, 17, 31, 37–8, 64, 78, 84, 109, 112, 120, 151
  legal 19, 72, 75, 128, 141, 159
  present-day 23–4, 122, 203, 213
  see also colonialism, neo-colonialism; hegemony; lawlessness; state of exception; United States as empire
Inca 23, 119, 124
Independent Petroleum Association of America 116
India 7, 22, 27–8, 80, 96, 111, 114, 132, 154, 166, 199, 203, 206–7
  Bhopal catastrophe 154, 166–7, 212, 267
  Kerela 207
  and "neem" tree 86, 203, 206
  Panchayat 207
  see also Coca-Cola
Indonesia 126, 182, 199, 210
inevitability thinking 76
institutions, reactive 75, 95, 137–41, 143, 144, 165–6, 180, 200, 212–13
intellectual property 48, 83–8, 95, 203, 224n, 226n
  Andean "maca" 205–6
  collective inventors 87, 203
  "cool hunters" 86
  copyrights 84, 85, 98–9, 177, 206
  open source movement 206
  Sonny Bono Extension Act 99, 177
  trade-related aspects of intellectual property (TRIPS) 84, 85–6, 206
  see also Africa, karité butter; agriculture; AIDS; India, "neem" plant; internet

International Convention on the Rights of Children 164
International Court of Justice 25, 79, 80
International Criminal Court 150, 151, 154, 178
International Dispute Settlement (IDS) *see* Alternative Dispute Resolution (ADR)
International Financial Institutions 16, 19, 35–7, 45, 57, 75, 77, 81, 144, 172
  harsh lending conditions of 57–8
  initial prestige 55
  as interventionist 50, 58–9
  lack of accountability 58, 213
  politicization of 55, 97, 200
  and sovereignty/conditionality 50–1, 54, 57–63, 87, 140, 204
  see also Bretton Woods institutions, debt; development; neo-liberalism; Washington Consensus
international law 22–3, 25, 68, 71, 75–6, 119, 121, 123, 131, 150–4, 158–64, 172, 177, 178–9, 187, 231n, 233n, 236n
  see also Geneva Convention
International Monetary Fund (IMF) 3, 14, 19, 30, 40, 42, 45, 48, 58–9, 63, 134, 145, 201, 222n
  creation of 54
  see also Bretton Woods institutions; structural adjustment
internet 83–4, 88, 202, 208
  American influence on 83
  "digital divide" 83, 88
  and first possession 88
  see also intellectual property
intervention 15–17, 32, 38, 48, 54, 96–7, 112–13, 122–34, 152–3, 233n
  redistributive 139, 149, 212
  see also structural adjustment
Inuit of Baker Lake 105
invasion 103, 115–16, 118, 124, 126, 136, 203
Iran 116, 121, 180
Iraq 3, 22, 112, 114–16, 117–19, 122, 131, 179, 180, 201, 224n
  civil code 29
  "Desert Storm" 121
  see also Abu Ghraib; Bremer, Paul; Gulf War; oil
Islam 7, 19, 32, 72, 78, 109–10, 120, 121, 123, 125, 144, 148, 220n
  Islamic jurisprudence 29, 72, 110, 122, 148, 232n
  see also judge, *qadi*
Israel 4, 25, 109, 117, 121, 124, 152, 154, 186, 187, 203
Italy 51, 129, 130, 155–8, 162, 170, 178, 181, 185, 202–3
  Italian Susa Valley 202

Jamaica 131
Japan 16, 19, 20, 53, 66, 75, 158, 191, 212
Jefferson, Thomas 105–6
Jesuits 14
Johnson, Lyndon 70, 149, 212
judge, *qadi* 78, 110
justice 5–6, 7, 14, 15, 18, 48, 74, 93, 96, 127, 152, 157, 158, 160, 165, 169, 172, 201–2, 210, 221n
  injustice 107, 110, 115, 202, 211, 213, 269
  market for 160, 162
  motive 73, 89, 200, 203, 206, 208, 209
  natural 67, 72
  privatized 3, 78–9

Kappa, Elle 185
Kayapo 85–6, 203
Kelo v. City of New London 208
Kelsen, Hans 93
Kennan, George, straight power doctrine 3, 182–3
Kerry, John 186
Keynesian economics 43, 45–6, 48, 54, 56, 93–4, 95
Khalidi, Rashid 119
Khomeini, Ayatollah Ruhollah 32
Klare, Michael 113
Kohl, Helmut 51
Korea 29, 70, 121, 180
Korematsu v. United States 138, 170
Kosovo 126
Kruschev 29
Kucinich, Dennis 192
Kuwait 152, 225n
  see also Gulf War

labor 48, 50, 51, 69, 112, 128, 131, 165, 170, 172, 203–5, 208, 210, 221n, 223n
  law 30, 148, 204
  wages 60–2
  see also slavery; unions
lack, theory of 4, 65, 67, 98
  institutional 128–30
  as justification 70–5, 143
    for development 78
    for intervention 20, 31
    for invasion 16, 110, 122, 127
    for jurisdiction 162

Western 75, 148, 162, 216
see also civilizing process; positional superiority
Lafontaine, Oskar 51, 220n
latifundio 69
Latin America 4–5, 15, 20, 27, 28, 31, 37, 42, 50, 56, 62, 68, 69, 71, 72, 73, 78, 95, 96, 99, 112, 121–2, 130, 131, 133, 154, 160, 167, 184, 199, 200, 206
law
diffusion 17, 19–20, 59–60, 76, 77, 81, 95, 125, 143, 159, 167, 209
discovery 146, 159–60, 161, 166
ideologies 88, 90–1, 96–7, 123–8, 150–4
illegality 3–4
examples of 11, 22, 70, 118, 121, 130–1, 173, 184, 187, 207, 210, 230–1n, 236n
notions of 8, 39, 59, 93, 152, 154, 189, 202, 231n
see also harmony ideology; rational law; rule of law
law and economics 48, 71, 74, 91–3, 95–8, 111, 131–46, 148, 168, 169
lawlessness 3, 4, 26, 115, 166, 195, 213, 215
lawyers 12, 26, 28, 48–9, 139
as social engineers 90–1, 94–5
US-trained 75, 145–6, 161, 163, 167
Lebanon 109, 126, 203
Lee, Barbara 187
legitimacy, providers of 31, 74, 81–110, 111, 200, 122–3, 125, 137, 138, 150, 152, 154, 168, 171, 177–80
Leninism 43
Lesotho 16, 165
Liberia 126
library records 188
Libya 117
Linan y Cisneros, Archbishop 119
Lincoln, Abraham 186, 191
Llewellyn, Karl 90–1
Lloyds report 1993 135
Locke, John 67, 71, 74, 84
Lopez, Francisco Solano 69
Love, James 87–8
Lula da Silva, Luiz Inácio 136

MacArthur, General Douglas 19
Madison, James 13
Madrid, Miguel de la 37, 96
Magna Carta 12
Maine, Henry 82, 147
Mair, Balakrishnana 207
Mali 61, 87, 128–9, 151, 267
Mandel, Ernest 199
manifest destiny 102
Marshall Plan 32, 70
marxism 13, 18, 43, 210
Marx, Karl 26, 111
Matteoli Commission 158
MAUSS (*Mouvement Anti-Utilitariste dans les Sciences Sociales*) 214
Maya 23
Mazzili, Ranieri 70
McCarthyism 101, 192, 194
Mead, Margaret 215
media 18, 33, 87, 90, 113, 121, 124, 147, 152, 174, 182, 186, 190, 193, 195, 203
Melainine ould Belay, Cheik 183
Menem, Carlos 40, 42
mercenaries and "private security" 22, 63, 164, 172–3, 183
Merrill Lynch *see* Wall Street
Mexico 37, 77, 96, 115–16, 134–6, 202–5, 238–9n
Articulo 27 136
Assembly of Peoples of Oaxaca (APPO) 205
Chiapas 136, 203, 204
Oaxaca 77, 136, 202, 204, 205
Solidaridad 135
Middle East 21, 23, 29–30, 34, 109–10, 116–19, 152, 214
military industrial complex 44, 114–15, 169
Milosevic, Slobodan 126, 150, 152, 154
missionaries 26, 31, 73, 78, 102, 108
Mobil 116
Mobutu, Sese Seko 55
Monroe Doctrine 28, 69, 133, 178, 200
Monsanto 86, 112
Moody's 130
Mooney, James 103–4, 227n
Morales, Diego 30, 134
Morgan, Lewis Henry 106, 107
Morgan Stanley *see* Wall Street

Nakba catastrophe 124
Napoleon 19
National Broadcasting Company (NBC) 193
Native America(ns) 13, 16, 20, 67, 84, 103–7, 133–4, 228–9n, 230–1n, 238n
Dawes Allotment Act 104
Indian Claims Commission 104
Red Power movement 107, 228–9n
Shoshone/Paiute 104–5
Sioux 103, 224n
and toxic waste 100, 104, 107, 147, 153, 159, 228n
see also Inca; Inuit of Baker Lake; Maya; Steward, Julian; U'wa

INDEX

The Nature Conservancy 108
Nazis 32, 139, 155, 157, 158
see also Holocaust
Nehru, Jawaharlal 28, 132
neo-liberalism 7, 23, 35–53, 58, 62, 74–5, 79, 137, 163, 173, 220n
and authoritarianism 52
definition 43
economic rationale for 60–1
and electoral process 51–2
as expansionist 46, 49, 50–7, 59, 145
parallels with colonialism 5, 30–1, 40, 144
see also development; good governance; international financial institutions; universalism
New Deal 16, 94
New York City Bank 112
New York University Law School 76
New Zealand 167
Nicaragua 122
Nigeria 30, 201
Nixon, Richard 149, 175, 199, 214, 236n
Nobel Prize 88, 92, 147
non-governmental organizations (NGOs) 23, 77, 144, 147, 160, 210
Noor, Queen 114
Noriega 55
normative blindness 102, 216
North Atlantic Treaty Organization (NATO) 16, 59, 121, 144, 151, 154, 203, 225n
North American Free Trade Agreement (NAFTA) 4, 77, 135–6, 205
Nuremberg trials 65, 150, 154, 157
Nyerere, Julius 28

Occidental Petroleum 115
Occupational Safety and Health Administration (OSHA) 4
O'Connor, Justice Sandra Day 176
Office of Strategic Services (OSS) *see* Central Intelligence Agency
Oil 22, 25, 30–1, 44–5, 55–7, 93, 111–19, 127, 164, 168, 201, 204, 212–13, 267, 222n
Anglo-Persian Oil Company 116–17
Arab oil embargo 115
Iraq Petroleum Company 117
pipeline 31, 113, 115, 127, 163
Turkish Petroleum Company 117
see also Organization of Petroleum Exporting Countries
Oliphant, Herman 90
Omar, Mullah Mohammed 152
Organization for Economic Cooperation and Development (OECD) 59
Organization of Petroleum Exporting Countries (OPEC) 50, 55, 56, 117–18
orientalism 2, 16, 33, 110, 122
Ottoman Empire 4

Pacific LNG 134
Padilla, José 185, 186, 187
Paine, Thomas 214
Palestine 109–10, 124, 126, 130, 203
Paraguay 69, 108, 158
Parmalat 175
Partnoy, Frank 40
patents *see* intellectual property
Patriot Act 180, 187–91, 193, 195
patriotism 6, 53, 103, 113–15, 188, 191–4
Peace of Westphalia 124, 152
People's Global Action (PGA) 204
Pepsi 207
Perez, Roberto 115
Peron, Domingo 43
Persian Gulf 109, 114, 116, 117, 225n
see also Gulf War
Peru 15, 52, 115–16, 202, 205
Petróleos Mexicanos (PEMEX) 115–16
pharmaceuticals 85, 86, 161
see also AIDS, Bayer
Philippines 182, 194, 206, 210
Pinochet, Augusto 15, 52
Pizarro, Francisco 32, 124
plunder
bio-piracy 205–6
bio-prospecting 206
definition 11
and development 6, 49
ideal conditions for 46–7, 63
see also colonialism; development; international financial institutions; neo-liberalism; profit motive
Poland 69
Polanyi, Karl 10, 196
Popper, Karl 88, 93
Portugal 1, 17, 64, 68, 196
positional superiority 15, 17, 20, 24, 33, 50, 100, 103, 112, 114
see also lack; racism
Posner, Judge Richard 74, 94, 175
Potosi *see* Bolivia
poverty 20–2, 24, 27, 37, 47, 49, 51, 56–7, 61–3, 87, 128, 132–5, 176, 197, 199, 209–10, 213, 238n
Powell, John Wesley 103–4, 106–7, 228n

prisons 52, 63, 113, 130, 132, 139, 149, 172, 193, 199
Convention on Prisoners of War 186
see also Abu Ghraib; Guantanamo Bay
privatization 5, 43, 46, 95, 118, 128, 132, 134, 136, 147, 165, 173, 204
economic rationale for 60–1
of security *see* arms trade
see also water
profit motive 59, 112, 169, 200
"external" costs 196–7, 210–12
rational maximization of utility 21, 89, 92, 97–8
propaganda 24, 26, 29, 32–3, 113, 121, 123, 152, 173, 194, 195, 213
property rights 15, 50, 65, 67–8, 71, 124
eminent domain 164, 208
see also intellectual property; water
Putin, Vladimir 51, 121

Quadros, Janio 70

racism 25, 32, 90, 112, 199, 219n
essentialized "other," depictions of 16, 19, 33, 127–8, 144
see also lack, theory of
railways 61, 770, 128–9
rational/natural law 14, 16, 49, 66, 74, 84, 88, 104, 158
Reagan, Ronald 45, 94, 211, 236n
Reagan/Thatcher revolution 33, 43, 44, 48, 89, 120, 212
monetarist policies 56–7
and worldwide recession 56
Reed, Richard 108
regulation 44, 46, 48, 63, 93–4, 97, 140, 165–6, 207
and protection of stronger markets 47, 59, 62, 131, 223n
Rehnquist, Justice William 176, 177
resources, distribution of 7, 13, 24, 44, 49, 61, 63, 66, 89, 95–8, 117, 125, 136–41, 145, 149, 169, 196, 199, 201, 204, 221n, 232n, 234n
see also property rights; welfare state
Reynolds, Earle 101
rights, affirmative and negative 43, 50, 66–7
see also human rights; property rights
Rivera, Geraldo 193
Roberts, Justice John 91
Roosevelt, Franklin D. 43, 125, 174, 211
Roosevelt, Theodore 43, 106, 107
de Rosas, Juan Manuel 69
Royce, Charles 106–7

Ruiz, Ulysses 205
rule of law
buzzword 10
as commodity 31, 45, 73, 95, 200
and courts, extraterritorial 68, 140
as double-edged 18, 26, 208
efficiency in 35, 44, 46, 60–1, 72, 75, 78, 85, 92, 94–8, 146, 148, 157, 168
fictional jurisprudence 3–4
Euro-Americanization of 64–80, 144–9
British Common Law 64, 65, 76, 170, 207
and colonialism 26, 65, 117
image of court neutrality 44, 65, 91, 171
as decentralized 66–7, 145–6, 154
and independent academic institutions 66, 138, 171
lawyers as social engineers 66–7, 90
and powerful independent judiciary 65, 149
and negative individual rights 66
and universal jurisdiction 39, 66, 140, 158, 162–4
written constitution in 66–7
as ideal 3, 5, 25, 32, 125, 203
as implicitly positive 10–11, 16
meanings 14
see also good governance; rational law
as negative limit 15
origins 10–11, 12–13
uses of
as justification of plunder/oppression 5, 16, 22, 55, 67, 71, 84, 117, 119, 122, 124, 125, 184, 198
legitimization 5, 13, 65, 93, 197–8
order 3, 15, 63, 127, 137, 139
definition of illegality 4, 93
see also civilizing process; democracy; double standards policy; law; universalism
Russia 20, 43, 47, 51, 95, 120–1, 180
see also Soviet Union
Rwanda 151

Salinas de Gortari, Carlos 135–6
Sanchez de Lozada, Gonzalo 134
sanctions 122, 130
Sandino, Augusto Cesar 122
San Martin 68
Savage Co. 128
Sayigh, Yosuf 117
Scalia, Justice Antonin 176, 186
Scandinavia 15, 43, 120, 212
Schmitt, Carl 139
Schroeder, Gerhard 51
Schultz, William 183–4

Securities and Exchange Commission 42, 174, 175
Sempra 134
Senegal 61, 128
September 11th, 1973 183
September 11th, 2001 6, 25, 113, 171, 179, 187, 191–2
Sharon, Ariel 186, 187
Shiva, Vandana 71
Shivji, Issa 22
Sierra Leone 30, 126, 182
slavery 5, 20–1, 23, 28, 61, 138–9, 158, 170, 193, 199
Smith, Adam 27, 74, 92, 111
Smithsonian Institution 103, 106
socialism 26, 28, 29, 33, 43–4, 46–7, 93, 98, 120, 125, 148, 149, 197–8, 215
Somalia 121, 122, 123, 124, 126, 164, 177, 210
  "Restore Hope" 121
South Africa 27, 85, 126, 185
sovereignty 15, 66, 112, 141, 148, 150–3, 163–4, 218n, 224n, 225n
  see also human rights; international financial institutions and sovereignty
Soviet Union 5, 28, 43, 44–5, 46–7, 48, 149, 213
Spain 20, 23, 28, 35, 51, 237n, 239n
  conquistadors 20, 23
Speck, Frank 107
Sri Lanka 126
Steward, Julian 104–5, 107, 110
Sudan 121, 126, 180
sugar 102
Switzerland 63, 67, 158, 210, 212
Stalin, Joseph 125
state of exception 25–6, 112, 122, 172, 174, 193
St. Johns firm 70
stereotypes *see* ethnocentrism, the West, the "other"
structural adjustment 16, 38, 40–1, 53–7, 58–9, 61, 89, 95, 132
  "comprehensive development frameworks" (CDF) 50–1, 53–4, 60, 97, 128, 143, 201
  evaluation in 50
  first phase, "stabilization loan" 63
  second phase 63
  structural adjustment plans (SAPs) 49, 50, 60, 62–3, 87
  tool of development 54
  see also Bretton Woods institutions; international financial institutions; privatization
Suharto 55
Sunstein, Cass 206
Syria 121, 180, 185

Taft, William H. 112
Taliban 32
Tanzania 22, 28, 151
terra nullius ("empty" land) 4, 84, 88, 101–2, 104–5
  and "discovery" principle 16, 67–8
  lex nullius 110
terror 25, 30, 35, 53, 110, 124, 177, 192, 194, 203
  war on 121, 122, 129, 178–90, 193
Texaco 212
Thailand 210
Thatcher, Margaret *see* Reagan/Thatcher revolution
Third World 37, 40, 46, 48, 53, 55–6, 57, 59, 62, 73, 75, 96, 115, 132–3
Tibet 130
tobacco 214
  Framework Convention on Tobacco Control (FCTC) 214
  Network for Accountability of Tobacco Transnational (NATT) 214
de Tocqueville 65
tort law and "reform," U.S. 6, 153, 158, 161, 162, 168, 169, 170–1
Truman, Harry S. and Fair Deal 149
Tucker, Vincent 53–4
Turkey 20, 116, 163–4
Twain, Mark 194

unilateralism 121, 154, 177
  see also Bush, George W.; intervention
Union Carbide 112, 166
unions 52, 147–8, 204–5
United Fruit Company 29, 69, 112
United for Peace Resolutions 151, 235n
  see also United Nations
United Nations (UN) 55, 59, 119, 122, 124, 130, 150–2, 154, 178, 187, 231n, 235n
United States 65–7, 142–9, 158–67, 168–95
  constitution 66–7, 138, 158, 170–1, 180, 184–6, 192
  Department of Justice 104–5
  as empire 17, 25, 45, 54, 121
  as global law graduate school 66–7, 73, 76, 167
  military industrial complex
    Military Commissions Act of 2006 184
    Uniform Code of Military Justice 184
  "open door policies" of 68–9, 71
  political parties 45, 98, 120, 121, 147, 152, 178, 186, 195

reputation 25, 31–2, 68, 72, 149, 171, 175, 178, 180–2, 190, 198–9
suing in *see* rule of law, Euro-Americanization of and universal jurisdiction
Supreme Court 25, 91, 99, 121, 138, 164, 170, 176–9, 184–6, 208–9
and UK 54–5, 57
see also California; Central Intelligence Agency; Chicago School economics; corporate capitalism, executive power; Florida; Guantanamo Bay; Iraq; oil; Marshall Plan; Monroe Doctrine; Native Americans; positional superiority; September 11th, 2001; Wall Street; Washington Consensus
Union Oil Company of California (UNOCAL) 113
universalism 7, 17, 20, 47–8, 49, 50, 66, 74–5, 84–5, 86, 88, 89, 94, 108, 123, 127, 129, 150, 153, 225n
Urban II, Pope 124
Uruguay 69, 73, 79, 136
US Steel 70
U'wa 115

Vargas, Gertulio 69
Vasquez, Tabare 136
The Vatican 159
de Vattel, Emerich 67, 71, 74
Vauro 178
Veblen, Thorstein 93
Venezuela 116, 122, 206
Vidal, Gore 191
Vietnam 29, 32, 33, 149, 193, 212
violence 4, 5, 11, 13–14, 29, 32–3, 36, 52, 55, 60, 63, 82, 112–13, 115, 119, 126, 130, 144, 150, 179, 189, 193, 198, 205, 207, 209, 211
see also genocide
Vivendi 175

Wall Street 8, 35, 36, 39, 40–2, 56, 173–5
Warren, Justice Earl 138, 172, 179, 198
Washington Consensus 4, 23, 25, 35, 36, 41, 51, 59–60, 80, 112, 143
see also international financial institutions; neo-liberalism
water 4, 80, 109, 135, 203, 207–8, 210
wealth *see* resources
weapons of mass destruction 8, 45, 117, 122, 203
Weber, Max 72, 78, 110
welfare state 43–5, 47, 48, 58, 61, 93, 140, 148, 169, 198, 211–12, 213–14
see also economics, efficiency in; privatization; Reagan/Thatcher revolution
Wilson, Horace 132
Wilson, Woodrow viii, 32, 191
World Bank 14, 15, 16, 20, 48, 50, 54, 58–9, 68, 73, 74, 75, 78, 97, 114, 128–9, 204, 207, 223n, 238n
"comprehensive legal system" 50
creation of 54–5
see also Bretton Woods institutions; international financial institutions
WorldCom 113, 173, 174, 192
World Trade Organization (WTO) 4, 5, 30, 50, 55, 68, 79, 84, 112, 131, 132–3, 140, 190, 206
World War I 26, 114–15, 117, 191
World War II 26, 32, 43, 54–5, 100, 101, 117, 125, 142, 148, 154, 157–8, 180–2, 198, 212
Japanese American internment camps 138, 170

Yanomami 88
Yemen 121, 186
Yoo, John 185
Yugoslavia 16, 122, 150–1, 152, 154, 177
Yalta agreements 125–6
see also Kosovo

Zapatistas 204
Zapotec 77
Zinn, Howard 191

10-29 Film: Direct Orders

anthrax vaccine although unapproved by FDA.

↳ discharged w/o taking
↳ relation to Gulf War Syndrome
↳ "misguided experiment"

↳ experimentation
↳ unusual side effects of vaccine - earringings "grey outs"
↳ no consent required if in interest of natl sec
↳ Gulf War syndrome - name given to "emotional disorder" - not emotional - physical consequences. - auto immune disorder cognitive issues (memory
↳ question of informed consent
↳ article 15 : less than honorable discharge
↳ demand trial by court marshall
↳ 21 k fine
↳ jury not allowed to hear full story
↳ use of music in documentary (like a commercial/prop for military)
↳ army did all research - owned patent

* This is pre-911 late '90's - ? - look up

354 B
M 1-2
W 2-4

↳ bioport manufactures
↳ ~~squaline~~ squalene found in blood
↳ indemnify ??
↳ Eygptian/Kuwaiti soldiers who fought same war w/o vaccine do not experience Gulf War syndrome

↳ after bioport shut down - still administered not sure where manufactured
↳ everyone in film after this shut down

Jason Samwitz
convicted felon for refusing

What does it mean to be informed?

10-31 Duty to Rescue
Renteln – "cultural defense"
universalism vs. cultural relativism
right to culture - international covenant on civil rights (ph?)

ranking of rights – priority

right to a name
↳ symbolic representation of iden
↳ practical consequences to not being able to name children.
↳ ex) Messiah – Tennessee mother names
↳ employment opportunities
onomastics (process of naming? sp?)

Good samaritan? Luke 10: 25-35 (policy) parable/narrative
humanitarian impulse

ius gentium – looking for univerals in law
comparative approach to law

civil law vs common law
legal duty to rescue — anglo-american
no tradition (inquisitional process) — precedent – inherently conservative
presumed innocent (accusational process)
France, neth, italy colonies

rescue – failure
↳ kitty genovese, sherrice iverson, princess diana, yu
↳ abuse – extortion china – hosp bills + assumption of guilt
- bad samaritan laws punish those that fail to help
- good law is immunization from suit bc of help
- can be meaningless (criminalization of rescue) bc ppl don't know about it.

- Code pink
- R2P? International –
- Gaza flotillas
- suggests Peace corp + americorp expansion

Made in the USA
San Bernardino, CA
30 September 2013